John Lewis Peyton

**Rambling Reminiscences of a Residence Abroad**

England--Guernsey

John Lewis Peyton

**Rambling Reminiscences of a Residence Abroad**
*England--Guernsey*

ISBN/EAN: 9783744729680

Printed in Europe, USA, Canada, Australia, Japan

Cover: Foto ©ninafisch / pixelio.de

More available books at **www.hansebooks.com**

# RAMBLING REMINISCENCES

——OF——

## A RESIDENCE ABROAD.

## ENGLAND—GUERNSEY.

——BY——

## J. L. PEYTON

AUTHOR OF "THE AMERICAN CRISIS," "OVER THE ALLEGHANIES AND ACROSS THE PRAIRIES," "HISTORY OF AUGUSTA CO., VA., ETC., ETC.

"Much have I seen and known ; cities of men
And manners, climates, councils, governments."
—Tennyson.

STAUNTON, VIRGINIA :
S. M. YOST & SON, PUBLISHERS.
MDCCCLXXXVIII.

[All Rights Reserved.]

# TABLE OF CONTENTS:

## CHAPTER I.
London Past and Present.................................... 1— 12

## CHAPTER II.
The Dark Side of London Life—The Social Dregs ............. 12  27

## CHAPTER III.
The Kew Gardens and Richmond Park—Ruminations over some of John Bull's Peculiarities................................... 28— 39

## CHAPTER IV.
Further Experiences of Richmond—Gypsies—John, Earl Russell, &c. 40— 48

## CHAPTER V.
Windsor Castle, Past and Present—George IV—The Lawless Lords of Other Days—The Royal Stables—The Parks, &c........... 48— 59

## CHAPTER VI.
The Inauguration of the Second World's Fair in London—The Fine Art Department—American Exhibition—Letter to the "Times" —New-Made Friends....................................... 59— 71

## CHAPTER VII.
Letter to the "Times," referred to in Previous Chapter—Gladstone, Bright &c, &c............................................. 72— 76

## CHAPTER VIII.
The Shaw Farm of Prince Albert—English Agriculture—Stock Breeding, &c.,—Political Influence of the Landlords—Duke of Somerset............................................... 77— 86

## CHAPTER IX.
Hampton Court—Mons. Assolant—Cardinal Wolsey.............. 86—101

## CHAPTER X.
Harrow-on-the-Hill—Byron's Early Days—Hampstead Heath—Rural Sports—Kissing in the Ring, Highgate, &c,............... 101—116

## CHAPTER XI.
London Law Court—The English on America— The Duke of Somerset—The Land Laws, &c,—The Courts of Queen's Bench and Exchequer—Nomination of Sheriffs—Lord Mayor's Banquets—The Right Honorable William Cubitt, M. P., Lord Mayor of London—A Village Graveyard—Curious Epitaphs. 117—130

## CHAPTER XII.
Sanitary Science—House and Town Sewerage—Its Influence on Health and Longevity..................................... 131—142

## CHAPTER XIII.
The Royal Mint—A Distinguished Man and a Club Cub—Sir John Shelley—The Illusions of History......................... 143—150

TABLE OF CONTENTS.

CHAPTER XIV.
The Derby Day—British Love of Sport—The Popularity of the Turf
—The Celebrated Racer Eclipse.......................... 151—160

CHAPTER XV.
Dover—Fashionable Society on the Seaside—The past and Present
—Dangers on the Old Road............................ 160—167

CHAPTER XVI.
Dover—The Cinque Ports—Ancient Customs—Walmer Castle—
Deal—Death of the Duke of Wellington—The Middle Age
Monks—Religious Intolerance......................... 168—176

CHAPTER XVII.
Folkestone—Club Life—Martello Towers—Shorncliff Camp and the
Organization of the British Army—Visit to a Country House—
Lord Ellenborough—Etiquette, &c........................ 176—184

CHAPTER XVIII.
Visit to a Country House—Lord Ellenborough—Matters of Etiquette
—Osmond Priaulx—Tourists............................ 184—188

CHAPTER XIX.
Romney Marsh and Dungenees—The Military Canal—Napoleon
—Plans for the Invasion of England—The Origin of English
Lighthouses—A Type of the Modern British Politician........ 189—199

CHAPTER XX.
From Folkestone by Dover, Deal and Canterbury to London—The
Cathedral—The "Ashes" of Kings—The Fate of Sovereigns, &c. 200—208

CHAPTER XXI
Chatham—Faversham—Rochester—Sir Francis Doyle—Gads' Hill
—Cobham Hall—Mss Letters of Sir John Peyton, Governor of
the Tower and of the Island of Jersey—Edmond Beales The
Reformer ............................................. 208—217

CHAPTER XXII.
Seven Oaks—Montreal—The Amhersts—Sir Philip Sidney—Knoll
Castle—Showmen— Towbridge Wells—Battle Abbey—Return
to London ........................................... 217—231

CHAPTER XXIII.
The Anglo-Norman Isle of Guernsey—Literature &c.,—The Sporting Club—The Institutions of the Island, &c.—Hauteville
House, Victor Hugo, Private Theatricals, &c.—Public Lectures, &c.—St. John's Readings—Lectures on Electricity—
Workingmen's Association—Remarks by Colonel J. L. Peyton—
Physical Features, Former State, &c.—The Island One Hundred Years Ago—Religion, Past and Present, &c .......... 231—268

APPENDICES.
APPENDIX A.—Trees—Lines by Georges Metevier............. 269—270
APPENDIX B.—Letters of Dr. Benjamin Franklin.............. 271—297
APPENDIX C.—Prominent Guernseymen since 1600............. 298

# RAMBLING REMINISCENCES.

## CHAPTER I.

### LONDON PAST AND PRESENT.

On the 22nd of November, 1861, after a boisterous voyage across the South Atlantic from Charleston, S. C., by the Burmuda and Azore Islands, in the Confederate man-of-war, *Nashville*, Capt. Robert W. Pegram, commanding, we found ourselves comfortably ensconced in a West-end (London) Hotel.— Every one has heard of London and its November fogs — Few Americans know what either exactly is. Daniel Webster, after his return to the United States, was asked what he thought of London, and replied, "I have not yet done wondering." This language gives expression to the sentiment with which it has always inspired us, and we are sure we shall never cease to wonder at London or a genuine London fog, dim, dreary, sullen as it is, particularly in November, when it is a vile, double distilled fog of the most intolerable kind. Winter has already scattered his shafts, and this penetrating fog comes like a demon in search of the dead strewn in town and country, through forest and field. It is cold, it is wet, it is dark, it shrouds all things in a ghostly gloom, a smoke like darkness. But for the gas lights it would be black as the ninth plague of Egypt at mid-day. Looking out of our window in Trafalgar Square, the morning after our arrival, we saw the town wrapped in a vast winding sheet of gray mist and yellow smoke. It was eleven o'clock, still there was no sign of day ; gas blazed in street lamps and shop windows. The smoke was thick, the mist thicker, the sky black ; few persons were abroad ; fewer cabs, and the drivers of these few shouted apparently at the darkness through which they slowly groped their way. About one o'clock the fog for a few moments cleared up, and seemed sneaking off into the country. The blackened sky became yellow, and the sun loomed as through a glass darkly.— Our spirits were reviving when the sun quickly covered himself again with the clouds of night and sailed unseen across the sky.

Stiff in every limb, with tender feet and heavy head, the effects of a winter voyage across the ocean, a tour round our chamber contented us on this our first day in the great metropolis. Looking out on the cloudy, muggy, dark and wretched streets, strangely illuminated with flickering gas-lights, if the writer did not for the first time in his life, wish himself another man, he certainly wished himself in another place. The vitality of our youth was not to be quenched, however, by such surroundings, and substituting the philosophy of maturer years for any depressing heaviness under which we were suffering, we soon plucked up spirits, and in a few weeks commenced those explorations which have left us ever since, like Mr. Webster, "wondering."

Let us take a glance at this grim old metropolis: There is no romance about the London of the present; tourists have rummaged it from end to end—it is known the world over from Belgravia to Bethnel Green, from Camberwell to Campdentown. Yet it still interests and fills the stranger with astonishment. The more he knows of it, the more he wishes to know. Widely understood as it may be the number familiar with that great capital is infinitesimal when compared with the sedentary world who are almost totally ignorant of all but its name. This is some excuse for re-telling the old story of its wonders and mysteries.

The stranger in London is bewildered at its extent, its gloomy grandeur, its grim magnificence  He sees before him a labyrinthine confusion of streets, straight, broad and spacious, narrow, crooked and filthy, according to locality, and intersecting each other at every possible angle. With a correct general idea of the metropolis, gathered from a chart, he cannot find his way from one quarter to another without the aid of a guide, or even retain his knowledge of the points of the compass, unless he remains in the vicinity of such leading thoroughfares as the Strand, Oxford Street or Piccadilly. He may spend weeks with all the ardour of an explorer, perambulating the side-walks and visiting the principal objects of curiosity, and still have an imperfect idea of the place. The mass of highways and byways is still as intricate as a Chinese puzzle, though during the last decade large sums have been expended in straightening old and opening new avenues for the purpose of simplifying the system of streets, and more readily accommodating the traffic.

The city of London proper commences at Temple Bar, and covers an area of little more than one square mile, and contains a population of 111,784 persons only. As the gateway is without beauty and obstructs the most crowded of London's thoroughfares, its retention is a striking illustration of the conservative character of the English mind, of the tenacity with which our ancestors cling to whatever is old.

Passing this so-called barrier, we are in the city proper. It is not the city of former times, full of densely inhabited houses and fine residences, belonging to the chief merchants, the landed gentry and the nobility—the great landlords of the country; the city, as it once was, of small and narrow streets, of mean lath and plaster houses on rickety wooden frames and of all imaginable sizes and shapes; the city of badly cleaned and foully smelling streets, and of desolating plagues bursting forth from time to time and carrying off myriads of people. On the contrary, it is the city *par excellence* of the trade, business and commerce of the modern world. The city of the Bank, the Mint and the exchange of Lombard Street, Cornhill and Mincing Lane, of warehouses and Counting rooms, of vaults and offices, in a word, of those great commercial houses whose extended operations embrace the entire globe. The city where the Bankers, brokers, merchants, stock jobbers, money changers, Jew and Gentile, most do love to congregate, and where they regularly cast up the accounts of the world.

Fleet street and the Strand are the great arteries of the city, and, passing by Temple Bar from Charing Cross, extend to Ludgate Hill, where St. Paul's rears its towering front. Here making the circuit of the Cathedral and thence branching into Cheapside, Poultry, Cornhill and Cannon streets. These are a few only of the great arteries through which the tide of population and business flows. Thousands of others in all directions are daily choaked with vehicles and myriads of human beings who swarm like bees on every spot.

Around this focus or centre of business have grown up, with incredible rapidity, the different quarters known as Brompton, Hammersmith, St. John's Wood, etc., which with the "city" constitute what is known as the Metropolis, or the Metropolitan district, spreading over an area 18 miles long by 14 wide, and containing a population of about 3,800,000 souls. This is the monster London which has been so well styled a province covered with houses. The houses are built almost entirely of brick and are generally inferior in size, architectural ornament and imposing appearance. They inspire no idea, indeed, that they are the palaces of the rich and great. The humid atmosphere, causing the smoke to settle down upon the dwellings, soon changes their color, the brick becoming of a dingy gray, the whole assuming a dreary and dismal appearance. Buckingham Palace, the residence of the Queen, and on which vast sums have been lavished, during the reign of George IV and since, is not equal to many of the country seats of the nobility, and St. James' Palace, where the Royal Drawing-rooms or receptions are held, and which was the town residence of the royal family until the accession of Queen Victoria, is a low, red brick building resembling a lying-in-hospital, for which purpose it was originally intended. Excepting St. Paul's Cathedral, Westminster Abbey, the New Parliament Houses, Somerset House, the British Museum, the University of London, the principal club houses, and some of the fine old historical residences, such as Northumberland and Chesterfield houses and the new hotels, there is little in the way of architectural beauty or symmetry of which London can boast. It is a monotonous wilderness of brick and mortar, where the stranger sees little evidence, save upon stated occasions of solemn processions, of the existence of an opulent aristocracy and brilliant court. The paucity of fine private residences in this great city, the seat of the wealthiest of commercial empires, is striking, and can only be explained upon the hypothesis that the money which would embellish any other capital is elsewhere expended. And this is, indeed, the fact. In England the proprietorship of landed property carries with it greater dignity and influence than in any other country. Hence the nobleman directs his attention specially to the improvement of his country estates. On these he spends the chief part of his time, his talents and capital in making agricultural experiments, in rearing fine stock, and in growing large crops. Here, if he belongs to the old nobility, he keeps up a baronial castle or a stately hall, dispensing a princely hospitality. If he is of the class of new rich, he builds a spacious mansion and endeavors to rival "my lords." These large estates have grown out of the feudal system and the law of primogeniture, which Dr. Johnson rather justified, because "that it makes but one fool in a family," and constitutes one of the peculiar features of England.— Among the most magnificent we remember to have seen, during a long residence in the country, may be mentioned in passing— those of the Marquis of Breadalbane, whose property extends on a straight line from his mansion a distance of 100 miles, and the Duke of Sutherland's, which covers a whole county in Scotland, extending from sea to sea. The Duke of Norfolk's park in Sussex, is fifteen miles in circuit, and the Island of Lewis, containing 500,000 acres, is owned by a single individual! The process of absorption is still going on, the larger domains growing larger and larger as the number of proprietors decrease. A hundred years ago there were 250,000 proprietors in England and now there are only 30,000. This is a great evil certainly and must be remedied. Urgent necessity there is of *nationalizing* the land, as the present state of affairs both in England and Ireland show. Against this increasing evil John Bright, the late J. S. Mill and the Manchester party generally, have raised their voices and are proceeding to "agitate" the country.

The English nobility and the landed gentry only know London during the season. What the metropolitan mansions lack, however, in exterior ornament is more than compensated by the expensive and luxurious style of their interior decorations and furniture. In the inside, everything is of a sumptuous and elegant description. Nothing is wanting which refinement, taste and cultivation can suggest or gold purchase. Costly paintings adorn the walls—they are often more costly than meritorious. Every niche has its statue. A simple list of the houses of the principal nobility and gentry where valuable collections of art treasures may be seen by any one taking the trouble to make application, would cover pages. The finest of these is Stafford House (St. James' Park) which was built by the Duke of York, second son of George III. It is at present owned and occupied by the Duke of Sutherland, who is little else than a titled booby. In Bridgewater House, the residence of the Earl of Ellesmere, the collection of paintings at the death of the Duke of Bridgewater in 1803 were valued at $750,000. The collection now contains three hundred and twenty-two paintings of the estimated value of $1,500,000. We give these figures because the English are a people whose imaginations are not transported by figures of rhétoric. They are a people with whom, not excepting glory itself, everything ends in money.* If offered to the competition of connoisseurs this collection would doubtless fetch a larger sum. In no country in Europe are the arts so patronized and encouraged by the wealthy classes.

It is impossible for the stranger, amidst the confusion produced by the multiplicity of objects and images that dance before his eyes and glide away, to take a comprehensive view of the whole capital. A description of each quarter and all the wonders presented to his contemplation, would exceed our limits—require volumes. We shall content ourself with giving the result of a *coup d'œil* of the capital from the most commanding spot in the city, the summit of St. Paul's Cathedral. Beyond question this

---

*The British government votes to her victorious generals and officers of inferior grade, under guise of public testimonials and swords of honor, magnificent pensions and huge sums of ready money. After Sir Garnett Woolsey's successful campaign in Ashantee land, he was rewarded by a lump sum of £25,000 sterling, and on his return from Egypt raised to the peerage, with probably a further sum of money by way of supplying him the means to keep up the state and dignity of his Barony. Lord de Sausmarez, after his brilliant naval victories, was voted $10,000 a year for his life and that of his son and grandson. These are only a few instances which occur to memory among those whose families are known to the writer. All the world knows the large grants in the way of money, lands and houses made by Parliament to such heroes as Marlborough and Wellington.

is the most eligible position for seeing the metropolis, and the stranger no sooner mounts to the dizzy heights than he is dazzled and bewildered by the extent and variety of objects spread out before his eyes—one illimitable expanse of streets, courts, alleys, squares and parks, alive with restless activity and teeming millions. In the section immediately surrounding this centre, all the financial transactions of the country are carried on, principally in Lombard street, the resort of the bankers, and Capel Court, the haunt of the money brokers and stock jobbers. Here, beneath the surface of the streets, the private bankers have their vaults, which with those of the Mint and the Bank of England contain the treasure of the Kingdom. In the circumjacent streets the wholesale business is conducted. In a word, it is the heart or core of that busy world of London, belonging to the toiling millions, and in which a drone is *rara avis in terris*.

Sweeping across the southern horizon the eye takes in those populous districts to the south of the river, Camberwell, Lambeth and Peckham. These are crowded with artizans and the laboring classes generally, and it is from the lofty chimnies of this region that thick volumes of smoke constantly arise and spread like a pall over the scene. To the east appear the lofty spires and gilded domes of Greenwich, surrounded by the deep green of the wooded heights, while midway between the Northern and Southern limits of the city the river flows. This is crowded with forests of masts, smoke-stacks and funnels far as the eye can reach. Along the Thames the eye wanders from Westminster Bridge to Victoria Docks, a distance of more than ten miles, which comprehends the entire line connected with the harbour and the naval and commercial operations of the kingdom. All the streets and wharves on the line are crowded with vehicles carrying off the goods which have been landed, or bringing down cargoes for vessels to be freighted. The busy crowd which gathers here is entirely different from that seen near the Bank and Exchange, and is composed of another class of those enterprising men who contribute so much by their labor to extend the commerce and add to the wealth and glory of England. This is the peculiar haunt of shippers and importers. About midway in this line stands that huge edifice known as Somerset House, where all accounts of the Kingdom are audited and affairs connected with the internal revenues of the Empire are settled, and on a line with it, but further down the river, is the Custom House, the never failing barometer of the national prosperity, on which fleet after fleet bears down and whose ponderous cranes are perpetually at work transfering to the gaunt and dreary looking ware houses, which cover this quarter, the immense stores contributed by the world to the wealth and energy of the British people. Also the coal exchange and Fish Mongers Hall, the latter the headquarters of one of the most ancient and wealthy guilds in the Kingdom. Here also is "Shameless Billingsgate," the famous fish market, the resort of drunken sailors and oyster wenches so celebrated for its vulgar wrangles and intolerable stenches.

On the same inclined plane but higher up the river, in striking contrast to the Fish Market, are those quiet and delightful gardens extending in sloping greens to the water's edge which belong to the inner and middle Temple Inns of Court, wherein a large portion of practising barristers have chambers, wherein also, as in colleges and universities, so many young men live together upon terms of easy freedom, and are supposed to be engaged in the study of law, but are in too many cases engrossed with the pursuits of pleasure. Lower down again stands that remarkable monument of antiquity, the Tower, the chief object of curiosity with the majority of strangers.

> "The Tower of Julius, London's lasting shame,
> With many a foul and midnight murder fed."

This ancient fortress cannot be visited without awakening in the mind the recollection of memorable scenes and tragic stories. Hard by is that lofty monument erected in remembrance of the great fire of 1666, of which Pope said, in allusion to the inscription it bears, accusing the Catholics of burning this Protestant city.

> "London's high column, pointing to the skies,
> Like a tall bully, lifts its head and lies."

On this line also, are found those extensive docks constructed upon a scale to accommodate the shipping of the world and which are without a parallel among the public works of this or any other country, and near by, burrowing beneath the bed of the river, is the Thames tunnel, that wonderful triumph of modern engineering skill. Diverted from its original purpose it is now used by the Chatham and Dover railway, numerous trains daily passing through it from the two sides of the river.

In the opposite direction, two miles from St. Paul's, is Trafalgar Square, and the Royal Academy. Sir Robert Peel once declared in a moment of patriotic enthusiasm, that this was "The finest site in Europe." The most important work of art in this square is the column dedicated to Nelson, which rises alone in solitary majesty, with its base at once decorated and guarded by the bronze lions of Sir Edward Landseer. Here the famous West-end begins, in which are grouped the Parliament Houses, the Abbey of Westminster, the Royal Palaces, the Home and Foreign offices, the

Headquarters of the Army, the Admiralty and the Government offices generally. Also the Club Houses, the residences of Court retainers and all those most distinguished for rank and wealth, and who make up the fashionable world. This is the quarter whence issue those endless lines of showy equipages which roll with stately grandeur along Rotten Row through Hyde Park and Kensington Gardens.

To the north of Hyde Park lies Tyburnia, a handsomely built modern city, principally occupied by successful merchants and bankers, the *noveaux riche;* all those who are undergoing, in the significant language of the club houses, the transitorial state between commerce and fashion. Tyburnia is a sort of *Hades* or purgatory where aspirants for Belgravia and Mayfair are prepared to enjoy those Elysian fields.

The health, beauty and comfort of the West-end are increased by three grand parks, the largest of which, Hyde Park with Kensington Gardens, contains 688 acres. In the district, popularly known as Bayswater and Nottinghill, there are likewise many noble squares, and it is in reference to these squares and parks which, indeed, exist in every quarter of the metropolis, that it has been truly said, they are the nostrils and the lungs of London.

There are few meritorious statues in the public places of London; a peculiarity due, the Londoner will tell you, to the English climate, which quickly destroys such works of art when exposed to its action, but which a stranger is more disposed to attribute to a want of appreciation of the fine arts—sculpture more especially.

Notwithstanding its extraordinary size, the health of London is better, as the bills of mortality show, than that of any large city in Europe. This fact is rightly attributed to the excellent, but still inadequate, system of drainage. The rapid increase of the Metropolis has made the subject of drainage one of growing difficulty and embarrassment, especially since it became evident that the sewers could no longer be discharged into the river. Under this system the river itself was but a vast sewer, and the banks were all but insupportable. During the summer the air was filled with noxious vapors and fatal fevers generated, notwithstanding the temporary expedients resorted to for correcting the evil, such as scattering lime and other disinfecting agents on the water and over the slimy shores. It was the pressing importance of this question which led, in 1858, to the formation of a vast system of sewers, or subterranean tunnels, 12 feet wide and 9½ feet high, to run by the sides of the river to a point 15 miles distant, where they discharge into the river at high tide, that the ebb tide may remove the refuse. The total length of the great receiving sewers is 72 miles, and the estimated cost $15,900 000.

From this *coup d'eil* we gather the fact that London so far exceeds the capitals of other countries that it may be regarded as, *par excellence*, the metropolis of the world. It is not only the most populous, but most wealthy, if not the most enterprising. The population is greater than that of the kingdoms of Hanover or Westphalia, and nearly double that of Greece. It is nearly as great as that of the City and State of New York, the most populous of the United States, and little less than that of Scotland. London may be likened then to a kingdom concentrated upon the territory of a very small province. Nowhere, in such a space, can there be found gathered such vast interests, so much luxury, so much misery, so much pleasure, such sorrow, so much wealth, such poverty!

A retrospective glance at its mutations will not be uninteresting. Little over two and a half centuries ago, at the accession of James I, the population was 150,000—less than half the population of a dozen modern cities within a day's journey of Pall Mall. It had increased to only 675,000 in 1700, and in 1801 had just reached 860,000. The progress has since been more rapid, and in 1870, as we have seen, the population exceeded three and a half millions.

Queen Elizabeth, and subsequently James I and Charles I, were alarmed at the increase of the inhabitants, and sought to retard the progress of the population. By royal proclamations Elizabeth prohibited the erection, within three miles of the city gates, of any new house or tenement "where no former house hath been known to have been." James I and Charles I, issued similar proclamations, the latter declaring that if larger it could "neither be governed nor fed." Charles was perfectly correct in this opinion. But for the invention of steam, London could not be fed at this day, and to govern it requires an army of 10,000 policemen. In the time of Charles I the city was without an organized police, and was the receptacle of thieves and robbers who stalked abroad in daylight, setting all authority at defiance. Nor was it lighted at night, nor supplied with water, nor indeed, any of the modern appliances for securing health, comfort or security; and it is not surprising that royal minds should have been filled with misgivings at the prospect of its increase.

The Strand, in the time of Henry VIII, was merely a country road leading through green fields to Westminster, and was so full of ruts and holes that the King ordered it to be paved at the expense of the owners of the adjoining lands. The Churches of St. Martin's-in-the-field and St. Giles'-in-the-field were so called from having been originally erected literally in the fields. During the reign of Elizabeth, when it was first rated, the Parish of St.

Martins contained only one hundred persons who were liable for poor rates. West of this was the open country, where now stands St. James, Piccadilly, Pall Mall, Regent Street and the West-end quarter. The present fashionable Mayfair was distinguished as a dairy farm, and the region of Dover street and Berkeley square was famous for game. Oxford street, then known as Tyburn road, lay through a country district, of which Pennant wrote about the middle of the last century: "I remember Oxford street a deep, hollow road and full of sloughs, with here and there a ragged house the lurking place of cut throats; insomuch that I was never taken that way by night, in my hackney coach, to a worthy Uncle's who gave me lodgings in George's street, but I went in dread the whole way." What a contrast to the brilliant Oxford street of to-day.

A hundred years ago the inhabitants of Kensington, intending to visit London during the evening, collected in large numbers and marched in a body for defence and mutual protection. The managers of theatres in Islington announced in their play-bills, "A horse patrol will be sent in the new road to-night for the protection of the nobility and gentry who go from the squares at the end of the town." It was not considered safe to cross Lincoln's Inn Fields on a dark night, or Hounslow heath after dark. The streets were badly lit with oil burners. So much so that links were carried before carriages and foot passengers as late as 1805, and these linkmen and boys were amongst the most numerous and disorderly classes of London.

Bethnel Green and Spital-fields were in 1805 rural districts. — Now they are probably the most populous districts of London, and there are miles of spacious streets in even these, which are considered the most inferior town quarters.

What is true of them is equally true of the districts south of the river, as far as Dulwich and Camberwell, now a dense mass of human dwellings extending in all directions. In the 17th century this was simply a wild and unenclosed tract of semi-swamp land.

In the 17th century the river Fleet ran between Temple bar and Ludgate Hill, flowing into the Thames near Blackfriar's Bridge. Barges sailed up this stream to discharge their cargoes at Holborn hill. In the course of time the Fleet became a nuisance, nothing more than an offensive sewer, and was covered in, and is now one of the main underground drains. On the north, the present district of Moorfields was simply what its name bespeaks, a moor or fen. So was the present site of Finsbury, which takes its name from the *Fens* on which it is built and which were first drained in 1527.

Few houses were built of brick previous to the great fire in

1666; there were some few built however between 1616 and 1636. The most interesting of those are in Lincoln's Inn Fields, Covent Gardens, Great Queen street, St. Martin's lane and Aldersgate street. The best specimen of old English domestic architecture in the city is Crosby Hall in Bishopsgate street, which was erected of stone and timber in the 15th century. When built it was considered the finest house in London, and is full of historic interest, being referred to by Shakespeare as the residence of Richard III. After the great fire, the city was rapidly rebuilt and extended westward, but as late as 1708 the papers spoke of Sir Robert Walpole when minister, thus: "The right Honorable Premier comes to town this day from Chelsea." It takes less time now to reach London from the sea coast at Brighton or Hastings!

Notwithstanding the already gigantic proportions of London, it is annually increasing at the rate of 80,000, and for many miles after leaving what is technically known as the Metropolis, it is difficult to define where the country begins and the town ends. The everlasting tide of brick and mortar rolls on, covering fields, parks, towns and villages. Silent villages, sleepy hamlets are obliterated by masonry; fields and parks are mapped out into squares, crescents and streets, shops, public houses, cab and omnibus stands, school houses, churches and suburban residences appear, and the country becomes incorporated into the town—an embodied part of the great city.

There seems to be no limit to its growth, while the country advances in wealth and prosperity, unless it be presented in the obstacle to which Charles I. alluded—the inability of all means of transportation to bring the population food. This difficulty may paralyze its growth; it does not appear that any other is likely to do so. Good dwelling houses for the poor, spacious streets, squares and parks, an abundant supply of pure water, thorough drainage, will keep off plague and pestilence—can railways and steamboats prevent famine?

Having given the reader, briefly, a tolerable idea of London, without encumbering the account with figures, we shall have occasion in subsequent pages to make him acquainted with the metropolis in other aspects, and give him a glimpse of its social condition and of some of the subdivisions of its mixed population, their modes of life, manners and customs and actual condition.

We will not say that those who have not seen London have seen nothing, but they have failed to see a great and curious spectacle. Under its one aspect of magnificence it is without a rival in modern times, and in its other of degredation, poverty and crime it undoubtedly surpasses all other cities —ancient or modern.

In the West-end, the rallying point of its rank and wealth, it is gayer, brighter, more resplendent with fashion, glitter and gold than even Paris, and in its remoter districts sad and dull without a parallel. Whatever pretense of life lingers about these regions is highly suggestive of still-life, if not of death itself, which renders them more truly appalling, more ghastly than Pompeii.

## CHAPTER II.

### THE DARK SIDE OF LONDON LIFE.—THE SOCIAL DREGS.

Having in the preceding chapter presented a general idea of outside London, we shall introduce the reader in this to some interior views. He will not see in them the most pleasing, interesting or popular aspects of metropolitan life, but there are plenty of writers who riot in descriptions of the *beau monde*, by which we mean the world of fashion, for neither wit nor learning are elements in it. On the other hand the number is small indeed, of those who are willing to take the less attractive, not to say revolting part, of portraying scenes where vice wears no veil and decency forever blushes. Let it be our part, at least, to touch upon them.

During a long residence in London, the author gathered the information embodied in this chapter from various sources and by personal visits to the haunts of the destitute, and the dens of thieves. He was sometimes accompanied by a clergyman of the District, but more frequently by a brace of well armed policemen. The scenes disclosed to him deepened his convictions that London forms no exception to the rule that sunshine may fall upon the earth and bless it, but the shadow is ever at its side. To know London you must see both sides of the picture —its dens of misery its regions of squalid poverty and perennial suffering, as well as its West-end mansions and shops, its noble squares and extensive parks. Prominent as is the mighty Babylon of our day for its wealth and grandeur, it is equally disgraced by its exceptionable regions of poverty which excite pity, and of crime which awaken fear. While it is undeniably a pleasant thing to contemplate man in all the exaltation of his wisdom and virtue, it is also of service to us to occasionally look into his obliquities and to distinctly remark how great and portentous are his follies, his crimes and his sufferings.

Penetrate into remote quarters, and you find behind the smiling exterior of West-end wealth and splendor, masses of miserable, over-crowded houses, immured, as it were, in close and narrow streets, from which narrower alleys radiate, where the sun never peeps and broad daylight is never seen; swarms of poverty stricken people, pale with grief and suffering, emaciated, toiling men and women, by the side of beggars and thieves, and all maintaining a desperate struggle with want—literally fighting for life. No belle, glittering with jewels, rolls in her coach to the Queen's Drawing room without startling the ear of dying poverty in some hovel of wretchedness and despair. No gaily dressed congregation reaches its fashionable church without encountering the fumes of taprooms and gin palaces, and mixing with their crowd of squalid, drunken customers. Thus is exemplified the truth:

> "Wherever God erects a house of prayer,
> The Devil always builds a chapel there."

The Royal Palace has its disgusting back-ground of reeking sinks, slums and hovels in Pimlico. The opera has its counterpart in the low, vice-engendering penny theatre, and the balls of the aristocracy are set off by the costermonger's two-penny hop. The fine shops of Regent street and Piccadilly draw their supplies of silks and rich stuffs from the poverty stricken dens of Spitalfields. The gayest and most brilliant streets of the West-end are close upon St. Giles, the darkest London haunt of crime and misery. Hordes of beings rise every morning without as much food as will serve them through the day, and who derive a precarious existence by sweeping the crossings, selling matches, gathering bones or rags, riddling cinders out of dust holes, retailing apples or oranges, collecting and selling the refuse vegetables of the markets, running errands, and, worst of all, girls selling their perishing charms for the wherewithal to buy bread and meat.— The stranger dreams not of these things when sauntering through Piccadilly or Pall-Mall, where a beggar is rarely seen, and the panorama of which is but a successive procession of prosperous industry and superfluous wealth. The moral geologist of London however, can map out the localities of the different classes, each having its haunt, as clearly as the physical geologist does the chalk and clay, marl and gravel deposits of any given section of country. Each of these localities is known to them. They can point in an instant to the retreat of the burglars, the shop lifters, the coiners, the dog stealers, the pick-pockets, the garroters, the murderers, the house burners, the hiding places of the infamous generally, where no policeman dare venture alone. The spots where are gathered the social dregs, the lees, the offscourings of the great city, the Pariahs, outcasts and outlaws, whose hands like the hand of Ishmael, are against the world.

Formerly one of the most notorious of all these haunts was St. Giles, one of Dickens' favorite resorts for studying low life and obtaining materials for his inimitable sketches. St. Giles was, however, broken up by the extension of Oxford street through its heart. The inhabitants did not cease to exist, and the army of beggars, knackers, thieves and murderers, thus unhoused, settled down and crammed themselves in the district about Saffron Hill and Smithfield, a region where are still seen, as in Hogarth's day, over gin sellers' doors, "*Drunk here for one penny, dead drunk for two pence, and clean straw for nothing.*" Not even is it safe for the clergyman to enter this district without police attendance. In some parts it is a huge bagnio, in others a thieves' caravansary; in others are ware-houses of stolen goods and manufacturies of decaying poisonous food; the whole district being a sink of nauseating stenches and moral putridity.

But it is not in such outlaying districts alone that masses of human beings are huddled together in filthy courts and alleys.— The Royal Palace is close upon the sinks and stews of Pimlico, the streets of bagnios and the dens of thieves who are the tenants of the Dean and Chapter of Westminster. Eaton Square, in famed Belgravia, closely adjoins one of the still worse drained and most squalid parts of the West end. All around Westminster Abbey are reeking rockeries, under the very noses of the law-givers of the land. This is equally true of the fashionable quarter of Regent street—it lies in the midst of rookeries, filled with human beings for whom modern civilization and progress has done absolutely nothing. The largest and finest streets and quarters, indeed London over, have their back ground of wretchedness. In these favored localities the fine buildings are but screens for misery behind them, which shocks the mind and from which men avert their gaze. In too many cases industrious, hard working families are huddled together in a single room, a sitting room by day, and by night a bed-chamber. Many spots like Agar's Town have been squatted upon, and it is found impossible to remove the squalid inhabitants. The ground is undrained, houses foul, the streets filthy, water scarce and a clean life impossible. It is the same case in the minories, Shoreditch, Whitechapel, Wapping, and in their antipodes Paddington, Bermondsey and Lambeth.— The disreputable and the criminal classes and the working people are environed with nuisances and live in dwellings which barely supply the most elementary wants of our being, and where the moral as well as the physical atmosphere is full of poison, especially for the susceptible nature of youth. If there be goodness, generosity, nobility in any toiling inhabitant, it is poluted and cramped by the poison and penury of all around. But of these redeeming qualities there is, we fear, but little. The majority of the resident families are drunken and destitute, and filth and immorality abound to an extraordinary extent.

In the districts occupied by the better class of laborers—the the porters, policemen and such like—there is likewise extreme poverty. Though their wages are high, so are their rents. Can any one wonder that rent troubles exist in England as well as Ireland? There is another drain upon them, the almost constant presence of sickness in their dwellings, and the want of medicines and medical advice. A few years ago, the philanthropic Lord Shaftsbury made a visit to one of the favored localities, as they are regarded, near Golden Squares, and thus describes it : "It is a quarter inhabited by the most respectable of the laboring classes. They were all deeply sensible of the misery brought on them by the condition of their dwellings and the impossibility of keeping them tidy, and by the fetid smells to which even habit had not reconciled them. These families have each but one room, about twelve feet square, in which they sleep and live, and some in addition carry on their trade. I found many of them full of steam, exhaling from clothes hung up across the room to dry, after having been washed, many of them in the same water, owing to its scarcity. In every family we heard of sickness and death; some had lost two thirds hardly any less than one-half of their children. Their houses had been for the most part once inhabited by separate families of some fortune, and were partitioned off into lodging rooms, at weekly rents, varying from 1s.6d for a very bad cellar, to 5 shillings for a large upper room. In no case had they any but an intermittent supply of water at the bottom of the house, which in some cases was kept in water butts of decaying wood. Some of these rooms were in overcrowded cow houses, where cows diseased by the badness of the air, supply the neighborhood with diseased milk, some close to slaughter houses."

From this description it is readily seen that the mortality must be frightful. Indeed it is said to exceed that of a well regulated hospital, and is far beyond any losses England sustains in Afghan and Zulu campaigns. Typhus fever is a constant denizen. What else, indeed, is possible when each small house is occupied on an average by seventy? The lessee who pays from ·£20 to £30 rent, sublets the rooms at from two to three hundred per cent. on the original rental. It is common for thirty and forty children to sleep in a single room 18x20 feet. These are the scenes of defilement and pestilence in which thousands of children are reared. Their only education is obtained in such *homes* and in the streets round about them. They are constant witnesses of drunkenness which grows out of this state of physical defilement, and thus become familiar with beastly scenes.

From these dens and haunts issue the lawless, roaming and deserted children of the Metropolis, over fifty thousand in number. One half of these dine out, living on garbage and sleeping under porticos, sheds, carts, the dry arches of bridges and viaducts, in out houses, saw pits, stair cases, in the open air, or in those cheap lodging houses where forty are placed in a small room 12x18, the floor of which is covered with straw, shavings or old rags, and where they pay a penny each for the night's accommodation. It is in such haunts that the larger part of the crime which is committed is concealed. They are but nurseries or breeding places for the prisons; the homes of wild, neglected, lawless children. These *gamin* are seen in every part of London. They are bold, pert and dirty, half starved, half clad, haggard, yet vivacious. They talk obscene slang, raise the shout of laughter at the reeling drunkard, pick pockets and prowl in all directions in search of prey. Their only education is obtained in their lodging houses or gathered from the festering gutters. The principal part of their education consists in learning the art of picking pockets and committing other crimes without detection. To facilitate the work of instruction, the professors, who are aged and experienced old rogues, who have retired from active life, resort to many ingenious devices and contrivances. Among those for testing the ingenuity and skill of youth aspiring to become a pick-pocket, is a *lay* figure suspended by a small elastic cord from a bell fastened in the ceiling. Stuffing the pockets of this figure with port-monies, pencil cases, hankerchiefs, etc., they are then buttoned up and the senior class of light fingered gentry is brought in for instruction. The professor now diligently practices them in all the arts and ways of emptying the pockets of the lay figure without sounding the bell. Those who perform the task again and again with dexterity, are graduated and sent abroad to prey upon the public, while those who do not, are soundly flogged. If after repeated floggings and months of instruction, they do not acquire the requisite delicacy of touch and agility of action to perform such *sleight of hand* feats they are permanently passed into another class and become apprentices to less difficult branches of the robbing profession.

In the complicated state of modern society there are many causes operating to produce the crime that nestles in the streets of great cities, which meets us at every turn in the rural districts, which haunts us in our going out and coming in, which spares neither age nor sex. It may be born of ignorance, of depravity, of want, but above all it must be set down to intemperance ; to the whiskey bottle and the ginpalace. These are the fruitful sources of the frightful demoralization of the people. In London there are 180,000 gin drinkers, who spend $15,000,000 a year in this spirituous drink alone. During a period of thirteen years 249,000 males and 183,920 females were taken in custody in London alone, for being drunk and disorderly. Of the ten or twelve thousand charges entered annually at Bow Street police station, one-half are for being drunk Samuel Warren, author of "*Ten Thousand a Year,*" who was in 1871 Recorder of Hull, in the course of a long and luminous charge to the grand jury, recently said : "As all crimes have their origin in intemperance or ignorance, there are two causes to which it is your duty to pay particular attention." 30,000 persons are annually committed to prison in Scotland, 40,000 in England and it is estimated that 90 per cent. of these crimes arose out of the drinking custom of society. These are terrible facts.

The existence of the dangerous classes, to which we have referred briefly, in the midst of modern society, under the shadow of our churches, schools and libraries, is one of the most deplorable incidents connected with the vaunted progress of the age. Classes who owe nothing to society but a bitter grudge—who owe nothing to, as they never derive anything from civilization. The ferocity of these classes was brought to light in Paris by the French Commune—classes of whose existence scarcely any one had previous knowledge, and greatly added to the horrors and terrors of that era of crime and bloodshed. Assi and his associates were little else than "tiger apes" or demons in human shape. They were gaunt, inhuman, merciless and savage ; a frightfully demoralized brood, who sprang as if from the earth, and filled the streets of the city, the halls of the Tuileries and the saloons of the aristocracy. All law and order was overturned and these barbarians held for a time supreme command. Everybody knows the excesses and crimes of that second "reign of terror." There cannot be a doubt that London contains an equally savage race of "tiger apes" ready to rush forth on the least occasion, to commit equally savage and revolting excesses. The world is not their friend, or the world's law. Nor have they any idea of the governing authorities than that they constituted an armed despotism which prevents their earning a livelihood. They hate all law because they are taught to believe that it is but a tyranny administered for their oppression. They have no idea of religious or moral principles, and when they are aroused, what is to restrain the exercise of their grossest passions? Society has no greater enemy than these neglected classes – the wretched—the half fed dregs of the nation, who fester in the cesspools of all great cities. All must shudder at the flood of crime which, like a lava stream flowing from a volcano and destroying the vineyards of the sunny land, is apparently, in spite of repression and detection, withering the good of the world and scorching its promises into the ashes of disappointment. Yet in our opinion there is no reason for despair. The earnest and thoughtful know that below, deeper than all these bad influences and more powerful, there is the true spirit bubbling up, through the hot crust of evil and neglect, in springs of purity—that truth and falsehood are grappling and no one has ever known truth to have the worst of it, in a fair and open encounter. This spirit is pouring itself forth by a thousand channels, is making religion its minister and science its handmaid. It is sent forth in sermons, essays, lectures, pamphlets, novels, poetry—in a thousand ways we are told that refinement and barbarism are contending powers, and in order that the rich may enjoy their luxury the poor must be elevated; that one class of the family of man can never be happy while others are miserable. This is the voice which urges noble men to give to the poor parks, picture galleries and libraries, baths and wash houses, improved dwellings which will enable them to live with some decency and refinement. In short, the true spirit of the times is one directed to the improvement of the moral and social state of the masses. This spirit has already accomplished much since these notes were penned, in eradicating and repressing the evils of which we have spoken, and when it was impossible utterly to eradicate them, to mitigate their evils. Let us hope that this great and beneficent work will be ceaselessly prosecuted until the holy mission is accomplished. It is no doubt painful to have seen, at times it may be depressing to reflect over such things and scenes as those just described. The man, however, who has a heart to appreciate and a brain to understand, cannot but be improved by such extension of his knowledge. No matter where he may be afterwards placed, he has laid up for himself mental food for life.

Charity, curiosity and philanthropy have united to portray with uniform accuracy all the incidents in the life of the London poor. Home missionary societies, newspaper reporters, adventurous philanthropists, and the intelligent foreigner have penetrated into their retreats and have brought to light innumerable details, curious, sad and revolting. The darkest recesses of their social state have been revealed to us. An elaborate inventory has been made of their defects, physical, moral and spiritual. We know what their dwellings are, how they live, the amount of their incomes and how they spend them, what they save or rather what they do not save; how they are taxed and what usury they pay ; how many can read and write, what they eat, drink and wear, how many live in one house and sleep in one bed, and and finally how much sooner they sink into graves than the comfortable classes. All has been investigated and lies exposed to the public gaze. The physician has inspected their sores, and the magistrate their vices. The Divine knows how many do not attend church, and the teetotaler how many frequent the gin shop.

It was highly desirable that such information should be obtained. Having procured it, those who are willing and able to aid the poorer classes in their efforts to elevate themselves, now know what measures to take, how the existing evil may be remedied.

It is not our purpose to enter into these grave questions. We shall confine ourselves to giving some of the details of the daily life of the 50,000 prowlers of the streets. The people and authorities of London will doubtless know how to grapple with the subject in its practical bearings.

The nomadic population of London, the vagabonds or Metropolitan Gypsies, or those who live upon the settled classes at large, is composed pretty much as follows : Beggars of all kinds, bone grubbers, mud larks, patterers, costermongers, fruit-and-fish sellers, dogsellers, hawkers of all kinds, finders, sifters, street artists, musicians and showmen, acrobats ; in short, the entire loose and wandering population. The "finders" are a leading class and live by picking up in the public thoroughfares, bits of coal, ends of half smoked cigars, bones, rags. and such like odds and ends, which they manage to sell for money.

In addition to the *waifs*, in the way of lost articles, picked up by these Finders, they in the course of their trade of living in the thoroughfares, occasionally find the way into the pockets of the inexperienced and unwary. Indeed it is believed that the larger part of the "findings" of these light fingered gentry, are of small articles which have never been lost. The largest and most influential division of the street Bohemians goes by the name of the costermongers, and this class includes fish sellers, retailers of vegetables, oranges, ginger beer, pop-cock, fruit and such like articles These wandering traders, people who carry their stock upon their backs or in a hand barrow, are the hucksters and greengrocers of the streets, and supply a large portion of the working population with food, little comforts, and the lighter articles of dress. The "upper ten" of these occasionally own a donkey and cart. Many women and even children belong to this roving body of tradesmen, and scarcely any of them can read or write.— Amongst these the percentage of Irish is very large, and they are said to assume a place among the lowest strata of society in other great provincial cities, as well as in London. A fact, if true, strangely in contrast with the settled position the Irish win in America by their steady industry and many noble qualities.

Leaving the class of itinerant hucksters, we next come to the patterers, or distributors of wayside literature, the street musicians or organ grinders, the sellers of water cresses, the keepers of coffee stalls, where a black mixture, one-half chicory and the other half possibly catsup—it tastes like it—is sold at a half penny per cup; the cat's meat retailers, whose stock consists of the carcasses of defunct horses and dogs; ballad singers who parade in front of the best houses, about eleven o'clock p. m., making night hideous with their shrieks; play bill sellers and purveyors of dubious news; bone grubbers and mud larks; crossing sweepers, street performers and show men; travelling menders of chairs, umbrellas, clocks and pots, and the professional tinkers; sellers of bonnet boxes, toys, stationary, plaster statuary, songs, ditties and last dying speeches; vendors of tubs, pails, mats, crockery and blacking; of lucifer matches, which won't light, corn salves, clothes pegs, brooms, sweet meats, commonly called "cholera pizen," razors, which like those immortalized by Peter Pinder, were not meant to shave but sell; dog stealers and venders of dogs, dog collars, birds, coals and sand; scavengers, dust men and many others. It is believed that not fewer than 60,000 individuals belong to this class, and like the 50,000 mentioned previously, find their living in the streets.

As the wine and spirit business is the final resort of old army and navy officers, who wish to add to their pensions; of broken down gentlemen, and of prodigal sons, who are indeed their own best customers, so the costermonger's trade is taken up by speculators of a lower grade, when all other avocations fail. It often happens that you will find among the patterers, those who have been clergymen in the established church, and among the orange and herring sellers, those who have been at one time in their lives mechanics or laborers. As a general rule, however, the costers are a distinct people. The children of the costers grow up costers, as gypsies' children grow up gypsies. They acquire the slang, the wandering habits, and the vocation of their parents; and rarely in after life settle down to any fixed employment. When efforts have been made by benevolent and well intentioned people to reclaim the children, it has been generally found impossible.

The author was informed by his friend, Rev. Francis C. T. Moran, brother-in-law of Sir Hardinge Gifford, present Solicitor-General, Incumbent of St Philipps, the Evangelist, Peekham, one of the worst quarters of South London, that a young girl of twelve years of age, whom he had taken from her parents to bring up as a domestic in his family, was in a few months so oppressed with the confinement, the ease, comfort and plenty of a well regulated household and the restraints of civilization, that she availed herself of an opportunity, when sent out upon an errand, to return to her poverty and the Arab freedom of her street life, and no persuasion on his and Mrs. Moran's part could induce her to give it up again. She preferred the bare existence she could pick up in the streets with its liberty, to all that religion, civilization and plenty could give her when restricted to the conventional rules of society among domestics. And had she been acquainted with the poet's lines would have probably quoted them, "give me again my hollow tree, my crust of bread and liberty."

"Bless you," said one of these wild wanderers when asked how they live, "we don't find a living at all, it is only another way of starving." While this is true of a majority, some of them do well, especially the dealers in fish and vegetables, the higher grades of whom make fair earnings, but unfortunately they are spent as quickly as made. The costers are a gambling, improvident set, fond of cards, liquor and tobacco. After business hours they retire to their dens, and with only the feeble light of a tallow candle pass hours at all-fours, blind hookey, or cribbage. When excited they lay heavy bets, but play principally for beer and gin. A majority of costers belong to what are called the "sporting community;" are fond of pugilism, horse racing, dog fighting and rat killing. They are always present at places of amusement, such as penny gaffs, two penny hops, and three penny theatres. The boys are early taught to fight, or as it is called in their slang to "work their fists." All disputes between them are settled in the ring, where no interference is allowed by the umpires, but the antagonists are permitted to fight it out. Of these arenas there are several in each quarter. located generally in underground London and these encounters usually take place at night, and are witnessed by men, women and children. Serving out a policeman is the most noted exploit of a young coster. Until he has served out at least one of the legal custodians of public order, he has no standing in the burrowing community. The policemen are called "Bobbies" or "Peelers." They are so called in memory of their founder, the late Sir Robert Peel, under whose auspices they were introduced to supercede the "Charlies," and

Bow street runners of the preceding generation. Thus says Burns:

> "At length attacked by runners three
> Peg fell, besmeared with wounds so gory,
> And Bob was hanged on Tyburn tree,
> She died for love and he for glory."

Between the bobbies and the costers there is perpetual war. Strategy, tactics, treachery and cunning are employed by both sides to secure victory. When a coster has been unlucky and is captured, and some of them have been in prison a dozen times, they are looked on as martyrs by their comrades. After their imprisonment and return to their friends, they are invariably relieved and rewarded by a general subscription. Long inured to this war with the Peelers, they acquire the skill, cunning, and treachery of savages. The coster endeavors to take the peeler or crusher by surprise, and often crouches at the entrance of a court until his foeman passes, when a stone or brick is hurled and the coster immediately vanishes till the effect of the blow is known. If the crusher is brought to the ground, he is quickly mauled with his own *baton* which the coster carries off in triumph to his retreat. Here it is used for the first night to stir a bowl of gin toddy, after which it is burnt, as they cannot gratify their pride by preserving their trophy longer than one evening, seeing that the peelers are pretty sure to give the coster haunts a visit after one of their number is served out; and it would go hard with those found cherishing such a souvenir of victory. The love of excitement as well as a fondness for gambling is universal among the fraternity of costers; even the young are desperate gamesters, and no effort to mitigate the evil and eradicate the taste has ever been of the slightest avail. On the contrary, the very exertions of the police to put a stop to it, have seemed to increase their desire to indulge in it. These incorrigible scamps hold with Solomon, "stolen waters are sweet, and bread eaten in secret how good is it." Pie boys and butchers' apprentices will toss each other for their stock; ill luck only increases their recklessness, and they will proceed until they have gambled away their caps, coats, cravats and even shirts.

The chief place of amusement for the drama-loving costers is the "Vic," or Cobourg theatre which holds in its galleries about 2,500 persons. On star nights it is so crowded, that at the back it is common to see boys piled on each others shoulders all around. The rules of this theatre do not require a full dress circle but rather its antipodes, and the heat on such occasions being extreme, the costers generally divest themselves of their coats and waistcoats while the "ladies" hang their bonnets and shawls over the iron rail in front.

A not uncommon incident in these theatres is thus graphically and poetically described:

> Pat Jennings in the upper gallery sat,
> But leaning forward, Patrick lost his hat.
> What shall he do? pay at the playhouse door
> Three shillings for what cost when new but four!
> While thus he ponders overwhelmed with grief,
> George Richards whispers, "Take my handkerchief."
> "Thank ye," says Pat, "but one won't make a line,"
> "Take mine," cries Soper, and cries Green "take mine."
> A motley cable now Pat Jennings ties,
> Where Spital fields with real India vies,
> Down darts the varied chord of Iris hue,
> Brown, black and yellow, speckled, pink and blue,
> George Bond below with palpitating hand
> Loops the last kerchief to the coster's band,
> While to the applauding galleries round him, Pat
> Made a low bow and touched the ransomed hat.

An occasional burst of the full band is heard by gushes as if a high wind were raging. Recognitions take place every moment, and "Bill Smith" is called to in a loud voice from one side, and a shout in answer from the other, asks, "What's up?" Or family secrets are revealed, and "Bob Triller" is asked where "Sal" is, and replies amid a roar of laughter, that she is "a-learning the 'pi nanney.'" The conversation ceases suddenly on the rising of the curtain, and then the cries of "Silence! Ord-a-a-r! Ord-a-a-r!" make more noise than ever. Whilst the pieces are going on, brown, flat bottles are frequently raised to the mouth, and between the acts a man with a tin can, glittering in the gaslight, goes round crying "Port-a-a-r! who's for port-a-a-r!" No delay between the pieces will be allowed, and should the interval appear too long, some one, referring to the curtain, will shout out, "Pull up that 'ere window blind!" or they will call to the orchestra, "Now, then, you cat-gut scrapers! Let's have a ha'porth of liveliness!" But the grand hit of the evening is always when a song is sung to which the entire gallery can join the chorus. Some actors at the minor theatres make a great point of this, and in the bill upon one night, when we visited the "Vic," under the title of "There's a good time coming, boys," there was printed, "assisted by the most numerous and effective chorus in the metropolis," meaning the whole of the gallery. The singer himself started the mob, saying, "Now, then gentlemen, the Exeter Hall touch!" and beat time with his hand, parodying M. Jullien with his baton. An "*angcore*" on such occasions is a matter of course, and, despite a few murmurs of "Change it to Duck-legged Dick," invariably insisted on.

The morality of the costermongering community is, as may be imagined, low. They do not believe in the sanctity of the marriage vow. Not one-tenth of those living together are married. They consider it a waste of time and money to go through the form of wedlock, when they can live together and be quite as highly esteemed by their fellows without it. Among them marriage is not honorable, or concubinage disgraceful. The unmarried women living with her lover stands quite as high as the married. These unions last only so long as they are agreeable to both parties, and are dissolved by mutual consent or otherwise, as the case may be. New ones are formed and costermongerdom is not scandalized. The two penny hop is usually the place where matches are made, and the affair is generally settled the first night of meeting. The boy coster is probably not over fifteen and the coster girl is under twenty. Having taken the first step in life by their match they set up costering on their own account.

The religion of the costers is as low as their morals. Few if any ever attend church. Some have never heard that there is a God. Few read and those who can hate tracts which "gives them the 'orrors." In religious matters the costers are not more ignorant than the bulk of the poor population of London. Few persons even in England have an idea of the practical heathenism in which vast numbers are growing up. While this terrible condition of affairs prevails at home, the sympathies of the Christian people of England are sought to be aroused in behalf of the African blacks and the Chinese mulattoes! And in the 19th century it is still true as in the days of Shakespeare, "in England they will not give a doit to relieve a lame beggar, but will lay out ten to see a dead Indian."

Upon this subject a recent writer, one who has investigated the condition of the poor of London minutely and elaborately, remarks "that a class numbering 50,000 should be permitted to remain in a state of almost brutish ignorance, is a national disgrace. If the London costers belong especially to the 'dangerous classes,' the danger of such a body is assuredly of our own creation; for the gratitude of the poor creatures to any one who seeks to give them the least knowledge is almost pathetic."

The ragged schools supported in the neighborhoods of the poor and depraved are not patronized by the costers. Their children are never sent, and the only education they get is acquired like that which made Sam Weller "sharp," in the streets, and is in a word, an education in crime.  In everything connected with the supply of their immediate wants without labor, in procuring money without working for it, they possess a precocious acuteness.  As a natural consequence, they have an irrepressible repugnance to any settled industry, and despise nothing so much as honest labor.  It could scarcely be otherwise when we recollect the moral atmosphere in which the coster grows.

Strange as it may seem, certain rude principles of honor exist among them.  Such property as they possess is always exposed and they leave their stall in charge of a competitor in the same line of business without the slightest fear or suspicion.  Their table, their hand-barrows, the stable containing their donkeys, are unwatched, unguarded by lock or bolt, but the coster sleeps soundly and securely, relying upon the honor which prevails among thieves.  This is somewhat remarkable when we consider that the donkey is included among the unguarded property of the coster.  All costers have a hankering after these little animals.  The strongest tie of affection in the coster's heart is that which binds him to his donkey.  He is kind to his donkey, however cruel he may be to others.  Ill treatment to his donkey he resents as a personal affront.  However meagre his fare the coster shares it with his donkey, always giving it the larger portion of his bread, and his confidence in the intelligence of his donkey is unbounded.

"It is all nonsense to call donkeys stoopid," said one, "them's stoopid as calls them so; they'se sensible, sensible to the last.  Not long since I worked to and from Guildford with my donkey, cart and a boy; Jack, (the donkey,) was slow and heavy in coming back, until he came in sight of the lights of Vauxhall and then he trotted on like one o'clock,—he did indeed! just as if he smelt it was London, besides seeing it, and knew he was at home."

"There was a friend of mine," said another man, "had great trouble with his donkey a few months back.  He was doing a little work on Sunday morning at Wandsworth, and the poor thing fell down dead.  He was very fond of his donkey and kind to it, and the donkey was very fond of him.  He thought he wouldn't leave the poor creature he'd had a good while and had been out with in all weathers by the roadside, so he dropped all idea of doing business, and with help, got the poor dead thing in his cart, its head lolloping over the end of the cart and its poor eyes staring at nothing.  He took the place of the donkey between the shafts.  He thought he'd drag it home and bury it somewhere.  It wasn't for the value of it he dragged it, for what's a dead donkey worth, even for cat's meat?  There were a few persons about him—mourners.  They were quiet and seemed sorry for the poor fellow and for his donkey. The church bells struck up, and up came a crusher and took the man up (for violating the Sabbath) and next day he was fined ten shillings, I can't exactly say for what. He never saw no more of his animal, and lost his stock as well as his donkey."

The costers, like all other persons, when "tight up," are made the victims of the rapacity of usurers. Not having the *capital* to become the owners of the tables, carts and hand barrows used in their business, they hire these from persons who make a support by letting them out. It is a good living too; on every £100 of value in hand barrows, thus advanced by the owners, they derive an annual interest of not less than 20 per cent. per week, or one thousand and forty per cent. per annum. This is a usurious rate of interest quite up to, if not beyond that of the most inexorable modern Shylock. The cost of a barrow is when new, about £2, but no instance is on record of a coster having saved money enough to become the owner of one. They prefer to pay 1 or 1½s per week for its use. If they had the money they would not purchase; and on several occasions when benevolent persons have presented them with barrows, they have immediately sold them at a deduction of fifty per cent. to realize ready cash—nothing being in their eyes so desirable as immediate money. The owners of the barrows live like Lords. One man owning 120 barrows worth £240 derived from them a net income of £360 a year. Many of these owners who let barrows on a large scale, become wealthy in the course of a few years, and often retire to ease and independency in an ornamental cottage or a suburban villa.

With these meagre details we must here stop. It is a painful subject inasmuch as it exhibits a vast number of human beings living in a degraded state, abandoned to mere sensual life. The darkest clouds, however, are lined with silver and this picture is not without some cheering light. Evidence is not wanting, in even these wretched beings, of human goodness which would bring forth the richest fruit with proper culture. We have never felt, when visiting these haunts, any other sentiment than that of commisseration for these unhappy victims of neglect. It is not difficult for the well-fed moralist, seated in his easy chair, his slippered feet upon the fender and a bottle of ruby wine within reach, to expatiate on the depravity of human nature and the beauties of virtue, knowledge and religion. Aye, preaching is indeed easy. We first stigmatize these victims of misfortune as brutish, stolid, wicked —then reap the rewards of their labors and deny them the dignity of citizenship, take from them all incentive to perseverance, all desire to be respectable, all future hope, and then declaim against their recklessness, their disorderly habits, their ignorance and their wickedness! In other words we never want a plea for our own shortcomings and misconduct.

Could the moralist so easily stand the wear and tear of poverty? Were he subjected to their trials what would become of him and his prudence and self denial? Where would be this well wined and well dined homilist without hope to stimulate and port to fortify? If instead of his leisure to moralize upon the frailties of human nature, he were confined to some irksome employment from dawn till dusk, fed upon insufficient food, married to an overworked and underfed factory girl, deprived of the enjoyments opened up by education, with no place of recreation but the pot house or the two-penny theatre, we imagine the complacent moralist would be little better than those he looks down upon from the heights of his prosperity and enjoyment. As no life is pleasing to God but that which is useful to mankind, would it not be wiser and more virtuous to labor to redeem these wretched people, instead of denouncing them? If after providing them healthy employment and remunerative wages, suitable amusements for hours of relaxation, books, newspapers, lectures, concerts and exhibitions; in a word, doing our duty, putting our neighbor in possession of all the advantages we enjoy, they continued incorrigible, it would be soon enough to inveigh against their sins, the sins of suffering humanity. But some people will never learn anything, for this reason: because they understood everything too soon. He is a good divine that follows his own instructions, and these railing moralists would be more useful men and more reliable guides if they preached less and worked more, since it is agreed that the distinguishing characteristic of a man of merit is to be ever active in laudable pursuits.

## CHAPTER III.

THE KEW GARDENS AND RICHMOND PARK—RUMINATIONS OVER SOME OF JOHN BULL'S PECULIARITIES.

So powerful was the effect produced upon us by the strange experiences we had now acquired, and which we have detailed in the preceding chapter, that we resolved, for our heart was troubled, our spirits depressed, to turn for relief to nature, for all nature breathes the language of hope and mercy. Experience teaches the soothing influence of the country, the beneficial effects of from time to time looking upon green fields and bright flowers ; of giving the mind an interval of repose while 'the body wanders over scenes of beauty, and the heart expands under the canopy of heaven.

Thankful for the opportunity of leisure which enabled us to enjoy at this time, rural sights and scenes, we set forth with alacrity, in the direction of Kew and Richmond. We went forth determined to see, in the limited time at our disposal, as much as possible of life in villages and hamlets, farm houses and cottages ; in palaces and castles, parks and gardens ; to attend fairs and festivals—in a word, to mix with the people and study their habits and customs, if possible, in all the conditions and walks of life, persuaded that the character of a people cannot be obtained by confining one's observations to a metropolis, however great that metropolis may be.

Our route was down Parliament street to Westminster, which stands in the centre of that remarkable locality which may be regarded as the heart and core of the British empire. From this centre go forth the veins and arteries which give vitality to the most distant parts of England's dominions   Here are grouped the Parliament Houses, in which the Peers of the Realm and the representatives of the people—the Lords and Commons—assemble. Here also the innumerable offices for the transaction of all public business, civil and military ; Buckingham Palace, the town residence of the Queen, St. James' Palace, in which the drawing rooms or receptions occur, and Marlborough House, the residence of the Prince of Wales ; Westminster Hall, in which for nearly eight hundred years the superior courts of justice have held their sittings ; the Horse Guards and the Admiralty—the respective head quarters of the army and navy ; Westminster School and

Westminster Abbey ; within a few stones' throw Lambeth Palace, the official residence of the Archbishop of Canterbury. On every side are the evidences that the multitudinous affairs of the British Empire are here transacted ; that this is the arena upon which has been solved the theory of the British Constitution ; that here her great and enduring institutions have been moulded into sh⁀pe; the arena where battles have been fought, which if of less thrilling interest, have not been of less importance, in their influence on the affairs of men, than those which follow the shock of contending armies – the arena where noble hearts have pulsated and a long array of illustrious orators and statesmen have passed, whose names and deeds will be gratefully remembered wherever Christianity and civilization find an abiding place.

Pursuing our course up Constitutional Hill we reach Hammersmith, and then the long-wished-for country of green hedges and cultivated fields. The day was bright and joyous, a rich, soft sunlight descended upon the landscape and fell in golden streaks upon the river. Carried forward at a brisk trot in the Putney 'bus we were soon in the streets of the antique village of Kew.

Kew is one of those quaint old towns, so common to England, abounding in the disorders of architecture, where are seen side by side, long low fronts and narrow, high gables, broad windows, with French plate glass and narrow ones with diamond panes, some mullioned, others bay windows projecting over the walls, latticed piazzas and high porticos, houses of red brick and others of grey stone, some with one wing and others with two and where two, most usually unlike ; some roofs that are flat and others steep and the whole without regard to congruity, yet where there is in the general aspect a certain harmony and decided picturesqueness.

Rich in its ancient historical reminiscences, Kew carries us back to the fantastical days of hoops and farthingales, of full bottomed wigs and snuff colored coats, of silk breeches and dangling swords; of pointed shoes and cocked hats, all of which were in full vogue during the earlier period of that Georgian era from which these far famed gardens date their foundation. Those were the days during which men systematically and as a measure of common prudence executed their wills and bade farewell to their families before starting on the perilous journey from London to Bath; when upon the side of the rumbling stage coach were duly enumerated the towns it would pass through and the inns it would stop at. Old England, however, has passed away with the stage coach, and while she has bequeathed to us much to be grateful for and much to admire, her work has been done. It is with young England we have to deal now—the England of railways and telegraphs, of steam boats, of the penny post, of gas lit cities and cheap newspapers, of lyceums, libraries, etc.

Crossing Kew green we saw in many windows cards offering apartments to let. Wishing to know how these compared in various ways with those of London, we rapped at one of the doors, and were introduced by a dowdy servant girl, her sleeves rolled up above her elbows and her face smudged with dirt and blackened with smoke, to her mistress, Mrs. Jones. Mrs. Jones was quickly discovered to be a representative woman of her class, and with a real woman's volubility. As she conducted us through the house she almost stunned us with a torrent of words in which she set forth the advantages of Kew in general as a place of residence and her edifice in particular, as the most eligible and desirable of Kew lodging houses. The impulsive landlady went on to declare that she had been uniformly patronized by the quality, such as Sir John McLeod and Lord Claud Hamilton, who came there annually to fish; by the Percys of Homedale, not the Homedales of Percy, a junior branch of that ancient race, and that if we came to her she would guarantee us every home comfort and all reasonable luxuries. Notwithstanding our haste to see the vegetable prides of Kew, we suffered ourselves to be detained until she had counted up among the gentle-folks she had entertained, a considerable part of the peerage, and, what seemed to us the larger moiety of the landed gentry.

The house, a roomy, rambling one, was ordinary enough in appearance and appointments. The lodgings, however, were higher in price than similar suites in London Expressing surprise at this fact, she informed us with an emphatic toss of her head, which caused her cork-screw curls to tremble in the still air, as her cap darted in the direction of the opposite wall in a parabolic curve; that Kew was most decidedly a fashionable town, not so large as London, but by no means small, and quite charming. "Besides," said she with a triumphant air, as she straightened herself up, throwing back a pair of square shoulders and advancing a protuberant bust, "I live in the same street with the Duchess."

Incredible as it may seem to American readers, a feeble impression only was made on our minds by this earnest advocate, and we backed out of the front hall without having engaged lodgings.

Recrossing the green to the Brown Jug, a respectable looking inn, we heard from the barmaid while despatching in the parlor a glass of the inevitable 'arf and 'arf; a girl robust in figure and fresh in complexion—that Mrs. Jones not only lived in the same street, but on the same side of it, with the Dowager Duchess of Cambridge, and that she was in the habit of entertaining many "high judicial gents and other official functionaries." This fact accounted at once for the good woman's credit and consequence, for the indignant toss of her head and the high price of her apartments.

A rain coming on it was decided that we should pass the night at the Brown Jug. After a European repast in the shape of a "meaty tea," we established ourselves in a fireside chair and began to ruminate.

A century's residence is by no means necessary in the mother country to make the stranger acquainted with the abject servility of the middle and lower orders towards the nobility. The deity of rank is absolutely idolized by them. The successful man of business, be he banker, merchant or manufacturer, considers nothing more desirable than to bestow his daughter, she may be beautiful and accomplished, upon the son, though an unworthy son, of a Lord. On the other hand it must be admitted that the impecunious Viscount is not too proud to replenish his coffers by an alliance with a wealthy tea dealer, beer brewer or cotton spinner. It is a fair bargain and an understood thing that the money offsets the rank. The eagerness, however, with which the middle classes pursue their high game, and their pride at bringing it down, is marvelous. Few things connected with the commercial classes so much excites Republican surprise as this gross want of self respect. That sense of equality to which Americans are bred, finds no place among the inferior orders in Britain. Instinctively they *kotou* to it the moment they are confronted by superior rank. This obsequiousness is peculiar to the shopocracy—as deeply implanted in them as the Sepoy's abhorrence of a greased cartridge. To them a title outweighs all earthly considerations. To be patronized by a Lord is a great stroke of good luck and will make the fortune of a tradesman, or a green grocer or fish monger. Everybody is sure to patronize those whom nobility patronizes. To be surrounded by the odor of aristocracy is a safe card for a fortune. And this though the ancient nobility is principally sprung, as they should know, from the twenty thousand adventurers who landed at Hastings in 1066 and of whom it has been truly said: "These founders of the House of Lords were greedy and ferocious pirates. They were all alike, they took everything they could carry, they burned, harried, violated, tortured and killed until everything English was brought to the verge of ruin. Such, however, is the illusion of antiquity and wealth, that decent and dignified men now existing boast their descent from these filthy thieves. Or if you come down to later times, of which a faithful record has been left by Grammont, Pepys and Evelyn, from prostitutes taken from the theatres and made duchesses, and their bastards, Dukes and Lords."

When a shopkeeper has amassed a fortune, he retires to Tyburnia, on the route to the West-end or some fashionable watering place, and seeks the means of introduction into a higher circle. In a country enjoying the commercial prosperity of England, the number of such aspirants is large, and they often find it no easy matter to accomplish their wishes. The affluent "upper ten" are ever on the alert to head off intruders and preserve the exclusiveness of patrician realms. Relying solely upon their wealth, the new rich endeavor to acquire, through its instrumentality, the "open sesame." It is their only card; luckily it is a trump, and the best of trumps—the long trump. In the end they always succeed. The advertisements in the supplement to the *Times* furnish many striking evidences of these facts. Among the more recent we have seen is the following: "Home offered free of expense. A married lady of good family and highly connected, offers to receive as her guest for the winter season or longer, any lady or young lady of good birth, who in sole return would procure introduction for them to the leading society of either Dover or Leamington. All traveling expenses and further advantages paid. A happy home offered. Full particulars, with the best and highest references given. Address, L. V., Portman Library, Baker street, Portman Square, London, W."

The same feeling, in a modified form, shows itself in all classes —even in the Peerage, where the gouty old Baron turns up his humor-eaten nose and his watery eyes in contempt at modern degeneracy and the new creations—the new Peerages.

In the piping times of peace the principal avenue to success is through the law—a lawyer of eminent learning and ability rarely failing to make his way into Parliament and thence to the peerage. Two cases of the kind occurred during our residence in England. Sir. Wm. Vernon Harcourt, who was a rising barrister in 1861, (and who, by the way, married a daughter of the American historian, John L. Motley,) ten years later was a Member of Parliament for Oxford and Solicitor General And Sir Hardinge Gifford, who was little known beyond his Inn of Court in 1861, was in 1875 Member of Parliament for Guilford and is the present Solicitor General. These conspicuous men, who owe their success to their bright intellectual endowments, their erudition and persevering industry, are sneered at by the older Peers, who superciliously style them "Law lords." They seem to have forgotten that the power, wealth, and influence of a country lie not so much in the higher as in the middle classes; not with the aristocratic few, but with the plebian many. What true man is there, however great his pride of race, who would not rather owe his position to his powers of heart and intellect, rather than to the mere accident of existence which brought him into life as the heir of a nobleman instead of the son of a peasant. That class designated more particularly as our ancient nobility—those descended from the first Norman invaders or old Saxon nobles, are in general very proud of their descent, and most of them disdain all familiar intercourse with any of those among their fellow subjects, whom they think a degree below themselves, or if they condescend to speak to them, and admit them to some kind of familiarity, their condescension is such an odd mixture of urbanity and haughtiness, that it proves very disgusting to men of any parts and spirit. During our first visit to London in 1851-52, the writer had the pleasure to become acquainted with a "city magnate," Mr. Jones Lloyd—one of those enterprising merchants whose operations extend to the farthest corners of the earth. On his return to London ten years later, he was much gratified to find Mr. Loyd's great merits and success had been recognized, and that he had been raised to the Peerage, as Lord Overstone. We were not a little disgusted, from time to time, to hear these illiberal and narrow-minded old fogies still haughtily speaking of Lord Overstone as Jones Lloyd. Men like Lord Overstone smile at such impotent malice, while the mass of the people regard it as "all right as matters go" and are ever raking among the musty records of the Herald's Office to trace their origin to some one of the above mentioned twenty thousand Norman adventurers. A rage for titles exists and where the title of a woman is higher than that of her husband, it is not dropped, but ever paraded in contrast with his, which is construed, "how wonderfully I have condescended to marry him."

In every paper you see, during the season, such announcements as the following taken from the *Times* : "Frances, Countess Waldergrave and the Right Hon. Chichester Fortesque, M. P. (her fourth husband, her title being derived from her first) received a select party at dinner on yesterday," and "The Countess of Guilford and Mr. Elliot will leave town on Wednesday next for the Continent"—Mr. Elliott being her second husband.

If a man belongs to an order of Knighthood, he never forgets to sign after his name letters by which he is known, as John Bull, C. B., meaning Companion of the Bath, and Richard Roe, K. G., Knight of the Garter.

A country gentleman informed us that it was common in the rural districts for wives of Members of Parliament to have engraved upon their cards, "W. M. P ," meaning wife of a Member of Parliament, but as no case of the kind came under our observation, we must presume that he was indulging in chaff. A dingy looking dealer in milk and cheese opposite our lodgings sent us his card which ran as follows: "*Harry Patmore, P. A. R. F.*" Not understanding the meaning of these letters, and presuming that he could hardly belong to a learned society or the most recent batch of *new creations*, we had recourse to our landlady who solved the mystery by explaining that the title he bore was "Purveyor of Asses Milk to the Royal Family."

The daily papers chronicle the most trifling incidents connected with the Royal family, so that they may be said to live constantly in the full gaze of the public—to have no private life whatever. If the Prince of Wales should come to town for a day from his country seat, Sandringham, the details are gathered by the penny-a-liners and Jenkinses of the press and all the circumstances of the journey to and fro are minutely detailed, as if the route he took to the railway station, and the persons by whom he was attended, were matters of the greatest public importance. The public is informed that his carriages were close and not open ones; that the carriages on arriving at the station did not draw up at the public entrance, but passed on to the Queen's private waiting room; that there was a platform, and moreover a platform covered with crimson cloth, and that the Royal party alighted on said platform—that the Prince and Princess appeared in excellent health and spirits, and that instead of passing on from the platform to the waiting room without condescending to notice the spectators, they actually "bowed very graciously to the bystanders." The dress of the Princess is described with the minuteness and particularity of a mantaumaker, and the Prince, we are told, wore a wide-awake instead of his usual chimney-pot hat. The names of the officials who received the Royal party on the crimson cloth platform and escorted it therefrom are duly recorded, and before the perilous journey is commenced the farther additional information is vouchsafed that the "State saloon was placed in the centre of the passenger train," and that notwithstanding these tremendous preparations, "the train left at the usual hour," and travelling by certain stations with its illustrious inmates—the only stations by which it could pass—arrived at the usual hour at the London terminus, where we are further told, every preparation was made by the railway authorities for the reception of the Royal party, who are said to have stood the fatiguing journey of two hours remarkably well. Every incident is now again detailed how they left the train, what carriages they entered; through what streets they passed; how his Royal Highness, seeing a chimney on fire, expressed the opinion that the public health required that all families residing in the Metropolis should adopt the Derby patent for consuming their own smoke; how the public assembled in front of Marlborough House to catch a glimpse of the future king and queen, and how they were disappointed by the Royal party which turned up Piccadilly and down Constitution Hill and alighted at Buckingham Palace.

In extenuation of this snobbery, the stranger is told that these published details are collected by the newspaper reporters from footmen, butlers and kitchen maids, and are not communicated by the "noble lords and ladies" themselves; that he must not fall into the error of making them responsible for the prying curiosity and vulgar weakness of the Jenkinses of the journals who believe that the human race is divided into men, women and the British peerage. An explanation doubtless true in the main, as we regret to see in our country a similar system of *espoinage* growing up, and the private gatherings at our houses published to the world, and the remarks even of our guests not unfrequently passed in review in some sheet which lives on the profits of what is styled in the phraseology of the day, sensational journalism.

Whatever truth there may be in the Britton's explanation of these peculiarities, the stranger cannot be long in the country without observing that there is an extravagant homage paid to rank and title. It is the weak point in the English character. Whatever they may say, the fact is undeniable, they *love a lord.* During our protracted residence in Britain we have rarely known a public meeting of any kind without a lord in the chair. One of the sacred animals is, after the custom of certain eastern people, always placed in the van. Even the Scientific Societies insist upon having a lord for President. The Royal Geographical had Lord Ashburton for its presiding officer for years. It does not matter to them whether he has or has not attainments—he has a title—that's what they want, not the booby who sports it. Science does not prostitute itself to ignorance. only to rank. No institution of learning—school or college—is founded without having titled patrons or visitors to satisfy the popular requirements These are selected from among the aristocracy, whatever their want of qualifications, the more glaring the want of qualifications, the higher sounding must be the title. The title of Prince or Duke will cover with the mantle of charity even Egyptian ignorance. There is no learned or literary society in England which would not be proud to have a Prince or Royal Duke in the chair, so deeply rooted is that popular veneration for the consecrated race.

The injurious effects of this prevalent feeling is seen in the conduct and bearing of many of the nobility, and it is only strange that it does not ruin the whole race. A man has very little chance of knowing how to conduct himself in this world who has from his infancy been the object of slavish adulation. First worshipped by his nurse, then flattered by grooms, stable boys, peasants and hangers-on of the family, then todied by tutors, he enters college only to find his caste held sacred, and when he enters the world he finds himself delivered over to the adulation of the entire public. It is not surprising that they are sometimes arrogant. If people prostrate themselves before them why may not the people expect to be trampled on? It is not the fault of the lord, but of the people.

Much to be regretted is the fact that instead of worshipping rank, class or caste as do the Hindoos and Brahmins, they do not confine their reverence to purity of character, great thoughts and noble deeds. Here all the world could unite with them. The popular reception or value set upon a title by the lower orders gives the title its value—if people ceased to worship it, no one would desire it. But no sooner is a man invested with a title, got a handle to his name, than he finds himself invested with new power—a power that does not reside in himself, but in the hearts of those who fawn upon him. It is the aristocratic spirit and sympathy which pervades the entire mass of society which gives the aristocracy their power.—The English are at heart aristocratic and never cease struggling after its honors. They spend their lives, giving up comfort and happiness, to reach its ranks, or that their children may do so. The growth of centuries, this spirit is supposed to have had its origin in the Norman conquest and the feudal system. However this may be, ages must pass before it can be eradicated. The feudal system still exists in a modified form in England. The law of primogeniture—the accumulation of vast landed estates in a few hands, the laws of entail, &c., which have been thrown off by all Europe, by America, and by the English colonies throughout the world, still continue in force in the sea-girt island. The laws are still made by the aristocratic few, for the benefit of the patrician classes. The privileges and immunities of this class being found in ancient usage and the customs of bygone ages, they cultivate a reverence for the past, disparage everything new or modern, and thus seek to strengthen their position by encouraging the growth in the minds and hearts of the people, of sentiments of respect for the law-givers of a semi-barbaric age in which these privileges had their origin. This well known sentiment, we may add, is turned to amusing effect in the new operetta, styled "*The Pirates of Penzance*," which is now being successfully performed at the Fifth Avenue Theatre, New York. In an encounter between the pirates and the police, the latter are conquered. The condition of the police seems hopeless but the sergeant is not without resource.

> SERG.—To gain a brief advantage you've contrived,
> But your proud triumph will not be long lived!

KING.—Don't say you're orphans, for we know that game.
SERG.—On your allegiance we've a strong claim.
We charge you yield in Queen Victoria's name !

This is an appeal that no Englishman, not even a pirate, can resist. The King and his crew at once surrender.

KING —We yield at once with humbled mein.
Because, with all our faults, we love our Queen.

The General orders them to be marched off in custody, when Ruth enters:

RUTH.—One moment; let me tell you who they are—
They are no members of the common throng,
They are all noblemen who have gone wrong!

This announcement has an electrical effect on the General and the police, who at once kneel in homage at the feet of their late foes.

GENERAL.—No Englishmen unmoved that statement hears,
Because with all our faults, we love our House of Peers.

This is no overdrawn picture, yet we find a certain class of British tourists in this country, with true Cockney audacity, ridiculing what they style the American's love for titles. These carping faultfinders are offended with the existence of military and naval titles in a country uncurst with a standing army and an invincible armament. They forget that we have a bellicose militia. We are willing to admit that the average American is not altogether without something of the "Britisher's" love of gewgaws, nor are "his sisters, his cousins or his aunts," but nobody in this country attaches the slightest importance to these militia titles. They do not enhance the credit or consequence of the persons who bear them, are often conferred in merriment by boon companions. But if we are to take as true the moral of the operetta, so recently and admirably represented by amateurs in Staunton, we could hardly be charged with an ill-regulated and false ambition, if we ranked the Admiral of one of our yacht squadrons with the "ruler of the Queen's navee."

But whither are we wandering? What has become of Kew? *Revenons nous a nos moutons.*

The pleasure gardens of Kew constitute its chief attractions, though many of the disciples of Isaac Walton frequent the Thames hereabouts, pursuing their favorite pastime. These famous gardens have been improved with much taste, and show, notwithstanding the level surface originally, a considerable variety of scenery. The botanic gardens are noted for their exotic treasures collected from every part of the world, which flourish in the Palm house, the largest glass structure we have seen, save the Crystal Palace, "unconscious of a less propitious clime."

On entering the gardens from the village, one of the first objects which attracts attention is the willow, an offspring from that which overshadows the tomb of Napoleon at St. Helena. We were surprised to find at this early season, in full bloom in the open air, many flowers of vivid hue; scarlet geraniums, crocuses, yellow callecolaries, hyacinths and heliotropes.

Among the rare trees pointed out to us were 2,000 Chinconas, from which the sulphate of quinine is manufactured. For some years prior to 1860, the British government was successfully engaged in the task of supplying these trees to the East Indies. They are produced at Kew from seed brought from South America. Much fear was felt of the entire destruction of the tree in South America, when the British government hastened to fit out an expedition under one of its ablest admirals, with C. R. Markham as botanist, to proceed to Chili and Peru to collect trees and the seed of the tree, as a means of preserving and propagating it in its own equatorial and other fever stricken colonies. These labors have been crowned with gratifying success, and the day is not far distant when the price of quinine, so expensive now, will be within reach of the poorest sufferer. Worthy of all praise, we trust this enlightened policy may be pursued by the authorities of our Gulf States. The climate of the cotton States is doubtless well adapted to the growth of the Chincona tree; it is certainly prolific in the diseases in which quinine is taken with good effect.

From imperial Kew we passed on to Richmond and soon reached the terraced road on the hill which leads directly to the Park. This road, lined and shaded by great oaks in the gnarled majesty of old age, commands an extended and beautiful view of the Valley of the Thames, which is covered with country seats, farm houses and villages. The line of beauty was never more faithfully depicted in landscape than by the course of the broad and beautiful river. So regular are its windings, so just are the length and curvature of its sweeps, and so well proportioned are its width and the space it occupies in the rich valley through which it flows, so tranquil and lake-like is the surface of the water that at first sight we cannot divest ourselves of the idea that nature has called in the assistance of art, and has ornamented the scenery beneath us with reference to the most approved principles of landscape gardening.

In a few minutes more, we entered the celebrated Star and Garter Inn, which is situated just outside of the main entrance to the Park, and after indulging in some of the expensive dainties dispensed at this establishment, leaving our baggage, we set off for a stroll in the enchanting scenes of the park, more than 1,000 acres of which are covered by a dense forest. From Oliver's mount, in the park, St. Paul's Cathedral and Windsor Castle may be seen on a fair day. Yet you cannot penetrate a half mile into the dark recesses of the forest without feeling that you have taken leave of civilization and the haunts of men.

The park occupies a portion of the ancient hunting grounds of William the Norman and his regal successors for centuries, and the sites of many of the lodges of the rangers, around which are strewn masses of ruins, are still pointed out to the stranger. How are times changed! The days of Robin Hood and his merry men are gone; the sound of the hunting horn no longer awakes the echoes in the solitudes of the few forests which have survived the desolations of centuries; the swineherd no more attends his charge under the mighty oaks, and the lady of high degree, attended by her knights and retainers, cannot now be seen, cantering on her palfrey with falcon on her fair hand awaiting the flight of the heron. The great law of change has acted here as elsewhere. Old things have passed away and all traces of them are rapidly disappearing. No where more so than in the vicinity of London. Buildings are starting up in every direction and anon speculative builders and joint stock companies will overlay beautiful Richmond with brick and plaster. Such is the progress, the utilization of the age. The lovers of the philosophical science of esthetics must unite to preserve the beautiful and sublime in nature and art, or both will perish in the din of machinery and the smoke of factories.

## CHAPTER IV.

### FURTHER EXPERIENCES OF RICHMOND—GYPSIES—JOHN EARL RUSSELL, &C.

While sojourning in Richmond, we wandered on one occasion to the outskirts of the Park looking over the waste of an adjoining common, inhaling with pleasant exhiliaration the unbreathed air of the heath. Soon our attention was attracted by a thin, vapory column of smoke ascending from a ravine, about two hundred yards distant. Approaching the spot, we saw a ragged tent, around which several swart, sun-burnt children were playing. On the opposite side of the tent stood a shaggy pony yoked to a rickety cart. Several men were busy packing away goods and chattels belonging to the party, which was evidently about to strike tent and be off. We recognized them at once as a party of gypsies. Our appearance seemed anything than agreeable to these Bohemians; the children scampered off, while the men appeared perfectly unconscious of our presence. An old hag hobbled from the tent at this embarrassed moment, her dishevelled hair streaming over her back and shoulders, her glassy eyes distilling rheum, and introduced herself by asking if we wished to have our fortunes told. She accompanied this question with the encouraging remark "that our faces were lucky." Declining to appeal to the fates upon the question of the future, we scattered a few pennies among the children, who were momentarily becoming bolder and lessening the distance which divided us. The unsympathetic men who witnessed what was going on from the corners of their furitive eyes, now advanced, as if we were friends, and became as amicable and communicative as could be desired. Our intimacy increased rapidly. In a half hour we ascertained that they had no accurate knowledge of their own origin and history, that there was nothing peculiar to the habits of this particular party—that they were simply common-place strollers.

This singular and unhappy race, for it is unhappy, as can be seen from the expression of vacuity and melancholy in their faces. is generally believed to have had its origin in Hindostan where they belonged to the lowest class of Indians. They are supposed to have taken to flight early in the 15th century when India was ravaged by Timur Bey for the purpose of spreading the Mahometan religion, and thousands were put to death. Their exit was through the Southern Persian Gulf to the mouth of the Euphrates, thence to Bassora into the great desert of Arabia, afterwards into Arabia Petrea and so into Egypt by the Isthmus of Suez. They claim, however, to be Egyptians and account for their vagabond life by referring it to a judgment of God upon their forefathers who refused to entertain the Virgin Mary and Jesus, when they fled into their country. Every effort to conform them to the usages of civilization and systematic labor has proved futile. They adhere to their wandering, almost savage mode of life, picking up a scanty support by petty thieving, peddling, tinkering, jugglery, legerdemain, fortune-telling and general cheatery. Wherever their camp fires are seen glimmering at night there are sure to be twisted necks and vacant nests in neighboring hen-roosts. Among themselves they speak a language of their own, which is not the slang of thieves, but the language of Romany, which has sprung from the Sanscript and the Zend, an ancient Persian dialect. A dictionary of this tongue has been prepared and the Bible translated into the idiom by Barrow. But their language is on the decline and the race passing away. The number in England does not now exceed 15,000 and as the commons are enclosed and the land brought into cultivation, they are gradually losing the spots on which they have so long pitched their tents and lighted their camp-fires. In some sections of the country in both England and Scotland, particularly in the latter, they have intermarried with the rural population and become much assimilated in manners and customs. When about to leave, one of the girls was brought forward (she was not over fifteen years of age) and sang with considerable taste and power "The Gypsy's Tent," commencing as follows:

> "Our fire on the turf, and our tent 'neath a tree—
> Carousing by moonlight, how merry are we!
> Let the lord boast his castle, the baron his hall,
> But the house of the gypsy is widest of all.
> We may shout o'er our cups, and laugh loud as we will,
> Till echo rings back from wood, welkin, and hill;
> No joys seem to us like the joys which are lent
> To the wanderer's life and the gypsy's tent."

Rewarding the sun-burnt denizen of nature with a few pence, we left by a path leading to Pembroke Lodge.

When visiting Scotland in 1852, we had the pleasure to meet Lord John Russell, who had recently resigned the seals of office as Premier. He was driven to this course by the unpopularity of his ecclesiastical titles bill, and the secession of his old colleague,

Viscount Palmerston. Aggrieved at the course of events, he had sought in the bracing air and marvelous variety of scenery in Caledonia, some relief from the bitterness and melancholy which seized upon him as his policy failed ; his old friends dropped off, and enemies arose out of the darkness, as pigmies wax bold when a giant falls.

An admirer of his liberal principles, political and religious, like a few of his British party friends, who loved him well and stood staunchly by him to the last, in good and evil report, we never wavered in our respect for Lord John. His course from 1861–65, when Foreign Secretary, did not meet our approval in so far as it referred to America's relations with Great Britain. At this period, when disappointed and irritated at his management of the foreign office, in connection with American affairs, we spoke of his Lordship in far from complimentary terms. It was unbecoming in us and unjust to him. His foreign policy was then, in our opinion, liable to grave objections, whether considered with reference to British or American interests. Time has entirely changed this opinion. Now, that there is no longer passion to cloud the reason, may the manes of the deceased statesman be appeased by this frank avowal.

During the many years that we were on one side of the Atlantic and Earl Russell upon the other, our time occupied with private affairs, and he controlling with consummate ability the destinies of the British Empire, we never lost sight of him. Immediately on our return to Europe in 1861, we met him again, not through relations established with the British Foreign Office by Mr. Yancey or Col. Mann, then resident agents of the Confederacy in London, but through Sir William and Lady Hutt, with whom we had formed cordial relations, which soon ripened into affectionate friendship. For months during the season, we met him almost daily at the houses of mutual friends. Sir William was a member of the Cabinet, being Vice President of the board of trade and M. P. for Gibside, and the life long friend of Lord John. Lady Hutt was a member of the Walpole family, and thus a cousin of Lady Francis Russell, the wife of Earl Russell's younger brother, Lord Francis Russell, R. N., and daughter of the late Rev. Algernon Peyton, D. D., Dean of Ely, by his wife, Lady Mary Walpole, daughter of Horatio, Earl of Oxford. Lady Hutt's connection with the Bedford family, and her kinship to the Peytons, caused the Hutts to take no small interest in us, which they exhibited at this time and during the long period of our sojourn in England, by innumerable acts of hospitality and kindness. Lady Hutt always claimed us as an 'American cousin,' a claim which we good humoredly allowed without an appeal to family records.

Their disinterested friendship caused us to feel much less solitary and more secure than would otherwise have been possible, and contributed much to the pleasure of our sojourn in England, and to our travels on the continent, when we crossed the channel together to enjoy an "outing" in beautiful France.

In another place we have spoken of Earl Russell as an eminent man, author, statesman and diplomatist, but better acquaintance with him considerably modified our early impressions. We had recently visited him—a visit the details of which we shall spare the reader who cannot be much interested in the way in which one gentleman meets another in his family, or in which a man eats his dinner with the assistance of half a dozen footmen and a butler. This visit to Richmond, however, furnishes the opportunity for a more extended notice of him than has appeared in "The American Crisis," and which few men more richly deserve. We can give the salient points in his character and career very much as we received them from Sir William Hutt and others, partly now and partly at subsequent periods.

After his last retirement from office, Earl Russell took up his Residence at Pembroke Lodge, in Richmond Park, which was granted to him for life by favor of the Queen. ' Since he has led a secluded life, taking little interest in what is said or done by the outside world, and had perhaps less knowledge of the general public and of the men who most influence their fellows, than any political leader has had during the present century. Here he was passing his old age, hale, hearty, affable, resigned to its condition, thoroughly experienced, philosophic, full of judgment, learning and sobriety. It is here that he met, during the recesses of Parliament, the small coterie of whom he was the especial favorite ; and the leaders of that old whig party of which he was at once the historian, the centre and the traditional idol. Few, if any, of the public men of the country have been more mixed up with the political affairs of the nation during the last forty years than Earl Russell. None of these notabilities have rendered more important services to their parties, yet we have not found one of his contemporaries, and we have conversed with many of them, willing to admit that he is an eminent statesman and still less a great man. In reference to his public career it is said that it was no evidence whatever of his possessing fine parts. That some of the most momentous events in English history occurred under and were controlled by the feeblest and most insignificant minds known to her parliamentary annals. That the majority of the cabinets who directed and often misdirected Wellington throughout the Peninsular, he who won Waterloo, imprisoned Napoleon, partitioned Europe and disposed of the fortunes and nationalities of millions of the human race all over the world—the Bexleys, Sidmouths, Vansittarts, Bathursts, Liverpools and the rest—were miserable mediocrities, execrated for their mingled feebleness and ferocity while living, and despised when dead, "forgotten as fools or remembered as worse," as the satirist says in his lines on Sheridan, who was the victim of these malignant incompetents.

Whatever may be said by the rivals and contemporaries of Earl Russell, all impartial men will agree in the opinion that his abilities, if not of the first, are of a very high order, almost raising their possessor to the rank of genius. One of his marked characteristics, said Sir Wm. Hutt, is caution, still he has always had the reputation among friends and foes of being rash, headstrong, self-willed and indifferent to consequences, provided he can carry, or thinks he can carry his point. It was this reputation which caused the celebrated remark of Sydney Smith that Lord John would undertake the command of the Channel fleet or the most difficult operation in surgery with equal *sang froid*, such was his self sufficiency and precipitancy. Nothing could be be more unjust than this estimate of his character. Though he has occasionally given utterance to indiscreet phrases and indulged in intemperate language, a retrospect of his career will show that he has always been prudent and painstaking. The best evidence of this is the fact that at an early age he was put forward by his party, the old Whigs of the Holland House School, as the conductor or manager of the leading questions of the time. To discharge the duties of this position required rare powers, and among the most essential of them was supposed to be those of a good debater. For forty years he took the lead and obtained the ear of the House of Commons, discharging the duties of his responsible position with success, though he has no pretentions whatever to eloquence, or what is called in America, fine speaking. As a speaker he has had to contend with physical difficulties of the most discouraging description—a small, insignificant and undignified presence; *petite*, inexpressive and common-place features; a harsh, dissonant and monotonous voice; an embarrassed, ungainly, confused, stammering, yet didactic and somewhat pragmatical manner; all these made up the aggregate drawbacks to his rhetorical success. Yet he overcame them all and for a score of years, led the House of Commons, which is regarded in England as the most fastidious audience in the world, but which in reality does not excel in its acumen our own House of Representatives. During the long period since his first entrance into public life, he has figured prominently in connection with every public measure of importance, has held together his party with matchless skill, always kept an eagle's eye on his opponents, never gave them an advantage, was always on the lookout for their weak point, and rarely missed an opportunity of inflicting upon them a serious political injury. Such are the rare qualities which have enabled him so long to maintain himself at the head of the liberal party. However his rivals may ridicule his shortcomings in comprehensive legislation; however intellectual radicals may sneer at his mental and literary deficiencies; however economists may object to his multiplication of places for *proteges* of his own family ; whatever general exceptions may be taken to him ; as a tactitian and party leader he had no rival in his day; hence in hours of disaster the liberals still instinctively turn to him. He never appears so well as when surrounded by obstacles, difficulties and impediments; is always greater in opposition than when in office at the head of a triumphant party. Notwithstanding his external frigidity and apathetic hauteur, there is about him, when you get to know him, and especially in his own home, a great deal of geniality and kindness of feeling. His adversaries declare that he is a politician in contradistinction to a statesman, the first belonging to that numerous class who are constantly thinking of what the country will do for them, while the latter belong to that class of patriots who are ever thinking of what they can do for the country. There is more satire than veracity in this witticism when applied to the Right Honorable Earl. A close examination into the history of his public career has satisfied us that there is little in Earl Russell's course to justify this severe judgment, nor do we believe it will be that of a non-partizan and passionless posterity.

At the early period of his life when he essayed to attain fame as a dramatic writer and poet, his personal friend, Tom Moore, dedicated to him some verses in which the immortal bard undertook to persuade his lordship to leave Parnassus and stick to Parliament; at the same time he reminded him of the responsibilities which attached to the house of Russell. It is not known whether Moore was envious of Lord John's frequent draughts at the fount of poesy, or whether he really believed his friend was never likely to become a favorite with the muses, and in kindness to his literary infirmities, tendered him gentle reproofs in poetry, on which he could not venture in person. The lines, however, had the effect of chastening down Lord John's exhuberant taste for metre—his poetic mantle was soon thrown aside and exchanged for the dignified robe of the legislator.

Earl Russell was born in 1792 and entered Parliament as a member for the "rotten borough" of Tavistock in 1814 ; in 1820 he was member for the Huntingdonshire ; for the town of Bandon in Ireland in 1830, and for Devonshire in 1831, which seat he vacated in 1834, on his appointment to the office of Secretary for the Home

Department, and was the guiding spirit of Lord Melbourne's administration. From 1841 to 1846, whilst Sir Robert Peel was in power, Lord John Russell led the opposition, and on the defeat of Peel this year succeeded to the Premiership, which he held until 1852. In office, he showed an indisposition to take the initiative in any marked measure of progress and advancement. As a consequence, he could only depend on a small and uncertain majority in Parliament; and the inefficiency of his ecclesiastical titles bill, accompanied, nearly at the same time, by the secession of his colleague, Lord Palmerston, forced him into retirement. Under the administration of Lord Aberdeen, he was Foreign Secretary for a short time and then Lord President of the Council. Lord Palmerston now became Premier, and in 1855 appointed Lord John Colonial Secretary, and he represented England at the Vienna Conferences, and in consequence of the dissatisfaction caused by his diplomatic course, again resigned. In 1859 he resumed office under Palmerston as Minister for Foreign affairs, and bore a conspicuous part in the solution of the important questions which occurred in political affairs in different parts of the world. Amongst these may be mentioned the protests made by the British government to that of Russia against the oppressions practiced on the Poles; its endeavors to deter the great German powers from pursuing an aggressive policy towards Denmark, and the disputes which arose between England and the United States during the civil war. It must be admitted, with reference to some of these vexed questions, that however unsuccessful the efforts of England may have been, through the backwardness of allles, in averting the evils it sought to counteract, the sincerity of its intentions, as evinced in its diplomatic action under the auspices of Earl Russell, has been clearly manifest. We, therefore, who felt at the time, or now feel, any bitterness towards the mother country for her course towards the South during the civil war — her apparent want of sympathy— should now, that the hour of passion has passed, be ready to unite in according to her the meed of praise for having been wiser in that great crisis than we ourselves were

During his active political life, such was his patient, persevering industry, that he contributed largely to the literature of the day. Among his best known works are his Life of Lord William Russell, his Miscellaneous Essays and "Memories of the Affairs of Europe," "A Concise History of the British Constitution," "The Nun of Arvouca, a tale," and a tragic drama styled "Don Carlos." His most recent work composed during his retirement, is entitled The Rise and Progress of the Christian Religion in the West of Europe, from the reign of Tiberius to the end of the Council of Trent. This work illustrates how happily and usefully the evening of his days was passed, how far he was removed from those discontented, querulous, ill-conditioned, gouty old men, who ludicrously contend against the grave—a burden to themselves and a nuisance to all around. He did not indulge in the vain regrets of those who regard death as the "evil day." Death, he knew, could not be staved off, however our energies may be economized, that in the end we are all brought to bay; there is no more thread on the reel; for the fates together have spun the whole web of our existence and there is an end. The ancients lamented old age and the grave, because not believing in the immortality of the soul, there was no hope beyond it — nothing but everlasting night. When the flower of youth is passed, says one of the pagans, it is better to die at once, and he prayed that he might be struck dead at sixty. These unnatural pagan sentiments exaggerate the value of bodily strength and animal spirits, the joy of the wine cup and the delights of love. They evince an imperfect idea of the pleasures of matured intellect, of calm sagacity and of that tranquil wisdom which looks before and after without terror and without excessive regrets. Christianity corrects by its sublime teachings alike the pagan's morbid love of youth and his dread of old age. And Earl Russell lived and died an humble, sincere and pious Christian.

Before leaving Richmond, where we had passed so many happy hours, and which we have since revisited many a time, with the old pleasure, a word more must be ventured as to its past.

In the early part of the last century it was much frequented as a watering place. A mineral spring in the park was supposed to possess valuable curative elements. Both pleasure seekers and invalids were attracted to its gay halls and life giving streams. Grand hotels, pump rooms, baths, squares, terraces and crescents were erected or laid out in eligible and commanding situations. The son of a dead baron, or some such sprig of nobility, was always installed as master of ceremonies, and an eminent rural M. D., the cousin of a living Viscount, if such could be had, as well doctor as an analytic chemist, was sure to receive from the managing committee the appointment of resident physician. Dowager whist players, half pay officers, old maids, fortune hunters, widows without fortunes, but ready for the matrimonial game, people of good family and questionable morals flocked to Richmond Spa.

This is now all changed. The spring still flows, but seems to have lost its virtues; and in Richmond's palmy days was probably more "doctored" with tinctures of iron and sulphur than were the shaky valetudinarians who here resorted for the tonic or aperient waters.

The grand houses of the past are now business places, and steady going people replace the Jackanaps and Jack-a-dandies, simpering maids and old blades of 1750.

No intelligent foreigner in London fails to visit Richmond, either to enjoy the scenic beauties of the park or dissipate the spleen by its water, which, if without mineral ingredients, are much purer than those of the Metropolis; or to enliven the imagination and improve the understanding by learning the associations of the place and reviving the instructive history of the past.

## CHAPTER V.

WINDSOR CASTLE, PAST AND PRESENT—GEORGE IV—THE LAWLESS LORDS OF OTHER DAYS—THE ROYAL STABLES—THE PARKS, ETC.

A friend, who is ever ready to impart information in an agreeable way, has recently expressed the opinion, in our hearing, that we love pleasure. The innocent lamb may prefer work, but not the straying sheep. A man of nice perceptions, our *fidus Achates*, rarely fails in a diagnosis. We do not cousider it worth while, therefore, to deny the "soft impeachment." Yet we would not have our reader imagine that we love nothing but pleasure because, instead of returning to the dingy atmosphere of London, we shall penetrate forthwith deeper into the country, and possibly to the heart of the Royal county of Berks.

During the annual absences of the Queen, the State apartments in Windsor Castle are thrown open to the public, and joining the "madding crowd" of sight seers, we bade adieu to Richmond, and made the best of our way to this ancient seat of British Royalty. No season could have been more favorable for our excursion.

The trees were in leaf and the country clothed in verdure. Pleasant parks, well cultivated fields, quiet homesteads and patches of common and garden enlivened and beautified the landscapes on the entire route. The sky was of a sweet opaline blue—something one does not see every day in England. Looking out upon the Heavens and the earth, we came near startling our neighbors in the railway carriage, by exclaiming, how pleasant to live sometimes!

But the train stops. Our dream is fulfilled; there stands the Round Tower; in a moment we are hastening to the Palace gates. We stop to scan the exterior of the building, we run through it, we return and linger to study it, and feel when it is over a certain sense of disappointment.

The castle is an old stone edifice, with turrets and battlements more like an antique fortress in exterior appearance than a domestic habitation. Has somewhat the cold and sombre aspect of a prison, and its gaunt buttresses and dim archways, and high and broad ramparts plainly tell the history of its feudal origin. The narrow, meanly built streets of the town of Windsor extend on one side to the very gates, and the visitor emerges from them to pass immediately into the palace court. But for its situation on a lofty hill and the surrounding park and forest, with its wild and picturesque scenery, Windsor Castle would be the most cheerless and unattractive of homes, though it has been much modernized and has so many of the adjuncts of domestic life, that its appearance has ceased to create the idea of one of those rugged fortresses destined solely for war, whose gloomy towers suggest to the imagination only dungeons, chains and executions. Nevertheless, it carries us back to the time when anarchy and violence glowered over England, to the age of the Norman and of feudalism, when there was no distinction but that of soldier and serf. To the time when the fair-haired and blue-eyed Saxon was crushed by his haughty Norman conqueror, and who, while biding his time, breathed against his oppressor curses not loud but deep. Windsor, as it now stands, and regarded as a simple specimen of its particular style of architecture, is unequalled in England for grandeur and magnificence.

This spot, we are told, was selected as a residence by William the Conqueror, who was drawn to the neighboring forest by his fondness for the chase. The country now embraced in the Royal county, was then as famous for wild boars, as it now is for Berkshire pigs. William I., built, according to tradition, a rude fortress on the spot occupied by the present edifice, and that or some other Royal building occupied the ground till the 14th century when the existing castle was erected. The old building had gone much to decay when George IV. awoke to the fact that it was the only specimen of a Royal Palace of any antiquity or pretentions in England, and determined to preserve it, if for no other reason than as a memorial of the past. Accordingly the government in 1824 undertook its restoration and spent on the work—so says the guide book—£900,000. An idea may be formed of its extent from this fact. From that time it has been the country residence of the Royal family (it causes Berkshire to be styled the Royal county;) though the Queen has from her enormous wealth—she is said to be the richest woman in Europe—secured several more congenial country seats, one, Osborne, in the Isle of Wight and the other Balmoral, in the Highlands of Scotland. The latter was built at the request, so it is said, of Prince Albert, a man of good sense and much taste, not like a castle, but after the modern style of a gentleman's residence.

On the north side of Windsor Castle the State apartments are situated and consist of nine large rooms in a suite, the first being the Queen's grand audience and the last, Her Majesty's grand presence chamber. We could see no particular reason why they should be so styled, though like the rooms of all palaces they are capacious and abound in gilt. They are approached by a wide stone stair case, the *grand* stair-way of course, which is gaudily painted with fabulous stories from Ovid's Metamorphasis, and at the head of which stands a stature of George IV. whose great ambition was to be styled, as he was on the slenderest possible grounds, "the first gentleman in Europe "

George IV. was one of the most wretched specimens of a man who ever existed on or off a throne, uniting in himself the sot, dissembler and roue. The late Sir George Jackson, in his recently published volumes, photographs the life of the early part of the present century. He speaks of the Prince of Wales in 1804 (afterwards George IV.) and of an illness which arose from the fact that the Prince and the Duke of Norfolk had been so drunk for three whole days, that the former at last fell like a pig, and would have died like one, but for prompt and copious bleeding. How rude the "first gentleman" could be when he chose, even to his wife, is well known. At a drawing room, held by Queen Charlotte in June, 1807, when the Prince and Princess of Wales were present, he took no notice of the Princess. Turning his back upon her, he stood between her and the Queen, and as long as the Princess remained he kept up a conversation with his sisters, thereby preventing them from addressing a word to his wife. This feeling against his wife he paraded everywhere. He was jealous of her popularity—quite unnecessarily, for she made herself ridiculous, and the subject of scornful criticism, by her lavish display at evening parties of her protuberant beauties. At these parties the Prince would stare at ladies whom he knew, without speaking to them. His condescending speech was addressed only to his first wife, Mrs. Fitzherbert and her sister, Lady Hagerstone. The first of these ladies lived at Brighton with the state of a Queen and the spirit of a goddess of mirth. Meanwhile, his Royal Highness flirted with "his future Duchess," the Marchioness of Hertford. He knew how to play a good part at times. In 1811 he gave a grand fete at Carlton House at which Louis XVIII and the sad looking Duchess of Angouleme appeared. The Prince received Louis as a Sovereign *de facto*. "I am only a Count of Lille," said Louis modestly. "Sir," said the Prince, "you are the King of France and Navarre," and he treated his guest accordingly. Both the Prince's wives, Mrs. Fitzherbert and the Princess of Wales were at home by themselves, but the favorite of the hour was commanded to attend. It cannot be denied that English society needed refinement in the first decade of the present century. And I may add, some of the foreign society was quite as free and easy.

We never think of George IV without the caustic lines of Thackeray recurring to memory. "I try to take him to pieces and find silk stockings, paddings, stays, a coat with frogs and a fur collar, a star and blue ribbon, a pocket handkerchief prodigiously scented, one of Truefitts best nutty brown wigs reeking with oil, a set of teeth and a huge black stock, underwaistcoats, more underwaistcoats and then nothing. There was nothing of him but a grin and a bow."

But we will never get through Windsor if we linger after this fashion before a statue, even though it be that of a Monarch. The ceilings of all the suite, constituting the State apartments, are painted in imitation of fresco by Antonio Verrio, an Itallian artist invited to England by Charles II. He is little known to fame but made a fortune decorating Palace walls. His forte consisted in painting gods, goddesses, nymphs, naiades and the whole host of heathen mythology, in the brightest colors and the most extraordinary attitudes. Instead of giving this fabulous host the graceful attitudes of divinities, they are oftener represented as semi-nude and sprawling in all sorts of grotesque contortions. The general effort of Verrio's pencil, however, is decidedly ornamental. These rooms are furnished obviously at great cost, and are elaborately decorated with paintings, many of which have faded, with gobelin tapestry, wearing the appearance of having been moth eaten, and with much statuary etc. They look, on the whole, more like public galleries than as if they had ever been the scenes of private life and domestic comfort. There could be nothing really comfortable in them. No fire, however large, could heat them, and as for preventing draughts, it would be impossible without sealing them up. It is not surprising then that the Queen has provided herself with modern mansions.

In one of the apartments our eyes were attracted by a portrait, taken from life, of Mary Queen of Scots. Mary was a lovely woman, with an expression of great sweetness and sincerity of character She is represented as holding a crucifix in her right hand and in her left a breviary. The painting bears a lengthy and high-flown Latin inscription which in substance represents her to have been by right Princess and legitimate heiress of England and Ireland, as tormented by the heresies of her people, overcome by rebellions, and deceived by her relation, Queen Elizabeth, perfidiously detained a prisoner for nineteen years, until the English Parliament, stimulated by religious animosities, by an inhuman sentence condemned her to death, when on the 18th of February, 1587, she was beheaded by the common executioner in the 45th year of her age and of her reign.

The next room, of elegant dimensions, is the dining room, or Waterloo chamber, as it is called, from the fact that William IV gave dinners in it in commemoration of the victory of the 18th of June, 1815, surrounded by all the surviving commanders who took part in that famous battle It is the repository, too, for the portraits of all those connected with the memorable field. Among these portraits is one of George IV, who is said to have—under a hallucination of mind—affirmed that he was present at the battle, and to have repeated the tale so frequently that he finally came to believe it himself. On one occasion, having appealed to the Duke of Wellington, His Grace, with infinite presence of mind replied, "Sire, I have often enjoyed the honor of hearing your majesty relate the anecdote." The banqueting hall or State dining room is, says the Hand Book, "two hundred and thirty-four feet long, thirty-four feet broad and thirty-two feet high," which we are prepared to believe and accordingly take on credit. The ceiling is emblazoned with the armorial bearings of all the Knights of the Garter, from the institution of the order down to the present time, all dead, all buried, all forgotten. How can one look upon these records without a cloud of melancholy stealing over the heart.

At the eastern end of the gallery stands the throne. The guard room is full of ancient relics in the way of old armor hanging from the walls, warlike and sporting implements of different ages and countries, the whole furnishing food for curious and amusing speculation The last of the rooms exhibited is the Queen's presence chamber, a capacious apartment much like the others.

Of course nothing like a description can be attempted of the decorations and furniture, articles of virtu, etc., in or about the castle, nor would such a catalogue interest any but a guide book compiler, or a cockney reporter of the Jenkins type.

Passing into the court yard on the way to the chapel and looking upon the old castle, around which the ivy twined its solemn arms, we could but reflect upon how many a venerable pile time has moulded into beauty, which in the day of its power was only terrible! The age of chivalry seemed to pass before us, the turf to heave beneath our feet, strange vibrations seem to run along the dead that slumber there, and forth they come again, with their stern, earnest faces; the mailed warrior, the representative of an age long passed away—the white stoled priest, the minister of the old faith; the serf with the wassail bowl, and the most strange and eccentric of all, the rude jester of the old baronial hall. For a moment they all live again, while we catch once more rude snatches of their mirth and music, revelry and song. Such is the poetry of an old castle, of an old baronial ruin! In the days of the castle and baron, however, they were terrible things. In the age of King Stephen, A. D., 1134-1158, when the Barons exerted their greatest power and indulged in unlimited feudal insolence and feudal tyranny—an age of castles —when 1,500 were built and garrisoned, all the laws of God and man were trampled under foot, and the castle was little else than the stronghold of robbers and highwaymen. "Every rich man made his castles" (says that old chronicler, John of Salisbury,) "and held them against the King, and the land was filled with castles. Grievously they oppressed the people with their castle works.— When the castles were made, they filled them with devils and evil men and then they seized every one who was supposed to have any property—man and woman, both by day and night, and put them in prison for their gold and silver, and punished them with such inexpressible torments as none of the martyrs ever suffered. They hung them by the feet and smoked them with foul smoke; and they hung them by the thumbs or by the head and hung fire to their feet; they put knotted cords about their heads and twisted them till they pierced their brains. They put some in dungeons where were adders, and snakes, and toads, and so tormented them. Others they placed in a Crucet House, that is a chest which was short, and narrow and shallow, and they put in sharp stones, and pressed people in them till all their limbs were broken. In many of the castles were things very horrible and hateful—these were "Lachantages," that were as much as two or three men could lift, and they were so contrived that the man was fastened to a beam with sharp iron about his throat or neck, that he could neither sit nor lie down, nor sleep, but was always compelled to support that weight. Many they tormented with hunger. I cannot tell all the sufferings and all the torments which the wretched people bore during the nineteen years of Stephen's reign. They laid tributes upon towns, and when the wretched people had no more to give, they ravaged and burnt all the towns, so that you might go a long day's journey and not find a man dwelling in the town, or the land tilled. Then was corn, and flesh, and cheese, and butter dear."

Some may be inclined to regard this as an exaggerated account. Far from it. It is matter of history, that during the reign of Stephen, England presented one continued scene of confusion and bloodshed. David, King of Scotland, espoused the cause of his niece, Matilda, daughter of Henry I, youngest son of the conqueror; by his wife Matilda, daughter of Malcolm III, of Scotland, and niece of Edgar Atheling. This marriage united the Saxon and Norman lines. Henry I usurped the dukedom of Normandy, and by this act, brought England into collision with France and laid the foundation of the wars which ensued. Matilda, niece of David, was the widow of Henry V, Emperor of Germany, and David invaded England to maintain her right; he was defeated at the battle of the Standard, but Matilda, who soon landed in England, was acknowledged by the clergy, but during the civil wars was expelled. It was during these times of civil commotion and wars for the succession that castles multiplied in England and the land was desolated by the rival barons and their retainers.

Such having been the condition of affairs during the reign of Stephen, we are not surprised when our chronicler adds "many abandoned their country, others forsaking their houses, built wretched huts in the churchyards, hoping for protection from the sacred character of the place. Whole families, after sustaining life as long as they could by eating roots, herbs, dogs, and horses, perished at last with hunger, and you might see many pleasant villages without one inhabitant of either sex. In this King's time all was dissension and evil, and rapine. The great men rose against him they had sworn to support, but with whom they maintained no truth. They built castles which they held out against him."

This is the poetry of old castles to which we flock in the present day with such eager curiosity, over which we indulge in so much sentiment.

From the State departments we proceeded to St. George's Chapel, which stands on the spot of the ancient edifice, built by Edward III in honor of St. George of Cappadocia, Primate of Egypt in the fourth century, and Patron saint of England. St. George was put to death by the Pagans of Alexandria. Though he gave them ample provocation still having been slain by detested Pagans, it was enough, with a little legendary coloring, to make him a martyr. The crusaders read of him in their calendars and martyrologies, and under the winning appellation of St. George the Victorious, he was installed among the Christians of the East. These circumstances and the assistance which they imagined they had received from the beatified St. George, at the siege of Antioch, led them to adopt him as the patron of soldiers and tutelar saint of England. He was, as one tradition avers, in reality a Cappadocian tanner, but be this as it may, he has been for many a century a favorite with all sorts and conditions of Englishmen, thus—

>"Our ancient word of courage, fair St. George!"

was the invocation of the fierce Crook-Back upon his last battle field of Bosworth, and Shakespeare, with strong, double-edged wit, makes the bold bastard Falconbridge refer to him, as

>"St. George who swinged the dragon, and e'er since
>Sits upon horseback at mine hostess door."

On entering the chapel, our admiration was excited by the beauty of the architecture, which is elaborately ornate. In one of the chapels is the beautiful cenotaph of the Princess Charlotte, the unhappy daughter of George IV. Here are buried a long line of Royal personages and illustrious heroes "by all their country's wishes blessed." While lingering among the tombs, Addison's beautiful lines recurred to memory: "When I see Kings lying by those who deposed them; when I consider rival wits placed side by side; or the holy that divide the world with their contests and disputes, I reflect with sorrow and astonishment on the little competitions and debates of mankind: when I read the several dates of the tombs, of some that died yesterday, and some six hundred years ago, I consider that great day when we shall all of us be cotemporaries and make our appearance together."

In allusion to the fact that the rival Kings of York and Lancaster sleep here, side by side, Pope wrote:

>"Let softest strains ill-fated Henry mourn,
>And palms eternal flourish round his urn;
>Here o'er the martyr King the marble weeps,
>And, fast beside him, once fear'd Edward sleeps,
>Whom not the extended Albion could contain,
>From old Bolerium to the German main,
>The grave unites, where e'en the great find rest,
>And blended lie the oppressor and the oppress'd."

The choir portion of the chapel is appropriated to the performance of divine service and the ceremony of installing the Knights of the Garter. The stalls of the Knights are arranged on either side of the choir—over each stall are mantle, sword, helmet and crest of the Knight by whom it is occupied. Above these is the banner on which are his armorial bearings and at the back of the seat, on engraved brass plates, are recorded his name, style and titles. The brass plates of former occupants for centuries are preserved as a perpetual record of the distinguished honor each has in his lifetime borne; amongst them is that of Sigismund, Emperor of Germany in 1418, Casimer IV, King of Poland, in 1451, and Robert Peyton, who assumed the surname of Ufford and was Earl of Suffolk in 1349, who was one of the founders of the Order.

George III and IV and William IV all died at Windsor and lie in the Royal Dormitory, to the east of St. George's Chapel, where all the members of the Royal family who have died in England have been placed since its application to the purposes of a mausoleum, with the exception of the Duke of Sussex, who, at his own request, was buried in Kensal Green Cemetery, and the unhappy queen, wife of George IV, who was removed to Brunswick. One cannot visit such a spot, rife with royalty in its ruins, without its suggesting the moral of the poet: "The glories of our blood are shadows, not substantial things." It sinks deep into our souls that God is "no respecter of persons," and there is "no king saved by the multitude of an host." Such visits seem to urge the admonition upon the mighty and the lowly, "Be wise now, O ye kings; be instructed, ye judges of the earth. Serve the Lord with fear and rejoice with trembling." It is "appointed unto all men once to die:" but after death the judgment! The mind is startled from the engrossing pursuits, the cares and anxieties of this world, and we apply these texts in all their force. How impressively do they counsel the wisdom of seeking pardon and peace from that Saviour by whom alone we are saved.

On the next morning we attended service at St. George's Chapel and saw a number of the gallant veterans called the "Military Knights of Windsor," who have residences in the immediate vicinity of the castle and small annual pensions. The only duty imposed upon them being a regular attendance at church and constant prayer for the prosperity of the sovereign.

There are two parks at Windsor. The little park nearest the castle, contains 500 acres, which is enclosed by a brick wall. It is studded with clumps of trees and abounds in promenades, the finest being the "long walk," which is lined with elms. Here are the Queen's stables, wherein, like those of Branksome Castle, "a hundred steeds feed free in stall." These stables, plain and substantial, are built on the most approved plan for securing fresh air, light and uniform temperature, for the comfort of the animals. The heat is regulated by a thermometer and is not allowed to rise above 65° Far., or to sink below 50. The system of ventilation is by openings near the ceilings, constructed so as to prevent a current of air from passing over the animals. The light is uniform and without any glare, and the rooms are ceiled so as to prevent dust from the lofts getting into the eyes of the horses and the ascending gasses from lodging in the hay. The stalls are level and have clay floors—inclined stalls and plank floors have been universally abandoned in England, as they fatigue and injure the horses. The stalls are roomy so as to encourage the animals to lie down, and no straw is ever put in them for bedding.

The Queen keeps the full complement of forty carriages in different styles and one hundred blooded horses for use while at Windsor. The kennels are near the stables, where Her Majesty's fancy dogs are kept, embracing almost every kind and variety of dog, foreign and native. It is a unique collection in which the Queen is said to take much interest.

The dairy and farm buildings are extensive, and combine every accommodation and modern improvement. The great park contains 1800 acres and is much admired for its varied and picturesque scenery. This park was a famous place as early as the 12th century, when Henry II not only kept his deer here, as the legend goes, but "diverse strange beastes, which were sent unto hime from foreigne countries farre distante, such as liones, lepardes, linxes and porkupines."

The park is at present well stocked with deer and pheasants which furnish excellent shooting and a constant supply of game for the Queen's household. In this park lie the Home and Shaw farms, two of the model farms of Prince Albert. The only work of art in the park is a colossal equestrian statue of George III, which terminates the "long walk" at a distance of at least three miles from the castle. There is a handsome school building near the farms in which the children of the servants connected with the castle and property are educated. It was established by Prince Albert. The boys receive a good English education and are instructed in the practical operations of farming and gardening, while the girls are taught sewing, ornamental needle work and domestic affairs.

In the southern extremity of the grounds lies the celebrated lake entitled *Virginia Water*, the lovely natural scenery of which has been heightened by the aid of art. A road has been constructed around the lake, so that all the best views may be seen in an afternoon drive. The shade trees are principally larch, pine and fir.

At the head of the lake the road crosses an embankment having a rustic stone fence on one side, covered with moss and ivy, and from which a road leads over a bridge across the water and to the Fishing temple, an elegant pavilion, surrounded by grounds ornamented with fountains, flowers, plants and statuary. The roof is painted in various colors and ornamented with dragons and other grotesque figures. This building was erected for the use of George IV and those members of his family and household who were fond of angling. The lake is sufficiently large to admit of piscatorial amusements upon a large scale. In a romantic glen below the lake stands a fine ornamental ruin styled "the temple of the gods."

The scenery here is singularly wild and sweet. It is a kind of sacred valley of delightful solitude, which makes one dream of nymphs and shepherds.

A more delightful country than that in the vicinity of Windsor we have nowhere looked upon. The scenery, though not romantic, is extremely pleasant. The winding Thames pursues its course through fertile meadows and well cultivated fields, with a back ground of sloping hills and woodland heights. A favorite resort of the pent-up denizens of London for a day's outing, a thoughtful man finds abundant material for study, whether wandering beneath the wide spreading trees of the parks, basking in the sunshine of the castle walls or walking along the streets of the good, quiet town. Not only will the busy crowd of passers by, the scenes of excitement presented, and the incidents of each moment suggest reflection, but the houses will be as books with open leaves full of moral instruction and practical hints. Those dwelling places are proofs and expressions of ingenuity, skill and social habits, and thus they illustrate the superior nature, the inventive mind, and the soul of sympathy and affection with which God has endowed man. How diversified are the habitations in architecture, style and appearance! under what different circumstances, from what various motives, for what diversified ends were they planned and built? They remind one of the innumerable forms, the many tinted hues of man's condition, characteristics and feelings. What changes have occurred since the edifices were reared! What a new era has dawned on our civilization since yonder time-worn mansion was raised! How many have passed into eternity since then! What changeful aspects have the families within those walls presented from time to time! People have come and gone, children have been born, parents have died : the rooms have witnessed weddings and funerals, joys and sorrows. The contrast between the outward look of some of these abodes and the inner feelings of the occupants, how startling ! Here perhaps, where all seems so splendid, where many a proud equipage sweeps up to the door and powdered footmen rise at the rap, and distinguished visitors are announced and aristocratic names echo in the halls, hearts are wasting with ambition, envy, disappointment, fear.

shame, remorse ; whereas in yonder humble tenement, peace may dwell, for "Faith shuts the door at night, and mercy opens it in the morning." The houses of princes and peasants exhibit alike the same moral phenomena.
Here we bid adieu to our didactics, to Windsor, the town and castle. Windsor Castle ! Its antiquities and its pleasantness cannot be comprehended in a visit. Its annals, memoirs, legends, would fill volumes and they must be pondered ere one can enter into the spirit and philosophy of its history, or understand the famous men who have figured in its courts. Let no one, however, be kept back from a visit—not even the bird of passage, or the summer tourist, for the visitor of a single day will see much to deeply interest, though he may see more that he does not understand. He will come away in any case with a fund of knowledge which, though a little mixed and undigested, is yet strangely pleasing. Stored up in the memory these experiences will constitute the agreeable musings of old age. If at times when recalling the past, melancholy should mingle with the retrospections, as is apt to be the case, it will be found to have something in it sweeter even than pleasure.

## CHAPTER VI.

THE INAUGURATION OF THE SECOND WORLD'S FAIR IN LONDON—
THE FINE ART DEPARTMENT—AMERICAN EXHIBITORS—
LETTER TO THE TIMES—NEW-MADE FRIENDS.

The opening of the great international exhibition of 1862 occurred during our sojourn in London. The only notes of this grand affair which we have are in the form of two brief letters to a friend in Virginia, from which we make the following extracts: "The international exhibition was inaugurated in this place on the 1st of May. Nothing could have been more propitious than the weather on the opening day. The sky was calm and cloudless, the air bright and genial. For weeks before the 1st, a continuous stream of visitors had been pouring into London from every quarter. The papers had already announced the arrival of Frederick William, Crown Prince of Prussia, of Prince Oscar of Sweden and Queen Christiana, of Spain, with their respective suites. The Japanese Embassy was also here, minus the ubiquitous "Tommy," who created such a stir among the spinsters of New York ; there were commissioners from almost every country. It was apparent to me long before the opening day that this great and noble enterprise would be a complete success.

I left my lodgings, 39 Bedford Square, about ten o'clock in the forenoon, and found the streets filled with gaily dressed people wending their way to the West-end. On reaching Hyde Park corner, I saw tens of thousands who had already assembled. Flags were suspended across the streets and floated from windows which were gracefully decorated with awnings and filled with cheerful faces. In the distance were seen the lofty domes of the exhibition building, enlivened by the flags of every nation. The procession of carriages with elegantly dressed ladies, extended from Apsley House (the Duke of Wellington's) in the direction of Brampton and the marble arch, far as the eye could reach. The road from Buckingham Palace up Constitution Hill was lined by a dense mass of human beings in holiday attire ; along the whole route detachments of horse guards in their brilliant uniforms, and metropolitan police were interspersed through the crowd, the whole forming a scene of gaiety, excitement and confusion of the most pleasant and exhilirating character. London was evidently in all her glory.

Leaving the Park I took a position near the entrance of the building, where I had an excellent opportunity of observing the distinguished arrivals. The chief object of interest with the masses seemed to be the Queen's, or what was styled the Royal party, the Ministers of State and the Lord Mayor, and as each of these arrived, the delighted multitude loudly cheered—made the welkin ring. The coaches containing the Royal party were draped in black, and the occupants and servants were in deep mourning. The contrast presented by the mournful procession to the gay and brilliant equipages by which it was preceded was deeply impressive, and suggested many painful associations in connection with Prince Albert, with whom these enterprises—international exhibitions—originated. The Royal carriages contained Prince Frederick William, who wore the uniform of a Prussian General, and Prince Oscar of Sweden, with their respective suites. The Prince of Wales, whom it was hoped would be present and officiate in the opening ceremonies, in place of his father, was, to the general regret, absent in Egypt. It is said that he was sent abroad to divert his mind and heart from a young lady, the daughter of a distinguished Cambridge barrister, with whom he became acquainted, and for whom he formed a passionate attachment while at the University, and with whom he wished to "link his fate"—the marriage act of George III to the contrary notwithstanding.

The Royal party, government officials, distinguished foreigners and others to the number of about 30,000, having assembled in the building at one o'clock, the procession was formed in what was styled "Procession Court," and after a grand flourish of trumphets, took up the line of march for the spot from which the Exhibition was, with imposing ceremony, to be declared open.

As the procession moved on, Lord Palmerston, who is a popular favorite, was repeatedly cheered, as also, Lord Derby, who is a feeble looking old man who gets along by the aid of a cane. Nothing could exceed the brilliancy of the spectacle presented by the moving crowd in which the uniforms of soldiers were mixed with the black gowns of the Judges and the white robes of the Doctors of music and the ten thousand hues of the ladies' Spring dresses.

When the Commissioners had taken their seats the first verse of the National Anthem was sung by more than 2000 musicians, and then the special music composed for the occasion to the following appropriate words by Alfred Tennyson, Poet Laureate.

> Uplift a thousand voices full and sweet
> In this wide Hall with Earth's inventions stored
> And praise thee, Universal Lord,
> Who lets once more in peace the nations meet,
> Where science, art, and labour have outpour'd
> Their myriad horns of plenty at our feet.
>
> O, silent father of our King to be,
> Mourn'd in this golden hour of Jubilee,
> For this, for all we weep our thanks to thee!
>
> The world compelling plan was thine,
> And lo! the long laborious miles
> Of Palace ; lo! the giant aisles,
> Rich in model and design ;
> Harvest tool and husbandry,
> Loom and wheel and engin'ry,
> Secrets of the duller mine,
> Steel and gold, and corn and wine
> Fabric rough, or Fairy fine,
> Sunny tokens of the line,

Polar marvels and a feast
Of wonder, out of West and East,
And shapes and hues of art divine!
All of beauty, all of use
That our fair planet can produce,
Brought from under every star
Blown from over every main,
And mix't as life is mix't with pain,
The works of peace with the works of war.


O yes, the wise who think, the wise who reign
From growing commerce loose her latest chain,
And let the fair white-winged peace-maker fly
To happy havens under all the sky,
And mix the seasons and the golden hours,
Till each man finds his own in all men's good,
And all men work in noble brotherhood,
And ruling by obeying nature's powers,
And gathered all the fruits of peace and crown'd with all the flowers.

The Earl of Granville then delivered an opening speech in which he referred in eloquent terms to the National grief at the death of Prince Albert, and to the particular loss sustained by the Commissioners of the exhibition in their arduous labors, and to the popular disappointment at the absence of the Queen. He concluded with a brief history of the circumstances connected with the realization of the scheme for holding the Second Great International Exhibition in England.

The Duke of Cambridge replied, reading an address of intense respectability as to the language and style, but exceedingly dull and common place, after which, 'technicalities,' the Exhibition was declared open, amidst the cheers of hundreds of thousands in and out of the building and repeated salutes of Artillery in the Park.

I cannot, of course, attempt any description of the multitudinous display of whatever is most remarkable in British and Foreign products, as the results of the industry and art of every country—all contained in this gigantic building—volumes are required for a simple catalogue.

The *coup d' oil*, standing under either of the domes of the vast Exhibition building itself and looking down the nave, is one of almost unequalled beauty. The fine proportions and mouldings of the columns make the immense vista appear as if looking along a kind of iron lace work. As I wandered through the vast area of this great building, before countless stalls, my eyes dazzled and my senses filled with admiration, I felt the full force of the adage, "peace hath her victories no less renowned than war." What sight could be more glorious, what scene more noble than that here presented of the peaceful rivalry of the nations? What marks more strongly the progress of the age, the coming of that new era of universal brotherhood, in which the gentle spirit of Christianity, with all its humanizing and ennobling influences is to supercede the barbarism of the past, and to banish forever those relics which survive in the brutal contests of the present, in which might makes right, and virtue and patriotism are crushed to the Earth by the power of tyrants, or the frenzy of fanaticism.

Any attempt at a description of the infinite variety of articles on exhibition, as I have said, would be absurd and fail to attract attention at this remote period, but the following extract from a second letter written to our Virginia friend, in May, 1862, will not be altogether without interest as it contains some information as to one particular department, that of Art, and the contributions to it of a fellow countryman then in London, and with whom we formed a pleasant acquaintance, and the story of whose life is one of vigor, perseverance and energy :

"The fine art department of the International Exhibition of 1862, presents for the first time in the history of the arts, a collection of works of contemporary artists from every civilized nation. An opportunity is thus afforded the observant and reflective mind of comparing the styles of the various schools, and leading to a pleasant and instructive investigation of the causes which have produced those peculiarities and excellencies by which they are distinguished. The walls of this vast department are adorned by the labors of men of the greatest genius, and afford space for the works of persons noted for some bold innovations upon the generally acknowledged principles of art.

Without attempting to give any lengthened review of these varied productions or the impressions by which they have individually affected me, it may be at least useful to give you their combined result upon my mind. They may be serviceable to the future cause of the arts in our own States. The styles cf "schools" are quite as distinctly marked as the boundary lines which separate one country from another ; for no observant eye can fail after a few days examination of these schools to recognize their distinctive differences, and to see that their characteristic qualities are the effects of that system of teaching which prevails in the art institutions of each country. Hence it is that whilst Sir Joshua Reynolds was at the head of the English Academy, the young artists, whether pupils or not of that institution, followed his manner and received instruction as coming from an oracle in art. It is thus that the great mass in every profession are certain to follow, many slavishly, the theories and practice of those who either from genius, from management or from Royal patronage have attained to distinction and high rewards. So that the characteristics of a school are changeful, and according to the accidents of the success of individuals. At one period the method of Sir Joshua influences the great body of young aspirants, at another it is Sir Thomas Lawrence who rules supreme. Then Wilkie leads the way for a host. Finally, the English school has changed entirely from the masculine, dashing and effective style of Reynolds, until it has arrived at the effeminate, dry and ineffective manner of those who style themselves, however inappropriately, "Pre-Raphaelites."

These facts are readily gleaned from the large number of pictures displayed in the English department of the Exhibition, which extends over a period of a hundred years, during which they were executed. The departments of the French and other foreign schools, as they contain only the work of living painters, give a much more restricted scope for the study or elucidation of the principles which I have ventured to assert. In the French school we see no work which was inspired by the dry, academic and classic practice of David, Nicholas Poussin, or Le Brun—their works were those of academicians and founders of the earliest schools of France. I see now in their stead the influence of later masters such as Horace Vernet, De Laroche, Ary, Scheffer, the one differing as much as possible from the other.

The Belgian school being essentially French in character and derived from the teachings of Parisian masters, follows the same law and adds its testimony to the justness of my views. The Tuscan school presents in its leading work by Ussi, the Fruits of the Florentine Academy, under the late Presidency of Bezzuoli. Spain, Russia and other countries of Europe cannot be said to possess any school whatever, their leading artists having generally been students in Paris and their style and excellencies attributable entirely to its professors.

The American department contains a few paintings, six only, two by Cropsey and four by Kellogg, two portraits and two ideal pieces. The landscapes by Cropsey, one representing an Autumn on the Hudson, and the other a Cane brake in Louisiana, are two of the finest specimens of this kind of painting in the Exhibition. The atmospheric tints peculiar to the American Autumn, and the rich foliage of the forest and the brilliant sunset sky are admirably painted.

Kellogg's portraits are quiet and natural in color with serene and thoughtful expressions, the draperies well cast and carefully worked up, and the drawing admirably executed. The "Flower of the Seraglio" represents a Turkish girl seated at an open window, evidently contemplating with delight a flower which grows in a vase placed upon a table by the side of the Divan upon which she reposes. A glimpse of the neighboring buildings is seen through the lattice work of the window. At first view of this picture I was struck with the power and brilliancy of the sunlight which pervaded it. This quality of light brought to my remembrance several paintings belonging to the French school which, over all others, is pre-eminent in this essential and rare beauty in painting.

Passing this piece I next saw his "Bath Scene." This is a subject calling for many of the higher qualities in an artist, a foreshortened naked figure; one-half in a powerful light and the other in reflected light, partially derived from it, the whole figure being surrounded by stuffs of the greatest variety of texture and rich and varied colors. This principal figure is a girl reclining after the pleasures of the Oriental bath, and apparently just dropping into a gentle slumber amid the cushions which supported her.

This principal figure and chief point of interest is quite upon one side of the picture, the attendant features being situated on the other side, a very difficult and rare system of composition. This important painting which strikes the spectator at once with pleasure, is one requiring daring and educated qualities in the artist, both of which have been successfully illustrated in the piece which seems an emanation of the loving spirit which led the ancient artists to immortal renown, breathing a devotion to the truth of the subject chosen, which works out the result from an innate perception of beauty and propriety, and creates of necessity a manner of execution peculiarly its own, untrammeled by the dicta of academies or by the tyranny which tradition so often exercises over the artist mind. The pleasure which the study of the works of an artist who combined so much of freshness of thought, variety of style and beauty of execution was enough to make me desire to know something of the routine or system of education which had produced these happy results, and as Mr. Kellogg was an American, I soon found myself pursuing my investigations in his studio and amidst the evidences of his long and devoted labors. From my notes of conversation with him, the following brief account is given of the method he has pursued, and by which he has reached his high position in the practice of art. The example of his career cannot but be serviceable to the youthful artist of our country, who is striving amidst the darkness around him to fix on some system of study which will ultimately secure his success.

Mr. Kellogg, while still a lad commenced the pursuit of art, and though unaided by either fortune, powerful friends, teachers or examples succeeded in earning a precarious livelihood in the north western States which at that time, thirty years ago, lacked every means of instruction in the arts. The *Cincinnati Gazette* of January 9th, 1873, in an article referring to his early predilection for the arts remarks "some fifteen years ago in an old and leaning frame building that stood, or rather pretended to stand on a somewhat noted part of Main street, and whose second story was reached by a rickety flight of steps on the outside, were types, cases, presses and all the etceteras of one of our old time printing offices. And in this ancient office, at one of the cases aforenamed, stood a bright eyed, fresh cheeked, mischief loving boy, some twelve or fifteen years of age, who had "gone" (as the phrase was when youngsters here were too proud and independent to be "apprenticed" and mothers too weak to tolerate the idea of having their sons bound out) to learn the "art, trade or mystery" of a printer. With all his life and mischief he was yet a dreamy lad; and notwithstanding that he was not lazy, but on the contrary clever and active, he yet made but slow progress between the Monday mornings and Saturday evenings, in the important work of setting type. This was a mystery that required a little investigation, and on such examination taking place, it was found that some accommodating body had constructed a convenient drawer under his type case, which was capacious enough to hold an old violin, an eight keyed flute, two or three music books, divers pieces of crayon and many sheets of drawing paper, many of which were covered with grotesque groups of 'boss' and his 'jours,' and caricatured likenesses of that considerate and good natured class of gentlemen loungers, who have from time immemorial been in the habit of passing their morning hours around the tables of Editors to assist in hunting out news. Withal the youth mentioned was good natured and genial, and so when remonstrated with frankly confessed that his love of music and the pencil was greater than his regard for type, and it was decided that he or his friends for him had mistaken his vocation."

It was shortly after this period that urged by a love of painting and a noble ambition he left the West and worked his way to the Eastern States in search of examples and teachers. Here, however, his necessities forced him to abide several years in the interior of the State of New Jersey, which was as destitute of the means of instruction which he sought as were the states of the far West. His success in painting portraits enabled him in a short time to reach the State Capital, where he made influential friends and obtained a commission from the Legislature to execute a large portrait of Washington for the assembly rooms of the State House, which portrait gave such satisfaction that he was honored by the Legislature with a unanimous vote of thanks. Instead of resting a moment contented with the approval of his abilities, he used the means it furnished him to obtain the instruction he so much desired. He visited Washington City and there secured the favorable consideration of the Cabinet of President Van Buren, among whose leading members was Hon. Joel R. Poinsett, Secretary of War, a man of great learning and cultivated taste, who warmly interested himself in promoting the honorable views of the struggling artist. The result was that the President and Cabinet secured for him the friendly notice of the Professors in the Military Academy at West Point. Giving up the pursuit of painting for the present he proceeded to West Point, where through the gratuitous and able teachings of the Professors he was enabled in the course of a year to lay the foundation of a knowledge of perspective and other sciences connected with the art of design. With a mind trained to some system in the pursuit of a most difficult art, he resumed the practice, Shortly after he went to Tennessee and painted the likeness of General Jackson, ex-President of the United States, and the friendly intercession of the old hero resulted in obtaining for him several valuable commissions from the Government at Washington, by whom he was finally entrusted with despatches for the Minister at Naples.

Here he found himself in the glorious land of art, but without means and only one important commission. He diligently pursued his studies for three years amidst difficulties and privations of the most discouraging character, and as his means would not enable him to spend anything upon living masters, he determined to seek from the examples of ancient art around him, some knowledge of the principles by which they were produced. In the course of two years, he had by copying some of their best works and by a few original pictures acquired the means to study the human figure from living models and to obtain in the Hospitals of Florence a practical knowledge of the structure. osteological and anatomical, of the human form and also to sketch and take elaborate notes of the famous paintings in oil and in fresco which have given renown to the most splendid palaces of that great seat of medieval art. He had sent original paintings to the Royal Academy of Florence which received complimentary notices of the press and pointed out such admirable copies of Raphael's works as to have obtained commissions enough to allow him to venture to spend a season of study among the churches and other depositories of art throughout Lombardy and Venice. Determined now to see something of the arts of other countries he made a visit to Egypt and labored with assiduity in studying and drawing from its mysterious and mighty ruins. He then continued his journey, sketch and note book always in hand, into the desert of Arabia

Petrae to the Convent of Mt. Sinai where he spent some time in exploring this most interesting region of the ancient world. It is sufficient evidence of his thoughtful investigation and enthusiastic character to peruse his journal of this journey—a portion relating to this region being of such interest to Biblical scholars as to find a place in Dr. Kitto's work on the Scripture lands. After crossing the Desert of Hebron, he made a complete tour of the Holy Land and returned to Italy, enriched by a large collection of sketches of oriental scenes and characters. The next year his love of art and adventure took him again to the East. He remained some time in Constantinople, where the American Minister extended to him the hospitalities of a home at the Legation and the English Ambassador, Sir Statford Canning and his accomplished wife, Lady Canning, took a lively interest in his success. It was here that he formed the acquaintance of Mr. A. H. Layard, who afterwards disinterred Nineveh, with whom he made an extensive tour in Asia Minor, which laid the foundation of a mutual and lasting friendship. He now returned to the United States from which he had been absent seven years, where he remained four years prosecuting his profession, after which he spent three years more in Italy studying the old masters. He then removed to Paris determined to glean all that was possible from the theories and practices of the most excellent of all schools of modern art. After a residence of four years he came to London where he has been established for the last five years.

I have thus traced briefly the career of an artist who starting from a sphere where art was literally unknown, and without any means of obtaining either instruction or fame, has travelled extensively through remote countries, and is now settled with honor in the Metropolis of the modern world, with port-follios filled with subjects sufficient to keep his pencil profitably employed during the remainder of his life.

Probably nothing could give stranger proof of Mr. Kellogg's accurate knowledge of the works of the old painters than the possession of so many of their best productions, for it is only by such knowledge that a man of his limited means is able to become their owner. His collection is of rare excellence, many of the pictures costing him a very small sum, having been found in the most unlikely places, and sometimes in a dingy or injured condition—for some, however, as they came from well known galleries by public sale, something approaching their real value had to be paid. A few which have excited the interest of the most enlightened artist and critics are of such great importance, that I may be excused for speaking at some length as to the manner by which Mr. Kellogg obtained them.

When his collection had, by slow degrees and in the course of his travels in the different countries where they were found, increased to the number of more than one hundred examples of good masters, his attention was accidentally called in Paris to a small number of paintings, the property of a Swiss lady, who upon the death of her father had brought them from Switzerland to be disposed of for the benefit of his heirs. This was in the summer of 1855. Owing to the war in the Crimea and to the distress in financial circles it was impossible to obtain for them the notice they deserved. Mr. Kellogg examined them, and was so convinced of their value and so reliant on his own discernment, that although the price demanded for them was thousands of dollars beyond his means, he borrowed the money by pledging as security the whole of his own collection, and that too, without knowing the opinion of any other person as to the authenticity of the pictures, and thus he became their purchaser.

Among the pictures to obtain which Mr. Kellogg had thus advisedly risked the whole of his little fortune, were at least two which he believed to be of inestimable value. One was a "Herodias," by Leonardo de Vinci, and the other the "Belle Jardiniere" by Raphael. They had been so long hidden in the family of an humble connoisseur among the mountains of Switzerland as to have escaped the zealous researches of every biographer of those two most distinguished masters of the Italian school.

He kept these pictures in Paris for four years, where they were freely open to the visits of all lovers of art; the best artists and most impartial judges declaring them to be originals of the highest value.

The 'Belle Jardiniere' had, however, a rival in a painting of the same subject in the Gallery of the Louvre; which though acknowledged to be an inferior work, and its originality openly contested by able connoisseurs, had in its favor the prestige of some centuries existence in that great museum of art, and its authenticity asserted by the most indubitable documentary history. Notwithstanding these generally received opinions, he engaged earnestly upon the labor of examining every available record which concerned the history of that work. After exhausting the field of research which Paris offered to his industry, he made a visit to the famous exhibition of art treasures then open at Manchester and to several collections in London, to acquaint himself with every work attributed to Raphael which could there be found. Returning to Paris he prepared to leave that city and establish himself in London, when Count de Morny visited his collection, and was so struck with the beauty of the Raphael as to express a wish to see it by the side of the picture in the Louvre, and through his influence this was accomplished, and he obtained at the same time the long desired privilege for Mr. Kellogg of making a satisfactory examination of the two paintings side by side. After this was done Mr. Kellogg removed to London. Here his fine collection soon attracted the attention of many noblemen and lovers of art. For three years he pursued the study of his subject and finally published a pamphlet, giving the result of his "Researches into the history of a painting by Raphael of Urbino, entitled La Belle Jardiniere. (Premiere Idee du Peintre.)" *

Of course these researches included the history of the Louvre painting and all its traditional claims to authenticity. In the most laudable spirit of impartiality he abstained entirely from expressing any opinion regarding its merits, leaving these and the record of historical facts which he gives to decide the question of the relative value of the two paintings.

Without going further into this interesting subject, I may briefly state that the result of the critical labors of Mr. Kellogg have been to prove conclusively that his painting possesses stronger historical claims to originality than that in the Louvre, and to surpass it in many of those qualities which distinguish Raphael from all other painters.

Through losses and illness in his family, pecuniary embarrassment now pressed heavily upon him. Against those, however, he battled manfully, and the Civil War in America deprived him of every assistance from his countrymen. In this most gloomy condition of his affair he was induced to dispose of the picture he had so long cherished and which was so dear to his artistic spirit. Thus after seven years sojourn in the studio of the man who had the sagacity to appreciate its character and the courage to rescue it from oblivion, his judgment was at last triumphantly confirmed and his unswerving faith in its originality and patient labors to prove it to the world adequately rewarded.

The conviction expressed in the preface to the "Researches" that enlightened and impartial criticism will ultimately secure for it an elevated position among the precious monuments of Italian Art, was not founded on erroneous conceptions of the character of the picture, for it has, after passing the ordeal of the severest critics in Europe, been recognized as an original and at length reached an elevated position among the precious monuments of art which composed the noble collection of Lord Ashburton.

*Vide Art Catalogue published by the trustees of South Kensington Museum.

*Lord Ashburton purchased the painting for two thousand guineas and left it as a special legacy in his last will to Lady Ashburton. It now adorns the walls of Bath House, Piccadilly.

I have selected this interesting incident from among similar ones in the career of our artist to testify to the value of that course of study, which in the absence of Academic instruction, may sometimes lead to distinction in the practice of art and to a sound judgment in the appreciation of her noblest works.

Mr Kellogg's studio is filled with works painted by himself at various periods under the influence of the pictures of the old masters, which he was at the time studying. They illustrate by their different qualities and subjects, the comprehensive field which his mind has traversed in its search after knowledge. Refreshing himself at times from the fountain of nature, as the greatest and noblest of all teachers, he has secured himself from falling into that mannerism which is inseperable from the works of all the disciples of any one school.

I do not mean to affirm that he has pursued the only right course of study, since he himself laments the loss of many precious years of his youth in battling for bread, and that too in a district destitute of every means of instruction in his profession. That he has attained his present high position is due entirely to his natural talents and to unremitting labor and observation, wherever his lot was cast, owing nothing to any advantages of study which his own country had afforded to him in the arduous struggles of his youth.

From the foregoing reflections I have been led to conclude that if a country is ever to be honored by the presence and skill of native artists, it must afford its youth examples of the works of artists of every country who have attained to excellence, and I cannot too highly applaud the course of the alumni of the University of Virginia in founding an art gallery there. These are as necessary as is a library in the pursuit of literature.

It is also important that some system should be adopted whereby the general principles of art and the sciences, which are essential to its successful practice, can be taught in such a manner as to leave the student's mind free from prejudice in favor of any particular master's style, whilst it gives him the power of expressing in the readiest way his conception of subjects which shall henceforth occupy his pencil.

I am inclined forcibly to the opinion that Academies of Art are generally conducted on principles subversive of originality in the minds of their pupils by encouraging the belief that reputation and rewards are more certainly within their reach, if they follow the methods which are practiced by successful academicians and that their errors may be avoided and every necessary instruction imparted by including departments or Schools of Art in all universities similar to those of law or medicine.

## CHAPTER VII.

### LETTER TO THE "TIMES" REFERRED TO IN PREVIOUS CHAPTER—GLADSTONE, BRIGHT, ETC., ETC.

Immediately upon reaching London, Mr. Yancey requested me to write for the papers, a letter correcting certain reports industriously circulated in England as to the state of public opinion in North Carolina. Concurring with him as to the propriety of this course, the following letter was written and published in the London Times, on the 24th of November, 1861:

SIR:—"I have been greatly surprised to learn since my arrival in London that an effort has been made through publications in the English press, to create the impression that there is much disaffection towards the Confederate Government in all the Southern States of America, but particularly among the people of North Carolina, and that the proceedings of what purports to be a meeting of influential and respectable citizens of the county of Hyde, in that State, have been published as authority for the numerous statements made upon the subject.

I am directly from the city of Raleigh, North Carolina, having come on board the Confederate States war Steamer, Nashville, which left Charleston, South Carolina, on the 26th of October, and cast anchor off the Itchin, Southampton, on the 21st of this month, and have been since August, with the exception of brief visits to Virginia, constantly in the eastern portion of the State, where this disaffection is said to exist and the meeting to have taken place. I need not say, therefore, how much gratified I am that an opportunity is afforded me of pronouncing the entire story utterly devoid of truth in every particular. No such disaffection exists in North Carolina and no such meeting has ever been held. The people of North Carolina are united and enthusiastic in the support of the Confederate Government, and are determined, under no circumstances, to ground their arms till the independence of the Confederacy is acknowledged by our enemy. . Before the State seceded, there was in North Carolina, as in every Southern State, (as there will always be in every popular Government,) a divided popular sentiment as to the wisest policy to be pursued for a redress of grievances suffered at the hands of the Government of the United States, but the proclamation of Mr. Lincoln, in contravention of all law and authority, calling for 75,000 men, ostensibly to 'hold, occupy, and possess' a few dilapidated sea side forts and an armory at Harper's Ferry, a force utterly disproportioned to the end announced, aroused the whole Southern people to a sense of their danger, and the Act of Secession was passed in North Carolina by a unanimous vote of the Legislature. Subsequently it was ratified by a State Convention elected by a popular vote and representing the sovereignty of the people. This action occurred in the month of April last. Since that time I have not heard in my extensive intercourse with the people a single expression of opinion in opposition, but, on the contrary, a universal sentiment of concurrence in its justice, propriety and necessity.

Before I left America the State had sent to the seat of war in Virginia, 33,000 volunteer troops fully armed and equipped (infantry and riflemen), and a regiment of cavalry, numbering 1094. There were 6,000 troops on the State coast, and camps of instruction established at Raleigh, Ridgeway and Careysburg. War is always popular and the people were fired with enthusiasm, so much so that the number of volunteers still offering was so much larger than was needed, that General Martin, Commander-in-chief of the State forces, had, under orders of His Excellency, Gov. Clark, issued a proclamation informing the people that no further troops would be mustered into service.

A simple statement of these facts is a sufficient refutation of the idea which Mr. President Lincoln so earnestly and persistently seeks to create abroad, that there is a Union party in the Confederate States. It may suit his purposes to create such an impression, as a justification of his course in waging a wicked and atrocious war upon a gallant and noble people, whom he is perfectly aware he can only wound—never conquer, but he will find few charitable enough to believe him actuated either by truth or honor.

The further statements of the papers of the United States, which have been extensively reproduced in the British press, that large numbers—multitudes, indeed, of the people of North Carolina had, after the fall of Fort Hatteras, gone in and taken the oath of allegiance to the Government of the United States, are likewise devoid or truth. On the isolated and barren strip of land where Fort Hatteras is situated, there are some *wreckers*, who support themselves principally by decoying vessels to their destruction by displaying false lights, &c. Some of these desperadoes, who live without the sense of any duty they owe to God or man, and who do not wish to be disturbed by their new neighbors, may have gone in and taken the oath after the fort fell, but even this is doubtful. If the Yankees were dislodged to-morrow, they would take a second oath, with equal alacrity, to whoever might next occupy the waste. If any meeting favorable to Mr. Lincoln ever took place in North Carolina, which I do not believe, it could only have have been composed of these wreckers, acting under the auspices of their new fledged friends, the Yankee invaders, and the salutary restraints imposed by martial law and the guns of Fort Hatteras.

By giving this hurried note a place in your columns, where the statements it is intended to correct, have appeared, you will much oblige, Sir, your most obedient servant,

J. L. PEYTON.

'58 Jermyn Street, St. James,
London, Nov. 23rd, 1861.

P. S.—The statements in the alleged proceedings of the meeting in Hyde county, that the writ of *habeas corpus*, the freedom of speech and of the press, and the right of trial by jury, had all been suspended in North Carolina, are equally without foundation.

J. L. P.

This note had no sooner appeared in the *Times*, than large numbers of persons began to call, either to make more particular enquiries as to the condition of affairs in America, to express sympathy for the Southern cause, or simply to pay their respects and invite us to dinner. From this time our circle of acquaintance rapidly extended, and we received much civility and kindness from persons in all ranks and classes, and these amenities continued up to the period when we left on our return, years afterwards, to the United States.

Elected an honorary member of the Reform Club, we there met many of the celebrities of the day—statesmen, authors, lawyers, army and navy officers, etc. In the library of the Club much of our correspondence, for a time, was conducted and in the whist room we were initiated into the mysteries of short whist, which has superceded the game played in the days of Hoyle.

The most agreeable impressions were produced by our new made friends, by the ease and elegance of manners generally of those in good society, and the entire absence of any pomposity or assumption of dignity. Foreigners entertain many erroneous opinions as to the English. So far from being a surly, ill-tempered, rude, vulgar and unfeeling people, they are the reverse, and should be valued, and are, by those who know them well, upon their high breeding and upon, as a people, being *de bon coeur*, which in its real meaning answers with much exactness to the English adjective good-natured. Mr. Gladstone usually sat in the Club, when his onerous duties admitted of his being there, talking to a listening audience who gathered round about his chair, in an earnest and perfectly natural common sense way as if he meant what he said, and said what he meant. This remarkable man wields a vast influence—manipulates those about him like a musician the keys of his piano. However some of his followers may now and again oppose his measures, they do not long remain in in opposition—they are soon reclaimed by his eloquence. Few can resist the charm, the magnetism of his manners, the force of his logic, the persuasiveness of his discourse. He is never at a loss or unprepared, but ever ready. He knows what he is going to say and how to say it; is full of arguments, images, tropes and figures, and blends them with his facts, with matchless skill. He is never cold, dull or monotonous, but always the enthusiast as talker, writer, orator and statesman, uniting the originality of the man of genius to the erudition of the scholar and the graceful manners of the gentleman and man of the world. He unites the sallies, the incidents, the surprises, the picturesque of language, with reflexion, sequence and thought, and draws his resources and his power alike from the premeditated and the unseen, from the vigorous precision of art and the simple graces of nature. We venerate the man; his heart is warm, his hands are pure.

John Bright walks about the rooms with his hands in his breeches pockets, chatting familiarly with his friends, and entirely free from any affectation, self-assertion or starch. These great men are civil, polite, attentive to stranger acquaintances, acting as if they felt an interest in them and their comfort—never on any occasion do they indulge in vulgar boorishness or neglect of others. Though a little reserved on first acquaintance, they soon establish relations of personal friendship with those to whom they are introduced and with whom they are thrown in the same social position, or who are of similar tastes and pursuits. They do not display what are called company manners, as do so many coarse and underbred people. The manners of high bred English people are always the same at home and in society. They never swagger, lounge, or carry into even the family circle the actions proper to the dressing room.

Among our most intimate friends in this club, and our relations subsist to this day with many who survive, were, Dr. Charles Mackay, the popular poet and for many years the American correspondent of the *Times*, Mr. de la Prime, a nephew of the great Thackaray, Osmond de Beauvoir Priaulx, a distinguished author and graduate of Cambridge, Sir William Hutt. M. P., T. Colley Grattan, author of "Civilized America," A. J. Beresford Hope, M. P., and many others.

We were also honored by an election as Fellow of the Royal Geographical Society, and spent many hours in their rooms, talking to the accomplished secretary, Dr. Shaw, to Captain Bedford

Pim, R. N., Dr. Rae, Sir Edward Belcher, R. N., and other celebrities. Many evenings were passed this winter and afterwards in Burlington House, Piccadilly, listening to the interesting and instructive lectures of travelled Fellows of the Royal Geographical, such as Sir Rutherford Alcock, who gave his impressions of Japan; Dr. Rae, who told us of out of the way places in Canada, and C. R. Markham, who gave an account of his travels in Peru.

In connection with the Society there is a social club called the Cosmos, where we partook of many fine dinners. The English love good eating and are a little too fond of talking about it. At the Cosmos we were much interested in the conversation of such famous guests or members—we do not know which they were— as Girard, the French lion hunter, and Paul du Chaillu, the African explorer and the first person to introduce Europeans and Americans to a knowledge of the gorilla.* With the editors of nearly all the daily papers, Messrs. Delane, Mowbray Morris, and Sampson, of the *Times*, Thornton Hunt, of the *Telegraph*, Mr. Johnson, of the *Standard*, etc., we were on familiar terms of intercourse. We understood the power of the press and sought its aid on our behalf—that irresistible power which is more mighty than armies, religions, legislatures or kings; more rapid than the winds, more boundless than space, as intelligent as thought.

While our time was much engrossed with affairs of serious import we did not altogether neglect society. On the contrary, we entered into its blandishments with keen zest. Who does not feel the need of society? Man is a social creature, and though some have divested themselves of social affection to a great extent, or confined it to very narrow limits, the social principle can never be eradicated. What man could be content with all the wealth and power the world affords, if no one could taste of his happiness but himself? What pleasure could wealth bestow, unless it was imparted and mutually enjoyed? What is desirable in power, but the exercise of it in good deeds? Who is savage enough to choose a solitary felicity?

---

*In October, 1855, du Chaillu sailed from New York for Africa, intending to explore the then unknown region lying 2° on each side of the equator. He spent nearly four years in this region, penetrating to about longitude 15° east. During this time he shot and stuffed 2,000 birds, of which 60 species were previously unknown to naturalists and killed fully 1,000 animals, including many gorillas and 20 other species of animals previously unclassified. He published in London, in 1861, the history of this expedition, under the title of "Explorations and Adventures in Equatorial Africa." He sailed from England in 1863 and reached the mouth of the Ogobai river, Africa, in October. On his return to Europe he published an account of his experiences under the title: "A journey to Ashargo Land."

## CHAPTER VIII.

THE SHAW FARM OF PRINCE ALBERT—ENGLISH AGRICULTURE—
STOCK BREEDING, ETC.—POLITICAL INFLUENCE OF
THE LANDLORDS—DUKE OF SOMERSET.

The sudden death of Prince Albert, shortly after our arrival in England, investing everything with which he was particularly connected with more than ordinary interest, we availed ourselves of being at Windsor, to visit the Royal farms—more particularly the Shaw farm, of which the Prince was tenant from 1840 until his death in 1861.

This farm consists of 800 acres, and is cultivated extensively for the supply of the castle. Since 1849, it has been conducted under minute instructions from Prince Albert, who sought to make it a model farm, and who here made many scientific experiments. It was here that he undertook and carried through successfully his plan for perfecting, by judicious crosses, the short-horn breed of cattle. The Prince, in this line, was a worthy disciple of the celebrated Jones Webb, who acquired world wide fame for his improvement of stock at his estate of Babraham.

Of the Shaw farm only one hundred and twenty acres is arable land, the rest lying out in grass for permanent pasture or being woodland. Thirty laborers and six pair of horses are ordinarily employed, but during hay making and harvest an additional force is engaged. The great particularity with which the land is cultivated and every farming operation conducted may be inferred from the employment of this large force. And they were constantly at labor. The Prince, an energetic working man himself, allowed no idlers on the estate.

The farm horse in use is of the Clydesdale breed, a cross of the thorough-bred with the Flanders mare. The ordinary size of this animal is $16\frac{1}{2}$ hands high, with a weight, when in good condition, of two thousand pounds. They have clean, straight limbs, a light step and powerful muscular development, are hardy, good tempered, intelligent, and, notwithstanding their size, quick and active. Many of Prince Albert's have taken prizes at the agricultural fairs, and in passing through the stables, we observed that the premium cards were attached to the stalls of the successful horses. They were pointed out with much pride by our guide, Mr. Tate, the overseer of the farm.

The Prince was likewise successful in raising coach horses, a type of which is produced by crossing the Cleveland bay mare with the thoroughbred horse. The points of the coach horse are a deep and well proportioned body, short and clean bone under the knee, open feet, sound and tough. He possesses a fine knee action, lifts his feet high, which gives elegance to his paces and action. He carries his head well and has a fine elevated crest. The breeding and rearing of horses are carried on professionally in England, chiefly in Yorkshire, but many private gentlemen and farmers address themselves to it as a means of pecuniary profit, and the improvement of their stock. None have been more successful than Prince Albert.

While traversing the farm-yard, we were attracted by some good specimens of the white Windsor pig, a type of the swine family obtained by the Prince after a series of judicious crosses, and which is supposed to combine more good points than any other. We saw them in immediate contrast with a number of those celebrated black Berkshire pigs bred on the farm with a view to ascertaining, by actual experiment, which was the more valuable. Without entering into an examination of the question, or the points determined by the Prince's experiments, we gave an instant preference to the compactly built black Berkshire pig, with his short snout, thick jowls and erect ears.

Prince Albert paid particular attention to the breeding of every kind of live stock, made many experiments and demonstrated by his success in this, as in every other department of agriculture, the value of science to the farmer. He made it a point before commencing operations to analyze the soil he purposed cultivating, and with a knowledge of its composition, qualities and deficiencies, what crops it best suited and how its absent properties could be most economically supplied, he went to work with a reasonable assurance of success.

The Shaw farm is cultivated on what is called the four course or five field system, and two grain crops are taken in succession. The use of these terms indicate to what an exact and rigid science agriculture is reduced in England. The system or course of cultivation is designated in the lease and no covenants are more strictly enforced. The well to do man may find no peculiar difficulty in executing them, for he has plenty of cheap labor and all the requisite implements and machinery. But the number of these is small if the accounts, had in 1879, from England are reliable—accounts which represent the tenant farmers as throwing up their leases by the score in order to emigrate to America. The four course system means simply that the whole arable extent of the estate, whatever this may be, is equally divided between four great crops : thus, say the estate consists of 2,000 arable acres, then it would be most probably laid down thus: in wheat 500 acres, barley and oats 500 acres, seed and palse 500, and roots 500.

The landlord insists upon a rotation of crops and the importance of such system cannot be overestimated. It is well known that certain mineral salts or salifiable bases are essential to the constitution of vegetables. Indeed, it is asserted by chemists that no seed exists that is without a phosphate; and it is well known that the alkaline salts powerfully promote vegetation. Such is their ascertained influence, that tobacco, barley and buckwheat sown in soils absolutely without organic matter, but containing saline substances and only moistened with distilled water, are known to have produced perfect plants, which flowered and fruited, and yielded ripe seeds. Whence it follows, that the presence of saline matter favors remarkably the assimilation of the azote of the atmosphere during the act of vegetation.

The importance of considering rotations in connection with the inorganic substances that are assimilated by plants, was perfectly well known to Sir Humphrey Davy. "The exportation of grain from a country which receives nothing in exchange that can be turned into manure, must exhaust the soil in the long run," says the illustrious chemist, who ascribed to this cause the present sterility of various parts of Northern Africa and of Asia Minor, as well as of Sicily, which, for a long succession of years was the granary of Italy. Rome, unquestionably contains in its catacombs quantities of phosphorus from all the countries of the earth. Such startling facts teach us that. the extraordinary production of the cereals which is now going on in America is not an unmixed blessing. The spirit of luxury and extravagance which is growing in our country and which causes our farmers to over cultivate is impoverishing our soil; and unless counterbalanced by an improving system of agriculture, the importation of manures and a judicious rotation of crops will leave us in the course of time in the same condition as the people of Northern Africa—the possessors of a kind of desert which was once a garden. Recent intelligence of a grain blockade at Chicago, Illinois, tells the story of our excessive production.

"A grain blockade of prodigious proportions, is the feature of the grain trade in this market" says the despatch. "The elevators of the city, which contain an aggregate of sixteen millions of bushels, are very nearly filled to their utmost capacity, and several roads are refusing to receive grain for this market, because, when it arrives there are no accommodations for it. In this condition of affairs the Directors of the Board of Trade are considering the propriety of accepting as regular the receipts in the elevators and storehouses along the line of the various railroads. It is also in contemplation to provide temporary storage outside of the elevators, and to build new elevators in various quarters of the city. Large numbers of cars are lying along the track in the city loaded with grain and are unable to deposit it. There are in storage 8,000.000 bushels of wheat, 4,000,000 of corn and enough other grain to make the total 14,250,000 bushels, against 10,000,-000 at this time last year. There are also about a million bushels afloat in the harbor."

Windsor park furnishes large quantities of fern, which are used as litter in the stables and cow yards, and with the hay and straw distributed as fodder to the stock, produces an abundant supply of manure. On the Shaw farm, as generally, in England, no rule is more insisted upon than that all the straw produced upon the farm shall be consumed upon it. The land is thus kept in high condition. We were glad to observe that the wasteful practice of applying fermenting and half-rotted mature to the ground as a top dressing for grain, so extensively practiced in every county in England, which we have visited, does not exist on the Shaw farm.

In portions of France and Switzerland, the practice of top dressing lands sown with winter grain, is extensively practiced. The manure is applied when the blade is already above the ground, and the passage of horses and wagons over the fields does not materially injure the crop. Yet farmers generally avail themselves of a time when the ground is frozen to perform the process. The good effects of top dressing with unrotted straw, litter, &c., have been too frequently witnessed to make us doubt its value to the growing crop, but we are decidedly of opinion that a well rotted dung heap, charged with volatile gasses, ought to be immediately plowed under to prevent the action of light and air upon the mass, but straw, woody stems, leaves and weeds—what is called the litter of barn yard and the farm—which make good beds for the stock, ought to be applied before it has fermented, as a top dressing for winter crops and on grass lands. Often, when walking over the parks and fields, we have felt crumbling under our feet the dry fibre of what was once a mass charged with fertilizing properties, but which exposure to the light and air had dried up and dissipated. The most valuable qualities of a manure heap being gaseous, it is surprising that in England, where there is such a diffusion of knowledge, and so much intelligent investigation, such an ignorant system should continue. By immediately turning the manure under with the plow, all this waste matter would be saved. The fertilizing properties of the manure, acted on chemically by the substances composing the soil, would enter into and become a part of the soil itself, and the beneficial effects be felt for years. A top dressing of leaves or unrotted straw protecting or shading the surface, and causing decomposition, is no doubt of considerable value to impoverished soil and grass land, and is probpbly the best mode of applying unrotted straw, but how different is this from exposing to the action of the sun and air a mass charged with highly volatile gases? On a large majority of the English farms, during this and a previous visit to the country, we have seen the manure, instead of being collected in pits or vats, with the liquid refuse, scattered over the barn yards and perpetually exposed to the action of the sun and air. The advantage of such pits are acknowledged, but the tenants are unwilling to incur the expense of having them prepared. They are generally tenants for a single year and hold their property under rigid covenants. This system of letting from year to year has been adopted as a means, so we have been informed, of making the tenants subservient in political matters to their landlords. It is perfectly understood they retain their premises upon the condition that they vote as their landlord may dictate, thus surrendering up their elective franchises and becoming the pliant instruments of his will. This is what is called the conservative influence of the landed gentry. We have just laid down a copy of the "Morning Herald," of 1870, containing the following paragraph, which bears the conclusive evidence of the wrong and injustice practiced under this system :

"THE DUKE OF SOMERSET AND HIS TENANTS.—The following letter has been addressed to the editor of the "Western Morning News." The indignation of the inhabitants of Totness has been aroused by the serving of notices to quit on most of the tenants of the Duke of Somerset, who voted against his Grace's nominee, or abstained from voting at the recent election. This dirty work was commenced soon after the last election. The victims then were Mr. E. R. Turpin and Mr. Blackler, They have this quarter left Bridgetown and come into the land of Freedom—viz, this side of the river Dart. The victims this quarter include the occupiers of both houses and lands, and some of them have been tenants the last twenty years and were among the number who acceded to the compact entered into some years since for one conservative and one liberal member. The following have had notice to quit : Mr. John Penwill, Mr. W. Ellis, Mr. J. Willis, Mr. W. Byne. Mr. Robt. Lake, Mr. J. Mitchell. Mr. W. K. Hanniford. Mr.Wm. Harris, Mr. James Briggs and Mr. T. Tucker. Mr. Robert Earle has given notice and so has Mr. Lake. The movement goes far to fully confirm the belief that the Duke is determined to make every one of his tenants vote as he bids."

Many similar paragraphs might be quoted from the papers, and many which show that the spirit of Radical reform and change is fostered among the people by such ill-advised conduct. It behooves the landlords if they wish to retain their influence and power, and that they must so wish none can doubt, to do justice to their tenants and yield something of their ancient rights and privileges to the masses, whose growing intelligence renders them fit and safe depositories of much more political power than they now enjoy. The real statesmen of England should see, while it is yet time, that it is only by liberal concessions they can satisfy the just demands of the people and silence clamor.

By acts of tyranny and oppression the rulers of the old world have almost precipitated revolution over half of Europe within the last twenty years. And unless wiser councils prevail, the period is not distant when we shall see the champions of the divine right of Kings meeting foemen worthy of their steel in the champions of freedom. Recent attempts have been made upon the lives of the Kings of Italy and Spain and upon that of the Emperor of Germany. The Emperor of Russia lives in a chronic state of alarm which has been recently amusingly illustrated by the following supposed diary of his Imperial Majesty.

THE CZAR'S DIARY.—[From the "Court Journal.] "Got up at 7 a. m. and ordered my bath. Found four gallons of vitriol in it and did not take it. Went to breakfast. The Nihilist had placed two torpedoes on the stairs, but I did not step on them. The coffee smelt so strong of prussic acid that I was afraid to drink it. Found a scorpion in my left slipper, but luckily shook it out before putting it on. Just before stepping into my carriage to go for my morning drive it was blown into the air, killing the coachman and the horses instantly. I did not drive. Took a light lunch of hermetically sealed American canned goods. They can't fool me there. Found a poisoned dagger in my favorite chair, with the point sticking out. Did not sit down on it. Had dinner at 6 p. m., and made Baron Laischounowonski taste every dish. He died before the soup was cleared away. Consumed some Baltimore oysters and some London stout that I have had locked up for five years. Went to the theatre and was shot at three times in the first act. Had the entire audience hanged. Went home to bed and slept all night on the roof of the palace."

The visitor to the rural districts cannot fail to be struck with the insufficient and insignificant character of the farm buildings generally and the condition of dilapidation in which many of them are permitted to remain. This is one of the evil consequences of the present system of renting from year to year, and can only be obviated by long leases, which involve an abandonment of the landlords right to control the political course of his tenant; and a two or three year's notice to quit with compensation for permanent improvements. Unless some such policy as this is adopted, rent troubles will become as serious in England as they now are in Ireland; and no earthly power can avert a revolution which will rock the British Empire from centre to circumference.

A striking contrast to the general state of affairs is presented by the Shaw farm, which is admirably and completely equipped with buildings, consisting of a farm house occupied by the overseer, with all the necessary appurtenances; foremen's and laborers' houses, barns, granaries, stables &c., the whole arranged with much skill. The buildings are supplied with corn crushers, straw and turnip cutters and other machinery worked by steam power. The granaries are in the third story of one of the buildings above the threshing floor, and as the wheat is threshed and cleaned, it is delivered by travelling cups to the granary bins, whence it is sacked and delivered into carts outside by an overhanging crane and pulleys from the end of the apartment. The same steam power is used to grind food for the cattle, and the steam boiler is utilized in the preparation of every substance used as food by the stock. The cut hay or straw is mixed with turnips, mangle wurtzel, &c., which have been crushed by the proper machinery. This mixture is passed into a large steaming chest and being there subjected to the action of hot air, becomes more palatable and soluble, and readily gives up all its nutritive properties.

The Prince's plan for fattening sheep deserves to be mentioned. It is a shed with a sparred floor. Here they are tied up by the neck and fed from troughs, upon mixed diet, having salt and water at pleasure. At the end of every fortnight they are weighed to ascertain what progress they are making, and the house and pen carefully washed with chloride of lime. Under this system as may be imagined, they fatten rapidly.

The yield per acre of wheat on the Shaw farm is from thirty-five to forty bushels, and from forty to sixty tons of mangle wurtzel, and of grass at the first cutting 35 tons, at the second 28, at the third 21 and at the fourth 8, or a total of 92 tons per acre. And yet not an acre of the Shaw farm was originally superior, if indeed equal to the poorer lands in the Valley of Virginia. It has been made thus productive by intelligent cultivation, by labor, and by the steady application of manures.

The laborers work during the summer ten hours a day, from six to eleven, then eating, and again returning to work from one till five o'clock. The horses receive two bushels of grain and one of beans each per week, with hay *ad libitum*.

Liberal wages are paid the laborers. In this county the ordinary wages are from ten to eleven shillings per week. Out of this the laborer usually pays one shilling rent a week for his cottage to which a small garden is in most instances attached. The Royal Dairy for supplying the Castle with milk, cream, butter and cheese is situated on this farm. The interior bears an inscription mentioning the date of its erection, &c. It presents a handsome appearance, the floor being covered with fine Minton tiles, of a rich and recherche pattern, and the walls adorned with the same kind of tiles in various hues. The ground color of the ceiling is green, upon which are many elaborate decorations in various tints. The windows are of stained glass of the richest description. In niches around the wall are statues of the Queen, Prince Albert and the royal children. We could not help thinking they ought to have been occupied by statues of the best cows. An ingenious contrivance called the "ventilator," keeps the butter and milk cool in hot weather. It bears on either side the monogram of the Queen and Prince Albert, and is said to be one of the Prince's inventions. The interior is adorned with marble tables, upon which stand the pans containing the milk. Under these tables a constant supply of water is kept, which may be drained off at leisure by means of plugs. Three fountains constantly play, the most beautiful being one representing Gibson's "Tinted Venus." Among the articles kept in the dairy are some rare old china, presented to the Queen by members of the Coburg family. The patent churn produces in a half hour thirty pounds of butter. Clinedinst's water churn would do it in less time. The neatness, order and industry of the dairyman and his wife are perceptible in all departments of this establishment. By one of the regulations, the resident farm laborers are allowed a daily supply of milk according to the size of their families. Much taste and judgment are displayed in the model dairy, which is but another monument to the practical good sense of Prince Albert.

Among the peculiar institutions of the Shaw farm is a school and reading room established by the Prince for the use of the farm laborers. A register of those who attended the evening classes and their progress in studies was regularly inspected by him, and he never failed to reward the constant attendant and successful student. In connection with the school, he provided a small, well selected library for the use of all employed on the estate.

He always insisted that a mechanic or laborer might prosecute bodily and mental work at the same time, and by doing so, he secured to himself a constant source of delightful companionship. By reason of his books and the information he acquired from them, he provided himself with cheerful fellowship at all times. Without relaxing his labors, he might, said the Prince, by and through his books, be in all times and at all places. How different it is with his fellow workman who has no such resource—who has no such companionship within himself! If his mind is not an utter blank, it is filled with a world of trifling and debasing thoughts. A man, however, accustomed to think, to read, and to hold intercourse with a pure and lofty morality, has tastes above those of his illiterate companion, and might hold in whatever sphere of life a higher social position. In addition to the library which he provided, he encouraged and aided the workmen to purchase a few books for themselves, thinking that a well selected collection of these in a house was a pledge of domestic comfort, of happy fireside influences, and the best security for their continuance. These good books the Prince regarded as household deities, shedding light and intelligence, begetting feelings of friendly interest within each, to man, and every living thing, elevating his ideas of the works of God, expanding his views of this and the world to come, staying the downward tendencies of their natures, purifying, ennobling and enlarging their affections, and thus becoming the shields of the household virtues. These, he said, were the real, true household deities, and not the false gods set up by the Romans in their ignorance and superstition. In a word, good books were, in his opinion, the best protection of every social virtue, and the best security to domestic comfort and peace. Few people there are who will not subscribe to the justness of his views on this subject.

A monthly report of the operations of the farm was made to Prince Albert, who inspected them closely and issued instructions accordingly. This excellent man ever sought, in his farming operations, as in all the duties of life, to discover what was true and to practice that which is good.

During the period of our visit to Berkshire, the farmers were engaged in plowing their land for the spring crop, and the process, though *new* to us, was decidedly antiquated. They had five to six horses harnessed, one behind another, to the plows, and while one man held the handles, another managed the team. From this almost obsolete method of turning the sod is doubtless derived the old distich:

"He that by the plough would thrive,
Himself must either hold or drive."

The reason for using so many horses and not putting them abreast, was the stiffness of the soil and consequent heavy draught; that by employing more horses than is necessary they stand the work better and longer than when too hard pressed ; that part of the team consists of young horses, which are thus exercised and assist in the labor, without injury to themselves, and harnessed in a line ahead of each other, they do not injure the soft surface soil on the land side.

These are very plausible reasons for the plan, but we are disposed to believe nevertheless that it is better economy to employ only the horses required for the work, than supernumeraries to prevent possible injury to them; that before putting a young horse to the severe work of the plow, he ought to be well broken, so that he may perform his work steadily and thoroughly, making a full *one* in the team, and that five or six heavy horses, marching one after another, at the bottom of a furrow will do more injury to the land than if harnessed abreast. Accepting, however, without argument, the explanation of the British farmer, the question is submitted to our practical agriculturists, who will, if they have not long since done so, soon solve the problem.

## CHAPTER IX.

HAMPTON COURT—MONS. ASSOLANT—CARDINAL WOLSLEY.

Milton has observed that he who neglects to visit the country in the spring, and rejects the pleasures that are then in their first bloom and fragrance, is guilty of "sullenness against nature." If we allow different duties to different seasons, he may be charged with equal disobedience to the voice of nature, who looks on the bleak hills and leafless woods without seriousness and awe. Spring is the season of gaiety, and winter of terror; in spring the heart of tranquility dances to the melody of the groves, and the eye of benevolence sparkles at the sight of happiness and plenty; not so in winter, then compassion melts at the universal calamity, the tear starts at the wailing of hunger and the cries of creation in distress. But a truce to reflections on the changes of the seasons. Concurring in the great poet's views—never going to the country without finding something to revive our curiosity and engage our attention

—we accepted an invitation to visit Hampton Court, in June, 1862, with a party consisting of many agreeable persons, among them Dr. A. T. Bledsoe, Mr. and Mrs. F. T. Tremlett, Sir Henry de Hoghton, Lady Eardley, and three French gentlemen, one of them being M. Assolant, the vivacious correspondent of the *Courier du Dimanche*, whose letters from England during the Exhibition of 1862 created so much amusement in Paris and so much irritation in London.

M. Assolant is a good specimen of a Frenchman, gay, witty, frivolous, sarcastic, sardonic. His pictures of the English, like all drawn by his countrymen, are exaggerated until they become ludicrous, and while no one could read them without a laugh, it appeared simply ridiculous that John Bull should take them so much to heart as he appeared to do. Not only the *Times*, but all the other daily papers, belabored him soundly for his sketches. M. Assolant is a fine flaneur, or "snapper up of unconsidered trifles," full of anecdote—one of those travelling companions who shorten the longest journey. He kept us in a continual laugh and emerged from the train at Hampton Court covered with dust and applause. This clever man was born in Aubusson Creuse, in 1827; he finished his collegiate career about the year 1850. He was now, such was his scholarship, appointed to a professorship in the University of France, where he was successfully engaged for some years. A fondness for adventure led him to abandon his trust and travel in Central America and the United States. On his return to France he contributed to the "*Revue des Deux Mondes*," an article upon the adventurer, "Walker and the Americans," and two rather successful novels. It was thought that while in Central America, he took part with the fillibusters. In 1858 he published what was called 'une fantasie Americaine," under the title of "Scenes de la vie des Etats Unis," and since many other books, biographical, historical and fictitious. His most recent work, published about this period, was entitled "Historie d'un Etudiant." For some unexplained reason Mons. Assolant could not get on comfortably with the English, but found himself entirely at home, like most Frenchmen, with Americans. His whimsical ridicule of John Bull was exceedingly droll and amusing. He would stop at times and express in a comical way his respect for America and the Americans, an admiration and respect which he declared was based on the great qualities of both country and people. When told that the Americans were English, only born in another hemisphere, he dissented and declared that though made up of all peoples, the Americans were more Celtic than Teutonic, and that Brother Jonathan, with all his eccentricities and grotesqueness, was decidedly ahead of John Bull. John Bull, he said, even before the conquest, was made up of Britons, Romans, Saxons, Picts and Danes, and had no right to call himself an Anglo-Saxon. In fact, said Assolant, there is no such race as Anglo-Saxons and never was. He remarked that when it was customary to denounce King William as a foreigner, Defoe wrote "The true born Englishman," in which he instructs his countrymen as to the mongrel races which had conspired to form that "vain, ill-natured thing, an Englishman," and showed

>   A true-born Englishman's a contradiction—
>   In speech an irony, in fact a fiction ;
>   A metaphor invented to express
>   A man akin to all the universe.

In a serio-comic vein he ran over a list of the boasted privileges of the English, and said they were all legacies left them by Frenchmen. It was to the Norman Kings that England owed trial by jury, the amelioration of the condition of the vassals by laws curtailing the powers of the old barons, the equalization of taxes by which lords and commons paid alike ; the summoning of the first House of Commons that forced King John to sign Magna Charta. Here was the commencement of English nationality, said he, for before this period, English history was a mere history of elements, of their collisions and of the processes of their fusion.

At this point a young man, of the cockney type, not, however, of our party, who had listened to the discussion in uneasy silence, began to show signs of fight, and it required all of Mr. Tremlett's clerical authority, and the *aplomb* of Sir Henry de Hoghton to keep the peace. At the next station we were glad to see this lard complexioned youth, with fierce grey eyes, piano-key teeth, elongated legs and gooseberry mustache, leave the carriage.

The French are, as all the world knows, the most racy and delightful of conversationalists, and M. Assolant shines among his own people, in the famed salons of Paris. Yet even he is not likely to rival, in this direction, his illustrious countrywoman, Madame de Stael, who is represented as having been so fascinating that those who listened to her were not aware, on one occasion of a thunderstorm.

To the politeness, the manners and the accomplishments of the fashionable world, M. Assolant adds a thorough knowledge of men ; is indeed a man of the world, if not the spoiled child, whose caprices have always been laws, and who must,when a child, have broken the playthings he was refused. It is possible, therefore, that he was "buttering" us at the expense of John Bull, or he may have been amusing himself with both at one and the same time. Sir Henry de Hoghton was too much occupied with a flirtation with Lady Eardley to pay attention to the Frenchman, who certainly diverted the rest of the party no little.  Dr. Bledsoe, who gave the witty Gaul small credit for sincerity in his pronounced American prejudices, directed many heavy shot at him, which struck with telling effect.  M. Assolant is a man of middle height, handsome features, dark complexion, calm black eyes, thick, wiry mustaches, hanging like those of a Tartar.  His voice is sweet and musical and when he smiles his face assumes an air of benevolence..

The train, which had been gliding on with jerks of white vapor, now stopped with bragging puffs of smoke, and the porters throwing open the carriage doors cried out: "Hampton Court!"

Hampton Court is known the world over as one of the most interesting spots in England, whether considerered with reference to the historical associations with which it is rife, its extensive picture galleries, or the beauty of its gardens and parks, both of which have been elaborately and elegantly improved.

Therefore of Hampton Court we shall give a brief account: Entering its gates it is impossible not to pass in review at once the singular history and deplorable fate of the wonderful man by whom it was reared, and who here lived in an ostentatious style of more than regal state.  Without indulging in the extravagances of the stock tourist, who might here detain the reader several hours with his "contemplations" in the style of Volney's, "here once stood a populous city, the seat of a powerful empire," we shall content ourselves with a rapid resume of the principal events in the life of Cardinal Wolsey, who built the palace when at the height of his power, and with the deliberate purpose of making it surpass in size and magnificence any Royal residence in Europe.

Thomas Wolsey was born in Ipswich, Suffolk, in 1471, and was the son of a butcher.  Though not wealthy, his father's means were sufficient to enable him to bestow upon his son a liberal education, which he completed at Magdalen college, Oxford.  During his university career he exhibited extraordinary talents and industry.

The multitude of the offices and dignities, civil and ecclesiastical, which he afterwards filled is so curious, that at the risk of being tedious, we shall'run hurriedly over the list.  In 1504 he was chaplain to Henry VII, with dispensation to hold three livings, stations he acquired through the influence of Sir John Naphant, Governor of Calais.  Young Wolsey had gone to France shortly after leaving Oxford and took service under the Governor, and showed such remarkable diligence and discretion that he was recommended by Sir John to his sovereign.  His next appointment was royal almoner, and in 1508, Dean of Lincoln.  In 1510, he received a grant of the parsonage of St. Bride, and in the same year was appointed Canon of Windsor, and was a member of the King's privy council. He afterwards succeeded to the Bishoprics of Tourney, Lincoln and York, and Primate of England. He eclipsed the Archbishop of Canterbury and every churchman about him, and became Cardinal and Legate, receiving his Cardinal's hat from Leo X, and this year (1514) he was advanced to the office of Lord High Chancellor of England. The emoluments of these offices were enormous, but did not satisfy the Cardinal, who is known to have received gifts and pensions from the King of Spain, the Duke of Milan and other foreign potentates. He greatly applauded Leo X when he burnt Luther's books declaring him a heretic, and next received from his Holiness a bill granting him authority to visit the monasteries, and conferring on him the tenth of all the revenues of the English clergy. Henry VIII also empowered him, in the year 1518, to confer letters patent of denizen under the great seal; and then to make out *conges d' elire* (the writ to choose a bishop), royal assents, and restitutions of temporalities of ecclesiastical dignities, as well as to take the homages and fealty of all persons, which might be due to the crown for such temporalities—sources of the most extraordinary influence and emolument. He now became Bishop of Bath and Wells, and of the rich abbey of St. Albans; then the administrator of the sees of Worcester and Hereford. In the same year he received the grant of the office of Bailiff of the Lordship of Chestnut in Hertfordshire and park keepers of Bantingsly. He sympathized strongly with the Pope when Luther burnt the Pope's canon law and styled Leo a persecutor, a tyrant and the very antichrist. Leo X granted him authority, in 1521, to make 50 knights, 50 courts palatine, 40 apostolic notaries, whose privileges were equal to those made by the Pope himself, namely, to legitimize bastards, and confer degrees in arts, in law, medicine and divinity, and also to grant all sorts of dispensations. Another bull empowered him to check and put down the new Protestant heresies. The Cardinal this year sent an ambassador to the King of France and the Emperor Charles V, and he received a grant of 9,000 crowns from the Emperor besides 2,500 in lieu of a former grant.

During the year 1522 he held the see of Durham, and in 1524 received a new bull from the Pope confirming his power to visit and suppress disorderly monasteries, and in 1529 became Bishop of Winchester. In a word, he had bestowed upon him an amount of honor, preferment, and emolument for 25 years the like of which the world had never seen and will never probably see again. His revenues exceeded those of the King himself or of any Sovereign in Europe. His state, too, was in keeping with it. At mass he was served by Dukes and Earls, who took the assay of his wine on their knees, and held him his basin at the lavatory.

He was the steady friend of learning and of learned men—intimate with Erasmus and induced the Kings to invite both Titian and Raphael to England—he established seven lectures at Oxford, a college at Ipswich, and founded Christ Church, Oxford, in which the royal princes and the sons of the nobility to this day continue to receive their educations. He had a passion for building, and was always thus engaged, and his structures were remarkable for their superiority to those of the age.

When in the zenith of his prosperity he built Hampton Court 1516-1526. He was the actual ruler of England, both in Church and State by the favor of the King and the courtesy of the Pope. Flattered and sought by power and beauty at home, and by the crowned heads of all Europe, he was hated, yet feared by courtiers; haughty, arbitrary and vindictive; possessed of revenues to which the incomes of the greatest nobles were poor, he lived in a splendor and state such as became only a reigning Prince, and expressed his swelling vanity in the well known words, "*Ego et rex meus*"—I and my king.

His palace, composed of five courts and two hundred and eighty chambers for the use of guests, and rooms for eight hundred servants, was the only place where he could entertain the crowds that flocked by every road to pay him court. Such was the magnificence of the establishment that Grotius, the great jurist, who was envoy to England, in 1615, says of it: "If any Briton is ignorant of what is wealth, let him repair to Hampton Court, and thereafter having viewed all the Palaces of the Earth he will say, 'these are the palaces of Kings, but this of the Gods.'" His household consisted of fifteen knights, forty squires and eight hundred servants, many of whom were the seedy and beggard descendents of the proud old barons. His steward was a Dean, his treasurer a Knight, his Comptroller an Esquire—he disdained to have an ordinary person filling an office near his person. His head cook daily wore damask, satin or velvet, with a heavy gold chain about his neck. He held a levee every morning at which he appeared habited in red velvet, after which he went abroad in State. Affecting humility, he sometimes went abroad as a priest, mounted upon a mule, but the animal was always concealed under a mountain of trappings. His own attire was princely, and his retinue on these, as on all other occasions, numerous and brilliant. The saddle and saddle cloth were of costly crimson dye, fringed with gold. The costliest sables covered his shoulders, gloves of red silk his hands, and his shoes were inlaid with diamonds and pearls. Before him marched two priests carrying silver crosses, before them two gentlemen bearing silver staffs, before these went a nobleman of high order, bearing his cardinal's hat, and foremost of all rode a pursuivant-at-arms with a massive mace of silver. The train was made up of other officers and attendants. Such were the splendid gildings with which he covered his pretended humility.

The cardinal lived many years in this kind of splendor, long enough to learn that it was all vanity. He served a fickle and capricious master. A turning point came in his fortunes and he sank more rapidly than he had risen. The crisis in his fortunes was his remonstrance against the King's marriage with Anne Bolyne. The favor of the King was withdrawn, and a plot devised for his destruction. Arrested upon a charge of high treason, his parks and palaces, his treasures and revenues, all the sources of his princely income, were forfeited. Crushed and broken in spirit, he became a prey to melancholly and disease and soon descended into the grave. His head was thus saved from the block.

His fortunes and his fall are thus finely described by Dr. Johnson in his "Vanity of Human Wishes:"

> In full blown dignity see Wolsey stand,
> Law in his voice and fortune in his hand,
> To him the church, the realm, their powers consign;
> Through him the rays of royal bounty shine ;
> Turn'd by his nod the stream of honor flows :
> His smile alone security bestows :
> Still to new heights his restless wishes tow'r,
> Claim leads to claim and power advances pow'r :
> Till conquest unresisted, ceased to please,
> And rights submitted left him none to seize.
> At length his sovereign frowns, the train of state
> Mark the keen glance, and watch the sign of hate
> Where'er he turns, he meets a stranger's eye.
> His suppliants scorn him, and his followers fly !
> Now drops at once the pride of awful state,
> The golden canopy, the glittering plate,
> The regal palace, the luxurious board,
> The liveried army of the menial Lord.
> With age, with cares, with maladies opprest,
> He seeks the refuge of monastic rest :
> Grief adds disease, remember'd folly stings,
> And his last sighs reproach the faith of Kings.

The palace has been occupied since the days of Henry VIII by by many remarkable persons. His son, Edward VI, was born at

Hampton, where a few days afterwards his mother, Jane Seymour died. Here Henry VIII married Catharine Parr. Here Bloody Mary and her husband, Philip of Spain, passed their honeymoon. Here the Princess Elizabeth was entertained, and afterwards where the potent queen sometimes assembled her Court. Here James I of Scotland summoned his famous conference of bishops and Puritan leaders to confer on the settlement of religion. Here in 1605, was entertained Francis, Prince of Vandemois, son of the Duke of Lorraine, and a large company, the feastings and festivities lasting a fortnight, and here died in 1618, Anne of Denmark. Charles I was imprisoned here and made his celebrated attempt to escape from it November 11th, 1647. During the plague in London, Charles I and Katharine of Braganza fled to Hampton and remained there until it was over, 68,000 persons having perished. Here they were when the great fire occurred, which destroyed eighty nine churches, including St. Paul's, and 13,200 houses, and covered 436 acres of ground with ruins.

Thinking persons were all disposed to acknowledge the hand of God in these judgments, on account of the sins of both King and people. But in the midst of justice it was tempered by mercy, and that which at the time was a dire calamity, has since proved a lasting blessing; the ravages of the plague were stayed by the fire, which completely purified the atmosphere, and the old city with its narrow streets being destroyed, way was made for the erection of one more commensurate with the requirements of modern times; and the mighty city which excites the astonishment of foreigners, which is now the emporium of the commerce of all nations, and which is justly styled the metropolis of the world, arose from the great fire of 1666.

Here Oliver Cromwell, the destroyer of the monarchy and the founder of the short lived Republic, held his court, as well as at Windsor and Whitehall. There his daughter Elizabeth married Lord Falconburg and another daughter Lord Rich, heir of the Earl of Warwick. Like many modern Republicans, Cromwell courted rather than disdained a connection with the nobility. Here he devised his foreign policy which was so eminently successful, resulting in the defeat of the Dutch and the capture of Jamaica from the Spaniards, events which forced Mazarin to acknowledge him, and the Venetians and Swiss to seek his friendship. When wearied and worn with the strife of parties at Whitehall, disappointed in his hopes at home, and his life ma le wretched by the constant dread of assassination, here he retired for rest, and to contemplate the more agreeable prospect of his power abroad, where he was both feared and respected. And here no doubt he saw signs of popular weariness with the Protectorate, and may have feared, without disburdening his soul, the ruin of his Commonwealth based upon the bible, and the restoration of the son of England's murdered King. It was here that he lost his favorite daughter, Mrs. Claypole, who exhorted him on her deathbed to retrace his steps and seek forgiveness from God. Mrs. C. evidently believed in the divine right of kings, and feared that her father in seeking to give the English people a Republican government was engaged in the devil's work. It was while he was at Hampton that the founder of the Society of Friends, the celebrated George Fox, visited Cromwell to beg that he would put a stop to religious persecutions. His visits were much enjoyed by Cromwell, who is reported to have said to him on one occasion before parting, "Come again, George, come often, I feel that if thou and I were oftener together, we should be nearer to each other."

The year 1660 saw the end of the Republic and the restoration of Royalty in the person of the murdered King's son. It was one of the greatest misfortunes possible to the English people that Charles II ascended the throne without any restrictions to the Royal power, and without any security for the rights of the people. The merrie monarch immediately began his revels at Hampton Court where he assembled such profligate friends as his brother James, Buckingham, Jermyn, Grimmont, Rochester—his own and their favorites or shameless mistresses. Such diversions, such libertinism, such scoffing at religion, such abandonment of decency and such rampant licentiousness was never before seen at the English Court. Shortly after the rye-house plot, Charles left Hampton Court and boldly walked about the west end of London. His brother James meeting him one day in Hyde Park, expressed his surprise at his venturing abroad in such perilous times. "James," replied the King, "take you care of yourself; I am safe. No man in England will kill me, to make you king."

Charles II fell a victim to his excesses, dying in 1685, and was succeeded by his uncle, James II. whose arbitrary measures and open coalitions with the Roman Catholics, and his sensual life caused him to be driven out of the Kingdom. The English throne was now offered to William and Mary, who accepted it, and the glorious and last revolution in England, that of 1688, occurred. It gave the people freedom in the midst of servitude, order in the midst of anarchy. Representative Government as it now exists in England dates from this epoch—the people owe to it, under Providence, whatever of law, security of property, peace and happiness they enjoy. William and Mary made Hampton Court their principal, as it was their favorite abode. Subsequent monarchs, down to George I, have occasionally resided at Hampton Court, but nothing occurred of such a character as to be worthy of mention.

And in 1838 the Palace and grounds were thrown open to the public, after the custom of the French and other Continental nations, and the people are permitted to visit the galleries, gardens and parks on so many days each week.

The picture galleries contain more than two thousand paintings, the most celebrated of which are the Cartoons of Raphael, which were painted during the last years of the great master's life and have been called the "glory of England and the envy of Europe."

Raphael's peculiar genius is displayed in those great works in various respects. His power of invention appears in the most advantageous light and nowhere do we so correctly feel how deeply Raphael had penetrated into the pure spirit of the Bible as in these designs.

The first cartoon is the death of Ananias, which is distinguished by all the qualities which constitute and mark the genius of painting.

The second is Elymas, the sorcerer, struck blind by St. Paul. Then follows the lame man, restored by St. Peter and St. John. the miraculous draught of fishes—St. Paul and St. Barnabus at Lystra—St. Paul preaching at Athens and the Last Charge of Peter. These seven cartoons are all that remain of a number sent to Arras that tapestries might be worked from them. When they reached there, the weavers commenced their work of destruction, by cutting each of them perpendicularly into slips in order to work conveniently after them. In some unaccountable way, after the tapestries were taken to Rome, the paintings were neglected and remained buried in oblivion till Rubens, who knowing their value, urged King Charles I to rescue them. Investigations led to their discovery in a cellar at Arras. All but these seven were destroyed. The pieces of these were collected and reunited.

Some of the pictures in these galleries are *chef d' ouvres*, but many possess no merit. The frescoes are by Verrio, with whose peculiar style the reader is already acquainted. Wolsey Hall is hung with ancient tapestry, deliniating the history of Abraham. The first of them represents the appearance of God to Abraham, and the Patriarch's benediction, declaring that through him all the nations of the earth should be blessed—a fact strangely forgotten by those who at present cast such obloquy on the unbelieving Jew. The second represents the Nativity of Isaac, and the peculiar ceremony, still characteristic of the Jews, attendant on his birth. The third exhibits Abraham sending out a servant to seek a wife for Isaac, his son. The fourth sets forth the return of Abraham and Sarah from Egypt, laden with the gifts of the Egyptians. In the fifth is delineated the reception of the three angels by Abraham. The sixth shows Abraham as purchasing the cave of Macpelah as place of sepulchre for Sarah, his wife. The seventh represents the separation of Abraham and Lot, when they had resolved on following different courses. The eighth and last exhibits the Patriarch as about to offer up his son as a sacrifice. The tapestries look as old, if not as familiar, as the history they hand down.

The pleasure grounds, containing about fifty acres, are handsomely laid out and improved and ornamented with jets d'eau. Three large paths diverge from the principal entrance, which are lined with trees and fringed with flowers. The garden for fruits and vegetables contains twelve acres, in which there is a grape vine planted from a slip in 1769, festooned, under a glass house built for its protection, which bears annually from two to three thousand bunches of grapes. The gardner is allowed to charge a small fee for showing it to visitors, which yields him a handsome annual revenue. From the private grounds a gateway leads into Bushy Park, which contains about eleven hundred acres and is five miles in circumference. Here there is a stately avenue of chestnuts in which there is a circular piece of water ornamented by a statue of the goddess Diana. Space does not admit of any description of this or the other parks, gardens and pleasure grounds, which form so charming a feature in English scenery.

These grounds and park, which we have said are opened to the public, attract, owing to their proximity to the densely populated suburbs of London, large crowds, who avail themselves of the privilege to spend a day wandering beneath the leafy bowers and by the sparkling waters Upon holidays it is thronged by tens of thousands. On Sunday the working classes flock hither for rest and relaxation, the picture galleries being opened after ten o'clock for their especial benefit. The good use to which it is now turned, cannot fail to exert a happy influence upon the minds, manners and tastes of the people. Though there are many good paintings in the galleries and some master pieces, it would be difficult to find anywhere a larger collection of pictorial trash. They have not been executed by royal academicians, some of whom enjoy world wide fame. but who are sneered at on the continent as England's best—Europe's worst painters; on the contrary, these are generally the productions of Court favorites, who knew much better how to "crook the pregnant hinges of the knee," than to use their pencils.

Separating at Hampton from the party, to keep an appointment in another quarter, we hurried to Leatherhead, one of the prettiest villages in Surry, thence to Dorking, the loveliest country town in England. We had accepted an invitation to visit the Bouchiers, whose ancestors had lived in Virginia previous to the Revolution. Rev. Jonathan Boucher, or Bouchier, as the name is now spelt, was Rector of Hanover, then of St. Mary, Virginia, and subsequently Rector of St. Anne, Annapolis, previous to 1776. On the adoption of the Declaration of Independence, Mr. Bouchier, who was a Royalist in his political sentiments, returned to England. Some years subsequent to this period he published in London a work on the causes and consequences of the American Revolution. He always retained a friendly feeling for our country and people—more particularly the people of Virginia and Maryland—and transmitted it to his family and immediate connections.

With these hospitable friends we remained some days, during which time we made many excursions in the country—one of them to Deepdene, the princely estate of the Hope family, where Disraeli wrote Coningsby. While in this lovely rural district, mixing with the country people, we heard much of the territorial aristocracy and the evils attending the present land laws. The views we then heard have a present interest in view of the agitation in both England and Ireland for a change n these laws, rent tenures,&c.

The landless people complained that they were entirely ignored by the proprietors, who rebuked all who dared, in any way, directly or indirectly, to express an opinion about the lands which did not belong to them and in which, therefore, they have no concern. The champions of the people asserted that the land was originally the property of all, but by confiscations and other legalized forms of robbery, at various periods in English history, it had found its way into the hands of first one and then another Royal favorite. In process of time it has fallen into possession of a few privileged families; the number of landlords being only about 30,-000 in a population of nearly 20,000,000. They further alleged that it is kept in their possession by the law of primogeniture, by entails and by the difficulties thrown in the way of its acquisition and the enormous expense attending its conveyance. At present the sale and transfer of the soil is fenced round with difficulties and expenses, rendering them nearly prohibitory to all except persons of great wealth. One gentleman said he had rented a house at £45 a year and had paid legal expenses connected with the lease, of £15. It was the general opinion that the laws which were passed in former times by the aristocratic few, in order to secure their ill-acquired estates, were now producing the most disastrous results. The discovery of steam had opened a way for supplying England with the wheat, meat, cheese, &c. of America, Russia and other large grain and beef producing countries and this had entirely changed the position of the tenant and all those who derived their living from the soil. Yet landlords wished to keep up the prices of their land to the point they had reached when there was no such competition and the tenant was protected by corn laws.

This state of affairs has led to a surrender of many leases and there are no applicants for the farms An English friend in December last, (1879) in a letter to the writer, stated that the Earl of Abergavenny had seventeen farms thrown upon his hands in the county of Kent, and the Duke of Marlborough 4,000 acres in Oxfordshire. This same Duke, John W. Churchhill, is now Lord-Lieutenant of Ireland, and is charged by Mr Parnell with the partizan distribution of the funds raised by voluntary contributions in America and elsewhere for the relief of the starving Irish.— Many of those tenant farmers who have the capital are leaving, or preparing to leave England to become citizens of the United States. Heaven be praised, there is plenty of land here, room for all.

We have recently seen a statement of one of the great landed proprietors of the reasons which prevent his pursuing a more liberal course towards his tenantry. It is in substance, that his rents could not be reduced, because in addition to his own family, many others derived an income from his landed property. Tenants naturally enough reply that they do not care to cultivate land at a loss to themselves, merely for the purpose of supplying old dowagers and younger sons with the means of living in idleness and luxury.

At a meeting of his tenantry which recently took place, the Marquis of Ailsbury told a piteous tale of how he was encumbered with a whole park of poor relations. He said:

"Protection had been talked of as a remedy for the present distress, but he urged them not to expect it. Protection was altogether out of the question. No Ministry would dare to attempt it, for it could not be introduced without causing a revolution in the country. A tax on the food of the people was an impossibility. He had come into an estate which was most heavily mortgaged, and, in addition to a large family, he had three dowagers to provide for, who, it should be remembered, would not take twenty per cent. off their allowances because times were bad, and he had reduced rents that extent. As a consequence he, of course, had very little to live upon."

Consequently the heavily burdened Marquis, with his three country seats of Tottenham Park, in Wilts, Jerveux Abbey, in Yorkshire, and East Sheen, in Surry, and his London Mansion, could not do what he would have wished to do, namely, abate something considerable from the rents of his tenantry.

Unfortunate nobleman! His estates encumbered by the necessity of keeping up four establishments, that he may be said to "live pretty much like a gentleman," with the further payment of thousands to three dowagers, and these old ladies determined on maintaining their style and state, on keeping their coaches, butlers, footmen, horses and dogs, no matter how hard the times, how depressed the agricultural interest, how impoverished the tenants, how niggardly the wages of farm laborers. But the noble Marquis' troubles did not end here. He is still further weighted by a number of younger sons who must have their allowances that they too may be considered gentlemen. Our readers may wish to know what a gentleman is in this tight little Island. This is the picture of an English gentleman drawn by one of the greatest of Englishmen:

"Perhaps you think I should not class myself among gentlemen, and yet I have as good a right to the name as most of the set. I belong to no trade; I follow no calling; I rove where I list, and I rest where I please. In short, I have no occupation but my indolence, and no law but my will. Now, sir, may I not call myself a gentleman?"

Ask one of the dowagers to reduce their establishment by a couple of flunkeys and a carriage or so, in consideration of the impoverished state of those who furnish them the means of maintaining it, and you'll get an angry negative. Ask one of these younger sons to live upon a less income and he will tell you the idea is preposterous. "Demme, you insult me. How can I gamble for large sums on a diminished income?" Let farmers, laborers and all connected with the land go to grief, come to the poor house, be driven from the country, dowagers and younger sons and others, hangers on planted upon the land, will have their uttermost farthing.

Neither the Marquis of Ailsbury, with three dowagers on his back, and with tithe collectors, tax gatherers and younger sons at his heels, and overweighted tenants worrying his lands, nor those under him can compete with the United States in grain growing and cattle breeding, and therefore the end is close at hand.

Nothing but a thorough repeal of the land laws will render the soil as productive and remunerative as it might be. Some means should be adopted for preventing thousands and tens of thousands of idle and useless persons being quartered upon its product. A man should be enabled to buy an acre of land as easily and readily as he can a leg of mutton. That mischievous law of primogeniture which places immense estates in the hands of one person, who must either provide for a number of others out of its revenues, or by quartering them indirectly on the public, should be abolished.

In Alfred A. Walton's history of the landed tenures of Great Britain and Ireland he remarks on this subject:

"There can be no doubt that a considerable portion of our operative classes and manufacturing population, as well as a portion of the manufacturers themselves, would have been employed in agricultural pursuits, had the land not been to a great extent locked up against their enterprise and industry. And this must continue so long as the usurpation of the soil by the few to the exclusion of the many continues and the agricultural population kept stationary or non-increasing, which is the social effect of our present territorial arrangements, while the 'surplus population,' as it is termed, is compelled to take refuge in our large towns and centres of industry. It will therefore be seen that the freedom of the soil is of the highest importance to the whole community ; both to the operatives, the mechanics and artizans of our large towns as well as the trading community, and likewise to the farmers and laborers in the rural districts."

Every man, therefore, be he landless or landlord, is more or less interested in the laws affecting the ownership, the transfer and cultivation of the soil. In the present condition of affairs, English tenants cannot compete with foreign farmers; the system tends to pauperise the landlords as well as those dependent upon them. It encourages the breeding of a race of high class paupers that are too lazy to work themselves, but not too proud to live upon the labor of others. They are a curse to the country. In a word, however prized by the privileged few, the land laws must be repealed. Such are the views of the mass of the British people, whether English, Scotch or Irish.

But all the evils of the system in England are intensified in Ireland. In that unhappy country there are 20,000,000 acres of land, and 6,000,000 of acres are owned by 292 persons, and 744 persons own 9,612,000, or nearly one-half of Ireland is owned by less than 800 persons. And there are twelve men who own 1,310,000 acres or about 108,000 acres each. And the three or four millions of people who are the tenants of the great landlords and tenants at will, having no lease, and liable to have their rents raised, or to be turned out at short notice. Worse still, these great landlords do not live in Ireland, but receive and spend the rents they extract from their tenantry in other countries. And the absentees acquired their property by the confiscation of about 3,000,000 of acres in the reign of James I, of seven or eight million during the protectorate of Cromwell, and of 1,000,000 under William III. In other words, nearly all the land of the tenantry has been taken away from the legal owners and given to strangers. Since that period the penal laws of England have inflicted indescribable injustice and wrong on the Catholic population in Ireland—so much so that not more than one-tenth of the land, in recent times, has been in the hands of Catholic proprietors—the bulk of the Irish population.

With such a terrible history of wrong, cruelty and oppression, who is to blame in the present day, for Irish disloyalty and Irish famine. Who does not see that the time for a change in the land laws has come.

## CHAPTER X.

HARROW-ON-THE-HILL—BYRON'S EARLY DAYS—HAMPSTEAD HEATH—RURAL SPORTS—KISSING IN THE RING, ETC.
—HIGH GATE, ETC.

We had often taken counsel with the more intimate of our new made English friends, as to an excursion on foot to that metropolitan locality, Harrow-on-the-hill. Indeed it had been agreed that we should "do" the place on the first fine day. This was not long in coming. The 10th of May invited us forth. Our party consisted of some famous walkers, among them R. B. Barnwell, of Charleston, S. C., Haviland Burke, since M. P., for one of the South-western shires, the heir and representative of the great statesman and orator, Edmund Burke, and Dr. Granville, ("Old Granny," as he was familiarly styled) of the British Museum.

Our route lay through Westbourne Grove and Kensall Green. The days of May are ever fair in Old England, yet fairest and best of May days seemed this particular one. Pure, calm and sunny, we cannot describe how much we enjoyed the sweet, exhilirating atmosphere, the rustle of leaves, and the ripple of sound that gladdened the morning. The hedges were decked with a profusion of primroses, butter-cups, daisies, cowslips and other wild flowers unknown in America, except in conservatories. Across the highway the shadow of many an old oak was cast. Everywhere there was a divine fullness; a mysterious sense of expansion suggested the unseen effort of the sap in motion. Glittering things glittered more than ever ; loving natures became more tender. There was a hymn in the flowers, and a radiance in the sounds of the air. The widely diffused harmony of nature burst forth on every side. All things which felt the dawn of life invited others to put forth shoots. A movement coming from below, and also from above, stirred vaguely all hearts susceptible to the scattered and subterranean influence of germination. The flowers shadowed forth the fruit as young maidens dream of love. It was nature's universal bridal. It was fine, bright and warm. Through the hedges in the meadows children were seen laughing and playing at their games. The fruit trees filled the orchards with their heaps of white and pink blossoms. In the fields were primroses, daffodils, hyacinths, cowslips, daisies, violets, milfoil, speedwell. Flowering vines covered the thatched roofs with colored patches. Women were plaiting hives in the open air; the bees were abroad, mingling their hummings with the music of the air.

On one side of the road there was a firm, smooth raised sidewalk, about ten feet wide, which made the walking perfectly comfortable—as much so as on the pavements of a city. This attention to the wants of foot passengers is general throughout England. This makes it plain that the laws, even in aristocratic Albion, are not enacted entirely in the interests of those who ride in chaises. This particularity as to the comfort of walkers arises, in part, from the high value which is set by the English upon human life; which causes them to sacrifice to its preservation many considerations of interest and convenience. The high speed, too, with which they drive in the country, never stopping to avoid pedestrians, make these side-walks a kind of necessity.

While resting at an inn on the roadside, regaling ourselves with a glass of ale, each of us having ordered, "a pint of the bitter in the pewter"—one of those roadside inns, which we never see without associating them with the old coach and four, and the 'ostler in fustian shorts and yellow leggins, standing with a watering pail at the 'osse's 'ead's, a drove of sheep passed on to Smithfield market. The shepherd, who seemed hot and thirsty, stopped to have his 'arf and 'arf, and being a talking man, informed us, while emptying his mug, that his sheep would fetch £2.12 each from the butchers. "Ees, Ees they'll fetch that or the butchers be a precious lot o'ard screws. Ben't that lots o' money?" and without waiting for a reply he walked off praising his sheep, which had been well kept together by one of those intelligent creatures, the shepherd's dog.

On leaving the inn, we continued our way by a gradually ascending and winding road until we reached the summit of Harrow hill. The panoramic view which meets the eye of the spectator from this eminence is beautiful indeed—London to the east reposes like a huge monster under its clouds of smoke; to the south are the famous Surrey hills or Epsom downs, to the north, the village of Stanmore and the baronial seat of the Marquis of Abercorn, and to the west the distant turrets of Windsor Castle stand out in gloomy grandeur against the sky.

Harrow, which was formerly a market town and place of some consequence, has dwindled into comparative unimportance. It is a unique and antique town, marked by the quaint and picturesque architecture of the Elizabethan regime. Formerly the residence of the Arch-bishops of Canterbury, it is now only known and distinguished as the seat of one of England's four great schools. This school counts among its former pupils some of the most distinguished names in British history, such as Sheridan, Byron, Theodore Hook, the wit and novelist, Earl Dalhousie, governor general of India, Earl Hardwick, Earl Westmoreland, Sir Henry Lytton Bulwer, the Earl of Aberdeen and Lord Palmerston.

It was here that Byron was placed at an early period and where he was associated with Sir Robert Peel, Lords Clare, Powerscourt and De la Warr, the Duke of Dorset and other eminent men with whom he formed passionate friendships or contracted life long enmities. He made, as everybody knows, but little progress in his studies, but gave such evidences of talent that the Head Master, speaking of him about this time, said that he had talents which would add lustre to his rank.

The school was founded by John Lyon in the 16th century, and contains on an average 800 scholars varying in age from twelve to twenty. As we proceeded through the town from the King's head hotel, we saw large numbers of these healthy looking lads strolling through the streets or listlessly idling near the cake shops. The yard of the school house was also well filled with others engaged in play. Lyon took a deep interest in the school, and before his death drew up a set of statutes for its government, with full instructions for the disposal of the estates, which he intended to appropriate to its support. Among these statutes was one requiring a sufficient sum to be set aside for the support of four of the most distinguished scholars at the universities, two at Cambridge and two at Oxford. In selecting them, he required that preference should be given to his own kin, to natives of Harrow and to such as are "most mete for towardness, poverty and painfulness." To obtain the first position at the school is a high honor, and brings the successful pupil prominently to the public attention. His future course is watched with no small interest. Under the head of University intelligence, the success of the Oxford dons and the Cambridge wranglers is annually given through all the newspapers to the country. Thus the *Times* refers to a Cambridge commencement.

UNIVERSITY INTELLIGENCE.

CAMBRIDGE, January 24.

The following list of honors at the Bachelor of Arts' Commencement was issued to-day. The moderators were Percival Frost, M. A., St. John's; Robert Baldwin Hayward, M A., St. John's. Examiners: Arthur Cockshott, M. A., Trinity; Anthony William Wilson Steel, M. A., Gonville and Caius. Wranglers: Dr. Moulton, St. John's; 2, Darwin, Trinity.

[Here follows a list of forty-seven young men upon whom honors were conferred. Of the two highest the first and second senior wranglers, the *Times* proceeds to say :]

Mr. John Fletcher Moulton, of St. John's College, the Senior Wrangler, the third son of the late Rev. J. E. Moulton, a Wesleyan minister, was born at Madeley, in Shropshire, in November, 1844, and is therefore just twenty-three years of age. He was educated at Kingswood School, Bath, under Mr. H. Jefferson, M. A. Lond, until the age of sixteen, when he presented himself at the Senior Oxford Middle-class Examination and was placed first in the general list. For the next three years he was engaged in tuition, during which time he matriculated at the London University, and carried off the exhibition in mathematics, besides passing the honorary examinations in classics and chemistry. From this time he seems to have devoted his attention more particularly to mathematics, and his career has been one of uninterrupted success. In April, 1864, he obtained the first Minor Scholarship for mathematics at St. John's College, Cambridge, and in June gained the Mathematical Exhibition at the first B. A. Examination at the London University. He subsequently graduated there, gaining the Mathematical Scholarship. In October of the same year he commenced residence at Cambridge, and during the whole of his University career, he has been at the head of his college examinations. In June, 1866, he was elected a Foundation Scholar of his College.

Mr. E. J. Routh, of Peterhouse (Senior Wrangler in 1854), was Mr. Moulton's private tutor, thus adding another to the long succession of senior wranglers who have read under his care. The Rev. J. V. Durell was his college tutor.

Mr. George Howard Darwin, of Trinity College, the second wrangler, the second son of Mr. Charles Darwin, the well known author of the "Origin of Species," is in his 23rd year, and is a native of Down, in Kent. He was educated at the Clapham Grammar School, under the Rev. Charles Pritchard, President of the Royal

Astronomical Society, and Hulsean Lecturer at the University of Cambridge for 1867, the late Head Master, and the Rev. Alfred Wrigley, M. A., F. R. A. S., the present Head Master. In the Easter Term, 1866, he was elected a Foundation Scholar, and he has been three times Prizeman of his college. Like the Senior Wrangler, Mr. Darwin's private tutor was Mr. Routh, his college tutor being the Rev. R. Burn.

The schools of Eton, Rugby and Winchester hold equal rank with Harrow. The head scholars from each, who annually enter the Universities, compete on their new theatres for scholastic honors amid the anxieties of their friends and the general expectation of the public. The successful collegian is almost certain to pass, in time, from the University to some high position, sometimes into Parliament and sometimes at the bar. This was the case with William Pitt, Horace Walpole, Sir Robert Peel, Lords Aberdeen, Palmerston and many others. This fact refutes a charge brought against the English by the French that they are insensible to literary merit and heap honors upon actresses, danseuses and song-stresses, who have the entre to the houses of the first nobility, while a poor *homme de lettres* is is left to starve in a garret.

It is true that Milton sold Paradise Lost for £15, while Charles II, to whom the British Parliament granted six millions of dollars annually for his support, was spending hundreds of thousands upon his mistresses and bastards. Yet even then all England was not insensible to the genius of Milton, or enamored of the depravity of Charles. The poet's admirers were found among those from whom the chief glory of a nation arises, and the sovereign was the leader of society and those whom we might not inaptly style the "dangerous classes." The one was serving his God and country, reflecting honor upon human nature, and the other entailing a line of spurious nobility upon England. Ignorant people in our day look up to and reverence those whom we are taught to style "our betters," and who are they? Charles II, by his mistress, Lucy Walton, had a son whom he created Duke of Monmouth; by another favorite, Nell Gwynn, a second son, whom he created Duke of Richmond, and by Barbara Villiers he had three sons, one created Duke of Cleve and, the second Duke of Grafton, and the third Duke of Northumberland. These were a few only of his favorites and his bastards, and he indulged them to the utmost of his power. All these mistresses and their bastard sons were recognized at court and supplied with money to maintain their "exalted" rank. His unhappy Queen was obliged to humiliate herself and treat them with courtesy, even familiarity. The men who surrounded the King were of like character, and while Charles' reign was the most scandalous which England has ever seen, those of other and even very much later sovereigns have been disgraced by great and disgusting immorality and licentiousness. Mr. C. S Parnell, who is creating so much interest in this country by his eloquent appeals on behalf of his suffering countrymen, recently repelled, in a vigorous style, peculiar to himself, an attack made upon his veracity by Lord Alfred S. Churchill, brother of the Duke of Marlborough. When speaking in Springfield. Massachusetts, January 30, Mr. Parnell referred to Lord Alfred Churchill's cable dispatch and said ;

"This young nobleman says that my statement that the relief fund of the Duchess of Marlborough is being administered for political purposes is false. Now I have the best and most recent information from the distressed districts that my statement is absolutely true and that all persons out of favor with their landlords are precluded from participation. More than one parish priest also has already complained that the fund is being administered for sectarian purposes. The word of a descendant, on the one hand, of the notorious Sarah Jennings, mistress of the Duke of York, and on the other hand, of Churchill, first Duke of Marlborough, of whom Macaulay write as follows: 'That he owed his rise to his sister's dishonor, and that he had been kept by the most profuse, imperious and shameless of harlots,' will be scanned somewhat closely by the American people, who at least can boast that their ancestors were honest men and women."

This vigorous retort tells incidentally the story of the reign of George III. Society took its tone from the court, and we doubt not in the days to which we refer, a pretty ballet girl was more highly esteemed in West end society than a scholar, literary man or, statesman. Happily those days have passed away, let us hope never to return. Under the reign of Victoria, the Court has set an example of purity and domestic virtue, worthy of all praise. The taunt of the French in the present day is an anacronism.— However true it once was, it is not so in the present. This may be asserted with force, notwithstanding the many vices which tarnished the character of the Prince of Wales in his earlier days, and which he has been weak and wicked enough to carry into maturer years.

While the facts we have mentioned in connection with the distinguished University student, attest the favor with which the English of our day, look upon the successful student and literary man, it cannot be denied that the chief importance is attached to wealth and ancent lineage. When during the Premiership of the Earl of Derby—1867-1868—he was supposed to be dangerously ill and the politicians were casting about for a successor, the old grandees, their organs and supporters, spoke in the following deriding tone of Mr. Disraeli, who for many years was the intellectual leader—the man of brains—in the Conservative party. (Though this was evidently his position, it was years before the old fogies would acknowledge it.) Who, they asked, should be Premier if the failing health of Lord Derby made his resignation necessary? Mr. Disraeli? Well it can hardly be pleasant to Mr. Disraeli to find that very few think of him as the coming man. He is unconnected, landless, wanting in rank and social position, utterly unable to keep his party together, said even conservatives, and his opponents expressed themselves, we need hardly say, far more emphatically. In the popular mind it seemed necessary in a Prime Minister that he should be connected with the half dozen great houses, who are styled in England "our governing families;" that he should be a large landed proprietor, which would imbue him with what are called conservative influences; that he should if possible be a nobleman, that is to say be of such rank as would give him commanding social position. All this was supposed to be necessary, but the sequel has proved that they are not always so—that the world moves.

In spite of his social and pecuniary deficiencies, his jewish origin, his low estate, and the bitter hatred of an influential section of Parliament, that section led by Daniel O'Connell who denounced him as a miscreant and wretch whose "life is a living lie" and finally as the "heir-at-law of the blasphemous thief who died impenitent on the cross." Mr. Disraeli has risen by force of his splendid genius to the highest position in the state, having been twice Premier. During the latter and his present term of office, this remarkable man has extended the British Empire by vast acquisitions of territory in Africa and in India, made millions of British subjects and fenced them round about with what he called a "scientific frontier." He has also added the title of Empress to that of Queen of the United Kingdom of Great Britain and Ireland, or as it is colloquially said in England, 'made an Empress." At the same time, he has pursued his policy of "Empire and Liberty," and claims that he has preserved the *status quo* in Europe, and maintained for England, peace with honor. So much for a man of the people, for a man of genius. A man too who, as Mr. Bright once said, "has not a drop of English blood in his veins" and who consequently met unusual opposition, and had to overcome extraordinary prejudice. He has that which is better than blue blood—to wit, brains.

And now after his extraordinary career, his marvelous success, in his seventy-sixth year, he is not affected with the weakness of age, but is vigorous with the strength of manhood, having a seat in the House of Lords and possessing in a remarkable manner its confidence. There is only one other man in England to whom the destinies of the vast British Empire and the prospects of Ireland are likely to be entrusted with better results, namely: Mr. Gladstone, Lord Beaconsfield's life-long rival and political opponent. Of Mr. Gladstone it may be truly said that he is Mr. Disraeli's superior every way; more brilliant in oratory, more sterling in integrity, more sincere in his convictions, more statesmanlike in his views, more terribly earnest in all he says and does.— To him the fortunes of the British Empire might be, and in our opinion, ought to be, entrusted by that people who will never cease to celebrate his pure and immortal fame.

It was often said during our residence in England, that the Conservative party, without making any professions or promises, carried through more measures of reform than the so-called Liberals. There was some color of reason for this remark, the fact being that the Liberal party ever showed the way of reform to the Tories.— This was the case as to Catholic emancipation; the corn laws, and with the reform act of 1867. For many years previously, the Liberals preached in vain that the admission of the working classes to the franchise was required by the state of society, and that it would strengthen the constitution. When the Tories came into power, they who had always bitterly opposed the idea, faced about and passed the act extending the suffrage. Thus the Liberal party, with such leaders as Gladstone and Bright, has ever been the pioneer of reform, though the Tory ministers have from time to time sought to gain the popular applause and reap the fruits of victory by passing the best conceived and most cherished liberal measures. But to return from this digression.

Beyond the school house stands the Parish church, surrounded by generations of tombstones One of the first pointed out to us was that known as "Byron's Tomb," from the fact that it was his favorite resting place. He thus refers to it in his childish recollections:

"Oft' when oppress'd with sad, foreboding gloom
I sat reclined upon our favorite tomb."

It is said that he would spend hours here engaged in thought, chewing the cud of sweet and bitter fancies, brooding in lonliness over the first stirring of passion and genius in his soul, and occasionally, perhaps, indulging in those bright forethoughts of fame, under the influence of which, when little more than fifteen years of age, he wrote these remarkable lines:

"My epitaph shall be my name alone;
If that with honor fail to crown my clay,
Oh may no other fame my deeds repay;

That, only that, shall single out the spot,
By that remember'd or by that forgot."

Secured in the walls of the church is an ancient brass. It was taken from the floor of the church, where it was half concealed by a pew. It is engraved with a grotesque figure intended to represent the founder of the school, and inscribed with a highly eulogistic epitaph, in what then passed for English, but which is now, hardly intelligible.

After an uncommonly pleasant day spent in wandering about the streets and neighborhood of Harrow, we brought up at the Kingshead Inn for a 6 o'clock dinner. We had intended returning to London by a night train, but clouds were gathering in the sky, and before we were half through with "our mutton," gusts of wind, more like the blasts of March than the zephyrs of May, drove the rain drops beating in sheets against the windows. Arise and wander forth? No, it was quickly decided that we should spend the night under the friendly shelter of the Inn. "You have decided wisely," said a quiet gentleman, whose name we soon afterwards learnt was Evershort. This respectable looking person was the only occupant of the room when we entered, and was dining at a small table on a chop and a pint of stout. Dressed in the subdued habit of a rector, he had something decidedly clerical in his sleek appearance. "Yes," he continued, "we shall have a bad night. Better remain here, and if we can get some cards we may spend a pleasant evening in spite of wind and weather. I suppose you all play whist; for myself I am very fond of a rubber."

.This speech, following what some of our party regarded as Mr. Evershort's rather expressive silence, took us by surprise, and our conversation hung fire for a few minutes like a damp squib. Barnwell, however, who possessed many of the good points of a man of the world, and was devoted to the well known game, acted as our speaker. He politely responded to the advances of our civil neighbor, fell into a pleasant chat with him and quickly pledged us for a rubber. Meanwhile we had discussed, *solo voce*, whether we had not come upon a professional card sharper, who only wanted the opportunity to relieve us of our guineas in the neatest possible manner. The South Carolinian turned toward us, as Mr. Evershort left the room in search of his pipe, and reassured us by pronouncing the quiet man as of rigid views morally and ecclesiastically—in others words, said Barnwell, "he's the c'rrect card."

Our social meal over, a comfortable cloud was blown, the quiet man having rejoined the party, lit his pipe and ordered a glass of brandy and soda. The card table was now opened in front of the jocund fire under the brilliant gas chandalier and the rubber commenced. Time wore on without any noteworthy incident, and we separated for the night at twelve o'clock, little having been won or lost. Mr. Evershort, however, was indebted to Barnwell in the sum of thirty shillings and being short of change promised to hand it to him the following morning. This, by the way, he forgot to do no doubt in the hurry of leaving. When we descended next morning to the breakfast room, the waiter informed us that our sleek friend had left two hours before. Barnwell was "flabbergasted" at this communication, and positively declined to enter into any kind of fun over the "c'rrect card."

Immediately after our breakfast we began to consider of the most agreeable way of returning to town. This leads us to enquire, is motion synonymous with pleasure? and is it sufficient to agitate ourselves to be amused? In that case we take too much amusement. What shall we do this morning? What shall we do this afternoon? What shall we do this evening? It is the diurnal refrain, and there we go on foot, on horseback, in carriages, thinking of nothing, going everywhere, with enthusiasm, laughter and jests, which return with us, sit down at table with us, dance with us, sing with us and do not leave us even at the silent game and when holding the "c'rrect card."

But to proceed. Wishing to enjoy the refreshment of another country walk, we descended the hill on the eastern side and struck off for the northern heights of London by Frognal road and West end lane. This route led us to Hampstead and Highgate, two of the most charming environs of the metropolis. Near the latter the Right Honorable Angela Georgiana; Baroness Burdett-Coutts, to give her the full title recently conferred on her by the British government in recognition of her many shining virtues, resides in Holly Lodge, surrounded by beautiful gardens and grounds. The hills on which these villages are situated, though only five miles from the Thames, are from three to four hundred feet higher than the surface of the water at Blackfriars Bridge. Their elevation, the purity of the air and water and the existence of one or more mineral springs in the neighborhood, have long made Hampstead and Highgate favorite residences for commercial and professional men. Rents are consequently from twenty to twenty-five per cent. higher than in any part of London, but the West end, and all the country hereabout, is covered with attractive looking dwellings.

These stone, brick and stuccoed villas, with their well kept lawns and dainty flower beds, and surrounded by handsome grounds of from two to five acres, with Hampstead's free village life and retired haunts, render it the most desirable locality as a residence near London.

Hampstead Heath is a rough, broken common, covered with a stunted growth and famous for its bracing air. In early days it was a haunt of wild beasts. When these were driven off, it became a place of concealment for more dangerous characters, thieves, highwaymen, robbers, fugitives from justice and other outlaws. In the course of time the drivellers of fashion displaced the highwaymen and it degenerated into a disreputable watering place. About a century and a half since Hampstead occupied on the north the same position that Richmond assumed on the south side of the Thames. It was patronized by the idle, the opulent, the unscrupulous. The Royal family composed of George I, about the time he created his mistress, Sophia Walmoden, Countess of Yarmouth, were in the habit of "honoring" Hampstead with their presence. On every side there were houses of amusement and dissipation—ball rooms, gambling hells, gin palaces, and bagnios, and all patronized by the *elite*. It was also a kind of Gretna Green, where unfortunate lovers, east of Temple bar and Blackfriars road, were united in "private" for the public amusement. In a comedy acted at Drury Lane Theatre in 1706, entitled "Hampstead Heath," many amusing passages occur, which vividly describe the scenes and company in those days.

Half a century later "the Wells" figure as semi-fashionable haunts in the pages of Smollet's *Roderic Random* and Fanny Burney's *Evelina*, and yet a generation or two, and we find them satirized by Lord Byron in the *Childe Harold* as the Sabbath haunts.

"Where the spruce citizen, washed artizan,
And snug apprentice gulp their weekly air.
The coach of hackney, whiskey, one horse chair
\*   \*   \*   \*   \*
To Hampstead Brentsford Harrow make repair
\*   \*   \*   \*   \*
And many to the steep of Highgate hie.
Ask ye Bœotian shades the reason why?
'Tis to the worship of the solemn Horn
Grasped in the holy hand of mystery
In whose dread name both men and maids are sworn
And consecrate the oath with draught and dance till morn."

It must be remembered that the expression "solemn horn," in these lines bears reference to an ancient tavern known as "The Horns" at Highgate, the host of which was wont for many years to pledge novices in nut brown ale, never to eat brown bread when they could get white, or to drink small beer, when they could get strong, &c.—but with a saving reservation always, "unless you like the inferior article better." The custom has long since become obsolete, shall we add, the more's the pity?"

Steele lived here about the year 1712, for the then common purpose with people who were "hard up," of eluding the vigilance of his creditors. During this period he composed many of his contributions to the *Spectator*.

In Hampstead Church there is a tablet inscribed to the memory of one Mr. Waad, who is described as the English Columbus. Some account of his voyages are contained in a work published in 1536, in which it is said that Waad being a man of "goodly statue, and of great courage, and given to study of cosmographic, encouraged divers gentlemen and others, being assisted by the King's favor and good countenance, to accompany him in a voyage of discovery upon the Northwest parts of America, wherein his persuasions took such effect, that within short space, many guests of the Inns of Court and of the Chancerie, and divers others of good worship, desirous to see the strange things of the world, very willingly entered into the action with him. They embarked at Gravesend for Cape Breton and New Foundland, where they suffered from famine to such an extent that they cast lots and devoured each other! Finally such of them as survived, among whom was Waad, were relieved by a French vessel in which they returned to England."

Whether this monumental eloquence is fact or fiction does not appear. It strongly reminds one, however, of the witty remark of a wanderer through a modern cemetery: "Here lie the dead, and here the living lie."

Hampstead is not now what it was. This is fortunate. With characteristic fickleness, fashionable society long since abandoned it for other haunts of folly and dissipation. The heath still remains to some extent, the same savage wild, swept by cool blasts and healthful breezes; the quaint red brick mansions of Tudor date or brown and yellow edifices of Hanoverian respectability still remain monuments of its departed greatness; the old crowd of court bucks and ladies, "all air and no dress," are no where to be seen nowadays. We are glad of it. The place still has, however, many charms, and on holidays, presents no common scene of gaiety. A new company, recruited from other classes, occupies the vacant places and enlivens the scene with its coarse but honest jollity. It is now the resort of the inhabitants of the densely peopled districts of the city who fly at every opportunity from their sweltering confinement to luxuriate in a country atmosphere and upon the sight of green fields. The splendid saloons of the past, radiant with youth, beauty, wealth and fashion, wit and all the seductive allurements of polished vice, have given place to dimly lighted tap rooms, the stale joke of the fat grocer, and the rough fun of the butcher boy and bar maid. In other words, plain but honest people replace the royal, noble and blackguard snobs, swells, rakes, blades and rascals of other days.

Our visit to the heath occurred on the occasion of the Easter Monday holiday when thousands of the "bold peasantry, their country's pride," were mixed up with the denizens of London engaged in rural sports. The English are remarkable for their love of rural amusements. One of the sportive games was dancing on the green. A large party were assembled, having a "set to," as they called it, to the music of a violin and flagolet. The music was—

> "Moll in the wad and I fell out,
> And what d'ye think it was about,
> She had money, I had none,
> And that was the way the row begun."

The dancing was full of the logic of the toe, not to say the fantastic toe. Double quadrills, eight on a side, making a set of thirty-two, were the popular figures. Dancing on the green is one of the most ancient popular amusements of the rustics. The spirit of the game consists in movement, restless activity, the excitement of motion. The young folks bound from the ground as if on a spring board, advance and recede, grasp each other by the waist and fly about like whirligigs, or as Dean Swift himself, much given to witness and even participate *incognito* in these rustic frolics, well expresses it in his "O'Rourk's Bridal."

> "Hand in hand they dance around,
> Cutting capers and ramping ;
> A mercy the ground
> Does not burst with the stamping."

Everything about the crowd when we saw it was natural, unaffected, full of simplicity,—their features, complexions, dress and attitude corresponding, and we must confess that we looked on with approbation, if not admiration. We venture to record this while concurring in a general detestation of those fashionable round dances so much patronized at this day by the gay world. A reprehensible kind of dissipation which has caused it to be said somewhat axiomatically that a woman however virtuous she may be, ceases to be so after a waltz of three or four hours. It is a physiological phenomenon, which we limit ourselves to mentioning, that it is no longer a woman who is held in the beau's arms, no longer a thinking, reflecting human being, but if it may be so expressed, only a sensation ready to quiver at the least contact.

At a short distance another game was progressing, called "kissing in the ring." As this game is played with some difference, we will describe it as we saw it. A ring is formed on the green by the young people of both sexes joining hands. There are often as many as a hundred in a single ring, a half dozen young girls or more then enter the arena, and moving around, each selects the handsomest young man, to whom she throws her handkerchief; she then bounds away, breaking through the ring and flying over the common, the young man in pursuit. He does not find it difficult to overtake the blushing girl, and after considerable resistance, and no small amount of rough embracing, but devoid of vulgarity, she is brought back to the enclosure, where in the presence of all she is saluted with a smacking kiss. They both then join hands and take their position in the ring. After all the girls have thrown the handkerchief and gone through the process of being kissed in the ring, the young men enter the circle and throw a bandanna to the romping girls. They in turn fly and are pursued and brought back and saluted in the same hearty manner. Frequently as many as a dozen pairs are in the circle at the same time paying the soft penalty. While this is going on those who form the ring are pulling and swaying to and fro, indulging in all kinds of merriment and not infrequently huzzaing the too evident gusto with which some rustic beau takes his kiss. This is a favorite game with maid servants and sailors, and many matches date their origin from this custom. Whatever objection the refined and elegant may find to this promiscuous assemblage of the sexes, it is doubtful whether anything more full of innocence and gayiety could be devised for the amusement of young folks. We are satisfied that these recreations in which the women share or humanize by their presence, are in the highest degree conducive to the health and rational enjoyment of the lower classes and that the objection to them comes from old maids whose sensitive natures are unduly frightened at the idea of collecting both sexes for the purpose of recreation. If music and square dancing are innocent for the higher orders, why are they sinful for the lower?

Notwithstanding all the maiden blues can do, all the care taken by the ancient prude and spinster to banish everything like merry making from all but the rich, with a view to the public morals, female chastity before marriage is confessedly at a low ebb among the inferior classes, both in town and country. And we cannot but think that it is somewhat due to the course of our spinsters in discouraging open air amusements, as they unquestionably, to our mind, tend to virtue rather than vice.

A pleasant stroll of two miles through a shaded lane on the sides of which at suitable intervals, wooden benches are placed for the benefit of pedestrians, brings you to Highgate. These seats under the old oaks are favorite spots, where congregate comfortable looking nurses around whom cluster children of all ages, from the rosy Miss of two years to the stately gentleman of eight. We never cease to admire the English nurses. They have an especially maternal manner and appearance. Blue of eye, red of tint, broad of shoulder and kind of tongue, they are the centre of that solar system, round which toddle and tumble in eccentric orbits, those wonderful planets—little children.

Such notices as this on the wooden benches serve to protect them: "Do not abuse what is intended for the public benefit." Similar notices preserve the flowers and shrubs in all the London parks. In conspicuous places on boards in large letters the visitor reads: "It is hoped that the public will abstain from destroying that which is cultivated for the public gratification." This is perfect; the aim of every society is that each one should be always his own constable and end by not having any other.

On the opposite side of the Hill from Hampstead and near its base in front of a Tom and Jerry Shop, fixed in the ground, on the road side, is a small gray stone which marks the spot where the celebrated Whittington halted to rest and ruminate over his hard fate when leaving London for the country and where. he heard the peals of the Bow bells, which seemed to utter the gentle and heart cheering admonition, "Turn again Whittington, Lord Mayor of London town." Everywhere in this neighborhood you observe in the shop signs how highly the memory of this civil patriot and munificent benefactor of the poor is still appreciated. One establishment is called "The Whittington." Another "The Whittington Cat." Another "Whittington and his Cat," nor should we omit to add that one of the most thriving reunions of the London middle-classes bears the name of the "Whittington Club."

The Hill is crowned by Highgate church, from the cemetery of which a wide prospect of the surrounding country, including the metropolis, is obtained. Highgate, like its neighbor, has long been a favorite haunt of Londoners, but by reason of its closer proximity to the city, is rapidly losing its ancient rural characteristics and becoming a modern town. As an evidence of its remarkable healthfulness, it is said that not a case of the plague occurred here during the period when it scourged London in the reign of Charles II.

The unfortunate Arabella Stuart, who was like Lady Catherine Gray, in close proximity to the throne, and whose only crime was marrying the man she loved, was for some time imprisoned in a house still standing at Highgate. She disguised herself in a suit of men's clothes and escaped. Taking a boat on the Thames, she soon got aboard a French barque lying off Gravesend, where she wished to await the arrival of her husband, Lord Seymour, then a prisoner in the Tower, with whom the projected flight had been concerted. Her friends dissuaded her from this course and the barque dropped down the river and into the channel where anchor was cast. Meanwhile Seymour escaped from the Tower and proceeded down the river, but not seeing the French barque, engaged another vessel to land him at Calais, to which place he made good his escape. His absence from the Tower was soon discovered and several ships of war sent in pursuit—one of which overtook the barque containing his wife, which after a short engagement was captured and Arabella Stuart returned to London where she was confined as a State prisoner in the Tower. She bore her fate with cheerfulness, when she heard that her husband was safe in France, but her spirit was soon broken by grief and solitary confinement, and she became insane and died in this condition after four year's imprisonment.

At the period of the restoration Seymour returned to England and was created by Charles II, in grateful recognition of his fidelity, Earl of Hertford. He ever cherished a romantic affection for the Lady Arabella and named his eldest daughter by his second wife after her.

## CHAPTER XI.

A LONDON LAW COURT—THE ENGLISH ON AMERICA—THE DUKE OF SOMERSET—THE LAND LAWS, &C —THE COURTS OF QUEEN'S BENCH AND EXCHEQUER—NOMINATION OF SHERIFFS—LORD MAYOR'S BANQUETS—THE RIGHT HON. WM. CUBITT, M. P., LORD MAYOR OF LONDON — A VILLAGE GRAVEYARD — CURIOUS EPITAPHS.

When returning one day through Westminster Hall, from a visit to the House of Commons, we were struck with the countenances of a number of persons lounging in the neighborhood of a door, upon the left hand side and half way down the vestibule. "Easter term has just begun," said our companion, Dr. Norton Shaw, "let us take a look at the court."

"Easter term has begun!" What a tremendous meaning these simple words have for that unfortunate class of human beings called clients. Almost unconsciously we stopped to scrutinize the wretched people pressing towards the temple of judicature. Almost every passion which can excite the human mind was depicted in the countenances of that miserably agitated crowd. There was the eager, grasping creditor, gloating over the prospect of making good his "pound of flesh," and there his hapless victim, despair pictured in every line of his countenance, and there the sly, sinister-visaged scoundrel waiting the result of his cruel plans to over-reach the unwary victim. On every side the wretched victims of the law's uncertainty and delay, of the pettifogger's rapacity, the knave's talent for stirring up dissension, creating discord, and transferring to his own pockets the substance of the ignorant, helpless and unwary who have fallen into his hands and are at his mercy.

With a soothing sense of relief that we were non-litigant and non expectant, the thought occurred to us whether it was possible that any human being but a hungry attorney could look upon that picture of passion, of hopes and fears, and not feel that ignorance is bliss in everything connected with suits in law and suits in equity.

During a protracted residence in the mother country, we heard so much derogatory of American courts of the practical denial of justice in them that we formed a high opinion, indeed, of what was always held up to our admiration in contrast therewith—

namely, the British tribunal. It was a common thing to hear American courts spoken of as if such a thing as justice was altogether unknown to them. Returned cockney tourists, big with travelers' stories and virtuous indignation, declared that in the United States, more particularly in New York, it was not only the common, but the right thing, to bribe judge and jury, and to suborn witnesses. Shocking accounts of James Fisk's connection with the Erie railroad swindles were related, and of the manner in which he was encouraged and protected in them by the New York courts. With agreeable merriment, the Tammany ring robberies of the city treasury, New York, and the "brilliant career" of Boss Tweed were enlarged upon, and also the operations of Jay Gould, James McHenry and other railroad "financiers," as well as the "eccentricities" of Gen. Belknap and the whisky rings. All the facts were given with an extraordinary amount of fiction until the whole affair seemed very much like "Yankee Doodle," with variations. The substance of all these horrible narratives was that there was a total denial of justice in American courts, a collusion between judge, jury, witnesses, lawyers and suitors for the purpose of robbing litigants and enriching themselves on the spoils. Brigandage in Spain and Italy was represented as a flea bite in comparison with the luxury of going to law in America. A suitor when entering a New York court was said to take leave of hope as Dante represented was the case with the lost soul when entering the infernal region. So much in this spirit, vein and humor had been said in our presence, if not addressed to us—when addressed to us, of course, always in the politest manner—by our mellifluous and self satisfied British cousins, and always in contrast with what our modest relatives asserted was the unsullied purity of their own bench and bar, that we confess we approached the portals of one of England's principal courts with a respect much akin to reverence.

Years have since passed away and a long residence in Britain satisfies us that there was no occasion for emotion on approaching the courts of Westminster; that in fact, justice is about as indifferently administered in that venerable pile, as in our own much abused tribunals. Probably no where in the world is such high flown nonsense talked about justice as in England, and probably nowhere is it more difficult to obtain substantial, cheap, immediate redress for wrong or injury. The truth is there can hardly be said to be such a thing as a well defined and understood law governing any case. Shelves groan with books of precedents, but these conflict as often as they agree. Miles of statutes have been enacted, but one half of them contradict the other half. Hundreds of thousands of subtle and acute intellects have thought out "cases," but each is designed to upset some case which preceded it. The result is that instead of an easily understood, clear, comprehensive code of laws, the English are burdened with a veritable labyrinth of obsolete phrases and still more obsolete ideas, among which justice is eternally losing her way. No man can hope to do more than master certain parts of this inchoate and useless jargon, and so from age to age the abuse grows larger and larger, the courts become more and more expensive, and suits of all kinds more costly, more hazardous and more unsatisfactory when they are concluded. As laws are made by lawyers, it is difficult to understand where reform is to come from. It is this which really bars the way to judicial reform, either partial or extensive. But until there is reform in these matters and English justice becomes a little more just, and bears a less resemblance to trickery it behooves Englishmen to cultivate more modesty in their comments upon what they term the shortcomings of the American system Whatever bold front John Bull may show to the "intelligent foreigner" in favor of the stability of all British institutions, public opinion in England is ripe for a change not only in the land laws, but in the entire system of laws, both municipal and constitutional. A few year's residence in the country satisfied us on this point— There is not an intelligent man of business in England who has ever been engaged in legal transactions, who does not know to his cost the petty pieces of legerdemain by which solicitors, for example, divide with accountants every divisible fragment of a bankrupt's estate, leaving the unfortunate creditor in payment of his debts, a lithographic copy of the accounts, and the memory of a swindle. While the law makers are selected from the class who themselves fatten on the law, who can expect they will permit, much less foster, any measure which they fear will curtail their own incomes. This much we venture to remark on this important subject—some of it was applicable a few years since to our own country—and without intending to cast wholesale censure and accusations of fraud and folly against a whole body of men. Yet we repeat that it is not going too far to assert that lawyers favor the present obscurity of the law, and will always exert the whole of their vast influence to keep it involved. The means of their living they imagine is inextricably associated with its inextricableness. To simplify statutes and make criminal and civil offences less the jungle they now are, would be in their opinion to make lawyers a luxury instead of a necessity. And for this reason, if for no other, the profession in England has always been found voting against reform and impeding judicial progress. It is much to be regretted that the prejudice against everything American is so great that they do not try our experiment of codifying and simplifying the laws, the pleadings and all the procedures of the courts. Such a course has not been found in the United States to materially affect the profits of the profession to the honest practitioner. On the contrary, nowhere is it better understood that the man who acts as his own counsel has a fool for his client.

The English prejudice against everything American, we must say *en passant*, has been recently illustrated in a clumsy way by the Duke of Somerset, (to whom we introduced our reader in the sixth chapter as an oppressor of his tenantry,) in a work published last year by "his grace," entitled "Monarchy and Democracy." Monarchy in England he considers to be as good as dead already, although he thinks that there is danger of its being galvanized into a sort of life by the reckless action of those people who support Lord Beaconsfield in his efforts to exalt the Crown. To that extent he is right, except that he confounds with the English nation the electors who gave Lord Beaconsfield a majority in Parliament; in all the rest of his book he is altogether wrong. The twaddle of this aged driveler is in curious contrast with John Bright's recent speech at Birmingham. Mr. Bright showed that England had progressed wonderfully during the past 50 years through the growth of popular power and the gradual overthrow of political abuses. The Duke of Somerset thinks England has been going down hill during the past 50 years, just because so many political abuses have been overthrown. He looks back almost with tearful eyes on the state of things existing before the Reform act of 1832 was passed, the time when as he says "the aristocratic patron, the jobbing borough-monger, the self elected corporation, the venal freeman, and the drunken pot-walloper, nominated a considerable proportion of the House of Commons!" That was the golden age of England, he says, when the "glorious British constitution" was in its most glorious condition. True he would have preferred a rule of "aristocratic patrons" alone, without the drunken pot-wallopers and their allies; but as they were part and parcel of the same system he reverences them all. Will it be believed that in this year of grace 1880, a duke, who was once a cabinet minister, would have the effrontery to say this to the enlightened, liberty loving people of England, among whom Republican sentiments are growing daily? Yet so it is. The Bourbons learn nothing and forget nothing. The Duke devotes many chapters to sneering at and slandering all reforms and all reformers.— Frankness about the working classes, the *proletariat* as he calls them, is impossible with him. He writes thus: "In all accumulations of animal matter there is an immediate tendency to ferment, and a crowd of human beings is especially liable to *effervescence*." Here is a noble duke who compares the people of England to nothing better than putrifying "animal matter," and yet he is not only tolerated, but by a certain class is reverenced. In looking back upon the history of England we can find nothing good within a half century which has come from the Tory party of which the Duke is one of the leaders. The history of Tories is a struggle to preserve the *status quo* of class privilege and popular ignorance and subjection. Toryism is intense in proportion to the injustice or inequality of which it is the offspring. It contains many stupid people, no doubt, whose interest is more imaginary than real, but as a whole it is the party of privilege, and as such, hostile to change, however salutary it may appear to the philanthropist. There will always be tories, we fear, in England and in every country, for to abolish them would be to abolish selfishness and stupidity. To get rid of them would be to renovate the mind and conscience of mankind.

His grace traces all the tendency to change in England to the example of America and consequently he hates America and everything American.

This aged fribbler belongs evidently to that old nobility which is more venerable than valuable, and his friends, if friends such a man can have, will regret the closing years of his life in acts of charity and repentance, rather than in an exhibition of his narrow political views and his scoffing infidelity. Among the hideous spectacles of his declining years has been his malevolent attacks on Christianity. Nothing more is needed to make him appear odious. Americans can afford to let them pass in contempt, firm, as every true born American is, in a fervent belief in the principle of human solidarity, and in the ultimate reign of Democracy and fraternity the world over.

Let us get back to a more pleasing and reputable subject by rejoining our reader, whom we have left so long standing in Westminster hall in front of an imposing looking door, which interposses between the outside world and the dignified body of a British Court. Mounting a few steps and pushing open two doors, one within the other, and which move smoothly and noiselessly on their hinges, we find ourselves in the presence of—an old woman, sitting at an apple stall, supplemented with a collection of stale ginger bread and cheap lollipops, and close by the side of a roaring fire. This is the lobby of the Court of the Queen's Bench, and the huge fire is intended to heat the court room, which it does by a system of flues. The old woman who does not object to the temperature of Madeira, with her solitary apple and beer stall, is all that is left of the famous array of shops which once graced Westminster Hall, constituting its chief attraction and making it a fashionable promenade. The Court of Queen's Bench is so called from the ancient custom of holding courts before the monarch in person, and the writs of summons still run in the ancient formula, citing the litigant parties to appear before "ourselves at Westminster."

Leaving the roaring fire and the old woman in possession of the lobby now at a heat of, we imagine, at least 100 Fahr., we passed through another door and were at once in the presence of the court. The chamber is some forty feet square and as many in height. It is dimly lighted from a domed circular lantern in the roof. Under a carved canopy in front of the royal arms, raised upon a kind of dias, sit four yellow-tanned, mummy-like objects, their heads enveloped in immense gray wings, amplified by two side appendages that rest upon the shoulders. Their bodies were covered with scarlet gowns, redundant in material and disposed in ample folds and broidered with ermine tippets and cuffs. Though the dress is barbarous, it is imposing, and in a degree dignified, and seems to verify Shakespear's acute remark, "through tattered clothes small voices do appear, robes and furred gowns hide all." Below the judges sat on benches behind a long table covered with green baize, the registers and masters of the Court, and below these the lawyers engaged in the case before the Court; below these again the bar, opposite to and facing the judges. The heads of all covered with grey wigs which brought to our mind the exclamation of one who loved them not, "Oh, men, with heads clothed in horse hair and effrontery." The bodies of all these men of the law were enveloped in flowing black gowns, their feet cased in shining patent leather pumps with silver buckles, and from their breasts depended a couple of clerical looking bands of the finest cambric. A violet colored bag crammed to bursting was near each one, and a bundle of parchments tied with red tape. These learned gentlemen are the incarnation of legal wisdom and experience; the experts who handle the machinery of the law and expedite or frustrate as the case may be, the decrees of even handed justice. Below them, in a kind of pit, are the clients, witnesses and other interested parties. Behind these there are several consecutive rows of seats, filled with attorneys, barristers and the bar generally, and behind these, rows of benches rise, one above another, on which the public find seats. These, whenever an interesting case is before the Court, are filled to overflowing.— Notwithstanding the large crowd, the utmost quietness—the nearest possible approach to silence—prevails. The slightest noise or disturbance, a hum of voices, or a shuffling of feet, is quelled in a moment, by an admonitory "hush-sh—sh," which passing around subsides into stillness. These disturbances rarely arise with the spectators, but generally originate with the gentlemen in wigs and gowns.

Upon the occasion of our visit, the case in progress was on a motion for a new trial in a case of libel and seemed to create unusual interest in spectators and professionals  The counsel for the plaintiff, who interlarded every period with "my lud" and "yer lud ship" was zealously endeavoring to impress the bench with a sense of the profound injury his client had received from the libeler.— But the chief was not very penetrable to the counsel's arguments —seemed to understand just what was pertinent to the case and how much to credit to *bunkum*. He interrupted the "learned counsel" as his lordship styled him, with much courtesy, in the middle of a rather monotonous piece of legal rhetoric and questioned him as to certain admissions which the plaintiff had made to one of his own witnesses. These cannot be denied and they constitute in his lordship's opinion, a justification of the terms complained of as libelous ; and in two or three words the rule *nisi* for a new trial was refused. The counsel's unexhausted resources of wind were choked down for another occasion. The disconcerted counsel, his chagrin softened by the consideration of the judge, who interlarded every period with "my learned friend," bagged his papers and disappeared, his face flushed and his wig all awry, while the next case was called.

As the learned counsel retired there was no demonstration on part either of the bar or spectators. The decision was received as a decree of fate which must be submitted to in silence. The slightest demonstration of either approbation or censure would have been instantly checked by the court officials. This singular gravity on part of the spectators was something for which we were hardly prepared. Dr. Shaw, however, explained that they were for the most part *old stagers* at the law, who had in times past lost and won many a cause. The destiny of many had thus been decided for life, and from having long lived in the excitement of the courts, they could not live without it. Besides being always within convenient reach of the officer they served on many juries and thus picked up an honest penny and a poor living. There are not a few men of this kind, who without the slightest interest in any cause to be tried, are as punctual in their attendance as the judges, and who are never known to be absent during a single day or single hour while the court is open. "I have been a guide, showing people over the Parliament 'ouse, 'all, and habby thirty years," said a dirty stranger who held out to us a dirty paper, containing his testimonials of character and efficiency as a guide, and who essayed to scrape acquaintance with inveterate politeness of language and unassailable composure of manner on the prospect of being employed as a guide, "and 'ave never seen the Judge happear without *Hold Timmy Smith hand Freddy Butler*. People do say Timmy hunderstands more law 'an hany of the bar and that 'is Lordship 'ave been known to hask 'is opinion on a knotty pint."

The interesting manner, we may remark parenthetically, in which this cockney dropped his h's reminds us of an amusing anecdote or two in illustrating this inveterate habit with a certain class of English people. A student at one of the two British military academies had copied a drawing of a scene in Venice, and in copying the title had spelled the name of the city *Vennice*. The drawing master put his pen through the surperfluous letter, observing, "Don't you know, sir, that there is but one *hen* in Venice?" on which the youth burst out laughing. Being asked what he was laughing about, he replied he was thinking *how uncommonly scarce eggs must be there*. The master, in wrath, reported him to the Colonel in command, a Scotchman. He hearing the disrespectful reply, without in the least seeing the point of the joke, observed, "an a verra naatural observation too."

A barber while operating on a gentleman during the cholera epidemic, said, "After all, the cholera is in the hair." "Then ' replied the customer, "you ought to be very careful what brushes you use."

"Oh sir," replied the barber, laughing, "I did not mean the 'air of the 'ed, but the hair of the hatmosphere."

And one seasoned cockney tells another, "My 'ed used to hake ready to bust."

These illustrations of a vulgar habit are not given solely because they amuse, but because it furnishes us the opportunity to say that we regard the care of the English language as at all times a sacred trust and most important privilege of the upper classes. Every man of education should make it the object of his increasing concern to preserve his language pure and entire, and to speak it, so far as in his power, in all its beauty and perfection.

It must not be forgotten, however, that we are in the court room. In casting our eyes over the audience, it was not difficult to distinguish the old attendants from the rest of the listeners, who were now, many of them, for the first time in their lives before a court. They are excited and unable to settle comfortably in a seat. If they do so for a moment they are up and off at a tangent, as some sudden thought strikes them. Rushing to the apple stall to cool their fever with gin and a temperature of 100°, or to write a note at one of the desks in the rear, of which there are always several available, and thus to inform their counsel of some vital point forgotten till that moment, or perhaps never before imagined.

From the Court of Queen's bench we returned through the

lobby to Westminister Hall and entered the second side-door which introduced us to the Court of Exchequer. This Court exercises functions extra judicial, and keeps up the observance of certain traditionary customs and rites, as for example it regulates the election of sheriffs. As the English mode of electing the sheriffs is peculiar and unlike anything American it will not be uninteresting to give a brief account of it. Annually on the day after St. Martin's, November 12, a Privy Council is held to receive the report of the Judges, of the persons eligible in the several counties to serve as sheriff. The chancellor of the Exchequer sits upon the bench arrayed in a figured silk gown, trimmed with gold, (this is the only occasion on which the chancellor of the Exchequer takes his seat in this court). Next are the members of the Privy Council, the Lord Chancellor and Judges of the Queen's Bench and Common Pleas; below sit the Judges and chief Baron of Exchequer, and on the left the remembrancer or recorder of the Court. The names of three persons in each county who are eligible for sheriff are reported by the judges, when excuses for exemption may be pleaded. When the Privy Council have considered the list, the names are finally approved by the Queen in Privy Council, which is done by Her Majesty pricking through the names approved on a sheet of paper called the Sheriff's Roll. There is an exception to this mode in case of the sheriffs of London and Middlesex, who are chosen by the Livery, but are presented on the morrow of the Feast of St. Michael, in the Court of Exchequer, accompanied by the Lord Mayor and Alderman, when the Recorder introduces the sheriffs and details their family history, and the Cursitor Baron, an officer of the Court who attends at Westminster to open the Court prior to the commencement of each of the fixed terms, and on the last day after each term to close the court, signifies the sovereign's approval; the writs and appearances are read, recorded and filed, and the sheriffs and senior under sheriffs take the oaths, and the late sheriffs present their accounts. At this point the crier of the court makes proclamation for one who does homage for the Sheriffs of London, to "stand forth and do his duty;" then the senior alderman below the chair rises, the usher of the court hands him a bill-book, and holds in both hands a small bundle of sticks, which the alderman cuts asunder, and then cuts another bundle with a hatchet. Similar proclamation is then made for the Sheriff of Middlesex, when the alderman counts six horseshoes lying upon the table, and sixty-one hob nails handed in tray, and the members are declared twice. By the first service the alderman does service for the tenants of a manor in Shropshire, the chopping of sticks betokening the customs of the tenants supplying their lord with fuel. The counting of the horse shoes and nails is another suit and service of the owners of a forge in St. Clement Danes strand, which formerly belonged to the city, but no longer exists, while as to the manor in Shropshire, even a century ago no one knew where the lands were situated, nor did the city receive any rents or profits from them.

Annually on the 9th of November the Lord Mayor's procession takes place from the city to Westminster. It is conducted at the present day with all the barbaric splendor of early days, interferes with the business of the Metropolis and excites the ridicule of foreigners, but the English cling to it with a kind of childish delight. On the arrival of the pageant at Westminister, the Court of Exchequer administers the oath to the new Lord Mayor. At the same time the late Lord Mayor renders his accounts, and the Remembrancer invites the Barons to the banquet at Guildhall. This annual feast, where all that can delight the gastronomist is displayed in bounteous profusion, is one of the "institutions" of old England. It is attended by the Cabinet ministers, prominent M. P's. and other officials, the foreign Ambassadors and distinguished strangers. All the circumstances connected with this repast are too well known and are moreover not of sufficient importance to bear being communicated to the reader.

It may not be uninteresting to add to what we have said a brief sketch of the Lord Mayor holding office on our arrival in London and the munificent banquets which he gave during his year of civil mayoralty.

An invitation to attend one of these feasts led to our acquaintance with Mr. Wm. Cubitt, M. P., and we have rarely known a better specimen of a straightforward, blunt, honest man, whose true merits rest on performances. Mr. Cubitt belongs to that class of successful men, so esteemed the world over by right minded people, who have been the chief architects of their own fortunes and fame. He has had none of the advantages which attach to birth and aristocratic friends or to fortune, but has carved out his passage to wealth and distinction by his own skill, industry and enterprise. Mr. Cubitt's career is a refutation of the popular error somewhat prevalent in this country, that no one can rise in England without the prestige of rank and wealth. He is sprung, like Mr. Gladstone and very many others now eminent, from the middle class, and was brought up to business. By persevering industry, good sense and the practice of those homely and truly domestic virtues comprehended in "Early to bed and early to rise, make a man healthy, wealthy and wise," has risen step by step to occupy a distinguished position in station and society. The borough of Andover first honored itself by honoring Mr. Cubitt with a seat in Parliament in the year 1847, and this, too, in preference to a gentleman enjoying the honors of an escutcheon and the claims of an aristocratic birth. It was a fine tribute to his moral worth, for much as he is distinguished for his sound sense and good judgment, he is loved more for his benevolence, his virtue and honesty. "It is not," we may add in the words of Sir Walter Raleigh, "for their wisdom that we love the wisest, nor in their wit that we love the wittiest, but for their moral worth; the other qualities only make us proud of their acquaintance." Though possessing no parts of an orator, by his industry and application to his legislative duties, his zealous advocacy of conservative principles and his suavity of manner, he soon gained a strong position in the House. To his suavity he adds a felicitous good humor, an even temperament and happy disposition on all occasions. He has done since entering into political life what so few public men do, established a character for honesty and sincerity. Thus though possessing few of those shining qualities, which distinguish many of his colleagues, he possesses more weight and influence.

He has gained his position, not by the length of his speeches, has rarely been seen "on his legs," but by the silent, unwearied energy with which he watches and takes part in the progress of legislation. Though chosen by the particular district of Andover, he has always felt since the election that he served for the whole realm, that he did not enter the House for the specific duty of representing Andover, but for the general purpose of serving the public, that it was not for the single advantage of his own district, but for that of his country.

During numerous conversations we had the pleasure to hold with Mr. Cubitt, about the time and subsequent to the occasion of his Guildhall Hall banquet, he spoke to us of the secret of his success in life. The substance of what he said was that his rule had been deliberately to consider, before he commenced, whether a thing was practicable. If not practicable he did not attempt it.— If it was practicable he would accomplish it, if he gave sufficient pains to it, and having begun he never stopped till the thing was done.

Mr. Cubitt is now in his seventieth year, but in full possession of his health and faculties. Is of medium height, pleasing countenance and unaffected demeanor and more like a quiet country gentleman than an old politician long accustomed to public life and the blandishments of West-end society. A finer specimen of honest John Bull could not be found. Much as he has accomplished, evidently he is a man capable of greater things than he has performed. There are many such men in the world. They seem sent among men with bills of credit, which from a sense of their own strength; the plentitude of their own resources, a consciousness of their ability to secure when they please to put forth their power; they seldom draw to their full extent. Within six months of the period when these lines were written, we went to Sir William's country seat near Dorking, one of the most elegant homes of Old England, and amidst scenery unsurpassed for its beauty. And, alas, that it must be said, within a few months of this time the glorious old man sunk into an honored grave.

Returning from our visit to Mr. Cubitt's, we passed near Crawley and entered the village churchyard of Barstow.

During the short time we remained here we copied the following quaint and curious inscriptions from the tombs. They are now given *verbatim et literatim*, the grammar, rhyme and reason, capital letters, punctuation and orthography, just as we found them.

I.

All human things are subject to decay,
And when death summons mortals must obey.

II.

Of all things Certain unto our Eye,
Nothing's more Certain than we're born to die.

III.

Let angels guard the sleeping dust, My soul to Christ in whom I trust
And when I wake with great Surprise, in my Saviour hope to rise.

IV.

Spectators here behold the Earthly grave, from Death's due debts none my life would save,
Then weep not husband nor my children dear, I am not lost, but only sleeping here.

V.

We here doth lie turn'd to clay
Until the resurrection day,
When we account to God must give
How we on earth our lives did live.

VI.

Though suddenly from me my life was took
I hope the Lord has not my soul forsook,
Therefore dear friends, lament for me no more
I am not lost but only gone before.

VII.

I come into this world indeed, I saw it was in vain,
I therefore did return with speed into my God again.

VIII.

All you in strength that here pass by
Think on the Dead that doth here lie,
And when you think remember that
The grave you're sure will be your lot.

IX.

My glass is run, my time is spent
And Christ my God have for me sent.
Come trim your lamps and with your oil prepare to go
For God will call for you also.

X.

With my God I hope to rest, and with my Savior Jesus Christ,
The pains of Death I have gone through and so I bid the world adieu.

XI.

Censure not rashly nature apt to halt
That man's Onborn that dies without a fault.

XII.

Sleep on sweet babes and take thy rest
And live with Christ among the blest.

XIII.

O! husband dear my time is past
My love remained while life did last
Let none for me to sorrow take
But love my children for my sake.
My body now is turned to Dust,
My soul to Christ in whom I trust.

XIV.

While on earth I did remain
My latter end was grief and pain,
God took me when it pleased him best
My soul in Heaven I hope to Rest.

XV.

In youthful inscence my mind was cheerful bent
I did not dream of Death, till Death to me was sent
How soon the thread of life was Broke into with me.
Death may not seem near you and yet be at your feet
To meet you in that place whare joy never ends
How happy I shall be to meet there dear friends.

### XVI.

O fatal Death that could no longer spare, a tender wife and loving mother dear,
Her loss is great to those she left behind, a sincere Christian and a friend,
She has gone awhile before a debt to pay
Pray God prepare us all for that great Day.

### XVII.

When God cuts off the thread of Life
Then fatal death parts man and wife.
Therefore my Husband and children dear,
I am not lost but sleeping here.

### XVIII.

This world is a city full of crooked streets
Death is a market place we all must meet,
If life were merchandize, the Rich could buy
Then they would live and the Poor must die.

### XIX.

Here lies a woman who lived a sober life
A tender mother and a loving wife
A good neighbor and a faithful friend,
And as she lived we hope soon to end

It is remarkable that so many quaint and curious epitaphs should be found in one village cemetery. We were told the presiding genius of the place was the blacksmith. He must, however, have simply been the imitator of some preceding *genius loci*, as many of these memorials showed symptoms of great age. Leaving the sacred spot with many of Harvey's meditations passing through our mind almost as if they were our own, we stepped into a railway carriage and were soon again under the smoke of London.

## CHAPTER XII.

SANITARY SCIENCE—HOUSE AND TOWN SEWERAGE—ITS INFLU-
ENCE ON HEALTH AND LONGEVITY.

The present era is remarkable for the commencement of what may be called a new science, which has for its direct object the extension, so far as means may avail, of the average duration of human life. It would be culpable ingratitude not to hail with sanguine hope the energy of the sanitary movement which now pervades the land. It will not, perhaps, be until one or two generations, that much impression will be made by its agency on existing evils. But posterity will, probably, see the public mind submitting to be enlightened and the public will directed by men who have rendered themselves competent to the office. The result will, in all likelihood, be that, with God's blessing on the work, an incalculable amount of physical suffering will be averted, and a large accession of good in all senses of the word, obtained. Each successive generation will occupy a position, as regards health, beyond that of its predecessor, and will leave to its children a still greater immunity from the bodily ills that afflict humanity.

The health of communities may be improved, without their having any intelligent apprehension of the reasonableness of the means employed; cities and towns may be drained and ventilated, and both rich and poor participate in the advantage without one of the inhabitants understanding how the benefits were brought about. And on the other hand, influences adverse to health, may rise unsuspected from the soil, or exist in the water drawn from the bowels of the earth, and scatter disease and death broadcast through the community. While in the rural districts visiting and sojourning in many charming looking villages the general and deplorable neglect of sanitary drainage was brought prominently to our attention. No country is blest with a larger number of medical philosophers than England and in the great cities the sanitary authorities are ever on the alert. Yet in many of the towns and villages which we have visited there is no sewer system whatever and in others it is entirely inadequate. The death rate is consequently much higher than it would be but for the unnatural condition of living and the tone of health in those who survive lowered to such a point that, if they do not become actual charges on the public, they transmit an inheritance of physical weakness to their posterity.

Absolute health cannot be hoped for by any child of Adam.— We suffer for the sins of our forefathers and inherit disease and the tendencies to disease which they incurred. Causes of ill health have operated on the bodily constitution from birth. It is not in the power of more than a few, to select the circumstances under which they will live and to avail themselves of all the suggestions which the enlightened physician is now prepared to offer. The mass of mankind will remain subject to poverty. Unhealthy influences surround us unsuspected. The arts and employments life are often such as can only be rendered comparatively uninjurious. Toil of mind and body must be persisted in, although known to be excessive. Sorrow, care and anxiety must be endured by thousands, who are ignorant of the only remedy against them—a living union to God, through Christ—and necessity will continue to oppose obstacles, often insurmountable, to what the instructed judgment knows to be expedient.

There are few readers who have not been exposed to one or the other of these causes of ill-health, and who will not therefore readily concur, for the most part, in the justness of these observations. Nor is there any reason why they should not be made. They do not weaken the force of the advice, to strive to become as strong and well as possible. The whole of human life, very nearly, is a battle between good and evil; and in the matter of health, most of us have to make the best of what we would rather had been other than it is. Many will wish they had known in their youth what any one may know now, who once sees it to be his duty to try and be well. And many will wish that their parents had been taught that their children had bodies as well as minds, which also needed to be educated. But it is the rule of this life, however numerous the expectations may seem, that whatever is made the object of intelligent pursuit, is more or less completely attained. And the manly, rational determination to be well that we may be useful, will certainly have its reward. Space will not permit us to enter into a description of the various organs of the human body, and the functions to which they are subservient. Nor can we delay to consider what individual effort is required within the walls of people's houses and in the regulation of their habits in order to secure and retain good health. Common sense and the experience of mankind teach that personal cleanliness, that the function of the skin, with its millions of pores, may not be impeded; that regular exercise, proper nutrition, pure air and water are the conditions on which depend good health. There are also mental and moral causes of disease and ill health worthy of consideration, but it does not belong to our plan to refer more particularly to them at this time. It is enough for us to allude thus generally to these essential matters. We shall confine ourselves herein to a few remarks on the subject of sanitary drainage, and the deplorable results which follow its neglect.

The question has interested the writer for many years, and its pressing importance was revived in his mind, as above mentioned, by the almost total neglect of these matters in the lovely villages and towns scattered over England which he visited at the period when these notes were being collected.

It is only within a comparatively recent period that the vital importance of the subject has engaged the public attention, though the evils it is intended to mitigate, or altogether avert, are as old as civilization. The ancients fully understood the matter and the great men among the Jews, Greeks and Romans considered personal cleanliness and the surroundings of a man's dwelling, whether this was a tent, a hut or a palace, as of paramount importance. In fact in most Eastern countries, cleanliness makes a part of their religion. The Jewish and Mahometan religions enjoin various bathings, washings and purifications. No doubt the washings may appear whimsical to some, yet few things would tend more to prevent diseases than a proper attention to many of them. Were every person, for example, after visiting the sick, handling a dead body, or touching anything that might convey infection, to wash before he went into company, or sat down to meat, he would run less hazard either of catching the infection himself, or of communicating it to others. By negligence in this matter infectious diseases are spread in all places where large crowds are brought together in camps, hospitals, cities and towns. The Jews during their encampment in the wilderness, received particular instructions with respect to cleanliness, "Thou shalt have a place also without the camp, whither thou shalt go forth abroad. And thou shalt have a paddle upon thy weapon; and it shall be, when thou wilt ease thyself abroad, thou shalt dig therewith, and shalt turn back, and cover that which cometh from thee."—*Deuteronomy ch. 23, v. 12, 13.*

Pliny says the common sewers for the conveyance of filth and nastiness from the city of Rome were the greatest of all the public works; and bestows higher encomiums upon Tarquinius, Agrippa and others who made and improved them, than on those who achieved the greatest conquests. And the Emperor Trajan gave particular directions to his proconsul Pliny concerning the making of a common sewer for the health and convenience of a conquered city. ·It is, indeed, from the ancients we derive maxims to which nothing can be added. From an ancient Greek physician we get the cardinal hygienic formula, "pure air, pure water and pure soil." It was a marvel to ancient travelers on what a stupendous scale the works of Egypt were constructed to obtain a supply of sweet water from the Nile, and those of Babylon to get it from the Tigris and Euphrates. The ruins of the ancient aqueducts for supplying Rome with water from the Sabine and Albanian hills form one of the most striking features, (exciting the astonishment of all intelligent travelers,) in the landscapes of the Campagna, at the present day. The stone pavements also on which the ancient sewers were bottomed are still visible. No wanderer among the ghastly exhumations of Pompeii can have failed to observe the careful provision made for securing a supply of water, and must have viewed with astonishment and delight the many baths, some of them unburied in almost perfect condition, as they existed 2,000 years ago. Nor can the traces of the net work of drains which kept the city pure have escaped his attention.

During the dark ages when the forests of the North poured forth their hordes, wave after wave, in all the strength and vigor of primitive nature, unlettered and barbarous, the knowledge of sanitary needs perished from men's minds, and the medieval cities were cursed from time to time with plague and pestilence. During this long period of about ten centuries—from A. D. 476 to 1492—the death rate was so high from the neglect of the laws of health, that population increased at the rate of something less than one per cent. in ten years.*

A national passion for pure air and general cleanliness is supposed to have been revived in Europe by the Moors, who invaded Spain during the Middle Ages and remained there until about the period of the discovery of America.

All thoughtful men, whose attention has been directed to the subject of the public health in cities and towns agree as to the absolute necessity of a thorough system of underground drains.— Consequently, in populous communities like those of London, Paris, New York and other great cities enormous sums have been expended to attain this object. Engineers and architects tell us, if common sense does not, that the waste of such communities cannot be accommodated, or be rendered innocent by any number of cess pools, however numerous or well constructed; that a system of cess pools or open vaults tend to saturate the soil with fetid matter. Around each cess pool, for a considerable distance, the soil is poisoned. "External to this limit," says a high authority

---

*For an intensely interesting account of the Epidemics of the Middle Ages, the reader is referred to Dr. J. F. C Hecker's great work

on these matters, "the filth is destroyed by the action of the oxygen of the air, which is a great purifier. Within the limits named the animal matter preponderates either constantly, or at some period of the year. They may remain simply disagreeable without being dangerous, and may again, in a way whose details have as yet escaped investigation, become the seed bed or the nursery of the infection that breaks out in fevers and dysentery. The danger increases as the quantity of filth and the number of its receptacles increase. To cover them up does not necessarily remove the evil. The putrid matter soaks into the soil and moves upward and downward in it with the motion of the soil water."

It is a truism that the health of man requires that he should have pure air, pure water and clean soil. Common sense and practical experience alike condemn the pollution of the air we breathe or the water we drink. And it has been well said that "we live or we die, live well or miserably, live our full term or perish prematurely, accordingly as we shall wisely or otherwise determine." In other words, our lives are short or long just in proportion to the care we pay to the laws of health. It is a matter which addresses itself to the builder of an isolated house who, if wise, will make provision against allowing the soil to become polluted by the accumulation of waste which follows occupation. And by placing his kitchen, stables, pig sties and other outbuildings at such a distance as to render any necessary visitation of the air from them innocuous.

If these country houses on healthy sites and in the vicinity of running streams of pure water, are liable to become centres of disease, by neglect of cleanliness, how greatly is the danger increased as population grows and houses multiply and are brought together in cities and towns. The danger is intensified by the further fact that in a town the filth in one house is the cause of disease and death in others. It is not a private, but a public question, a matter affecting all, in what state each individual inhabitant of a city or town keeps his house or grounds. No one should be allowed, or is, in a well regulated town, to keep upon his premises any festering organic matter, cess pools, pig sties, decaying vegetables, or any other refuse that endangers the lives of his neighbors. The health of each is important to all and it is the duty of all to join in securing it. If they cannot be induced to do so by an appeal to their good sense, they should be forced to it by municipal regulations.

When the municipal authorities are so blind or indifferent as to disregard these laws, sooner or later they are spoken to in terrible language—the language of disease and death. It has been wisely ly said "that pestilence is the angel with which it would seem, it has pleased the Almighty to awaken the human race to the duty of self preservation; plagues are not committing havoc perpetually, but turning men to destruction and then suddenly ceasing that they may consider. As the lost father speaks to the family and the slight epidemic to the city, so the pestilence speaks to the nation."

In cities and towns it is obviously impossible for works of general drainage to be carried out by any than public authority. In some European and South American cities, notably in Cadiz and in Rio de Janerio, joint stock companies have been formed 'under municipal authority for general drainage. They are usually denominated "Public Improvement Companies," and all houses are required by law to communicate with the extensive ramifications of sewers thus opened, and to pay to the companies a certain annual rent. These companies keep the city clean and healthy, and usually declare a semi-annual dividend at the rate of from ten to twelve per cent. When such works are executed by the municipalities under direction of boards of health, the boards are invested with plenary powers to the end that the works may fulfil every proper condition. The boards require all houses within the corporate limits to connect with the sewers; they refuse to allow the erection of dwellings on unhealthy sites, they provide ventilation for the main sewers, constructed in a way to prevent the poisonous gasses from affecting the inhabitants, thus lessening the chances of the introduction of gasses from the public sewers into the private houses, and they require all private cess pools or other repositories of filth to be closed.

All authorities on the subject agree that the individual housekeeper has these problems to solve: "1. To protect his house against excessive damp in its walls, in its cellars and where practicable in the surrounding atmosphere. 2. To provide for the perfect and instant removal of all matter of fluid or semi-fluid organic waste. 3. To provide a sufficient supply of pure water for domestic use. 4. To guard against the evils arising from the decomposition of organic matter under the house. 5. To remove all sources of offense and danger which may affect the atmosphere about the house. 6. To prevent the insidious entrance into the house, through communications with the sewers, cess pools, &c., of poisonous gasses resulting from the decomposition of the refuse of his own household with which a common sewer may bring him into communication.

And in the sewerage of towns the main drain should conform to the following conditions: It should be perfectly tight from one end to the other, have a continuous fall from the head to ;the outlet, be perfectly ventilated, so that the injurious gasses that necessarily arise from the decomposition of matters carried along in the water or which are left clinging to the sewer walls, shall be diluted with fresh air, and shall have such means of escape as will prevent them from forcing their way into the dwellings through the traps of the house drains. It should also be constructed so as to admit of its being inspected and of its being flushed with pure water. This ought to be done several times during the week in summer. Its size and form should be so adjusted to its work, or to its flushing appliances that the usual dry weather flow may be made to keep it free from silt and organic deposits. A sewer deficient in any one of these particulars is unsafe.

Properly constituted drains, we may add, not only bear off the filth of towns, the source of atmospheric impurity, and thereby render unfit for occupation many of those damp, dark, unventilated basements which are so prolific in tubercular diseases, but lessen, if they do not altogether prevent, other diseases which are brought on by a cold, saturated air and the want of light and ventilation. The importance of light to health is worthy of particular mention in this connection. Whether your house be large or small, give it light. There is no home so likely to be unhealthy as a dark and gloomy house or room. Light is necessary in order that the animal spirits may be kept refreshed and invigorated. No one is happy who in working hours is in a gloomy house or room. The gloom of the prison has been considered a part of the punishment of the prisoner, and it is so. The mind is saddened in a house that is not flushed with light, and when the mind is saddened the whole physical power soon suffers. The heart beats languidly, the blood flows slowly, the breathing is imperfect, the oxydation of the blood is reduced and the conditions are laid for the development of many wearisome and unnecessary constitutional failures and sufferings. Without light none of the functions of nutrition or growth will prosper; it is positively necessary to digestion.— The evolution of the tadpole into the frog is prevented if the animal is kept in the dark. The narrow street and confined dwelling are prejudicial to health, not simply because the air is pent up, but because the blessing of light is scantily enjoyed. Gas light when introduced into these dismal cellars which many living beings are still permitted to inhabit in large cities, is the bearer and sustainer of life; it acts too, as a powerful disinfectant, counteracting putrifaction, and destroying the spores of disease, rendering harmless the poisonous vapors in the air. The fact was frequently mentioned to the writer while in England that small-pox seldom, if ever, entered the houses of those who used gas. We have also been told that children suffering with the whooping cough are quickly cured by frequenting houses where gas is used or manufactured.

While unable from actual observation to confirm these statements we have no doubt of their reliability and strongly urge in the cause of health the general use of gas light. By substituting it for oil we are delivered from the danger of explosions, of being burnt to a cinder, and banish from our houses the offensive odor of burning wicks, the grease and filth of the cheap and foully smelling lamp, and any ærial poison they may scatter through the apartments.

The principles on which houses and towns should be drained having been thus briefly explained, we must here point out the practical results, in the way of improved health, which have followed the introduction of a sewer system in a number of English towns.

Dr. Latham gives the following table, showing the effect on health of sanitary works in different towns in England:

| | Population in 1861. | Average deaths in 1,000 before drained. | After drainage. | Reduction of typhoid fever, rate per cent. |
|---|---|---|---|---|
| Banbury, | 10,288 | 23.4 | 20.5 | 48 |
| Cardiff, | 32.954 | 33.3 | 22.6 | 40 |
| Croydon, | 30.229 | 23.7 | 18.6 | 63 |
| Davis, | 23,108 | 22 1 | 20.9 | 36 |
| Ely, | 7,847 | 23.9 | 20.5 | 56 |
| Leicester, | 18,056 | 26.4 | 25.2 | 48 |
| Macelesfield, | 27,475 | 29.8 | 23.7 | 48 |
| Merthyr, | 52,778 | 33.2 | 26.2 | 50 |
| Newport, | 24,752 | 31.5 | 21.6 | 36 |
| Rugby | 7,818 | 19 1 | 18.9 | 10 |
| Salisbury | 9,030 | 27.5 | 21.9 | 75 |
| Warwick | 10,570 | 22 7 | 21 0 | 52 |

It must be remembered too, that this great saving of life has been the result of works that are far from perfect. The average reduction of typhoid rate was 47⅜ per cent., nearly one half. It is believed that perfect drainage and ventilation, with a supply of pure water and plenty of light, would prevent the occurrence of a single case. Comment upon such facts is unnecessary. They tell their own tale. It has been truly said that a man is born to health and longevity; disease is abnormal, and death, except from old age, is accidental, and both are preventable by human agencies.— Those, therefore, who recognize the close relations between disease and its preventable causes, should band together in every town and city, and unite with the public authorities in executing plans for promoting and securing the public health. The other class of ignorant, indifferent and slothful persons cannot be aroused until the outbreak of some malignant disease, when it is too late to commence sprinkling lime and other disinfectants in street gutters, cleaning out cess pools, lighting up cellars, digging drains and searching after a supply of pure water.

It cannot be denied that this important question is one greatly ignored in healthy communities and in towns which having long existed as villages, cannot realize its deep importance when they have grown into populous cities. There are few persons, indeed, whose attention has not been specially drawn to the subject, who realize the terrible significance of an increased death rate. It is a question which involves not only the health of individuals and communities, but the longevity of generations. In fact the greatest and most distressing obstacles to the advancement of the human race is the impairment of individual lives by defective health. If a whole generation of men and women could live through the present ordinary forty or fifty years of life, free from periods of illness so serious as to interrupt the full exercise of their bodily and mental powers, it is plain that the unimpeded physical labor and mental activity of such a generation would carry forward the economies and intellectual progress of the country in which they lived with a success and velocity not to be calculated. No sources of suffering or sorrow are more common in the world as it now exists than the spectacle of noble natures and noble enterprises reduced to failure and premature death In millions of cases the community invests, in no figurative sense, an extensive capital in the rearing and teaching of groups and classes of investigators, inventors and thinkers, and finds itself suddenly deprived by some malignant fever or wave of sickness of all return for the sacrifices it has made; and so the present generation is made poorer and the heritage of coming generations is made less. As all accumulation and progress is the result of labor, it follows that both must be obtained in the highest degree where the laborers enjoy the most vigorous health throughout the largest number of years. The poverty and backwardness of the Middle ages of Europe were mainly caused by the prevalence of disease and by a death rate so high as to limit the increase of population, as we have said, in some countries to less than ten per cent.

For many years in England, France, and in the Eastern and Northern States, the governments and peoples have been more or less systematically at work devising plans and executing improvements with a view to lessening the prevalence of disease and prolonging human life ; and for the last few years the force of public opinion has led the authorities of the larger cities, North and South, East and West, to regard sanitary control as an essential part of local administration. Such fearful scourges as the yellow fever last year in Memphis, Grenada and other Southern cities, have effectually aroused those afflicted communities to the necessity of action, and already extensive works have been carried out in some of them, notably in Memphis. There is reason to hope and believe that this enlightened policy will effectually protect them against future visitations of pestilence. In all of our larger cities a sanitary staff has been appointed, hospitals built for small pox and fever cases, and for the control and limitation of epidemic diseases. Among the powers conferred upon these sanitary boards or staffs, is the important one of demolishing unwholesome dwellings, and prohibiting the erection of houses upon unhealthy sites. These old buildings were the permanent seats of disease and crime.— Where and whenever extensive drains have been constructed and a supply of pure water has been obtained for domestic use and with which to flush the sewers, the most gratifying diminution of the death rates has indicated the favorable effects of these sanitary measures. This has not only been the case in England, as we have seen from Dr. Latham's tables, but in every European country and in our own. In fact the death rate has declined in almost exact proportion to the energy and extent of the sanitary measures.

It is to be hoped that these cheering facts may have their influence upon the authorities of our prosperous and growing "city of the hills," and that something may be done by them in this direction before we are reminded of the necessity of such works by a visitation of disease and the decimation of our population by death. When undertaken, let us hope that the work may be upon a comprehensive plan for the accommodation of every part of the city and large enough to meet the wants of a much greater population than Staunton can now number. That our population is destined to be very much increased by accessions from abroad and within a comparative brief period, there is every reason to believe.

With the introduction of pure water into towns, the abolition of under-ground and cellar-dwellings, still so common in the crowded parts of London, Paris and New York and all large cities; the construction of drains and sewers, ventilated by shafts fixed at their highest points and carried above the eaves of the houses, the rapid conveyance of all excretal matters long distances from the towns and the utilization of all refuse, animal or vegetable manure, typhus and typhoid fever, once so common in those centres of population has become of comparatively rare occurrence; and all other infectious diseases have been largely reduced in amount while the general health has been improved.

That in any large city among its working classes typhus and typhoid fever should be nearly extinguished implies a diminution of human pain and misery which cannot be estimated. How terrible is the condition of the widows and orphans deprived of the earnings of the husband and father by premature death at entrance or in the midst of the productive period of life, for the most prevalent and fatal forms of sickness among the poorer classes are deadly fevers. If typhus can be reduced to a very low point, a latent resource of civilization will be developed in a most obvious and beneficent manner, and a potent mode of enlarging the means of enjoyment and the possibilities of raising the race to a higher level of physical and moral health.

The philosopher's ideal of human health and the duration of human life may not be, with our present means and knowledge, Utopian, but it is a noble ideal to keep before us. Life extends naturally to five times the number of years required in the various orders of animals to arrive at maturity. The elephant is young at thirty, and lives to 150; the horse matures at five, and lives to 25 years; the lion and ox mature at four, and live to 20; the cat matures in eighteen months, and its full life is 7½ years. Man arrives at maturity at about twenty, and ought therefore to live to one hundred. The body ceases to grow at the end of twenty years, but it does not cease to increase till forty, at which age it reaches its most complete physical condition. During the next thirty years, or to the age of 70, called the period of invigoration, all the functions become or ought to become more certain, all of its organization more perfect. At seventy old age should begin and last for about fifteen years; from eighty-five to one hundred there should be ripe old age, not accompanied by disease or pain, but marked by a gradual subsidence of the vital functions.

The possibility of arriving at this great prolongation of the active, investigating, inventive and thinking years of human life is the most limitless of all the latent resources of civilization. With the present average longevity in the United States of thirty to forty years the course of public policy, peace or war, wisdom or folly, is determined by men of imperfect and misleading experience and reflection which are attained at about thirty. In a community living on the average twice as long as at the present, the control of affairs would be in the hands of men fortified by the large wisdom of 50 or 90 years; and every question, public or private, would be judged by men undisturbed in the exercise of their faculties by defective health or distressing pain. Consider even now what a bound forward we should accomplish if for a year there were not a single ailment in the land. Not only would the absence of pain and disease prolong and render more productive in every material and mental sense the application of human labor and enterprise; but among its earliest effects would be the development of the degrees of symmetry and beauty in the human frame. Deformity is no part of human nature and to any one who observes it is plain that nature never ceases in its efforts to diminish or cure it; and what is more, nature is ever on the alert to translate into perfection of faculty and form any improved circumstance of physical condition in food, clothing, shelter, or the abolition of degrading labor which may chance to be arrived at by the community; and so it comes about that the eye of reflective science, aided by the growing certainties of knowledge, can even now see that the tendencies toward a higher physical life within the reach of human power are beyond a doubt.

Human life is so transitory, under all circumstances, that no effort to prolong it should be lost. Pliny, the younger, thus speaks on this subject, and we cannot close this chapter better than by quoting the words of that intelligent and highly educated man. "Is there anything in nature," says he, "so short and limited as human life, even at its longest? Does it not seem to you but yesterday that Nero was alive? and yet not one of those who were consuls in his reign now remains! Though why should I wonder at this? Lucius Piso used to say, he did not see one person in the Senate whose opinion he had consulted when he was consul; in so short a space is the very term of life of such a multitude of beings comprised! so that to me those Royal tears seem not only worthy of pardon but of praise. For it is said that Xerxes, on surveying his immense army, wept at the reflection that so many thousand lives would in such a short space of time be extinct. The more ardent therefore should be our zeal to lengthen out this frail and transient portion of existence, if not by our deeds yet certainly by our literary accomplishments; and since long life is denied us, let us transmit to posterity some memorial that we have at least lived."

## CHAPTER XIII.

THE ROYAL MINT—A DISTINGUISHED MAN AND A CLUB CUB—
SIR JOHN SHELLEY—THE ILLUSIONS OF HISTORY.

Few strangers visit London without making an effort to see the Mint. One of the stock sights, it is pleasantly associated with new sovereigns and the jingling music of gold—"bright, yellow, hard and cold." Nor is the Royal mint without great memories, for the celebrated Sir Isaac Newton was once master of it. Antiquarians claim still greater associations for the spot, asserting that Cæsar coined money at this identical locality during the Roman occupation.

The American is not long in England, or, indeed, in any part of Europe, without learning that history is one thing and tradition another and a very different thing. What is commonly called history is worth knowing, though if we are to confide in Neibuhr, Miller and other modern philosophical investigators, there is more of fiction than of fact even in history. This is especially and very naturally the case as to ancient history which has found, as to the Romans, for example, such a learned sponsor for its authority as Rollin. As for the stories or traditions related by guides to gaping tourists, to be retold on the traveler's return home, and many of which find their way into the average guide book, they are the merest stuff and rubbish, pure inventions, baseless as the fabric of a vision. Stories no more to be believed than are those "interesting" relics to be taken as genuine which are manufactured wholesale at Birmingham, to be retailed by vendors of curiosities as relics from the various battle-fields of Europe; spots so industriously visited by pilgrim cockneys and such sort of peripatetics. These wanderers who annually go forth in search of the picturesque, come back heavily laden—not always, however, with new ideas. One has Josephine's watch; another Peter the Great's punch bowl, another the first cannon ball fired at the siege of Metz, and a fourth the sword carried by the Bertrand du Guelin in the French wars against the English. But to be serious, two classes of people generally go to Europe for the summer, instead of the watering places at home—pleasure seekers and merchants engaged in the foreign trade. The latter generally take their families, or two or three of them at least.

This increasing international intercourse produces only good results on both sides of the Atlantic. These gigantic steamers, flying to and fro between Europe and America, like shuttles in a loom, are weaving the nations closer and closer together. Trade is benefitted, opinions are modified, manners improved and minds are expanded. Traveling is, indeed, the very best means of education; and yet something beside travel is essential to the mere pleasure seeker.

> "A man may have studied and traveled abroad,
> May sing like Apollo and paint like a Claud,
> May speak all the languages south of the pole,
> And have every gift in the world but a soul."

It is to be feared that the majority of those who now travel abroad belong to the class described by Lord Bacon: "He that traveleth into a country before he has some entrance into the language, goeth to school and not to travel, and he knows not what things are worthy to be seen, what acquaintances they are to seek, what exercise or discipline the place yieldeth." In response to what kind of society the traveler should seek his lordship continues: "As for the acquaintance which is to be sought in travel, that which is most of all profitable, is acquaintance with the secretary and employed men of ambassadors, for so in traveling in one country he shall seek the experience of many. Let him also see and visit eminent persons in all kinds, which are of great name abroad, that he may be able to tell how the life agreeth with the same." How few are governed by this safe counsel! How many return, bringing only spurious relics and the fabulous lore of gossipping guides.

But starting out to strip history and tradition, in a single sentence, of some of their illusions, we are digressing into other matters. Let us return by assuring the reader that we want faith in all stories connecting the Roman Dictator with money making on the spot now occupied by the Royal Mint. "Money making" was something to which the great Julius never descended, though he would have excelled in it, no doubt, had he chosen. He possessed, as all the world knows, that kind of universality of genius and practical sense, which his modern imitator epitomizes in these words, "There is nothing in war," said Napoleon. "which I cannot do by my own hands. If there is nobody to make gunpowder I can manufacture it. The gun carriages I know how to construct. If it is necessary to make cannon at the forge I can make them. The details of working them in battle, if necessary to teach, I shall teach them. In administration it is I alone who arrange the finances." Without doubt Cæsar would have done all these as well if not better than Napoleon, but as we shall probably have occasion to refer to him again—to his management of his finances and his campaigns—before bidding adieu to the reader, we shall now pass on and occupy ourselves for the present with things belonging to the present.

Supplied with a permit to visit the mint, obtained from the master by our friend, Mr. William Boyle, of Somersetshire, we appeared one fine morning before the gates. Here we were politely received and ushured in by a liveried servant.

While in the ante room, we saw from a card on the wall the various parts to be visited. We shall be happy if our reader derives a tithe of the pleasure this visit afforded us from the necessarily short account we shall give of it.

Our guide, a man of much intelligence, of much suavity and patience, conducted us first to the smelting house, where we saw six burning furnaces and in each a pot full of molten gold. .

He informed us that the gold was received from the Bank of England in sets of 100 ignots in the form of bricks. The ingots weighing 14 carrots each are brought to standard gold by an alloy of copper or silver. While our guide was making these explanations, the preparations were going on to decant the fluid.

The inside of the moulds were rubbed with oil that the metal might run more freely. A workman then brings a pot full of the melted metal. As it is too heavy to be easily held or steadily poured, it is placed in a ring and supported by a crane. The vessel is steadied in the hands of the workmen by means of a rope attached to the lever and which is held by another person. He is thus able to empty the vessel into the moulds with ease and steadiness.

It was a most interesting sight and we never wearied of looking at the light orange hue of the stream of gold. As the metal ran into the moulds it was sometimes accompanied by small pieces of coke, but these from their less specific gravity floated to the surface and were easily separated. In a few moments the metal in the moulds appeared of a greenish white color, but this was merely a superficial crust, not thicker than a sheet of paper. The moulds were now disjointed, being formed of iron bars, and out came the blocks of gold which were immediately plunged into cold water.

While in this room a large number of unstamped sovereigns or blanks as they are called, were thrown into the pots, and then passed into the moulds. These imperfect coins, the cuttings, and all loose gold is thus disposed of, and the process of smelting entails a loss of only one and a half grains on the pound troy.

From this room we passed to the next, that was designated on the card we had seen, as the rolling room. Here we were literally surrounded by bars and sheets of the precious metal. The bars brought to this room to be rolled are about three-quarters of a yard long. They are presented to the rollers, by which they are laminated and reduced to the determined thickness, which is seven grains too heavy. The sheets into which the bars are reduced are of three kinds and of different thicknesses and are termed fillets, ribbons, or lengths, and to bring them to their proper conditions there are in this room six gradations of rollers. It not unfrequently happens that a difficulty occurs in the process of rolling, and that the gold when about three-fourths rolled becomes hard and brittle, and entirely unfit for stamping. When this occurs it is annealed in this manner: The lengths are placed in copper cases of cylindrical form, and are again subjected to the furnace. When taken out and dipped in water they become soft as lead.

While in this room we were shown the circular shears, or horizontal circles of iron, which are kept constantly revolving by machinery. These shears which "never tire" cut inch thick metal without a moment's pause or cessation. They are considered so dangerous that they are fenced in and secured by a guard.

In order to ascertain whether the fillets, sheets or lengths of gold are of the same thickness as the outside rim, several holes in a zigzag form are punched in them before the stamping process commences. Every evening before the men are allowed to leave the mint the gold that is weighed out to them in the morning is weighed back in the evening. During the day no workman is allowed to leave the mint, consequently there is a cooking room within the walls, where all are supplied with food. The cooking is all done by gas so as to prevent the necessity for bringing in coal, and to diminish the opportunities for dishonesty. Instances of theft are rare, but some instances are on record, of which the following are two:

An old soldier, who was once in the employment of the mint, watched a *moneyer*, (these were persons who formerly contracted with the government to coin gold and silver—a system now entirely abolished,) as he was carrying various bags of gold, struck him down and locked him in. The rogue then seized four of the bags and ran off and got upon board an American ship. He was soon tracked by those blood hounds of Themis, the Bow Street officers, and brought back, tried and hanged. The other case was that of a workman who was tempted by the gold passing through his hands to retain 60 sovereigns, with which he disappeared. Though the most vigilant search was instituted he was never afterwards heard of. It is surmised that the receivers of the stolen property murdered the man and disposed of his body. These robberies awakened the vigilance of the authorities, rules were established to prevent them, and they have consequently not been repeated.— To enforce the rules of the mint a company of regular troops are kept on guard at the establishment day and night.

Proceeding, we next arrived at the adjusting room, where all the fillets, sheets, &c, are carried for examination and adjustment. By adjustment is meant seeing that every part of the sheets is of exact size and weight of every other part. When the sheets are taken to this room they are seven grains heavier than necessary. Each length of gold is inserted about two inches into a flatting machine. The part so inserted is "pinched" half as thick as the remainder of the bar. It is then taken to a machine, called a draw bench, where the pinched part is inserted between the steel cylinders. The sheet being drawn through, is cut into four lengths, and passed to the "tryers" who take each length, and with a punch, the size of a sovereign, cuts out a block, and it is invariably the standard weight. In this room there are twelve cutters, or presses with an extreme pressure of one hundred tons. The action of these cutters is vertical, and at each descent it cuts a sovereign out of the golden sheet. The piece falls into a box below. While we were watching the process, our friend, the parson, counted nearly a hundred sovereigns which had dropped into the box. When full this box is emptied into trays, of which there were many in the room, each containing five thousand sovereigns or about $25,000. The remnants of gold left from this process are called "scissel" from the latin word *scissum*, to cut, and are re-melted. The sovereigns are taken from this room into what is called the sizing room, where each piece is weighed to ascertain whether it is standard weight, then reweighed by another set of men called cheatmen. They are then passed, if all right, to the *ringers*, who sound them on iron anvils and reject those which do not ring. The others are passed into the *strongholds*, which are fastened with formidable doors, with double locks, requiring two keys to open them, and these keys are kept by two different persons.

From these strongholds the blank sovereigns, which are very hard and brittle, are taken to the annealing room to be softened and tempered. These blanks, in iron boxes, are put into the furnace. They are then boiled in diluted sulphuric acid in order to remove every particle of impurity. They are then put into an oven to dry and are afterwards shaken in beechwood sawdust, that they may be clean and warm to receive the impression. Great care and delicacy are required in these processes, for the blanks if heated even a very few degrees more than enough, wonld run into a mass, and if not sufficiently heated, condensation would take place and the impression would be spoiled.

The blanks are now transferred to the press room where they are stamped and made coins. Our guide explained in an admirable manner how this was done. He first showed the lower part of the press, round the top of which he placed a milled collar. This collar rested on a spring. He then placed the blank upon the lower die, and showed how the spring causes the collar to rise. Then the upper die descends with great force, by mere impetus, stamps the impression and expands the gold till it fits and fills the collar, and at the same time the milling is transferred to the edge of the piece. The dies are made of cast steel very finely tempered and engraved.

The presses stamp upon an average sixty pieces per minute, or 3,600 per hour, or in a day of ten hours 36,000 pieces or $180,000. The eight presses in a room, if they were all in operation, would thus stamp in a day 288,000 pieces, or $1,440,000. The last room to which we were conducted was the weighing room, where the blanks are weighed in the most perfect of all weighing machines— Colton's Automaton Balance. These blanks subjected to the weighing process turn out to be three kinds, the heavy, medium, or light. The first and last are recast, the medium only are retained for circulation, although they are not quite standard weight.— Not one sovereign in a thousand is standard weight and yet by the balances in use the 1-150th part of a farthing's value can be weighed. The most delicate scales, deflect eight times out of ten with the thousandth part of a grain, the smallest fraction used for practicable purposes. The reason blank sovereigns only a little above the medium are rejected and remelted, when the merest touch of the file would bring them to the proper weight, is because there would be loss, waste and temptation, and besides it would be an imperfect mode of coining.

Walking out from this instructive visit we ruminated as we proceeded towards the tower, upon

"Gold! gold! gold! gold!
Bright and yellow, hard and cold,
Molten, graven, hammer'd and rolled;
Heavy to get, and light to hold!
Hoarded, bartered, bought and sold."

On our return from "the city" Mr. Boyle, who had previously asked us to dine with him, said that we should have the company of Sir John Shelley. We enjoyed much the prospect of meeting this veteran, having heard him speak two or three times in the House of Commons, and having heard a great deal in society of him, of his advanced liberal or Americanized opinions and his vigorous forensic efforts and encounters in the House with the champions of the tory party.

A few minutes before the dinner hour, Sir John made his appearance in company with a young man by the name of Henniker. This young gentleman had that well-known audacity of manner and address which belong to the "howling swell" of Picadilly or West end "Club Cub," a coarse bark-like laugh, and spoke with a drawl. He interposed his exclamations with many aw-aws, as "God bless my soul! aw." "You don't say so, aw." "I cawn't make it out! aw, aw!" and yawning slightly, he would subside for a time into a placid stupidity.

With Sir John, we need scarcely say, we were much better pleased. His presence and manner, let us add before going further, impressed us more in the parlor than in the Senate. His personal appearance was striking and his manner what the French style *distingue*. Though at first he was what the English are apt to be, a little stiff, awkward and embarrassed, he soon became easy, then free, (the sherry had passed several times before this) and finally delightful company. Under what the middle class styled his "aristocratic demeanor," we discovered a kindly nature and generous soul; an unpretending sturdy John Bull, uniting at once the gentleman and the man of business.

He evinced a strong wish to talk upon the subject of America and asked numerous questions as to the practical workings of our Republican institutions, making what we considered a just and sensible observation that he did not consider the question of Republican government, as at all involved in the issue of the civil war, that the war was something totally separate and apart from the principles of government, and the result of a difference in the property and institutions of the Northern and Southern States and in the people themselves. Republican government was not in his opinion on its trial in the United States, as the Tories wish us to believe, and however the war may end, said he, you will have only Republics, the U. S. Government restored, or Republics North and South. He further said that he had long advocated the assimilation of English laws to those of America, had favored the vote by ballot, the extension of the suffrage to all rate payers, and triennial parliaments. Indeed, said he, I have been ironically called the people's idol and seriously denounced as the mob orator. Hereupon he laughed heartily. And this, too, said he, recovering from his merriment, though I represent in my person the Barony of Sudely, which has been in abeyance five centuries, and which I claim and shall seek to have revived, and off he went again with loud laughter.

During the dinner he informed us that he was returned to Parliament for the first time at the general election in 1852 as a member for Westminster. His object in desiring a seat in the House was to assist in the development of the great work of reform, so far as it was compatible with the state of public advancement and the theory of the existing British Constitution. "I was then and I suppose I ought to say am now, a patriot devoted to the interest of my country," continued Sir John with a twinkle in his eye, "though Dr. Johnson once testily defined patriotism as the last refuge of the scoundrel." It is needless to say that this is not my definition. This remark and his comical manner again set the table in a roar. The conversation now branched off for some time into channels suggested by his remarks. After awhile, when we had subsided into a more quiet mood, Sir John said that his colleague in this Westminster contest was Sir de Lacy Evans, (subsequently so much distinguished as a Major General in the army of the Crimea,) and the Tory candidate, Viscount Maidstone, son of Sir Finch-Hatton, Earl of Winchilsea, and Mr. William Coningham.

This election gave rise to immense excitement, and in the midst of the *furor* it was thought the seat of Sir de Lacy was in great jeopardy, but on the close of the polls, the General was elected by a majority of 400, while mine was over 700. So much for a mob orator.

We informed him that we had twice heard him address the House, at which the Honorable Baronet seemed much gratified. We did not tell him our opinion, that while a frequent speaker he has no pretentions to oratory. His delivery is bold and rapid and without the slightest attempt at effect, he conveys to his auditors the most truthful expression of his political statements.

While the friend of progress and reform, Sir John has not, nor could he ever become a radical of the modern type. He sympathized largely with the young England movement, but he had "no objection to the lord, provided he was a gentle one." The course of the Tory party hurried him to lengths of which otherwise he never would have dreamed. He might have been utilized by a wiser aristocracy as a wiser Church of England might have utilized Wesley. However they lost their chance, and Sir John Shelley had come to entertain principles utterly at variance with any form of Toryism whatever. Sir John Shelley is proverbial in private life for his known uniformity of conduct; from temperament not less than policy, he is ever consistent; at all times conciliating; neither harsh nor dogmatical to those differing from him in opinion, but ready to extend the olive branch to his opponents when the heat of controversy has subsided. Through his active career as a public man he has been characterised by his strict sense of honor, his uniform urbanity and kindness. His whole career illustrates well the remark of Saurin, "True courtesy of manners is one of the fruits of the love of God. It is Christian benevolence carried into detail, and operating upon all circumstances of social life."

## CHAPTER XIV.

### THE DERBY DAY—BRITISH LOVE OF SPORT—THE POPULARITY OF THE TURF—THE CELEBRATED RACER ECLIPSE.

Sir Francis Bacon, administering some wholesome advice to his patron and friend, George Villiers, afterwards Duke of Buckingham, the favorite and prime minister of James I, declares that in the courts of princes "there must be times for pastimes and disports;" and he recommends the "riding of the great horse, the tilts, the barriers, tennis and hunting, which are more for the health and strength of those who exercise them, than in an effeminate way to please themselves and others." How far this sage counsel may have contributed to the modern prevalent taste, among all classes of English, for out-doors sports, it is difficult to say. That they love fresh air—boating, running, leaping, boxing, wrestling and the quoit—in a word all kinds of athletic games and open air exercises and manly sports, is undeniable. There never is a horse race without an Englishman being, if possible, there or thereabouts. The good effect of these habits, too, is easily recognized in the ruddy complexions and robust constitutions of both men and women in their breed of good horses. While the women certainly do not engage in steeple chasing, pigeon shooting and such like convivialty, they are great pedestrians and understand the importance to health, mental and physical, of exercise and wholesome sports.—Fond of archery, lawn tennis, croquet, some of them have been known in times past to act the jockey, many at the present day follow the hounds, and almost all attend the races.

The Empress of Austria, Elizabeth Amelia Eugenie, daughter of the Duke Maximilian-Joseph, and cousin to the King of Bavaria, an English woman in her tastes, who is specially given up to the chase, has within the past month of 1880, sent from Austria to Ireland, fifty hunters and a train of servants, that she might engage in this healthful exhilirating sport. Only four of these steeds are intended for her Majesty's own use, the others will be used by her attendants.

Such habits not only improve the physique, but refresh and invigorate the spirits, and the stranger quickly discovers, after mingling with the British in the mother country, that the merrie isle is inhabited by a jolly race. He is not long in learning that the common estimate of John Bull by the outside world is a false and erroneous estimate; that the sturdy Briton is not, as many imagine, of a cold and arid nature, morose, unsympathetic and deficient in the finer feelings of human nature. On the contrary, quite the reverse. Under his frigid exterior there lies a genial temper and kindly nature. Break through the ice and you find a living stream beneath. However reserved, haughty and blunt John Bull may appear to the world, he is in reality, as all discover who know him well, an honest, generous, good fellow, fond of society, of sport, of sherry. The heat of his nature may be latent, but it only needs the friction of society, the sight of woe, the presence of danger, to disengage, set it free.

Entertaining these views, we need scarcely say that we have found little among them to justify the remark of Addison in the Spectator: "The English are naturally fanciful, and by that gloominess and melancholly of temper which is so frequent in our nation, we are often disposed to many wild notions, to which others are not liable."

Decidedly British in our tastes we looked forward with no small pleasure to witnessing the great national Olympic on the Derby day. Roused up on the morning of the 4th of June by an unusual uproar in the streets, we quickly despatched our breakfast and issued forth. All London was astir for the Derby, the event with which the day was big. The streets were crowded with every description of vehicles from the coster-monger's donkey cart, to the fancy gentleman's four-in hand. Business was at a stand still and the mews and slums, as well as the squares and avenues, poured forth a continuous stream of human beings. Lords and gentlemen, bankers and merchants, shop keepers and workmen, men, women and children, all came forth, bent upon a spree. A single instinct seemed to animate the entire mass. Everywhere in the streets, vehicles stood taking in their living freight and no end of boxes of "wittels" and baskets of bottles. Flags were suspended from the carriages and the horses were gaily decked with ribbons; the common people hurrying on foot to the downs, where in their holiday attire, though out upon a "rough roll and tumble excursion," while the "swells" who were perched upon the tops of the omnibusses or peered from the cabs were smartly dight, and thickly veiled in light blue or violet falls. The fair sex mustered in immense force, in summer dress and crowded the vehicles or trudged on the side walks. Many of the lower orders who, doubtful of their powers to do the journey on foot in a single morning, even under the inspiration of gin toddy and rum bitters, had started the day before and were now camped upon the field or were setting forth on their journey from the road side pot-house. The roads leading to the course were filled with a double line of vehicles, crowds of horsemen and pedestrians and at the distance of twelve miles from London were so blocked up that frequent halts were necessary. From the windows of many of the houses on the route flags were displayed, the union jack and the tricolor, and indeed the flags of all nations, conspicuous among them the stars and stripes, notwithstanding the "Harvey Birch" affair, the Trent affair and affairs generally on the American side of the Atlantic. Many private ensigns fluttered in the morning breeze, giving notice of Tom and Jerry shops and other public places where cordials and bitters and other things good and bad might be had for the money. The road was further enlivened by rustics who gathered on the side walks and stared open eyed and open mouthed at the cavalcade.

Mounting a cob, we had been previously invited to make one of a party of four, we joined the crowd unwilling to lose so fine an opportunity of seeing the people and increasing our knowledge of their manners and customs. But for this wish to see them to the best advantage on a gala day, we should have made our way to Epsom by train.

The first public house of consequence which lay in our route was the famous South London Inn called the Elephant and Castle. Here great crowds halted for the refreshment of 'arf and 'arf or a gill of "old tom" the reputation of the E. and C. wines and viands being unbounded. Following suite, we too stopped to wash down the dust with the famous "hale." D. Forbes Campbell, the friend and intimate of Napoleon III, (a relative of Lord Clyde) and the translator of the Emperor's Idees Napoleoniennes into English, Osborne Stock, afterwards M. P. for Carlow burroughs, and Capt. Manners made up our party. After partaking of a mug of the bitter the writer wished to be off, but Manners insisted with such good natured pertinacity on the party stopping for a second tankard and a smoke, that we settled down until the white ashes had fallen from the ends of our Havannas. The gallant Captain assured us that the delay would be of service as the crowd must lessen and our journey be advanced by a little masterly inactivity. Remounting our horses after this delay we found the streets as full as ever. Threading our way onward as well as possible we finally reached the open country. Shortly afterwards, Stock, who was a politician always watching for a weak point in the Tory policy, discovered a "hole in the hedge." He had no sooner pointed this out to Manners than the latter leaped his hunter through the gap, we all followed suite and scampered onward over the sod as near to a gait of 2.40 as our steeds could approach. As we galloped on we fancied we could hear the furious voices of the indignant farmer and his servants crying after us, and the sharp prongs of steel pitchforks, flails, scythes and other rustic weapons floated across our excited imaginations. Our engagements at Epsom, however, did not admit of any delay to verify, had we desired, these suspicious sounds. The only effect of the discordant noises, so out of place on this happy day, was to urge our steeds to greater exertions. Soon we were beyond reach of the din and no longer disturbed in mind by that rustic force and those ugly looking and dangerous, though vulgar, implements of war.

At eleven o'clock we reached the course where not less than 200,000 persons were already assembled. The scene was what newspaper reporters style "brilliant," and while apparently the utmost confusion prevailed, there was really the best of order. Tents and booths were pitched in every direction and tens of thousands of flags fluttered in the breeze -vehicles were scattered over the vast area of sward, and horses were tethered far and wide. Equipages were arriving by every road and coming into collision with others returning. There was consequently a dismal spectacle of smashed panels, lost spokes, broken axles and jaded beasts. Crowds on foot were pouring in from all the roads and across the newly mown fields. On the ground or heath the people were indulging in a variety of rustic games. Every kind of character was present from the highest of the "old nobility" to the lowest of the houseless tramp. A glance in any direction showed you stupid looking German bands, swarthy Italian organ grinders, foot sore gypsies, montebanks of every description. Near us a female was crying shrimps for sale, while further off, near a crowd of women, a man bawled at the top of his voice, "Buy a box of patent lozenges, good for pains in the belly." The light-fingered gentlemen, from the thimble-rigger to the card sharper, in the highest spirits, were industriously plying their avocations. From a dirty, ill-conditioned looking fellow on his knees busily shuffling three cards, you heard in persuasive notes. "Pick out the face card, gentleman, and you'll win a sovereign." A number of sleeping, but by no means silent partners, stood round about and lost and won their money, generally winning, in order to entice the unwary. There was a party playing at the game of "Knock 'em down," very popular with aspirants for police service. There was another at the favorite amusement of "Aunt Sally," not far off. The arrows of an archery party whizzed incessantly through the air, and every moment you were startled by the sharp and rapid reports from the pistol galleries, while the course was all over dotted with groups engaged in the exhilirating sport of flinging cudgels at long slender wands, the tops of which were surmounted by tin or wooden tobacco boxes, velvet pin cushions and hollow wooden boxes framed to represent apples, pears and oranges. Young men sauntered about with long red pasteboard probocis, and viewed their friends through six-penny spectacles. Woman, their unkempt hair flowing over their shoulders, strolled about, followed by their promising offspring, the broods often as large as that of John Rodgers, and the mothers often, as with Rodger's wife, with one at her breast. Young ladies now and then screamed nervously at some strange sight; in a word, a scene of the most indescribable bustle and uproar prevailed. Notwithstanding, however, the vast assemblage and its mixed character, there was no disorder, no rowdy turbulence, no disposition for riot. We were much struck with this fact. It would be hard to assemble in France or the United States five thousand people without a profusion of black eyes and bloody noses. Here a ready obedience was paid to the few policemen who were present and every one seemed to be in the best possible humor. It was a fine illustration of the Anglo Saxon love of order—a thing which seems to be inherent to the English character and which must not be supposed to result from special repression in the laws. Nowhere are they more liberal than in England, whatever erroneous ideas to the contrary may prevail in America. Many of us imagine, in our ignorance, that ours is the only "land of the free and home of the brave." It is a great mistake; a stupendous blunder. Nowhere are the rights of the people more jealously guarded than in England, nowhere is there a greater spirit of resistance to tyranny. This the history of centuries proves. So far as our knowledge of England and the English extends—a knowledge derived from a careful perusal of her history and many visits, extending over a period of nearly twenty years, and long residence, we are satisfied that they have little to envy in the condition of others, even of those who assume to be the freest, happiest and best governed people on the globe. We cannot stop to explain how they are as free, why they are as happy, and in what they are as well governed as the best. Let those who doubt it examine her laws, daily becoming more liberalized, watch the operations of her enduring institutions and visit her homes.

But we must not forget that we are on the race course. The grand stand, perched at an immense distance in the air, was already well filled with spectators, as were the numerous smaller stands by which it is flanked. Conspicuous on the central platform, among the "modish fancy," were the Japanese ambassadors, who looked very billious, somewhat bewildered and decidedly bored though it was reported they had staked heavy sums and could not be indifferent to the issue. Lord Palmerston and many of his parliamentary supporters and opponents in both Houses of

Parliament, was also on the stand, smiling and bowing in his happiest mood. He wore a blue coat with a velvet collar, and was, as usual, sucking a rye straw. It was thought from his unflagging good humor, that he had made the opening of diplomatic relations with the Japenese Empire the occasion of pocketing the £30,000, which it was said and believed the ambassadors had staked and lost. The miscellaneous education he had received in early youth and his long official career seems to have fitted the veteran Viscount for every company and occasion, and at a horse race he was certainly as much at home as in the House of Commons in a desperate party struggle.

After preliminary races to which little attention was paid, the people were notified by the loud ringing of bells, that the great event of the day was about to come off. The thirty-two horses entered for the Derby, mounted by their gaily dressed jockeys were trotted out and took a preliminary canter. They were then drawn up in line, and after several starts, which were pronounced false, the flag fell and off they bounded, swift as an arrow from the bow, the victor reaching the winning post, a mile and a half distant, in something in the neighborhood of 2:40 to the mile.

The result was immediately announced. An "outsider," an unknown horse, against whom forty to one was bet, had won. The announcement was followed by a lull of a few minutes, when the people commenced hurrying away as for life or death, by every road and pathway—some to the railroad stations, some by the pikes, in vehicles or on horseback, and thousands on foot and over the fields. Boys from ten to twenty years of age, of whom there were multitudes, formed the larger part of the pedestrians. These urchins had walked out in the morning and were now setting out on their return. Not a few were limping like wounded hares, but their spirits were not only good, but hilarious. They set forward with that stubborn resolution, so characteristic of the English race, and which has caused it, in whatever part of the world, to endure all that is necessary to secure their object. In patient determination and dogged resolution, John Bull is indeed unsurpassed by the Ass. England has thus become the colonizer of the world, the spawner of nations. The physical and moral qualities of the British breed, we may say, *en passant*, so fit them for colonizing, that no other race can compete with them. If the French or Dutch establish colonies, they are sooner or later absorbed by the English. This has happened not only in America, but, more or less, all over the world. British love of adventure, hardihood, industry and bull dog tenacity, and the fertility of the British mother, have established the English speaking race in America, peopled the continent of Australia and the North Pacific Islands, South Africa, and have even made headway in the crowded population of India and China. Unto them this planet seems to be given. For this reason hard times, silent industries and financial panics, such as in recent years she has seen and such as would blight other nations only arouse old England to another of her great efforts. She thins her overcrowded population by emigration, and thus relieves distress by founding new colonies. Australia, Demarara, South Africa, Canada, and the United States offer broad welcome to English emigrants. For the best governed parts of the world, the regions of greatest happiness, freedom and comfort, are those where English is spoken. In short the English have issued forth from their tight little island and conquered half the world, and before the other half becomes aware of what is going on, they may find the "blarsted Britisher" in possession.

But we must return from this digression. It seemed strange that the people should hurry in this fashion from the race course which they had exhibited such a determined wish to reach. It appeared almost incredible that so many persons could have taken the trouble and incurred the expense of traveling nineteen miles, under a hot sun and through clouds of dust, for less than three minutes enjoyment, but so it was. Tens of thousands were now leaving. This was not the case however, with "the mass." "The million" held on, for they avail themselves of the annual return of the Derby to have a country frolic and inflate their lungs with pure air, which they call their champagne. No sentiment is more universal with our English ancestors than a thorough, genuine love of the country. On every occasion they fly to it, and when they retire from the pursuits of the world it is always to the country, the peaceful scenes of the country. They rightly think that this is the only way of securing when young the highest mental and physical development, the "*sana mens in sana corpore*," and when old the calm repose suited to age. No passion to the English seems so universal as that for the race, which is one of Englands's most ancient and popular amusements. It is not only an amusement in which everybody participates, but a science by which thousands make a support while others are ruined. Racing of some kind, has been from the earliest days one of the most popular sports of the British people. Foot races were common before the Roman invasion, afterwards chariot races were introduced and mithraic festivities were practiced in many parts of the country. At this period racing with horses after the custom of the Romans without riders was also practised. Mounted races came in with the Anglo Saxons and during the ages when a man who could read and write was considered an effeminate milk sop, only fit to be a clerk of a priest, it was usual for knights and gentlemen to ride their own horses.

During the reigns of Queen Elizabeth and James I. both of whom were good judges of horse flesh and addicted to the turf, it was patronized as now by the royal family and the nobility, or in a word the fashionable world. It was not uncommon at that period, nor is it now, for young gentlemen to ride their own horses at a match. The writer often saw them do so during his sojourn in England. The turf was in a flourishing condition and so continues, as everything in England must be upon which the *ton* smiles and lavishes its gold. Meetings regularly took place in Yorkshire and Surrey, at Endfield Chase and numerous other places During the reign of James I, the turf first assumed systematic dress and was scientifically and methodically conducted. This national sport flourished with fresh vigor under the "Merrie Monarch Charles," who established a Royal stud and spent large sums in bringing the breed of horses to perfection.— He subscribed plate to be run for at all the meetings, entered his horse in his own name, and was arbiter of jockey club disputes. It has from that period maintained the first place among British sports and has superceded and taken the place of the jousts and tournaments of the olden day.

Racing is nowhere so popular or so much supported as in England. This is seen in the inns and public houses, in the prints which adorn the walls of races, racers and jockeys, and in this year of grace, 1880, a turf club has been opened in the West end, patronized by Viscount Mandeville, M. P., son of the Duke of Manchester, and the leading nobility, to which Americans of distinction are admitted to membership, provided their tastes are "horsey." This is the result the Ten Broeks and P. Lorilard's efforts to prove, as they have pretty conclusively done, that the American bred horse is superior in speed and bottom to his English sire. This is equally true of cattle, and within a few years cattle bred and reared in New York from English stock have been sold at enormous sums to be taken back with a view to the improvement of the original race. The effect of the American climate is seen even more plainly, according to the testimony of many northern authorities, in the superior physique of the American born and bred descendants of English and other European ancestors. The average American, whether originally sprung from the English, Irish, German or Swede, is said to be taller, with a deeper chest, broader shoulders and fuller muscular development, greater activity and more energy and endurance than his European progenitor. While this, if true, is mainly due to our fine climate, it may in part be attributed to the abundant, varied and satisfactory character of our food supply, and the further fact that marrying in-and-in is very rare in the United States, while the union of cousins is too common on the other side of the Atlantic. This vicious custom has been carried to such an extent in some portions of Europe, notably in the Swiss Cantons and the Channel Islands, that epilepsy, imbecility, idiocy and insanity are the characteristics of the dwarfish and deformed offsprings of certain families.

An apology for mixing up these grave matters in a chapter on the Derby, may be found in the words of Shaftesbury: "If, whilst they profess only to please, they secretly advise and give instruction, they may now, perhaps, as well as formerly, be esteemed with justice the best and most honorable among authors."

But to proceed. We need not discourse on the Englishman's love of the horse. It is known the world over. He treats his horse like his best friend, his second self, and not unfrequently consigns him to an honored grave. During the latter part of the last century, the celebrated racer Eclipse, who won £25,000 for his owner, dying at the age of twenty-five, was buried in state, bitter ale and hot buns being distributed to the mourners, who mourned most, we imagined, that such scenes occured so seldom. Eclipse's heart had been previously taken out and was found to be of extraordinary size, which satisfactorily accounted, as the mourners fancied, for the many noble qualities and the great success of the lamented steed.

The passion for the race is, as we have said, universal, possessing all ranks and conditions, and strange to say, if possible, more intense with the women than the men. The ladies attended the races in great numbers, and have been known to ride at them.— One of these female riders was the wife of a Colonel Thornton, and evidently his better half. In 1804 she rode a match on which £200,000 were depending, and with so much success that she entered the arena again in 1805 against a celebrated jockey by the name of Buckley, and beat him. The fair equestrienne was not only an accomplished rider but something of a poet or poetaster, and has left some lively rhymes in which she apostrophised the delightful sensations of a match. Ladies do not now play jockey, but still lend their countenance to the turf. Petticoats are interdicted by the by-laws of the jockey clubs, not to say by an improvement in the public taste, but the fair sex has by no means abandoned that department of the fine arts connected with horse flesh.— Often of an afternoon we have admired the beautiful creatures superbly mounted, careening through Rotten Row. Their success in this Olympic exercise is so remarkable that the most vicious colts are often surrendered to their management. They are therefore sometimes called "pretty horse-breakers."

Races are now held in more than a hundred and twenty places

in England, the most important of which are Epsom Ascot, York, Dorcaster and New Market, at the latter of which places between four and five hundred horses are in constant training. Ascot and New Market are attended by the most select company, among whom is the Queen, and the meetings are conducted without the serious drawbacks which detract so much from those of other localities, such as Epsom where the attendance is rarely less than 150,000.

The Derby and Oaks were instituted by an earl of Derby near a century ago and the Derby day is now regarded as a great national carnival, in fact the University boat race and the Derby are the only great annual festivals of the people. Both Houses of Parliament adjourn for the Derby and it is attended by the Royal family, the nobility, by statesmen, tory and radical, the ministry, by judges and lawyers, historians, poets, novel writers and journalists, the aristocracy of birth and intellect as well as by every other class of the community, high and low, rich and poor. The "Oaks" is more slimly attended and principally by that portion of the community which sports the title of "fashionable," though the usual per centum of rogues and blacklegs are always on hand.

## CHAPTER XV.

DOVER—FASHIONABLE SOCIETY ON THE SEA SIDE—THE PAST AND PRESENT—DANGERS ON THE OLD ROAD.

We do not remember to have seen in England such a succession of fair days, so little rain and humidity in the atmosphere, so much genial sunshine and so much balmy air as during the autumn it was our good fortune to visit Dover and the southeastern counties. Every traveler will understand the additional zest with which the sight-seer follows his vocation with the accompaniments of good health and good weather, which are a sufficient guarantee for good spirits.

Before reaching Dover, lodgings had been secured for us by a London friend in Marine Parade, a pretty little terrace of lath and plaster villas (semi-detached) extending round the north shore of the bay. Behind was the town, flanked by towering chalk cliffs, and in front the dark blue sea. Pleasure and fishing boats, with the busy groups belonging to them, filled the beach from early morning to sunset, and on the channel were vessels of all sizes and nations—steam packets also arrived several times during the day from Calais, and enlivened the scene by landing their crowds of passengers. Marine Parade had long since come in vogue as a summer residence for invalids, for fashionable idlers, for gay Lotharios and wanton women, for all who wished to recommend themselves to notice by their dress, their air, and their civilities, and its villas during the season were rarely untenanted. Visitors always sought lodgings fronting the parade, where they perpetually enjoyed sea views and sea air within convenient distance of bathing machines. Our friend finding one of these villas vacant, took it for us and we found ourselves moored between two maiden gentlewomen, occupying the adjoining villa to the north, and a bilious looking Indian officer, on half pay, on the south. The fashionable promenade was a long, wide and smooth walk between the village and the sea and at certain hours all the world of Dover assembled there to listen to the band, to see and be seen. Those whom gout or "fastidiousness" kept from touching mother earth with their dainty boots, sat in their bay windows, ready to greet with smiles and recognitions their less squeamish acquaintances. This was a pleasant peculiarity of the terrace. There was another—the end of a blunderbuss telescope protuded, in pleasant weather, from almost every window. As the afternoon hour of 4 o'clock approached, one could see the straggling *haut ton*, wending their way to the walk for the ostensible purpose of enjoying "a constitutional." Though these devotees to pleasure had in a measure slept off the effects of the previous night's dissipation and fortified themselves with "bitters," they for the most part appeared jaded, heavy, wearied. For ourselves, we generally visited this scene about five o'clock, when all of Dover, ill and well, grave and gay, lively and severe, was on the tramp. The citadel officers, in their gay uniforms, mustered in strong force, and eyed with profound interest the new comers of the softer sex.

These Machiavelian bucks soon knew who the late arrivals were, where they were from and what they were worth. Whether they were heiresses or co-heiresses, wards in chancery or under the protection of *pater familias*. If so unfortunate as to have a father, his age and bodily condition were soon as well known to them as to the medical adviser of a life association, and it was certain to be discussed how, when the old fellow was gone, "he would cut up." This was the slang phrase, the true meaning of which is, will his estate, when divided, leave a handsome penny to one and all of his offsprings. If a pretty widow appeared it was quickly ascertained what was her "jointure," and whether she was encumbered with "kids" (i. e. children) or was all forlorn. Dover in the "season" is indeed, to make short of a long story, a lion's den, full of pitfalls, sunken rocks, snags and shoals, gins and springs set by the fortune hunting fraternity. During the forenoon the promenade was deserted except by limp and smeary children dancing to the music of the organ grinder, a half dozen workmen arranging the stand for the afternoon band, or making arrangements on gala days for a pyrotechnic display of colored fires; a few lank and weary female forms flitted to and fro between the Terrace and bathing machines, and a crowd of gossiping laundresses, fishermen and seedy looking sailors, who lounged about the sands, smoking clay pipes and spinning yarns. The parade only burst in all its glories in the post meridian hours.

Among the afternoon habitues of the mall were our neighbors the two gentlewomen and the bilious officer. They had struck up acquaintance with us by reason of our close proximity. Everybody at Dover is on the lookout for eligible "connections," anxious to increase their social circle. The cheerful ladies always walked forth, each having in leading strings a sore eyed dog. This is one way in which the stranger recognizes that he is in a fashionable community; it is entirely *a la mode* for a single woman to sport a poodle. Another way is to ascertain if the people have music with their meals. This is quite the oriental flourish adopted by aspirants for the *beau monde*. Establishing themselves on wire bottomed chairs our maiden gentlewomen passed the afternoon dividing their attention between their canine pets and the company. They seemed to lay in wait of game, with a view to charitable comment on any obnoxious looking individual, such as the gentleman with the diseased liver, who might appear. By these venerable lassies such a blade was always supposed to have designs on them, and was pronounced a dangerous man. The Indian officer, whose long acquaintance with jungles enabled him instinctively to scent the presence of an enemy, took pains to locate himself as far as possible from his wily neighbors. It was quite apparent to the casual observer, that however unsafe he might be, at times and on occasions, the damsels were in no immediate danger from him.

In Parade villas, as we have said, we took lodgings and found ourselves in the midst of this kind of a promiscuous and would be world of fashion. Much amusement we might undoubtedly have derived from a study of life on the sands, but our time and plans did not admit of such delectable dissipation. The town and neighborhood presented many objects of interest and with these we busied ourselves more agreeably if not more profitably. For the best part of the time, we gave the go by to the seething mass of humanity elbowing their way up and down the pathway and around the band of H. M. 24th foot. (This is the ill-fated regiment which lost 850 men at Isandula, Zululand, in 1879.) After the fatigues of a well spent day sight seeing and a four o'clock dinner, we frequently sauntered forth to the promenade to take a peep at vice and folly through the fumes of our cigar. The Lieut. Colonel commanding the 24th Regiment, George Vincent Watson and his family were old friends, and much of our spare time was spent with them. We often dined *en garcon* at the mess of the 24th and concluded the evening with a rubber. To Col. Watson and the officers of the 24th and the Artillery commanded by another old friend, Col. Singleton, we were indebted for much hospitality. They supplied us too, with a deal of information as to the leading people then in Dover. Among them we soon discovered our old friends, Sir Henry de Hoghton and Lady Eardley whose flirtation was still kept up with undiminished ardor. Miss Maria Turner, author of "The Garden of the Lord" &c., John Fradgley, one of the principal officers of the Bank of England, Captain E. Newstead Falkner, late of H. M. 30th foot, H. R. Fox Bourne, author of "The Lives of British Merchants" and many others..— The first few days of our sojourn in Dover were occupied with an examination of its ancient ruins of Roman, Saxon and Norman origin, and we entered upon the work with the zeal of a discoverer, notwithstanding our misgivings as to the value of much traditionary lore. Rich as is Dover in these memorials of other days, it is richer in its objects of present interest, and what with seeing the piers and jetties, the military works, the forts and harbors, its civil halls and church edifices, its museums and picture galleries and its lovely environs, we had little time while in our "Cottage by the sea" for anything else. From our lodgings it was but a half hour's walk to the summit (from 300 to 400 feet high) of the cliffs north of town. Upon these stand the renowned Dover Castle. It is said, by antiquarians, of course, to occupy the spot of a Roman fortress. Be this as it may, it is well known that shortly after the Roman legions were withdrawn, it was strongly fortified by the Saxons, afterwards by the Normans, and has ever since been regarded as one of England's strongholds, in fact, the English Gibralter. Walking round the ramparts, Col. Watson pointed out the French coast which could be dimly seen without a glass. From this point Queen Elizabeth's pocket piece, so tradition says, once threw a ball to the opposite shore, a distance of twenty-one miles.

This beautiful piece of brass ordnance was cast at Utrecht in 1544, and was presented by the States of Holland to the potent Queen Bess. The exterior is ornamented with various figures typical of the blessings of peace and the horrors of war, and bears a Flemish inscription of which the following is a translation: .

"O'er hill and dale I throw my ball,
Breaker my name of mound and wall."

The Flemish language having died out in England, this inscription has been variously translated. In the language of the cockney, it is thus rendered:

"Load me well and ram me down,
And I'll throw a ball to Calais town."

The almost inaccessible natural position as well as the extensive works render the castle impregnable. The present fortifications have grown up in successive ages and consequently offer to the eye a confusion of style in the several parts. The effect of the whole, however, is picturesque and romantic. Over an area of forty acres can be traced some uninteligible ruins which are said to be the remains of the Roman, Saxon and Norman fortifications. After the battle of Hastings the castle was besieged and taken by William the Norman. The castle is within itself one of the most extensive and most interesting works in Europe. From it the views are unsurpassed. To the west the eye wanders over the Valley of the Dour, through which runs the London turnpike road, until the view is intercepted by a range of hills; to the north the prospect takes in the "North Foreland," the Isle of Thanet, Ramsgate, the Downs, Calais and the French coast to and beyond Boulogne. In clear weather, the fields, houses and a wide extent of country are seen in the *Pas de Calais* and even the celebrated monument erécted in 1805 by the grand army at Boulogne to the Emperor Napoleon. The broad expanse of water in the downs is constantly enlivened by passing vessels, and presents such a variety as is rarely met with.

Here we shall take the liberty to detain the reader while we mount our Pegassus and make a course through the regions of the past.

The old road on the banks of the Dour was formerly the highway to London, and became very familiar to us at a subsequent period when we traveled on it part of the way to the metropolis. Though Gibbon, in his XXXI chapter remarks, "There exists in human nature a strong propensity to depreciate the advantages, and to magnify the evils of the present time," we confess while viewing the silent and deserted inns on this ancient highway, once so full of life and activity, that they aroused many suggestive thoughts in the opposite direction, and we by no means considered the present as a degenerate age. We reflected with satisfaction, almost gratitude, upon having made our *debut* into the world amid the wondrous scenes of this wide awake, progressive age. How much better and happier than to have droned away a sluggish and half fossilized existence in the "good old" medieval times. We realized, as such thoughts passed through our mind, that it was of considerable importance when a man was born, at what period he comes into the world. It was something to have lived after the advent of McAdam, and be able to travel in a stage coach without risk of life or limb, even if still liable to bruises and contusions. It was more to have followed Fulton and the steam engine; to have appeared on the theatre of the world after the introduction of telegraphy, and when gas had paled the ineffectual fires of the blinking, twinkling, stinking lamp, which at the best only made darkness visible, and since coal oil has come in, only this up to the time when the pent up combustible vents itself in some disastrous explosion. We experience not the slightest wish, however our mind might sometimes dwell with delight upon the past, as affording in some respects more real happiness than the present, to have back- the past with only the things of the past. We must conclude then that experience had in our case corrected that "propensity to depreciate" alluded to by the great historian as we think it will in all cases when mingled with a little sober cogitation.

When from time to time we have dipped into antiquarian lore, of that veracious kind which challenges our respect in this severe matter of fact age, in which so many cherished historical delusions have been destroyed, we have been not only amused but deeply interested with the accounts given by those grave, quaint men of the olden time of the misfortunes and adversities of their days. One of these relates how he was in danger of losing his way in the ancient north road, one of the best in the Kingdom, and how he actually did lose himself between York and Dorcaster. Another tells how in traveling with his wife in his own carriage, he twice lost his way in one short tour, and on the second occasion narrowly escaped the penance of passing a comfortless night on Salisbury Plain. In those days the condition of the roads was frightful, and travelers in bad weather were often delayed for weeks together. Sometimes the floods were so deep and impetuous that wayfarers had to swim for their lives, while the weak and inexpert were swept away. Thoresby relates that in the course of one of his journeys he with difficulty escaped drowning by an inundation of the Prent. He was afterwards detained at Stamford four days on account of the state of the roads, and then was extricated from his position only by a company of fourteen members of the House of Commons, attended by competent guides, and who compassionately took him in tow. In 1685 the Viceroy on his way to Ireland was borne through Wales in a litter, while his carriage, which had been taken to pieces, was conveyed on the shoulders of Welsh peasants to the seashore.

In those days it was the custom, before setting out upon this old turnpike road or indeed upon any of those roads leading from the country to the metropolis, to canvass the matter for months in anticipation and to spend weeks in anxious preparation for the event. Tender farewells were taken of friends and neighbors, a will was made and duly signed, sealed and delivered with all the solemnities of a death bed testament. Thus says Evlyn's diary: "Paris, June 27th, 1650. I made my will, and taking leave of my wife and other friends, took horse for England." The intending traveler's midnight dreams were haunted by visions of disaster, robbery and death; and his days rendered hideous by the lurid gloom which coming events cast over them. If he had survived these and the day of departure arrived, his remaining resolution was broken down by the parting scene—the wife hanging upon his neck, the children clinging to his knees and the sorrowful neighbors gathering to take a last look at their adventurous friend.

Foissart gives an account of a journey accomplished by the mother of Richard II, who at the time of Wat Tyler's insurrection in 1380, came in one day from Canterbury to London, for "she never durst tarry on the way."

Of course this event would not have been chronicled but it was considered a surprising achievement, though performed with the aid of all the resources of Royalty and on one of the best roads in England. A good idea may be formed of the general insecurity of traveling in those days by an account of the expense of transporting £1,000 to Prince Edward the I, in 1301. The treasure was brought to London by two knights on horseback, attended by sixteen valets on foot. It was not sufficient, however, that the money should be protected by men-at-arms. In the absence of hotels, excepting in towns, it was necessary to secure the guards from hunger. They were therefore accompanied by two cooks, whose duty it was to provide a "safe lodging" daily for the money, and to attend to the gastronomic wants of its conductors. One of them, after having accompanied the escort two days' journey between Chester and London, spurred on to the metropolis to herald the approach of the money. It may be of interest in these days to know how these £1,000 all in silver were conveyed to their destination. In the first place, ten panniers "wherein to truss the money," and cords wherewith to tie them, were provided, with cost 4s., 9d. Then these ten panniers were put across the backs of five hackneys, supplied of course by the companies of hackneymen established along the road. It took the guard eight days to arrive in London with the heavy weight, and six days to return to Chester without it. The knights each received one shilling a day; and each valet was well paid, at a third of the same stipend. The cooks had each two pence a day; but the one who was in the prince's service having to stay two additional days in London, in order to count out the money to the treasurer, received two shillings extra. The cost of hiring the five hackneys was thirty shillings; and the total expense of conveying the money in question was £6, 19s., 6d., currency of that day, or about £104, 16s., in modern coin.

More than two days were required for the journey from London to Oxford in the stage coach, in the reign of Charles II, a distance traversed now by trains in less than two hours. When in 1703, George, Prince of Denmark, visited the stately mansion of Petworth with the view of meeting Charles III of Spain, he was six hours in making the last nine miles of the journey. The carriages were frequently up set and injured; and one of the courtiers in giving an acconnt of it, said that he never once alighted, except when the coach overturned or stuck in the mud. The roads were equally dangerous in Virginia. In 1662, Col. Valentine Peyton, of Nominy, in the county of Westmoreland thus speaks in his last will and testament, "Being about to take a voyage to Jamestown, and knowing the life of man to be uncertain, I doe make this my last will and testament."

These were, however, considered the minor difficulties and dangers of traveling in those days. The country, particularly the neighborhood of highways, was infested by troops of robbers and vagabonds. Many of the roads were so insecure that armed knights were employed to scour them and perform the duties of the modern rural police. The custom at present in Italy, Spain and Greece, of taking rich passengers and holding them until a ransom is paid, was then common in England. The great terrors of the road caused merchants, bishops, monks, lawyers, literary men and others to travel in companies, which gave rise to Chaucer's description in his *Canterbury Pilgrims*. Such in a general way were some of the delights of traveling in early days, and cause us rather to felicitate ourselves upon having had our lives cast in modern times. Reflecting over the pleasant advantages we now enjoy and not having the fear of Gibbon before our eyes, we gave vent to our animal spirits piping the following lines:

> "What one has done, when one was young,
> One ne'er will do again;
> In former days we went by coach,
> But now one goes by train."

## CHAPTER XVI.

DOVER — THE CINQUE PORTS — ANCIENT CUSTOMS—WALMER CASTLE—DEAL—DEATH OF THE DUKE OF WELLINGTON—THE MIDDLE AGE OF MONKS—RELIGIOUS INTOLERANCE.

But to return from this digression. The castle constitutes the chief defensive work on the north of Dover, and together with minor works in this quarter, and the series of fortifications on the hills and slopes to the south, defend all the approaches whether by land or sea. There is an interesting feature and peculiarity about the works to the South of the town, namely, a winding staircase of two hundred steps, or military shaft cut vertically through the chalk cliff, thus giving ready access from the barracks above to the town. These works lie near the celebrated cliff, called Shakespeare's cliff, which the great dramatist made famous. In *King Lear*, Edgar addressing the Earl of Gloucester, gives the celebrated description, beginning,

> "There is a cliff, whose high and bending head
> Looks fearfully on the confined deep."

History, says a distinguished essayist, is a tissue of fables. There is no reason to believe that any one page in any one history extant, exhibits the unvarnished truth. When Sir Walter Raleigh wrote his history of the world, he was a prisoner in the Tower of London. One morning he heard the noise of a vehement contention under his window, but he could neither see the combatants, nor distinguish exactly what was said. One person after another came into his apartment, and he enquired of them the nature of the affray, but their accounts were so inconsistent that he found himself wholly unable to arrive at the truth of the story. Sir Walter's reflection on this was obvious, yet acute. "What," said he, "can I not make myself master of an incident which happened an hour ago under my window, and shall I imagine I can truly understand the history of Hannibal and Cæsar." President John Adams thus expresses himself on this subject :

"I have little faith in history. I read it as I do romance, believing what is probable and rejecting what I must. Thucydides, Tacitus, Livy, Hume, Robertson, Gibbon, Raynal and Voltaire, are all alike. Our American history for the last fifty years is already as much corrupted as any half century of ecclesiastical history, from the Council of Nice to the restoration of the Inquisition in 1815. If I were to write a history of the last 60 years, as the facts rest in my memory, and according to my judgment, and under the oath of *pro veritate historiarum mearum deum ipsum obtestor*, a hundred writers in America, France, England and Holland would immediately appear, and call me, to myself, and before the world, a gross liar and a perjured villain."

This view is not very encouraging and would seem to belie the maxim that time will clear up all obscurities. Nevertheless we will venture to enter into some of the received particulars of the history of this famous old sea-side town. If not fiction they possess the merit of being equally as interesting. Dover is the principal of the maratime towns constituting the association known as "Cinque Ports." This remarkable fraternity, so intimately connected with the coast of Kent and Sussex, is still in existence after a lapse of eight centuries. As early, if not earlier than the Norman times, Dover, Sandwich, Hythe, Romney and Hastings enjoyed peculiar municipal privileges, granted them on condition that they would furnish shipping to defend the Southern coast (England having no navy then) and maintain easy communication with the continent in time of peace. To them were afterwards added Winchelsea, Rye and Seaford. William the Norman separated the civil and military administration of these ports from that of the rest of Kent and Sussex and placed both under a Lord Warden, who was the governor of these havens and their dependencies, and had the authority of an admiral and power to hold a court of admiralty and courts of law and equity. This officer resided at the castle and exercised the functions of Lord-Lieutenant, sheriff and *custos rotoloum* as also admiral over this part of the realm. In the course of time the fraternity was enlarged by the admission of other towns, either as principals or members, and since the days of William I, each port has been governed by Jurats and Barons, instead of aldermen and freemen; the difference being not merely in name, but in some of the functions also. In the year 1347, Sir Robert Peyton, second baron Ufford, Earl of Suffolk was commissioned by Edward III., Lord High Admiral of England, and commanded the King's whole fleet and sailed from one of the Cinque ports, where his naval armament was formed and equipped to the coasts of the northern powers, and only returned to serve on land with the "black prince" at the battle of Poictiers where, says Burke, "his Lordship achieved the highest military renown by his skill as a leader and his personal courage at the head of his troops." The founding of the British navy and the silting up of many of the harbors, c ombined to render the Cinque

Ports a nullity so far as concerned this matter; but many of the old political and municipal privileges and usages continue to exist. The Cinque system may now be regarded as a curious relic of past days, retained because it is old rather than because it is of any use. The Constable of Dover Castle for the time being is Lord-Warden of the Cinque Ports; the clerk of the Castle is under-sheriff of the Cinque ports, and these two functionaries are concerned in the holding of official meetings called the Courts of Shepway, the Courts of Brotherhood and the Courts of Guestling. The Lord Wardens, (the office is now a sinecure,) no longer reside in the castle but during the period when in Kent fix their residence at Walmer Castle about seven miles north of Dover. Prince Albert was for many years and up to the period of his death Lord Warden. Afterwards Lord Palmerston was appointed, and in 1862 attended at Dover and held sessions of the three courts mentioned, though at the time nearly 80 years of age and Prime Minister. In addition to the use of the castle there is a salary of £4,-000 per annum attached to this now useless office.

Upon one occasion we made an excursion from Dover to Walmer Castle through the villages of Orkney and Ringwould. Walmer Castle is an object of much interest to all tourists, not only as the official residence of the Lord Warden of the Cinque Ports, and the scene of the last hours of the famous Duke of Wellington, but for its antiquity, having been built and provided with a moat and drawbridge by Henry VIII in 1539. We were surprised to find the chief part of the moat converted into a garden, and looking far more picturesque than military. In other respects the grim old castle is now intact, and at the period of our visit was occupied by the present Lord Warden, Earl Grosvenor. During the time Mr. Pitt was Prime Minister, he was, like Lord Palmerston, the Lord Warden and occasionally spent some days at Walmer away from the toils of business. The guide shewed us a room in which the "heaven born minister" and Nelson planned some of their great naval schemes. We were also shown the room in which the Duke of Wellington, who resided two months every year at Walmer, slept upon a narrow camp bedstead of iron, with a straw mattress and cotton coverlet. The room contained no other furniture beyond a camp stool and an iron wash-hand stand, with a small looking glass affixed. His simple tastes and his habits as a soldier caused him to prefer such a sleeping room to the most sumptuous bed chamber. His windows looked out upon the sea and a door admitted him to the ramparts, where he walked for two hours every morning. On the 4th of September, 1852, on his iron bedstead, in this small, plain room, the hero of Waterloo expired, having near him his son, Lord Charles Wellesley, present Duke of Wellington, an apothecary from the neighboring town of Deal, and the household domestics. This room to which visitors are now admitted, is reverently kept with as little alteration as possible. The gardens and shrubbery around are beautiful and the view from the ramparts over the sea, wide and magnificent; but the peculiar interest which attaches to a place, like Walmer is, at least for ourselves, its old associations. We imagine there is no human being who has not felt the magnetic power of such associations. They grow with our growth and strengthen with our strength. When old age comes creeping on and the pulse rises slowly, and the life blood runs colder from the heart, and the limbs begin to fail ; when the visions of youth and the hopes of early manhood and the ambitions of maturer years are obliterated and annihilated, when the grave yawns grimly before, and the thin white hair hardly covering the shrunken skull, when the winter of life arrives, then are these associations in their fullest force, and seem to say that winter is but the prelude to a new spring. Forgeting the events of yesterday, the old man sees clear and plain, as though he were a child again, the old haunts and the old faces, and his ears, deaf to the voices around him, hear old familiar voices, long since hushed in the tomb. The barren path of age winds through the green memories of childhood, recalling at every step, old thoughts, dead loves and perished remembrances.

This effort having exhausted our rhetorical powers, this hot weather, let us return from whence we came, to wit, to Walmer, from whence we proceeded, on the beach, to the famous old port of Deal. In its aspect and appearance it is directly the opposite of Dover. There are no hills or cliffs at this part of the coast, but the town stands upon an open beach fully fronting the sea. The harbor is good and from its accessibility it has long been provided with works as a guard against hostile invasion. In the reign of Henry VIII., Deal and Sandown Castles were built with this view. Both have abundance of draw bridges, round towers and turrets. We were informed by a friend who was industriously plying us with learned lore, that in the seventeenth century one Col. Henderson was long confined in Sandown Castle, suspected of being a regicide. Our considerate friend stopped short in his narrative, and we do not know who Col. Henderson was, nor do we know in what king's blood he wished to imbue his hands. But as one Charles was laying his head upon the block by order of Cromwell about this time and the other was a refugee among the Dutch at the Hague, it must be presumed that it was upon one or the other that this patriotic and blood-thirsty member of the Henderson family wished to vent his patriotism.

On our return to Dover we stopped three miles west of the town long enough to examine the ruins of St. Radiguns, "whose mould-'ring abbey walls, o'erhang the glade." This religious house, says the guide book, and we never fail to keep this faithful friend by us and to occasionally draw inspiration from its pages, was founded in the twelfth century for the Premonstratensians, a religious order of regular Canons or Monks of Premontre, instituted in the twelfth century in the Isle of France by Father Norbet. This devoted man is better known to history than Col. Henderson, and when only 32 years of age accompanied the Emperor Henry V to Rome, was ordained a Priest a few years later, founded this order when 40 years of age ; was Archbishop of Magdeburg six years subsequently, and a benefactor, though dead, is not forgotten ; was canonized by Gregory XIII, four hundred and forty-eight years after his death. We defy the critics to find any of this precise and we may add interesting, not to say recondite historical information in the guide book. Let them search its pages, however industriously, hold fast the volume with a tight grip, turn over the leaves with nervous twitching fingers, stretch every muscle of the brain to the fullest extent, until the veins start out upon their brows and their eyes grow dim, and they will find nothing of it in the cockneys' road book. We chuckle at gaining this advantage over those carping, fault finding, overwise (in their own conceit) fellows, at mystifying the Shank's mare peripatetic, who only from the itinerary, and at the same time gaining favor with our reader by giving him some evidence that we possess a little solid historical knowledge. Thus entrenched in the good opinion of our reader, he will travel in our company, with a gratifying sense of security, though we say it who should not. He will soon learn that he is not going to be deceived with legends, fables and such like romance, but be supplied with the sound pabulum of the historic muse. His guide, philosopher and friend may at times be a little discursive, but the reader is advised to cultivate the belief that he knows how to handle a subject, how to descend to particulars, enter into the details and come to the point, as he has evidently done in the case of Archbishop Norbet, with the most gratifying success.

To be serious, and to return to the main subject. This Abbey was founded for the White Canons by an Earl and Countess—everything must be started in England by a Lord or Lady, one or both. It was richly endowed in the reign of Edward I. Its abbots were summoned to Parliament, and in 1319 it was specially honored by a visit from Edmund II. Important historical information to be sure, cries the cynic who believes that all human affairs are so entangled that the truth cannot be told. We care not to be driven from our course by perverseness of this nature and shall continue with our history.

The ruins of the Abbey are extensive and the walls of great thickness. Many fine windows and doorways of elaborate workmanship still remain in tolerable preservation. Every part of England can lay claim to these traces of a monastic life which has altogether passed away from the country. There is scarcely any portion of the land in which the ruins of Abbeys, monasteries and priories are not to be found, lying in green, sheltered valleys, or retired among the hills, rising up amid the fertile champaign country, embosomed in majestic trees or perched upon grey promontories looking out upon the sea. Their architecture is unexcelled in modern times. They were great builders in what is called the "dark ages." But the monks of old were more than architects.— They were in fact the only literary class of their age. They were the repositories of all art, science and knowledge. They have handed down to us the great thoughts of the ancients. Whatever there was of morality and intelligence in their day they represented. In the midst of a rude, savage epoch these monks were paving the way for the reign of universal justice. In the midst of their religious meditations they pursued the arts of industry and cultivated science. In appreciating the civilization of our times it is only fair to do justice to the men of those days. The lives they led, the life of the monastery, is unsuited to our times. It is the duty of religion in this day to uplift and elevate the mass, to ameliorate the lot of all who toil, to work out a daily practical result. It cannot fulfil its mission in our day and generation living apart from the world engaged in abstract meditations.

The acute Hallam, in his "Middle Ages," very truly observes that the sole hope for classical literature depended on the Latin language which would probably have been lost if three circumstances had not combined to maintain it, viz., the papal supremacy, the monastic institutions, and the use of the Latin liturgy.— Through the first, a continued intercourse was maintained between Rome and the several nations of Europe, so that a common language became necessary. The parochial clergy were very ignorent, and the little learning that existed was among the monks, whose monasteries served as secure repositories for the books and MSS., which could scarcely have descended to us by any other channel. Thus Papacy and its concomitants, which Protestants are accustomed to condemn, were eventually of the utmost advantage to learning, and to the establishment of a more liberal christianity.

These are facts, and facts are stubborn things. If they teach nothing else, they teach that the world owes a debt of gratitude to the Roman Catholics for the preservation of the learned treasures of Rome and Athens and whatever vast influence they may have exerted upon mankind. In view of the obligations the world owes to the Papacy, it seems strange that the bitterness of religious bigotry and intolerance should be so persistently directed towards both high and low in the only church which existed for over 1500 of the 1879 years which have passed away since the birth of Christ; that the Priests should often be represented as beings without human tastes whatever may be their inner religious convictions, and the Pope himself be held up to the world as if he were all that is bad, the embodiment of evil and the worst foe of the gospel — This is not very fair nor will it have much effect in breaking down the vast fabric of the Roman Catholic religion nor in building up Protestantism. It will have little or no effect, for the simple reason that it is not true; is not fact. And it may be inferred with tolerable certainty that a time will come when the erroneous ideas and this blind zeal will no longer deceive the world nor the zealots themselves. Can any fair-minded man assign a reason why the Romanists should be less sincere in their religious convictions than any other class of Christians? Laying aside then any claim they may have upon our gratitude for the good they have unquestionably achieved in the past, why cannot we accord to them the same purity of motive we claim for ourselves? Unless we can do this we are intolerant as Bramin. "A Bramin" says Lord Macartney, "or any cast of Hindoos, will neither admit you to be of their religion, nor to be converted to yours, a thing which struck the Portugese with the greatest astonishment, when they first discovered the East Indies."

But to proceed. Though we do not go to the length of the matter-of-fact and mistaken Thomas Gradgrind in his theories of education, we seek in these memorials to adhere to the fact, and if fancy sometimes mingles with them it has always been kept subordinate to the serious object in view. Fancy, we hope, has never run away with us, whatever tendency there may be in active imagination to mistake thoughts for objects. While the enthusiastic Gradgrind is undoubtedly very clever and entertaining, he is not at all true. Let us, however, end our hackneyed common-places with the theory of this modern school inspector:

"Ay, ay, ay! but you mustn't fancy! That's it. You are never to fancy. You are not to do anything of the kind. You are to be in all things regulated and governed by fact. We hope to have before long a board of fact, composed of commissioners of fact, who will force the people to be a people of fact, and of nothing but fact. You must discard the word fancy altogether. You have nothing to do with it. You are not to have in any object of use or ornament that which would be a contradiction in fact. You don't walk upon flowers in fact, and you cannot be allowed to walk upon flowers in carpets. You don't find that foreign birds and butterflies come and perch upon your crockery, you cannot be permitted to paint foreign birds and butterflies upon your crockery. You never met quadrupeds going up and down walls, you must not have quadrupeds represented upon walls. You must use for all these purposes combinations and modifications (in primary colors) of mathematical figures which are susceptible of proof and demonstration. This is the new discovery. This is fact. This is taste."

With all respect for fact and many misgivings as to fancy, we cannot pretend to have been guided in our writings more than in our life by this so-called new discovery. While adhering to facts with what may be styled a "healthy" pleasure, we have not committed the error of attempting to enlighten the reader, by demonstrating that two and two make four as a means of convincing him that all we have said has been upon this principle, has led to this undeniable result. On the contrary we have so far swerved from the false theories of the immortal Gradgrind as to indulge without obstructing our narrative in sufficient commonplace, in the way of reflections, to enable the reader easily to pick out our theory of life, and the average reader has a fancy for understanding, reading the author as well as his works. As we do not write here, however, for the purpose of carrying out an idea, we do not consider ourselves bound to adhere to severe rules as to harmony and proportion In a series of disconnected sketches or rambling reminiscences, a latitude is allowed which would be inconsistent with a treatise in which every part bears a relation to the whole. Availing ourselves of this theory we must mention a fact, on the supposition that the reader has not discovered it for himself, which is unconnected with the matters in hand and yet pertinent somewhat to all we have said, namely that, like most people who affect to think, we have some notion about the world in general. We are not likely to have a better opportunity to lug in this affair than the present, and we derive an additional pleasure from doing so for the reason that our fine flow of spirits has now and again caused surprise to our friends, who are familiar with our diversified and eventful career, in which there have been more "downs" than "ups." Our animal spirits are unquestionably good and our temper of mind the reverse of despairing, and we have thus been led into a playful vein of irony from time to time, but we trust never to the ridicule of grave and serious subjects. Our philosophy, if the word is permissible to us, is that of optimism. As a matter of fact we think events are so arranged as to turn out happily in the long run. Upon this hypothesis the facts of life are explained by allowing plenty of time for arrangement and by pointing out the imperfection of our means of judgment.

"All nature is but art, unknown to thee,
All chance direction, which thou can'st not see,
All discord, harmony not understood;
All partial evil, universal good."
—Pope.

In other words there is strictly speaking, no evil at all in the world. If a man entertaining such views is not cheerful sometimes even unto gaiety, where under heaven is the sunshine of the mind to come from? and if such a man is sometimes merry may he not rely upon the indulgence of a generous public? Let us then combine not against the balm of Gilead, the Papists, the truths of history or anything that is good or anybody striving to do good, but against those who travesty human nature by charging that the mass of mankind are generally ready to combine against excellence, because we can never adequately understand that of which we have no experience in ourselves.

## CHAPTER XVII.

FOLKESTONE—CLUB LIFE—MARTELLO TOWERS—SHORNCLIFF CAMP AND THE ORGANIZATION OF THE BRITISH ARMY—VISIT TO A COUNTRY HOUSE—LORD ELLENBOROUGH—ETIQUETTE, ETC.

Among the agreeable people we met, when on a visit to Waldershare Park, the seat of the Earl of Guildford, and now occupied by the Dowager and her family, at the head of which stands her eldest son, Lord North, was an old gentleman by the name of Brockman, who, strangely enough, turned out to be the kinsman of our lady acquaintances in Marine Parade. Living on his estate in Kent, Mr. B. is a fine type of the squirearchy, intelligent, educated, prosperous, public spirited, and hospitable. The duties, privileges and delights of a country gentleman have been so well expressed by a charming writer, that we give them in his own words: "Indeed, I do not know a more enviable condition of life, than that of an English gentleman of sound judgment and good feelings, who passes the greater part of his time on an hereditary estate in the country. From the excellence of the roads and the rapidity and exactness of the public conveyances, he is enabled to command all the comforts and conveniences, all the intelligence and novelties of the capital, while he is removed from its hurry and distraction. He has ample means, occupation and amusement within his own domains ; he may diversify his time by rural occupations, by rural sports, by study, and by the delights of friendly society collected within his own friendly halls. Or if his views and feelings are of a more liberal and extensive nature, he has it greatly in his power to do good, and to have that good immediately reflected back upon himself. He can render essential service to his country, by assisting in the disinterested administration of the laws ; by watching over the opinions and principles of the lower orders around him; by diffusing among them those lights which may be important to their welfare ; by mingling frankly among them, gaining their confidence, becoming the immediate auditor of their complaints, informing himself of their wants, making himself a channel through which their grievances may be quietly communicated to the proper sources of mitigation and relief; or becoming, if need be, the intrepid and incorruptible guardian of their liberties—the enlightened champion of their rights."

One afternoon Mr. Brockman called to say that he had just seen his kinswomen in the adjoining villa, and had invited them to meet us at Beechborough on the 6th of October. He had repeatedly extended an invitation to us before this time, and now urged our acceptance in the heartiest manner. We afterwards learned that our friend, Aubrey Alexander, had written, asking him to call, which furnished an explanation of Mr. Brockman's generous warmth and pronounced politeness. After a conference with the ladies we accepted this invitation and promised to be with him on the appointed day.

Wishing to see as much as possible of the country, we expressed our luggage to Folkestone and set out on foot, on a bright September morning, for that place, by a path leading over the cliffs. Our friends promised to join us at Folkestone a few days later.— This pathway is never safe, except on such fine days as the one selected for our excursion, and many horrible stories are related of adventurous persons, who, attempting to pass it, have been blown into the sea below. During a storm these cliffs exhibited, as may be imagined, a striking combination of congenial horrors.

But seen by us when no driving storm darkened the face of nature with its portentious gloom, and when the rays of a bright, if not unclouded sun gladdened the sparkling waters of the deep blue sea, it awakened only pleasant thoughts.

Folkestone on-the cliff is one of the most fashionable agreeable and healthy spots on the south coast. The high town is composed of new, spacious and elegant residences, many of them belonging to families from different parts of the kingdom who annually occupy them during the summer. It supports, and this in no mean matter, one of the finest clubs out of London, called "The Radnor," of which the author was elected an honorary member and where he met many charming people and played many a rubber. Club life is one of the most agreeable features in the social habits of England and contributes largely to the happiness of the people. The English clubs, unlike those of France, are established entirely, or almost entirely for social purposes, while in Paris the object of assembling is solely for the interchange of political thought or for the direct furtherance of purely political ends.— Even the great party clubs of Pall Mall, the Reform and Carlton, are social first and political afterwards. This the author quickly learned, for he long enjoyed honorary membership in the Reform Club and daily availed himself of the comforts and conveniences of this palatial edifice. These elegant centres of reunion exist in all the cities and large towns of the Kingdom, and the author rarely visited a country town to remain a week that the hospitalities of the local club, such as the "Weymouth, and County club" at Weymouth, were not extended to him, and he had the "run" of several in the West End. Shortly after he reached Folkestone he was admitted to the Radnor and it contributed much to the pleasure of his visit. Among the best remembered men of mark whom we met in this 'club were Lord Elibank, the venerable Marquis of Tweeddale, aid-de-camp of the Duke of Wellington during the Peninsular war, Admiral Sir Dalrymple Hay, Pleydell Bouverie, Sir C. Eardley, Gen. Hankey, Dr. Henry Lewis, Earl Darnley and Mr. Charles Eyre, a London Solicitor, one of the best informed and entertaining talkers in the realm. After he had enjoyed a good dinner and a bottle of sherry, the charms of his conversation reminded us of a line in Statira's speech, where she describes the charms of Alexander's conversation. "Then he would talk. Good Gods! how he would talk." The officers from Shorecliff also came of an afternoon for whist or billiards, and not unfrequently a few from Dover. Among the most constant of those from Dover were Col. Watson and Captain Thomas. The latter, however, was not a part of the Dover garrison. Those who came with no view to the intellectual dissipation of cards, sipped Irish whiskey, smoked old pipes and discussed in a pathetic mood the progress of liberal idea, for two of the most conservative elements in the kingdom are the army and navy.

The old town of Folkestone, lying on the sands below the cliffs, is a curious place, full of narrow streets, blind alleys and stuffy courts. It is said to have been occupied by the Romans, and the ruins of one of their watch towers are still pointed out. In more recent times the old town was the resort of smugglers and pirates, and is now much loved and crowded by fishermen, harbor laborers, sailors and other boisterous spirits, male and female. Like all low lying fishing villages it is a foul smelling and uninviting place. At low water the harbor is a heap of mud and the stranger sees little but trains coming and going, steamers landing sallow, bearded and strange looking people from the continent and piles on piles of luggage.

While making our headquarters in this place, we visited many interesting localities on the coast of Kent, notably Romney Marsh and Dungeness Light House. It may not be uninteresting to give some account of them. Our route from Dungeness was along the cliffs by Sandgate, a bold line of hills lying back of a flat shore of shingle. As we pursued our way we passed at regular intervals a number of Martello Towers. These isolated towers are so called from the fact that the first one towards which the attention of England was directed was in Martello bay, Corsica. When the British naval force was operating against Corsica in 1784, a round tower at Marletto or Myrtle bay made so gallant a resistance as to attract the attention not only of the British government, but of all Europe; and the English resolved to construct a number of the same kind on their own coast The Marletto tower is a circular brick or stone fort of two stories, the lower divided into chambers for the reception of stores and the upper fitted up as a casement or vaulted chamber for the troops. The diameter usually diminishes from about 40 feet at the base to 30 feet at the summit; the height is about 30 feet, and the thickness varies from about five feet on the land side to ten or more on the sea face. The vaulted roof is so thick and strong as to be shell proof. The circular wall extends high enough to form a parapet, and on the circular space within this parapet is a gun working on a traversing platform. The doorway is at a height of about eight or ten feet from the ground, accessible by a wooden ladder, which is removed during a siege.— Many of them are surrounded by a ditch and glacis. They constitute a singular series of defensive works, of very little value since the invention of rifled cannon.

Sandgate the first place of any size after leaving Folkestone for Durgeness is an aspiring watering place and lies nestling between green hills and the sea. Passing it we reached Shorncliff Camp, situated up the naked hills and hence the name "Shorn" or "bare" cliff, remarkable for its healthfulness, which fact and its proximity to the sea has led to its selection as a camping ground for troops. It was first used for this purpose during the wars of Napoleon, when it was thought of the first importance to keep a watch upon him, and if he approached the English coast to have a trained force ready to meet him. During the Crimean war large bodies of troops were kept here as at present and in fact the camp has been a *rendezvous* since the year 1804.

A few brief words may here find an appropriate place as to some of the peculiarities of the British army organization. It differs from the French and American is this that in the English service there is no *Colonel Commandant of Regiments*, actually in command. By the English system, the lieutenant Colonel performs the duty of commandant. When promoted, it is not to a Colonelcy, but to be a Brigadier, then to be a Major General, and so on. After becoming a full general, he is often appointed to be the Colonel Commandant of a particular regiment, merely that he may draw the pay, as a reward for services. There are many, however, who when they have reached the rank of General are never appointed colonels, for the reason that the colonelcies of numerous regiments are conferred upon a single individual. It is a means of increasing the salary of a court favorite. Thus Prince Albert was colonel of half a dozen regiments he never saw, and received the pay of all, though by holding them he prevented the advancement of many meritorious officers to whom the pay would have been no small matter. Prince Albert consented to accept these positions and enjoy the pay though he was in the receipt of £30,000 per annum for his privy purse, and held other lucrative appointments.

His course was severely criticised by all but the Court party. He was charged with an excessive love of money, with selfishly obstructing the promotion of veterans; of taking pay he did not want and cutting off the means of support of old generals with large families who needed it; with a want of generosity in thus requiting a government and people who, notwithstanding his large private fortune, allowed him annually $150.000, not one cent of which he ever used, but which he placed at interest, and at his death disposed of in his will. It is obvious from these facts that he was considered as a man, like the rest of mankind, not without his faults. As however this excellent Prince was guided in his course by the genuine principles of virtue, was a good citizen, a good husband and father, and sought to direct the Queen in a constitutional course for the promotion of the prosperity and hap piness of her people, it would be neither fair nor generous to judge him harshly in this particular. In accepting this pay he must be presumed to have been actuated, as in the rest of his life, by virtuous and commendable motives.

On this occasion when passing Shorncliff we made only a brief halt, but subsequently visited the camp on several occasions. Our extensive acquaintance with the officers and with what is styled in England "military society," both here and in many other garrison towns, made the subject of English army organization more than ordinarily interesting. Let us proceed then with our remarks on this grave subject.

England possesses the weakest land force of any of the European powers, and if she be regarded according to the number of her troops, is only a second-rate power, not more formidable than Norway, Sweden or Spain. England, however, in her proud old days, when her history was written, possessed no larger army than she does at present. A hundred years ago in London might have been seen many foreign regiments in English pay; and instead of sending her own countrymen to the battle field, the armies even of the Iron Duke of Wellington were only half composed of Englishmen; the other half consisted of Spaniards, Portugese, Dutch and Germans. In the war of the American revolution, England hired mercenary troops from Hesse Cassel and Brunswick and instigated the Indians to attack her American colonies. It was the active hostilities of the Cherokees against the South Carolinans in 1776, and other frontier tribes north and south, which so greatly irritated the colonist against the mother country and embarrassed the operations of the American armies, which fought with foes in front and rear. And in the war of 1812 the British government continued this deplorable policy commissioning the Indian chief Tecumseh a Brigadier General in the British army, in which capacity Tecumseh and his red-skin warriors co-operated with the British and Canadian forces in 1812-14 and until he was killed on the 5th of October, 1813. We shall not stop to comment upon this conduct or to give the comments of Bancroft or any American historian, anxious as we are to allow the bitter animosities of the past to slumber in the grave. We cannot pass on, however, without expressing our regret that this kind of statesmanship still prevails with the Tory party, and during the campaign of 1879, in Zulu land, the British not only hired African savages to operate against Cetewayo, but bribed Cetewayo's own brother to deceive and capture the redoubtable chief. The Tories seem to have acted on the principle that all things are right or justifiable in war, without remembering the trite adage, though you should lose everything else, remember to preserve your good name. Let us not wander, however, too much from the point. The happy position of England as an island, which defends her from foreign invasion is far better than any other European state, permits England to rest contented with so small an army and to rely mainly upon a powerful fleet for her defense. Whilst other powers of the mainland, even in time of peace, are obliged to maintain enormous armies, that of England is not at present stronger than it was 30 years ago. The strength of the British army, has, indeed, for the last 50 years remained unaltered.

Whilst the continental powers have been engaged in army reform, the English army has remained upon its old footing. Instead of red coats the infantry of the line wear red jackets. They carry the best breechloading rifles; the artillery also possess better guns, and the service and drill regulations have been somewhat altered, but this is all the modification that has taken place. The English army is recruited from the lowest classes, and in fact the army has not been inaptly styled a reformatory school. It is owing to the fact that such numbers of vicious characters enlist in the army that desertion is so common. Last year with a home and colonial force of 169,000 men, the deserters numbered 7,685; whereas in the French army of 428,000 men the deserters only numbered 300, and it was equally small in the German army of 400,000 men.

The English soldiers are better paid, clothed and fed than any others in Europe, receiving in one week more than a poor Russian does in a month. The pensions, too, are much higher than are allowed by other European States. England can, under her present system, only bring about 180,000 men into the field; and should she go to war with a powerful Continental State, she would be obliged to have recourse to some other recruiting system. In England, the large field manœuvres, with mixed arms, which take place in European countries yearly, are unknown. In the whole English army, therefore, there is not a single general who has had under his orders 40,000 men. Should the English army, therefore, ever have to go to war with a European Power, and have to fight great battles, the want of manœuvering capacities of the troops, and the still less practice of the higher generals having under their orders 50,000 and 60,000 men, will cause them great prejudice. In the Crimean war it was shown that the English troops, in point of courage, were quite equal to the *elite* of the French army, but they were far exceeded in their manœuvering by the latter, and then the French manœuvered worse than the Germans who in this respect take the first rank in Europe. With respect to the improved military education of the officers since the Crimean war, great progress has been made in the English army. The Military Academy of Woolwich is excellent and the officers are well educated, and the same may be said of Sandhurst. But it must be admitted that the English infantry and cavalry officers are far behind both the French, German and American officers in military education. With respect to the improvement of the men, the officers seem to give themselves little trouble in the matter. It is left to the non commissioned officers The distinction between the officers and the non commissioned officers in the English army is still greater than in those of the continental armies. The purchase system has been abolished, however, and therefore a great evil in the English army is removed. This great reform, however, was so strenuously opposed by the Tory party that Mr. Gladstone was forced in order to accomplish it to resort to the Royal prerogative. The officers, especially of Guards and Cavalry almost exclusively belong to the aristocracy, and receive allowances from their parents. Without such allowances they are unable to live. The middle class as a rule do not send their sons into the army but place them in commerce, trade and manufactures.

This wise course is becoming common with the aristocracy, and the Duke of Argyle, whose ancestor 800 years ago was the most powerful subject in the realm, a man in whose veins flows the bluest of blue blood, (if anybody knows what that is,) has three sons in trade, brothers of the Queen's son-in-law, John D. S. Campbell, Marquis of Lorne and Governor-General of Canada, namely, Lord Archibald Campbell, a wine merchant, Lord Walter, a tea taster, and Lord ———, a cotton broker, and no right minded man thinks less of them, though descended from that famous Duke of modern times, thus immortalized by Pope:

"Argyle, the State's whole thunder born to wield,
And shake alike the Senate and the field."

The English officers are, everything considered, badly paid. An infantry lieutenant must at least have a private income of £100, and twice as much is necessary for cavalry officer. When off duty the English officers do not wear uniform, and seem as proud to be thought gentlemen as officers. The recent custom therefore of the Duke of Edinburg in wearing his uniform when traveling and generally when off of duty, as is the case in Russia and Germany, has occasioned much comment and of a kind far from complimentary to him. He has been advised that in England the civil power has always taken precedence of the military, and that no foreign customs will be tolerated which look to giving greater prominence to the military or naval; nor to the introduction into England of anything which smacks of personal government or Imperialism. This he has been advised of notwithstanding Baconsfield's success in adding to her Majesty's title the words "Empress of India."

## CHAPTER XVIII.

VISIT TO A COUNTRY HOUSE—LORD ELLENBOROUGH—MATTERS OF ETIQUETTE—OSMOND PRIAULX—TOURISTS.

Having now improved our opportunity of sight seeing to the best advantage, being able to converse in an intelligent manner about things in this locality, and the time having arrived for our visit to Beechborough, we completed our arrangements, and taking the Misses S., under our care we set forward for that hospitable abode. The mansion stands on a commanding height. We had often seen it from afar in our various excursions, and on reaching it we found it one of the stateliest of England's stately homes.

Originally built of stone or brick, it has been disfigured by a coat of stucco, and is now of a drab color. Standing in a widely extending park of undulating ground, it has an air of quiet and comfortable old age, the ancient porch overgrown with woodbine and ivy, the tall gables peeping through taller beech trees. On one side the windows looked out upon a sunny orchard and a green hill side, which slopes down to luxuriant meadows. From the opposite side are to be seen far down in the Valley, near the stock yard and barn, a pool of water, always lively with ducks, and on the green margin of which a flock of geese were always gabbling. Lazy cows chewed their cud over the rails of the enclosure, and fat pigs delved up the litter of the yards with their snouts. This was the headquarters of one of the tenant farmers.

Here we enjoyed a week's visit, finding our host and his company, for several others besides our party were in the house at the time, pleasant and agreeable people. There was a lawyer in the company, Mr. Hawkins, who always started some good topic;

the rector of a neighboring parish, Mr. Stanhope, a delightful companion, and a lord—nothing is complete without one of the conservative race—and one of the great lords, too—the venerable and distinguished Earl of Ellenborough. Though it has been said of this eminent man that he was more eloquent than wise, we found him such good and, indeed, improving company that we are inclined to think that if all lords were of his type, we should soon learn to love them as much as the average Briton. The company assimilated well and the time could not have passed more pleasantly—good breeding and general elegance of manners prevailing with all. A friend informed us that our venerable host took pains in the selection of his company, and never allowed the quiet of his country home to be disturbed by those so well known as "trashy London dashers." He generally had in his company a few officers and their wives, but not those who recalled too forcibly in their conversation barrack life; a traveler, if such could be found, unlike the stock tourist who travels far and sees nothing; a few writers or literary men to make a charming spice for all, but like all spices, he would not allow too much of them. These "literary fellows" want keeping down said he; otherwise they would turn his house into an Athenæum club. In their society, too, he said, you feel, if you venture to talk yourself, you should contribute something substantial to the "feast of reason"—a thing many find it, continued Mr. B., easier to speak of than do.

Before leaving this hospitable abode and the subject, it may be permitted us to interpolate something as to that remarkable man whom Guizot pronounced the most brilliant orator in the Tory ranks, Lord Ellenborough. Guizot, who was long French Envoy to England and no mean authority, expressed this opinion, and he was in the habit of hearing Lord Derby, Lansdown, Sir Robert Peel, Mr. Gladstone, Disraeli, and other British orators. Hon. Edward Law, afterwards Earl of Ellenborough, entered public life in 1828-9, under the Duke of Wellington, and by the Cabinet of Sir Robert Peel was made Governor-General of India, where he was guilty of vagaries which filled the Directors of the Company with the utmost alarm. Although a civilian, he inflicted intolerable slights upon the civil servants of the company. He reserved his favor and confidence for the military, yet endangered the discipline of the very army which he had endeavored to conciliate by imprudent and unjustifiable means. He made showy progresses, which brought ridicule upon the British name. He addressed proclamations to the rulers and nations of India, which appeared to sanction idolatry, and finally, in the bombastic and inflated language of his proclamation concerning the gates of Juggernaut, when brought back from Ghuznee, he reached a climax of absurdity which no Viceroy had ever attained, yet the British government stood by him. Not so the Directory—the Directory, composed of business men. They recalled the eccentric Governor-General. As soon as he reached England he was promoted to an Earldom, and in 1858 was again Minister for India, and soon became involved in a quarrel with Lord Canning, the then Governor-General, the result of which was that he resigned his position in the cabinet of Lord Derby—not, however in the usual way. Instead of handing his resignation to the Prime Minister, as if he had no superior in the cabinet, he laid it before the Queen.

In 1855, Lord Ellenborough addressed the House of Lords in a speech in opposition to the Government's Russian policy, to which the "Times" thus referred next day: "The most briliant audience in Britain was kept for above an hour suspended between platitudes which no one contest, and the paradoxes which no one could believe. Most of those present retired with the melancholy conviction that, although the country may be sorely in want of a powerful war minister, that heaven-born statesman had not been found in the accomplished orator who had commenced the discussion." During the Indian mutiny, Lord Ellenborough criticised the Government policy and the conduct of affairs until it led to a breach between Lord Granville and himself. He continued his course of opposition to the Liberals until he was denounced by that party as the greatest imposter among living statesmen—the greatest charlatan among living politicians. Yet he was considered, by many, as the best debater in either house of Parliament. We can scarcely render adequate justice to the charm and impressiveness of his manner even in private—the reader can form an idea of what it was in public. His voice is sonorous, full, clear and penetrating. The figure manly, the features handsome, the hair grey, with the snows of seventy winters, yet abundant. His gesture is easy yet dignified, his emphasis not too frequent, but decisive. His eloquence is perfection, and we could not but think that if he showed to such advantage in the private circle, the admiration of Guizot, as embodied in his fine phraseology was not unduly excited by his displays in the House of Peers. In his Toryism he out Heroded Herod, and was almost ferocious in his opposition to reformers and any change in the British Constitution tending towards Liberalism.

Our visit to this country seat suggests a few remarks on visits to country houses before we quit the subject. Since an Englishman's house is his castle, no one, not even a near relation, has a right to invite himself to stay in it. It is not only taking a liberty to do so, but may prove to be very inconvenient. A general invitation, too, should never be acted on. It is often given without any intention of following it up. An invitation specifies the persons whom it includes, and the person invited can never presume to take with him any one not specified. If a gentleman cannot dispense with his valet, or a lady with her maid, they should write to ask leave to bring a servant. Children or horses cannot be taken without special mention is made of them, nor is it good taste to take too much luggage. The length of the visit is always specified in the invitation. This saves a deal of trouble.. While on a visit you should make it a point to give as little trouble as possible, to conform to the habits of your entertainers and never be in the way. On this princip'e you will retire to your own occupations soon after breakfast, unless some arrangement has been made for passing the morning otherwise. If you have nothing to do you may be sure that your host has. Another point of good breeding is to be punctual at meals. A host always provides amusement for his guests—in fact the rule on which he acts is to make his visitors as much at home as possible; that on which the visitor should act, is to interfere as little as possible with the domestic routine of the house.

But we are again in Folkestone and must give the reader some respite by bringing this chapter to a speedy close.

During our many visits to the historical spots and other interesting localities and objects in this part of England, we were usually accompanied by our friend Osmond Priaulx, of London, a man of talent and learning. Mr. Priaulx dropped us a note when he heard we were in Folkestone and intended to remain there a month, to say that he would come down by the next train and spend the same time by the sea. Delighted at this intelligence, we immediately engaged him apartments near our own in Cheriton Road.— His active mind, which showed itself in a spirit of prying observation and incessant curiosity, his large stores of knowledge and his intimate acquaintance with this part of the world and many of the country people, made him not only a charming, but the most useful of companions. A man not only of talent but of genius, he was entirely unlike some with whom we have journied. We refer to those self satisfied, half witted fellows, who, because they have gone over certain ground and seen nothing, return as ignorant, confused and vapid as they started out on their travels, fancy that all that which a man of talent sees and describes has no existence out of his imagination. These snappy snobs who have now and again floated down the current with us, and who are destitute of observation and discrimination, incapable of deriving any benefit from travel, make themselves objects of ridicule by perpetrating comments upon the accounts of the more gifted class of tourists. Such fatuous individuals grope through the world in a kind of twilight, bewildered by the obscurity of their incapacity to see objects in their true colors and dimensions, and bring strongly to memory the significant words of a clever writer, that the chief point of difference between a man of talent and the man without, consists of the different ways in which their minds are employed during the same interval. They are obliged, let us suppose, to walk from Temple Bar to Hyde Park corner. The dull man goes straight forward; he has so many furlongs to traverse He observes if he meets any of his acquaintances; he enquires respecting their health and their family. He glances perhaps at the shops as he passes; he admires the fashion of a buckle, and the metal of a tea urn. If he experiences any flights of fancy, they are of a short extent; of the same nature as the flight of a forest bird, clipped of his wings and condemned to hop the rest of his life in a barnyard. On the other hand, the man of talent gives full scope to his imagination. He laughs and cries. Unindebted to the suggestions of the surrounding objects, his whole soul is employed. He enters into nice calculations, he digests sagacious reasonings. In imagination he declaims or describes, impressed with the deepest sympathy, or elevated to the loftiest rapture. He makes a thousand new and admirable combinations. He passes through a thousand imaginary scenes, tries his courage, tasks his ingenuity and thus becomes gradually prepared to meet almost any of the many colored events of human life. He consults by the aid of memory the books he has read, and projects others for the future instruction and delight of mankind. If he observes the passengers, he reads their countenances, conjectures their past history, and forms a superficial notion of their wisdom or folly, their virtue or vice, their satisfaction or misery. If he observes the scenes that occur, it is with the eye of a connoisseur or an artist. Every object is capable of suggesting to him a volume of reflections.— The time of these two persons in one respect resembles: it has brought them both to Hyde Park corner. In almost every other respect it is dissimilar.

Much more might be said upon this subject, but we are restrained by that laudable fear of tediousness' which authors should always have before their eyes.

## CHAPTER XIX.

ROMNEY MARSH AND DUNGENESS—THE MILITARY CANAL—NAPO-
LEON—PLANS FOR THE INVASION OF ENGLAND—THE
ORIGIN OF ENGLISH LIGHT HOUSES—A TYPE
OF THE MODERN POLITICIAN.

After a few further days spent at Folkestone, to which we returned from our numerous excursions in south-eastern Kent, as persistently as a Frenchman to his "mouton;" days given to the blandishments of sea-side society; the intricacies of short whist, and the excitement of fishing in a cock boat on the English channel, we set out once more by the Coast road to make our contemplated visit to Romney Marsh and Dungeness Light House. More than once the reader has been promised the details of this visit, but as usual, our numerous digressions have prevented his getting them. Instead of going forward by the direct line to the end of our journey, we have allowed ourselves to be drawn aside, like a child following a butterfly, by the attractions of Shorncliff and our interest in the British army, and our sojourn at Beechborough and the delights of society in a country house. These have been the natural and interesting causes of our delay rather than uncontrollable impulse in our pen to wander wantonly and wildly.

The coast road which we again followed, led us, as the reader is now aware, over the familiar path to Sandgate, Shorncliff and Saltwood Castle—the green cliffs of Albion being to our right and the sparkling waters of the deep blue sea spread out to the left. The sky was bright and the air bracing. It seemed but yesterday since the merry month of May. The flowers were gay, sweet and pretty as when in the Spring-time, they leap over the lea and cluster round our feet. The glad voice of what seemed a new spring made the woods and welkin ring. Yet evidence was not wanting that autumn presided over the land. Ripe corn was stacked in the fields, ruddy fruit bent the branches of many a goodly tree, the air was loaded with the scent of gathered hops. Mother earth, with a bounteous hand, scattered rich largess to her children. The plantations of wood were kindling into hues of gorgeous beauty, mixed and manifold; the stubble-field gleamed out like tarnished gold in the mild lustre of the temperate day; clouds in the azure ocean above floated away like silver barks—softly came and went the winds.

Looking out upon the smiling landscapes which presented an enchanting scene of peace and plenty, the lines of the essayist recurred to memory, "a beautiful prospect delights the soul as much as a demonstration; and a description in Homer has charmed more readers than a chapter in Aristotle."

About midday we reached Hythe, having lingered frequently to examine some object of interest or to take a "bitter." One of the chief objects of curiosity of the road was the crypt of St. Leonard's church, where we saw hundreds of human skulls ranged on shelves for inspection. These ghastly remains have sorely puzzled archæologists. The guide informed us they were the skulls of the Danes and Northmen who invaded England before the time of the Normans, information which we received with much gravity and many doubts. It is most probable they were dug up when the foundation of the present church was laid. Resuming our course we reached West Hythe and found ourselves on a plain something like a prairie, and covered with grass, with hardly a tree, bush or hedge, with few houses or inhabitants, but abundance of sheep. This is Romney marsh.

The military canal which crosses this country is a singular work of defence, constructed in 1804, when the English apprehended a French invasion.

Napoleon had assembled in 1803-4 a vast flotilla of flat-bottomed boats at Boulogne which was to be used for the invasion of England. He was at this time unusually active and energetic in his movements; had gone in person to *Ponte de Briques*, a small village three miles from Boulogne on the river Liane, (the writer has spent at Pont de Briques many a happy day fishing) inspected the harbor and public works; reviewed the grand army, had caused it to be published in the "Moniteur" that the Comte d'Artois had offered his services and those of the *emigres* to the king of England and roused the French people to a kind of frenzy by rumors that the inhabitants of *La Vendee* and the *Chouans* had set on foot a plan of general pillage and incendiarism. In such a condition of affairs all conservative people, all property holders, gave in their adhesion to the established government under the impression that there was no security but in absolute power, a strong man and a strong government. They consoled themselves at the loss of liberty, with the following arguments, which were, says Mme. de Remusat, in her recently published "Memoirs," which are destined to remain one of the principal authorities on the character and policy of Napoleon, perhaps justified by the circumstances: "After the storm through which we have passed, and amid the strife of so many parties, superior force only can give us liberty, and so long as that force tends to promote principles of order and morality, we ought not to regard ourselves as straying from the right road, for the creator will disappear but that which he has created will remain with us." This was order, though Napoleon claimed that with the French Empire in Europe, began the age of civilization, of science, of light and of law.

Three quarters of a century have passed away and what was argument in 1804-5 has become fact in 1880. Four Napoleons have perished and the idea represented by the last one, that of imperialism, which was a menace to the present Republican government and to order in France, has perished with time. Thus the man of the people, the creator of equality, the rewarder of merit in France has disappeared but that which he created remains and is now represented by the Republic of M. Grevy.

The fragment of the Bonaparte family still in France at the head of which stands Jerome, known by the nick-name of Plon-Plon, the son of Napoleon's brother by his Westphalian wife, is without influence. Jerome is a man of ability but an indolent voluptuary with a decided repugnance for the active career of a leader.— Strange to say, he has always been a Liberal in politics and is now the recognized supporter of the French Republic. He has no imperial disposition, has no party of followers, and is not likely to create disturbances. If he were so disposed, he could scarcely find anybody to urge his claims to a throne, which at best, never had anything but a pasteboard existence. The Bonapartes have never had anything in France except what was won by the sword, and the same royal road to power lies before all men of brains, audacity and cruel ambition. Napoleon created in the minds of Frenchmen a love of liberty and equality and brought order out of anarchy. He and his dynasty are gone—that which he created remains.

But to proceed. The course of this canal is nearly coincident with the Northern margin of the Marsh, is from Hythe to Rye, a distance of about 23 miles. It has an average depth of 9 feet and width of 70. It was constructed for the conveyance of troops and military stores along a route almost unprovided, in those days, with any good roads, but it has been seldom used; and indeed, though begun in 1804, it has never actually been completed. A raised bank is carried along it, as a cover for musketeers; as the line is purposely made in a series of zigzags. Each angle of the bank was intended to be defended by heavy cannon. Military stations for artillerymen and infantry were placed at intervals. The whole affair looks very dismal now; the stations are occupied by coastguardsmen, who have little or nothing to do; and a spectator is apt to wish that something useful could be made out of that which must have cost John Bull a deal of money.

Leaving this route at Appledore, we made our way in a covered cart to the Southeast, across the Marsh, to the town of New Romney. The covered cart is the only vehicle of any kind which traverses the Marsh—is the only means of accommodation for that almost infinitesimal part of the travelling public which seeks business or pleasure in these solitary regions. Without springs or cushions, with broad, heavy wheels, crowded with sacks of corn and casks of beer, to say nothing of a multiplicity of smaller articles, and tugged by ponderous horses of the Flanders breed, the covered cart is by no means a rapid or luxurious mode of conveyance. The traveller has ample opportunity, seated upon a sack of corn and bolstered by a bale of hops, to study the features of the country. Stowed away in the cart among a lot of general merchandize, we commenced our journey at the rate of two miles an hour. Some ladies who were in the party, were sadly dejected and wonderous fidgety at the going off, but soon resumed an air of cheerfulness when it was declared that our fashionable friends in Folkestone should not be enlightened upon the subject of how we journeyed across the English Australia. The marsh begins two or three miles beyond the musketry grounds, and extends to Rye. It is a rich grazing country and supplies some of the best beef in the London market. The air is, however, full of malaria and the ague and chills always present in autumn. The air is indeed bad in winter, worse in summer, and at no time good. There is a joke that the marshmen know so little of anything outside of the marsh, that they believe the world to be divided into five quarters—Europe, Asia, Africa, America and Romney Marsh. The area, about 44,000 acres, is so rich in grass that it maintains 150,000 sheep. The whole district has been much improved of late years by drainage. The marsh forms a kind of peninsular, jutting out to the South, so low, that if a fierce wind came from the East, the whole might be flooded in a very short time. To prevent this, a remarkable wall called Dymchurch wall, has been constructed of earth and rough stone facing. At about three miles from Hythe this wall begins, close to the sea. It is three miles long, 20 feet high, 15 to 30 feet wide at the top and spreading out to a broad base. The sea-face is defended by piles, groins and jetties; while sluices are formed to facilitate drainage. The sea wall or barrier was built altogether at the expense of the marshmen. From the interstices of the wall and in the low sections faxatile grasses spring up as also many fluviatic plants. Arrived at Lydd our last dispositions were made for visiting the principal object of interest to us, Dungeness light house. It occupies the extreme southern point of the marsh and four miles of rugged shingle separated it from us. Only vigorous excursionists undertake to make their way to it. We felt now that even the covered cart would neither be despised nor rejected.

"It cannot be done" was the irresolute exclamation of one of the ladies.

"What can't be done?" was the response of the strong minded woman.

"Why" said the first lady, "we can never walk across the shingle to the light house."

"It is a mere excuse," responded the strong minded lady. "Have you ever tried it? no never! well, we'll never give it up till you do" said the vigorous dame.

The hopeful words of this lady did not encourage the other who gave up in despair, while her companion made preparations to accompany the gentlemen, saying determinedly: "It can't be done! well, did you ever? it must be done, and what's more, it shall be done and by this little woman."

Mrs. Peyton and the first lady having decided not to venture upon such an expedition they commenced making themselves comfortable at the Inn, as the escort of the second lady, and that interesting lady herself started with us for the light house. A laborious walk of two hours and a half brought us to the desired object, which with two forts is situated on the sands at Dungeness. No particular description of either would interest. Both the forts and the light house are annually becoming more and more inland, the shingle increasing in breadth and thickness at the rate of a hundred yards every fifty years. This process has been going on for the last two or three centuries. The light house though 110 feet high is gradually losing its value. Already plans are discussed for the erection of another nearer the water. It would be difficult to find a more retired spot than Dungeness. Visitors are rarely seen there, and the light house keeper though in sight of the French coast did not hear of the revolution of 1848 until three weeks after the flight of Louis Phillippl. It may not be uninteresting to our readers if we delay for a moment to give a few facts in connection with the origin of English Light Houses.. Their history is interesting and curious. It was not until 1696 that they were introduced into England. Upon the Cornish coast, about fourteen miles from Plymouth, there is a dangerous reef of rocks against which the Atlantic waves beat and break with uncontrolable fury. These are the Eddystone rocks, so named from the wild tumult of conflicting currents among which they dwell. Standing in the highway of commerce, it is not surprising that many a noble ship went to pieces upon them ; nor strange that men's hearts should have been set upon devising some means of giving mariners a timely warning. In 1696, Henry Winstanley determined to devote himself to this task and commenced work upon the Eddystone rocks. During the next season he had raised a round pillar or light-house twelve feet high and fourteen feet in diameter. He labored incessantly upon it until it reached the height of eighty feet, when it was so far completed that he took possession of it and lit his lamp. The first night he lodged in his strange citadel was one of storm and tumult, and for eleven succeeding days not a boat could approach the beleaguered garrison. They clung manfully, however, to their duty and finally succeeded in taking supplies to the heroic light-house keeper. The kindly glimmer of his beacon, dazzling upon the troubled water was considered by all sailors of that day a providential interposition in their behalf. Winstanley soon found, however, that at a height of eighty feet his lantern was sometimes actually buried under the water. He therefore recommenced his work and carried up the building to an elevation of 120 feet. The first Eddystone light house stood until 1703, when requiring some repairs, Winstanley and some workmen landed upon the rocks. Poor Winstanley, in his strong self-reliance in the stability of his work, had often declared "he only wished to be there in the greatest storm that ever blew under the face of the heavens, that he might see what effect it might have upon the structure." The night he landed with his workmen was one of storm, a storm which is memorable in history for its wild fury and for the fearful destruction it wrought—the storm of November 26th, 1703. When the morning of the 27th arose on the troubled waters, not a vestige remained of the light house, of the architect or of his men. There is a wide distinction between presumption and courage, between self-confidence and an humble trust.

The next person who wrestled with the stubborn difficulty was John Rudzerd. One would scarcely have expected to have seen one with his antecedents—for he was a London silk mercer—engaged in such a critical mission. But so it was. He commenced the work in 1706 with such energy and skill, that in two years the light might again be seen shining like a star above the waves, at the height of 92 feet. This last tower, however, was of wood, weighted at the base by a considerable mass of stone work. After standing over forty years it was destroyed by fire, its three tenants escaping with difficulty.

At this time there appeared a man of real genius, John Smeaton, a native of Yorkshire. He had been articled to an attorney and afterwards followed the business of a maker of mathematical instruments. He was the first person who ever, in

England, pursued the business or calling of a civil engineer, and in fact may be said to have created the profession. He resolved to construct a tower entirely of stone and though the public authorities were opposed to it, they finally yielded their assent and lent him aid. Having decided upon the material, the next object of anxious consideration with him was the form of his tower. His thoughts set upon the study of nature's own type of strength—a grand old oak. He considered its spreading roots, which take such a firm, broad grip upon the soil of its mother earth; he studied the rise of its swelling base, which when it attains the height of above one diameter, is reduced by a graceful curve concave to the eye, which carries it to a diameter less by one-third than its original base. Now, then it runs up more perpendicularly in the form of a cylinder, and then, a preparation being required for the support of its spreading boughs, a renewed swelling of its diameter is observable. Now, (Smeaton proceeds to reason) were we to cut off the branches of our noble oak and in that denuded state, expose its bole to the assaults of wild waves at the base, instead of wild winds at the summit, we have a style of such a lighthouse-column as is best adapted to endure the peculiar tests of its position. This is the well known story of the conception of the idea of the Eddystone lighthouse.

In 1756 Smeaton commenced work upon the rock, cutting the surface in regular steps or trenches into which the blocks of stone were to be dovetailed. In 1759 his tower, 68 feet in height, was completed. The structure is a solid mass of stone to the height of twelve feet. On the 16th of October, 1759, the benignant light again shone out over the waters, a welcome gleam to the straining eye of the mariner, though it was but the concentrated light of a few tallow candles. And there was no better light till 1807, when Argand burners with silver copper reflectors were displayed. Such was the recent and humble English origin of those numerous and splendid lighthouses now standing upon every part of the coast. Among the most important of those which throw a beneficent glimmer of light from wild rocks and dark shores is that of Dungeness.

When reaching the inn on our return we found Mrs. Peyton and her lady friend still industriously keeping up their chit chat. We felt grateful to the old maid for having made her time pass so pleasantly. This worthy woman was unlike the pictures usually delineated of aged spinsters; her bosom was not the abode of indifference or malignity. On the contrary, she was always cheerful, useful to those about her, the dispenser of happiness to her circle. Could the reader have listened to her interesting, gossipping conversation he must have subscribed to the opinion that she had cultivated in no ordinary way "God's gift of speech."

The evening was passed agreeably in the inn, the social party having been reinforced by two wanderers to this region, and after a night's rest, we again turned our faces towards Folkestone. One of the previous evening's arrivals was a native of Kent, Lt. General Knatchbull, R. A., uncle of Sir Wyndham Knatchbull, Bart., of Mersham le Hatch. General K. had been absent from England, serving in the Indian army, the larger part of his life, and had recently returned to enjoy a green old age among his kindred. His companion, a young friend of the old veteran, by the name of—well, we shall call him Von Humbug—was a somewhat remarkable character, of whom we shall have a word to say presently. With both of them we subsequently became well acquainted and passed much time in their circles, both in London and in Jersey, in which latter place Gen. Knatchbull extended to us the hospitalities of his well appointed establishment, Claremount Court.

Suspending our narrative at this point, we shall anticipate the future by informing our readers that this young man, Von Humbug, was a rising politician of the toad eating type. He was pursuing Gen. K. with sycophantic servility, hoping thus to secure the entre to Mersham le Hatch, and ultimately the social influence and support of the Baronet. His wily arts became in the course of time a study to us, then so little acquainted with the ways of courtiers. Von H. was an embodiment of caution, and always careful to be on the right side whenever there were two or more sides to a question, the right side being of course the winning one. As a rule, Von H. pledged himself to no particular party but just as a party was entering upon power it was certain to find him heart and soul for it. He avoided meddling with questions about which it was doubtful which way public opinion would turn, but whenever it became evident that a measure would become truly popular, he would advocate it with all the heart and soul he possessed, which, however, was not very much. Thus he often got the credit of being a wise man, and a far-seeing man, and a man who had the interest of his fellow-creatures at heart. He was very careful as to who were his acquaintances. It was one of his principles never to have much to do with those people who could do nothing to advance his interests, but was ready to attach himself to the skirts of some powerful man, like General Knatchbull, whose arguments he would re-echo, and to whose utterances he always said ditto. Upon no one point would he bring himself to differ with his patron. He was perfectly aware if he could bring himself to eat a sufficient quantity of humble pie, and was careful meanwhile to fortify his position, as his patron rose, so must he rise, until at last he would reach the pinnacle of his ambition. He was always found hanging about in the society of those people about whom there is an undoubted air of respectability—persons of acknowledged breed and position. He was rarely heard to say an unpleasant thing, or known to do a generous act. For petty offices he electioned principally after dark and generally "spotted" his men before midnight. It was easier to extract a promise from them, however, than to get the right ticket deposited in the urn. Von H. often found that the men whom he had tickled, returned the compliment by "scratching" him. He was rich in promises, as well as in money, but it was generally found that those who depended upon him got more pleasant things said to them than tangible benefits given them. Behind the scenes where nobody was looking on he was not quite so pleasant and polite.

Those who did work for him in secret got little thanks and less pay. He was ever on the lookout for opportunities to reap the fruits of other men's labors. In his business, he utilized schemes which had been the thoughts of other men's lifetime. A good listener, he took in other men's ideas and retailed them as his own. He rarely tried a new scheme himself or ventured an opinion he had not heard from another and had reason to believe was the popular thing. He waited until it was evident a thing could be made to answer, and then he would step in. He kept a sharp lookout for new patrons, for when one patron could help him no longer, he quietly dropped him and played the toady to another. He and his family never formed a friendship with any family about whose social status there was a shadow of doubt; nor indeed, did they form a friendship with any one which could not be dropped when convenient. His own and his family's position being weak they could not venture to know doubtful characters. We doubt whether he was capable of friendship in the true meaning of the word—friendship which would result in no gain, direct or indirect, to himself. Certainly he would not indulge in a sentimental friendship which would retard his getting on in the world. And being informed by his patron that he was engaged to be married to a woman whose family connections were only apparently of the right sort, he severed the knot though it broke the girl's heart. But though Von H. was an adept at dropping people when it suited his purpose to do so, it was almost impossible to drop him. You could hardly insult him, he was impervious to slights, and would demolish without a grimace, any quantity of humble pie. He knew that he could advance himself in no other way than by sticking to people who could help him, and he was too sensible, for mere sentimental grievances, to throw up his chance of advancement. He felt that a day of reckoning might come; meanwhile he would vent his spleen upon those unlucky individuals who are under his thumb, and whose brains and hands are at his disposal. This toady loved the applause and good opinion of the world. To this end he essayed to get an office, to enter public life. Once a town councilor, a member of a board or in a petty office of any kind he would take the greatest pains not to endanger his seat. He would express no decided opinions, identify himself with no unpopular movement; make no inflammatory speeches. He would do his best to conciliate and curry favor with all men and all parties. He would never think of advocating a new measure, speak until others had spoken and the direction of popular currents could be plainly seen and least of all would he think of proposing a reform. If every one else were content to let things go on in the old groove he would be quite content to do so too. But if a reform was imperatively demanded he would not risk his popularity by opposing it—he would indeed, avail himself of the opportunity to speak in favor thereof. He always feels, for he is still flourishing in the West End, very comfortably, and mildly deprecates any attempt on the part of the people to demonstrate that all the world are not really so comfortable as he is. He takes a rosy view of things generally, and not even the recital of the deepest misery can destroy his airy cheerfulness. He is now, after the lapse of fifteen years, still constantly on the look-out for good things for himself and *proteges*,—for even this wretched fellow has come to have followers: He is ready upon all occasions, to lend a helping hand to jobbery when he can gain anything by so doing. And all he does is so very polite, so very quiet, so very meek! He has never acquired much influence, and never will, and strange enough, has so far never incurred the contempt he deserves.. People, as we have been recently informed by an English friend, have not yet discovered that he is only a time server, selfish sharper and shuffling hypocrite. They see that he is ever on the winning side and accordingly applaud his judgment which has just been fortified in their opinion by his election under the 'liberal party to a seat in Parliament, though for the last seven years he has been sustained by Tory pap administered by Lord Beaconsfield. He is now in Parliament but will undertake nothing but appear only as the follower of other men. He will make his influence pay, however, and will be certain to leave public life richer than he entered it. Though in a liberal house he will prove to be one of the worst enemies of progress, because he is, and we know him to be so, an enemy in disguise. It is somewhat surprising that Englishmen, who are supposed to love blunt, outspoken honesty, should be de ceived by him. They are however. We cannot believe that it will always be so. John Bull will after while penetrate his disguises, understand his tactics and be convinced, as other people are, of his insincerity. Before this takes place, however, Von H. will have no further use for Mr. Bull. He will have feathered his nest, be prepared to retire full of plunder and full of "honahs."

Having sufficiently anticipated events in the foregoing sketch of Mr. Von H's character, and career, we must resume our narrative where we left off. Notwithstanding the doubtful air of Romney Marsh, we were much invigorated in body and mind by a night's rest at the Inn, and proceeded in the best of spirits to visit on the way back to Folkestone some interesting ruins. These are the ruins of Saltwood, Landslip and Westhanger Castles. According to doubtful traditions it was in Westhanger Castle that Fair Rosamond was imprisoned before her departure for Woodstock.

The interest which attaches to these ruins is greatly heightened by the moral sentiment which is blended with them. These degraded castles, now so charming in their drapery of ivy, were formerly no better than the strongholds of robbers, the dens of murderers, the homes of rapine. Well has it been said that when we recollect that these castles were formerly the residences of petty tyrants, who, before the royal authority was sufficiently established over the kingdom, from thence exercised their self created rights of pillage, on their miserable vassals and even over inoffensive passengers who fell into their hands, we imagine, when viewing them, that we are contemplating the carcass or the skeleton of some huge, ferocious beast of prey.

Time does not admit of any description of ruins, however interesting, nor of lengthened reflections upon the sentiments which they inspire. Our leader was the strong minded lady who accompanied us to the Light House, and she soon conducted us to new Romney. Here we took an open boat manned by three fishermen, and setting sail soon made Folkstone harbor. The glowing serenity that pervaded the whole prospect of sea and sky on this calm and sunny day was most pleasing.

"The glassy ocean, hushed, forgot to roar,
But trembling, murmured on the sandy shore."

## CHAPTER XX.

FROM FOLKESTONE BY DOVER, DEAL AND CANTERBURY TO LONDON—THE CATHEDRAL — THE "ASHES" OF KINGS — THE FATE OF SOVEREIGNS, ETC.

After having occupied Folkestone as headquarters for some time, the porter was ordered in to cord our luggage, preparatory to our return to London. A square top cab drew up in front of our lodgings, on which our boxes were placed. Household domestics gathered round about for a final "tip." Our kind neighbors hastily threw open their windows, as the news of our departure spread abroad and human heads protruded from them as well as telescopes. Our cheerful neighbors seemed eager to get a last glimpse of the lady in the new "waterfall" and the gentleman in duck breeches.

Everything having been settled, we jumped into the cab, and soon reached the station, only, however, in time to see the train slide out of view with deafening shrieks. Here was a difficulty. We stopped a few moments to take in the situation. The station was becoming deserted. A few minutes later a single porter remained  No sound was now heard, but the rattling of the tight cords of the signal post and the murmur of the winds against the telegraph wires. Flurried at this unexpected mishap, we determined not to be defeated in our plans and concluded a bargain in a few words with "cabby," who, at the end of something over an hour, set us down in Dover. Proceeding to the office of the Deal coach, we took seats in an antiquated vehicle, a stage coach, or long stage omnibus, plying by Deal to Canterbury, and were soon climbing hills and plunging into valleys behind four vivacious greys. Placing Mrs. Peyton and Miss Turner in the interior, we mounted aloft and sat by the side of the driver. Drawing the duster around our legs and lighting a cigar from that of the gentleman on the right, we prepared to enjoy the drive and view the refreshing variety of scenery through the fog of our cheroot.

The day was fine, the air just fresh enough to brace the nerves and give us a fillip to enjoy anything of enjoyment that might present itself. Though baffled in our effort to catch the train and our subsequent experiences of the road in a springless cab drawn by a jaded hack, we did not feel greatly *de trop*. The country was soon reached, and we passed on amid scenes enlivened by pretty villas which extend, here and there, from the sea coast to Canterbury. These villas and cottages, with their fanciful porticos and miniature parterres, are veritable earthly paradises. Each one of them is a little world in itself. All are alike and each possesses its individual characteristics. What an interest they assume in the stranger's eye; what range of thought they call up! We soon passed these and came upon a region of semi-detached villas which usher in the village — those rustic settlements everywhere scattered over the surface of happy, peaceful old England, and so dear to the long imprisoned denizen of the city. The green verandahs, minionette boxes and pretty strips of garden give them a charming semi-rural aspect. The villages are quietly left behind echoing to the noise of wheels upon the rubble stones —the coach is in the country again, but one village is scarcely out of sight before the greys are approaching another. But we are evidently now coming to a more important place. The houses are larger and more independent looking, the villas are still semi-detached, but more imposing. From the summit of a long, gently sloping hill, a wide extent of country is seen. That fine old building amidst venerable trees, with a well trimmed lawn, stretching down to the water, is the squire's hall. It has a quiet, venerable air, and has seen many generations of occupants. Dynasties have passed over its head—the Tudors, Cromwell, William of Orange, the Guelphs. It still stands unmoved and the old race still sit by the hearth. What joy and what sorrow, what lamentations and merrymakings, have not rung through that old hall. Yet it lives on through the social revolutions which are following each other so rapidly, and of which the emblems are the steamboat, the railtrain, the telegraph and the gas lamp. But we have swept by the hall and the heavenward-pointing spire, where the "rude forefathers of the village sleep," after exchanging a life of continual labor for one of eternal rest; and the school in close proximity to the church, where merry children, full of life, romp near to spots sacred to the tears and sorrows of mourners; by cottages and farm houses where there are well to-do farmers absorbed in the risks and chances of the markets, with abundance of good wheat in their barns and little thankfulness in their hearts; by other towns and villages differing in no respect from these, and after viewing a long panorama of lovely country and rich and varied views we arrive at the ancient cathedral town of Canterbury.

The first object which attracts attention is the ramparts which seem of great antiquity and above which gracefully rise a solitary column. Entering the park which is handsomely improved and shaded with lofty lime trees, we proceed at once towards this spiral column which surmounts a high mound, and find that the ramparts, garden, mound and column are all of modern origin. A liberal and public spirited gentleman, presented the grounds to the city, and at his private expense improved them and enclosed two sides with the wall which is built so as to represent ancient ramparts. In grateful recognition of this munificent liberality the authorities caused the mound, 150 feet in height, to be thrown up, and the column to be erected upon it, to perpetuate his memory. This is called the "*Dane John*" from the fact that the mound was according to tradition partially thrown up ages before, by a man named John who was a Dane.

Canterbury is one of the most ancient cities of the Kingdom and has been successively occupied by the Romans, Danes, Saxons and Normans. By the Saxons it was called the City or Stronghold of the men of Kent. For thirteen hundred years it has been chiefly famous for its Cathedral and Church dignitaries.

In 507, St. Augustine commenced the work of christianizing the Britons in Canterbury, by baptizing Ethelbert King of Kent. A pagan temple was converted into a Christian Church and St. Augustine became first Archbishop of Canterbury and founded the Cathedral and an Abbey. During six centuries, and the turmoils between the Saxons, Danes and Normans, the city was subjected to great vicissitudes and the Cathedral was destroyed and rebuilt more than once. It was here within the sanctuary that Archbishop Thomas a'Becket was murdered. This act caused the Pope to suspend the services of the Cathedral for one year. When Sir Thomas a'Becket had been canonized, pilgrimages to his shrine became famous and were kept up for three hundred years. It was these pilgrimages, which gave rise to Chaucer's Canterbury tales

The Cathedral is built in the form of a double cross, having two transepst. Notwithstanding the different ages in which the several parts have been ended and the various kinds of architecture employed, there appears nothing unsightly in its general aspect, but on the contrary, the effect of the whole is pleasing. Immediately upon entering the church we proceeded towards the east in search of the chapel of a'Becket and where he so often performed mass. After his death it contained the shrine to which Pilgrims of every country flocked. No trace of the shrine remains, but the pavement around the spot, where it stood is worn away by the knees of devout pilgrims. Through the munificence of wealthy visitors this shrine was most lavishly adorned. Erasmus who visited it in 1510 says, "that under a coffer of wood, inclosing another of gold, which was drawn up from its place by ropes and pulleys, he beheld an amount of riches, the value of which was inestimable." He continued "gold was the meanest thing to be seen, the whole place shone and glittered with the rarest of precious jewels, most of which were of an extraordinary size, some being larger than the egg of a goose." All of this wealth was subsequently seized by Henry VIII, who at the same time ordered the remains of a'Becket to be burned and the ashes scattered to the winds.

By the dissolution of monastaries and religious houses by Henry VIII, the possession of 644 convents, 90 colleges, 2,374 chantries and free chapels, and 110 hospitals were annexed to the crown. According to Burnet, the annual value of this property was something over a million and a quarter of pounds sterling, besides a vast quantity of plate and jewels.

It was given out, in order to enlist popular feeling in favor of this measure, that it would result in relieving the King's subjects of all taxes and services of any kind, and that the revenues should be applied to the maintenance of an army of 40,000 men, 3,000 knights, 60 barons and 40 new earls. Moreover, that a better provision should be made for the poor ; and for the preaching of the Protestant religion. Strype remarks, "Nothing of this came to pass, for neither was there provision made for the poor, nor yet order set for preaching the gospel, and in fine, a great part of it was turned to the upholding of dice-playing, masking and banqueting." Of this immense income, only £8,000 was devoted to the endowment of six new bishoprics of Westminster, Oxford, Peterborough, Bristol, Chester and Gloucester. Among the innumerable monuments, tablets and mural slabs preserved in the Cathedral are those of Edward, the Black Prince, who died at the Palace of the Archbishop, in Canterbury, 1376, and that of Henry IV, son of Gaunt, Duke of Lancaster, and grandson of Edward III. Both of these elegant monuments are in white marble and on them are full length effigies of the Black Prince and of Henry IV., and of Joan, second wife of Henry IV. and daughter of the King of Navarre.

Every part of Canterbury is worth inspecting by those who have any taste for the architectural memorials of the past, but no description of them would interest. After a full examination, we continued our journey to Chatham, so famous for its dockyards and ironclads. The only point at which we stopped between the Episcopal City and the "City of Cottages," as Chatham is commonly called, was Faversham, the headquarters of the English oyster trade. Though we indulged in a bitter and a few "natives," while here, it was not to enjoy the luxuries of the table that we made a halt. On the contrary, it was to enter the church where once reposed the bones of King Stephen. They are no longer here. When the abbeys were dissolved, his corpse, and those of his queen and son were exhumed and their contents cast into the sea. The bones of sovereigns do not sleep quietly in their resting places. Some years ago we stood in front of a plain grey marble slab, in front of the high altar of St. Stephen's Church, Caen, in Normandy. It was intended to mark the sepulchre of William the Conquerer, but not an atom of his body was then beneath it.

The dreaded Conquerer was himself at last conquered, dying as every one knows at the monastery of St. Gervais, Rouen. It was a melancholy scene. His eldest son, to whom he had bequeathed Normandy, was away with the Crusaders. His second son William, remained by the side of his dying father only long enough to hear himself appointed to the Crown of England, then leaving him in his last agony he galloped off to the coast, eager to secure his prize. His third son Henry who received his legacy in money, departed likewise to the treasury, and after carefully weighing the silver, placed it under lock and key. No sooner had the fatal event occurred than nobles, knights, gentlemen, priests, all decamped to look after their own interest and the servants set to work to plunder. Meanwhile the body of the late monarch was stripped and deserted, till the charity of an obscure individual provided for its conveyance to Caen, where the King had expressed a wish to be buried. Here his body was refused burial till the sum of sixty cents (sous) were paid to a man who claimed property in the site of the grave. In 1542 the Bishop of Bayeaux caused the grave to be opened and the body of the conquerer was found in good preservation, and justified by its appearance the reports of Chroniclers respecting his tall statue. During an insurrection in 1572, the grave was violated, the coffin dug up and its contents emptied into the street. A pious priest gathered the remains and preserved them in his chamber till a subsequent insurrection when the whole abbey was plundered and all the remains lost but one thigh bone, which was reinterred and a monument raised over it in 1642. During the revolution of 1793 the mob rifled the spot and the last fragment of the Great Duke and mighty conquerer disappeared.

The remains of Henry I., who was buried at the Abbey in Reading, have likewise disappeared and no man knoweth his sephulchre.

This was true also of the restless and fiery Henry II., who died at the castle of Chinon, near the junction of the Vienne and Loire in France. The breath was scarcely out of the body of the dead man when he was stripped of every rag, his apartments robbed, and those who had lately trembled at his word hurried off to make court with his successor. The charity of a neighbor provided a winding sheet for the body which was removed for interment to the Abbey of Fontevraud, one of the wealthiest ecclesiastical establishments in France. Previous to the funeral, the body was laid in the Abbey Church when it is said to have shuddered convulsively at the approach of Richard, an undutiful son. The conquerer of Saladin, and hero of a hundred fights, Richard I. was also buried here, and Queen Eleanor of Guienne and Isabella d' Angouleme the Queen of his brother John.

In the old Scotch College in the rue Desbrosses St.Victor, Paris, were deposited in an urn of bronze gilt the brains of James II.— The mob in 1693 broke this urn and the brains contained in it were trampled upon the ground. The royal body which was deposited at the chapel of the English Benedictines was little less reverenced. At the time of the revolution the chapel was used as a prison, and among the prisoners was a Mr. Fitzsimons, who witnessed the treatment to which the body was subjected and who thus describes what he saw:

"I was a prisoner in Paris, in the convent of the English Benedictines, in the Rue St. Jacques, during part of the revolution. In the year 1793 or 1794 the body of King James II of England was in one of the chapels there, where it had been deposited some time, under the expectation that it would one day be sent to England for interment in Westminster Abbey. It had never been buried. The body was in a wooden coffin, enclosed in a leaden one, and that again enclosed in a second wooden one, covered with black velvet. While I was a prisoner, the *sans-culottes* broke open the coffins, to get at the lead, to cast into bullets. The body lay exposed nearly a whole day. It was swaddled like a mummy, bound tight with garters. The *sans culottes* took out the body, which had been embalmed. There was a strong smell of vinegar and camphor. The corpse was beautiful and perfect; the hands and nails were very fine; I moved and bent every finger. I never saw so fine a set of teeth in my life. A young lady, a fellow prisoner, wished much to have a tooth; I tried to get one out for her, but could not, they were so firmly fixed. The feet also were very beautiful. The face and cheeks were just as if he were alive. I rolled his eyes; the eye-balls were perfectly firm under my finger. The French and English prisoners gave money to the *sans-culottes* for showing the body. They said he was a good *sans-culottes*, and they were going to put him into a hole in the public church yard, like other *sans-culottes*, and he was carried away, but where the body was thrown I never heard." George IV tried all in his power to get tidings of the body, but could not. Around the chapel were several wax moulds of the face hung up, made probably at the time of the King's death, and the corpse was very like them. The body had been originally kept at the palace of St Germains, when it was brought to the convent of the Benedictines. Mr. Porter, the prior, was a prisoner at the time in his own convent.

During the French Revolution the mob further signalized their hatred of Royalty by scattering the ashes of the dead Kings and mutilating their Statues. The tombs of the French Kings buried at St. Denis were opened by the revolutionists and their contents emptied into the neighboring ditches. It was only in 1813 when some workmen were engaged in repairing the vaults at Windsor that they accidentally came upon the coffin of Charles I. A doubtful point of history was then cleared up, for the contents of the plain leaden coffin, on which was inscribed in large legible character, "King Charles, 1648," were examined in the presence of the Prince Regent, (George IV.,) Sir Henry Halford, Sir Henry Peyton, and others. Within the leaden coffin was one of wood, very much decayed, in which, carefully wrapped in cloth, was the body. The skin of the face was found dark and discolored, the forehead and temples had lost little or nothing of their muscular substance; the cartilege of the nose was gone; the left eye was open and full in the first moment of its exposure, though it vanished almost immediately, and the pointed beard so characteristic of the period of his reign was perfect. The strong resemblance of the face to that of Charles I on the coins, busts, and especially the likenesses of Vandyke left no doubt as to its identity. Upon removing the bandage, the head was found to be loose and was held up to view. It bore evidence of having been severed by a heavy blow, inflicted with a sharp instrument.

Nothing is known of the resting place of Lord Protector, Cromwell. After his State funeral and burial at Westminster, his corpse was disinterred and treated with indignity. His head was exposed from the top of Westminster hall, while his body hung from the gallows in Tyburn. After remaining sometime in these positions they were cast into a hole, but no one knows the locality of it, though some learned antiquarians suppose it was near Red Lion Square, London.

The ill-fate attending royal races—their vicissitudes in life—may be further illustrated by two instances, furnished by the successors of Charlemagne in France and the Jameses in England. The son of Charlemagne, Louis de Babonnaire, died for want of food, in consequence of a superstitious panic. His successor, Charles the Bald, was poisoned by his physician. Charles' son, Louis the Stutterer, was also poisoned. Charles, king of Aquitaine, brother of the Stutterer, met his death by a blow on the head from a gentleman he was endeavoring by way of frolic to terrify. Louis III, successor to the Stutterer, a gallant Prince, having cast his eyes upon a handsome girl, the daughter of a citizen named Gormand, as he was riding through the streets of Tours, pursued her instantly. The terrified girl took refuge in a house, and the king, thinking more of her charms than the size of the gateway, attempted to force his horse after her, but broke his back and died on the spot. He was succeeded by his son, Carloman, who fell by an ill directed spear, thrown by one of his own servants at a wild boar, although the dying Prince had the generosity to charge the beast with his death. Charles the Fat perished of want, grief and poison altogether. His successor, Charles, the Simple, died in prison of penury and despair. Louis the Stranger, his successor, was killed while hunting. Lotharius and Louis V, the two best kings of the race of Charlemagne, were both poisoned by their wives, to whose little indiscretions they had paid too much attention. Of the whole line, after a revolution of 230 years, there now remained one, Charles, Duke of Lorraine, and he, after a struggle in defense of his rights against the ambitious and active Capet, sunk beneath the fortune of his antagonist and ended his days in a lonely prison.

In England the Stuarts were steadily unfortunate.

Robert the III broke his heart because his eldest son was starved to death, and his youngest, James, made a prisoner. James I, after having beheaded three of his nearest kindred, was assassinated by his own uncle, who was tortured to death for it. James II was slain by the bursting of a piece of ordnance. James III, when flying from battle, was thrown from his horse and murdered in a cottage, into which he had been carried for assistance. James IV fell in Flodden Field. James V died of grief for the wilful ruin of his army at Solway Moss. Henry, Lord Darnley, was assassinated and then blown up in his palace. Mary was beheaded in England. James I and James VI are supposed to have been poisoned by Buckingham. Charles I was beheaded. Charles II was for many years an exile. James II lost his crown and died in banishment. Anne, after a glorious reign, died of a broken heart, occasioned by the quarrels of her favored servants. The posterity of James II have remained wretched wanderers in a foreign land.

We have again wandered a long way out of our path and we are not quite sure that our reader takes as much pleasure as we do in these flights. But what reader is satisfied to jog on forever in the same beaten track. It is usually, if not universally the case, that in what one reads and what one hears, one expects to find something with which one was formerly unacquainted. If this reasonable expectation is disappointed, and an author goes plodding on indulging in a trifling minuteness of narration, in prolix descriptions and an abundance of common places, he is sure to fill the reader with languor and disgust. Napoleon III, at a period of excitement in France, gave utterence to the sententious remark: "For order I will be responsible." We wish we could say with equal confidence, "For preserving our reader from languor and disgust we will be responsible." In any event the reader shall not be cloyed with trite and obvious thoughts as if he had no apprehension of his own. Be it our object to give him something on which to exercise his reason and entertain his fancy. His attention will be thus repaid and he will not only excuse but delight, as we do, in those excursions through the regions of the past, which interrupt our narrative, but which do not long prevent our returning to the starting point. Whether we pursue beaten paths or give reins to imagination we seek to be plain, and invariably, as brief as is consistent with perspicuity, though this is not always the best policy, as it cannot be dissembled, that, with inattentive readers, darkness frequently passes for depth.

In the next succeeding chapter, clearing our brain from all fumes of fancy, we shall resume our narrative, and conduct the reader— we flatter ourselves he does not belong to the inattentive class— more rapidly forward on the journey from the sea coast to the interior.

## CHAPTER XXI.

CHATHAM — FAVERSHAM — ROCHESTER — SIR FRANCIS DOYLE — GADS HILL.— COBHAM HALL—MSS. LETTERS OF SIR JOHN PEYTON, GOVERNOR OF THE TOWER AND OF THE ISLAND OF JERSEY— EDMOND BEALES—THE REFORMATION.

Emerging from the church at Faversham we saw the train approaching, the train by which we expected to reach Chatham. Hurrying to the station and stepping into a carriage we were greeted with glad surprise by one of our earliest and best English friends, Sir Francis Hastings Doyle, professor of poetry at

Oxford, who was returning to London from a jaunt in France. Sir Francis was an intimate friend of Osmond Priaulx, at whose house we first met him at dinner in 1862, and where we had been in the habit of meeting him under the same pleasant circumstances, every Thursday, for years. He was one of a small coterie of literary and political celebrities who assembled every week at each others houses.

Many of them are dead, some are superannuated and others have retired from public employments. How melancholy it is to travel from one's country, and to make acquaintance with estimable men abroad, whom we are never to see again. How rapid a career is human life! Happy the man who has it in his power to employ it in doing good. Sir Francis Doyle whom we now met with, so unexpectedly, is a thoroughly companionable and delightful man—not only a poet, but a distinguished poet. He writes with taste, abounds in elegance, wholly reproves the spasmodic efforts of the metrical manipulators of the age, adhering to nature in a pure and unaffected style, replete with chaste and classic diction. His impassioned thought is elucidated and ennobled in all the sparkling imagery of truly poetic and romantic inspiration. He is plain and unassuming in manner and attire, would pass very well for one of the squirearchy, is fond of the chase and the pursuits of the country gentleman. He has written and published a good deal of poetry and some lectures but they have acquired no general popularity. He often referred in a humorous way to their failure to attract public attention, and said: "I don't know why it is; people don't care to read what I write." It was not difficult for us to see that he attributed this indifference to the bad taste of the reading public. Though he took a rather saturine view of his position with the public, we soon discovered that no one was more favorably regarded by the literary world—his laurels were green, however conscious he was of it, though his locks were gray. Sir Francis Doyle, in his demeanor and personal appearance, is considerably above the common order, and is altogether a handsome and noble looking man.

Among the choice spirits in this particular coterie was the great novelist Thackeray, but we never happened to meet him at one of the reunions. On one occasion, shortly after our arrival in London in 1862, we received an invitation from Edwin de Leon, now (1880) of Washington City, formerly United States Consul General in Egypt, to meet Thackeray at dinner. A previous engagement prevented our acceptance, and we thus lost the opportunity of meeting that eminent man of letters. He was soon afterwards struck down with disease, and to the inexpressible grief of a wide circle of personal friends, and to all generous minds and lovers of literature, sunk into a premature grave. Would that it were in our power to say something to do honor to the memory of that great and worthy man—this is the best return posterity can make them for their noble works and virtuous principles.

To return: little opportunity was afforded us on this occasion of enjoying the society of Sir Francis Doyle. The train soon drew up at the Chatham station, where, after bidding adieu to our distinguished friend, we descended to have a look at the dockyards and some of those modern ironclads which have superceded England's wooden walls.

Chatham, which possesses considerable claims to antiquity, is one of those industrious manufacturing centres too much occupied with the work of the present to have time to talk of its ancestors. To all not specially concerned in shipbuilding it is the most uninteresting of towns, consisting of a vast collection of dreary, monotonous looking cottages, in which are crowded a working population of fifty thousand. This mass of human beings owes its support entirely to the government expenditures at this point. No one lives in Chatham unless employed in the great naval and military establishments. We quickly determined to "do" Chatham in the shortest possible space of time, and went to work energetically to see the sights, the sooner to shake the dust of the town from our feet.

A naval station has existed at Chatham since the days of Elizabeth, and by degrees it has grown into one of the first class English naval arsenals and dockyards. Especially has Chatham assumed importance since the introduction of ironclads, the appliances for building them here being somewhat peculiar to the place. Upon applying to be admitted, we found it necessary to enter in a book kept for the purpose, our name, profession and nationality. After this we were conducted to an office, where the order of admission was made out, and presented to a guide who preceded to conduct us through the establishment.

The dockyard extends about a mile and a half on the river, and consists of wet docks for repairing ships, an immense tidal basin, seven covered slips on which to build ships, a mast house, a boat house, with a store of ship boats, a rope house, in which cables, hawsers and other kinds of ropes are made, a store-house, a sail-loft, two mast ponds, workshops containing duplicates of Brunel's block-making machinery, a smithery with forty forges, giving out their fierce heat, and steam hammers of 50 cwt. falling on masses of glowing iron; hydraulic presses for bending thick plates for ironclads, a timber pond with a submarine canal for floating in timber from the river Medway. sawing mills with numerous vertical and circular saws, metal mills for making copper bolts, ship sheeting, and order articles in metal, and various other buildings necessary for the construction of great wooden and iron war ships. To describe these shops and the progress would require a volume.

More extensive than the dockyards are the military establishments which cover an immense area of ground. There are barracks for 5,000 infantry, constantly occupied by invalids from India and the colonies; extensive artillery barracks, with stabling for their horses; barracks for a corps of the Royal Engineers and for the school of Military Engineering, which is established in the suburbs and designed for teaching officers all that concerns siege operations and defence work. Likewise a military prison, where from three to four thousand criminals are confined, and various hospitals and other buildings connected with these numerous establishments. The whole stretch no less than two miles along the Medway and further into the interior. There is nothing peculiar about them which would justify a particular description. We were much gratified by a visit to the soldier's institute, an admirable place, in which soldiers can enjoy the advantages of a good library and news room, chess and bagatelle tables, fives and tennis court. The building is well warmed, lighted and ventilated. A subscription of 4d. per month is demanded, the institute being a private affair of the soldiers, kept up by contributions, and more than 3 000 soldiers are members of it.

Adjoining Chatham, and to a stranger apparently forming the more aristocratic or west end of it, is the quaint old city of Rochester, so famous for its ancient cathedral, founded in the eleventh century, the chancel choir and trancept of which were added in 1230 by a noble and wealthy gentleman, Sir William de Hooe, of the Hundred of Hooe, in the Isle of Grain in Kent, and the extensive ruins of its grand old feudal castle, the battlements of which are now 104 feet from the ground. Though we visited every spot and fragment of this venerable monument of antiquity with the liveliest interest, any description of it would but fatigue. The walks around it are sequestered and pleasing and altogether calculated to raise our admiration and give a more perfect idea of this beautiful specimen of an ancient fortification, but viewing it we could but exclaim, "sad are the ruthless ravages of time."

We availed ourselves of the opportunity while in Chatham to walk as far as Gad's Hill, so notorious in old times as a haunt of tramps, rogues, vagabonds, and all kinds of desperate and abandoned characters. It was here that Shakespeare places the scene of one of the pranks of Falstaff, Prince Hal, Burdolph and their companions. On entering the Inn standing on the summit of the hill and intended to perpetuate the fame of the fat knight, we saw hanging on the wall a likeness of Sir John, whose lips seemed to move with the words, "Shall I not take mine ease in mine inn." The proprietor of this inn is a man of education above his station and conversed with sense and judgment upon the subject of Shakespeare's plays and the writings of his neighbor, Charles Dickens, whose home is not more than a hundred yards from the Inn upon the opposite side of the road. He told us that Dickens was then at home, at least he had seen him the evening before, and that he was always glad to see strangers. We had not intended calling upon the popular novelist. While admiring his genius we detested his character. All the world knows that he was a snob, and it is generally conceded that he was a drunkard and an adulterer. Curiosity, however, seemed to take possession of us, and in a moment of freak we formed a hasty resolution to look in upon him. Proceeding at once to the entrance of his grounds, we were met by a decidedly inhospitable growl, and saw in large letters across the gate, "Beware of the dog." A servant who answered our vigorous pull at the bell protected us from the idiotic looking brute who guarded the premises of "Boz," and conducted us to the house. From her we learned that Dickens had gone to London a few hours before, and that the only occupants of the house at the moment were a son and daughter. Without stopping to see them we returned to the public house, and settling our bill, left by a lane passing Dickens' house, to make our visit to Cobham Hall. From this lane running across Gad's Hall, we saw stretching before us at a distance of three miles, the wooded hills and plains of this magnificent park. After passing through a pretty and highly cultivated country where many parties were engaged gathering the ripe hops, we arrived at the park enclosure, and crossing a platform entered the grounds by a foot path conducting almost directly to the hall. Wandering through the arbor walks of this elysian wilderness, it seemed like a land of enchantment. So artfully had the walks been planned, that they seemed interminable, and the grounds without limit. The beautiful and the vast blended together. In a central situation, sparkling in the sunshine, was a serpentine lake, upon which swans of snowy whiteness floated, and towards which the drooping trees bent their branches. Herds of deer fed upon the green savannahs blazing in the sunshine.

Arriving at the Hall, one of the finest old residences in this part of England, and always thrown open to the public when the family is absent, as was now the case, we were ushered into the private apartments and conducted through them by one of the servants who acted as guide. This place had been in the Cobham family for many years previous to the 16th century, and in 1559 Queen Elizabeth was entertained here in great magnificence. Shortly after 1603 when Sir Walter Raleigh was dastardly betrayed by Lord Henry Cobham, who was himself long confined like Raleigh in the Tower, and finally beheaded, the estate was confiscated. We may remark *en passant* that at the time of Raleigh's imprisonment Sir John Peyton, of Doddington, who had been a member of Queen Elizabeth's Privy Council, was governor of the Tower.— Among the curious MSS letters of Sir John now in the British Museum, presented to the national library of Great Britain by George III, are many letters written by Sir John to Robert Cecil, Earl of Salisbury, who was sole secretary of State in 1603.. While the author was in England he enjoyed the privilege of a reader's ticket to the library, and time and again spent a few days searching among this vast collection. The following are copies of two of Sir John Peyton's letters to the Earl of Salisbury, in which he alludes to some of the State prisoners. And in the house of this very Earl of Salisbury we were now examining the objects of interest and calling up the associations of the past.

SIR JOHN PEYTON TO THE EARL OF SALISBURY.

TOWER, July 21st, 1603.

*Right Honorable,*

*My very good Lord:*—"According to y'r L'dships directions I related unto my Lord Cobham, what course was best for him as his case now standeth, he being under a Kings justice, that is composed of all mercy. I urged him to use no manner of reservation, which course he vowed to God to hold in his relation, which I send enclosed to your L'dship as required.

"Sir Walter Rawley standeth still upon his innocence, but with a mind the most dejected that I ever saw.

"My Lord Grey continueth in the same manner he did. He is desirous to write to His Majesty, which I in good warmth denied, until I might understand his Majesty's pleasure. Then he entreated me to permit him to write to your L'dship, whereupon I assented, and his letter I send enclosed.

"In all these actions God has shown a protecting providence over our good King and the State, wherein my heart rejoiceth.— And so I most humbly take my leave."

Your Lordships servant &c
JOHN PEYTON,
Lieutenant of the Tower.

SAME TO SAME.

July 23, 1603.

*Right Honorable,*

*My very good Lord.*—"I must confess that since my attendance on y'r L'dship I have been more than gratified, by your noble passion towards my son and honorable letters to myself which doth double both our desires to do your service, beseaching y'r L'dship to command me as one in whom your Lordship hath had and ever may have confidence. The letters directed to Lord Gray were brought by a soldier once of the lower countries.

"I also send your Lordship a letter for my lord Cobham, who in all his speech doth in no way spare himself. I never saw so strange a dejected mind as in Sir Walter Rawley. I am exceedingly cumbered with him; five or six times a day he sendeth for me in such passions as I see his fortitude is impotent to support his grief. Thus I take my leave.

Your Lordships ever &c.,
JOHN PEYTON.

TOWER, this 23 July, 1603.

After the confiscation of the estate of the Cobhams, it became the property of the Duke of Lennox, who had the honor of entertaining Charles I. and Henrietta Maria, in the Hall. During the revolution and the Republic under Cromwell, the property was despoiled by the Roundheads, and after the restoration became the property of the Darnleys, and so continues. Though many of the rooms have been modernized there is a great deal of the Old World grandeur about Cobham Hall. The principal feature is the very extensive and select gallery of paintings, a large portion of them by the old masters.

From the Hall we crossed the Park to the village, visiting lime tree avenue, which is 3000 feet long, and the Mansoleum, which was built in 1782 for use as a tomb. In every part of the park the scenery is magnificent and the lime, cedar and oaks of majestic size and picturesque arrangement. Slowly and silently we wandered over the grassy lawns and through the solemn groves, anon lingering by the way to gaze a last farewell on that hoary and time-honored pile, to cast a parting glance on the glittering towers and the lovely scenery surrounding them, pensively musing as we walked along of the deep and bitter feelings that occupied the bosom of the last of the Cobham race, when he took a last adieu

[NOTE.—Sir Bernard Burke says on p. 412 of his Extinct Baronetcies that "Sir John Peyton, governor of the Tower. *temp.* ELIZABETH, and of the Queens privy council; afterwards in the reign of James I. governor of the Island of Jersey and Guernsey, to which office he succeeded Sir Walter Raleigh, was in the words of an old writer "educated after the politest manner of the age he lived in, by serving in the wars of Flanders under the most able and experienced soldiers and politicians of that time. Amidst the sunshine of a court and the affluences of a large fortune, his conduct was so regular and temperate that his life was prolonged to the age of ninety-nine years, in so much health and vigor that he is said to have rode hunting three or four days before his death."]

of the hall of his ancestors and was conducted a prisoner to the Tower, which he was destined to leave only for the block.*

The only object of interest in the village is the church, which contains thirteen monumental brasses of the Cobham family, which are generally esteemed the finest things of the kind in England. Some of them are five centuries old.

Leaving the church we returned to Rochester, arriving there at an opportune moment for witnessing some of the performances of that most remarkable of all the beasts in the European menagerie, the British lion. The British lion is not one of those unfortunate, mangy creatures of African descent, kept at Zoological Gardens, or carried about the country in a wooden box to amuse the people, but a living, two-legged animal of indigenous growth. He may be a literary lion, or a political lion—a Conservative or a Reforming lion, or belong to some other species too numerous to particuralize. To whatever species he belongs he creates a great sensation whenever he goes to a public meeting, as on this occasion, or a public dinner—the people always go to hear the lion roar, or to see the lion feed. Though very unlike the African lion in appearance, his supremacy among beasts is acknowledged.— Whether he roars from the pulpit, the platform, or the printing office, his voice is law. His mouth is as large and his lungs as strong as those of the African lion, and hence the British lion has long been regarded as the mouth-piece of the people, the exponent of popular opinion. The specimen I saw on this occasion was the Reforming lion, in the person of Mr. Edmond Beales, M. A., who was here to roar to a meeting of the Reform League, to denounce the injustice to which the British were subjected under their constitution and laws, and the necessity for radical change. Mr. Bright is the great reforming lion of the land, who stands before the people in awful majesty as the peculiar champion of their rights and redresser of their wrongs, but much of his work is done by young cubs who beat the bushes and scour the plains, starting up the game, eventually to be brought down and secured by the King beast. Mr. Beales, M. A., most decidedly belongs to the breed of cub lions. After listening some time to the music of his voice, we were reluctantly brought to the conclusion that the British lion is not always a remarkably wise beast—wise beasts are less obtrusive and make considerable less noise.

We cannot afford space to report the roar of the lion of the species of Mr. Beales, M. A. It is enough to say that he has been

---

*Lord Cobham was hung in chains and burnt in London in 1407. Warpole speaks of him as a man whose virtues made him a reformer, whose valor made him a martyr, whose martyrdom made him an enthusiast. His ready wit and brave spirit appeared to great advantage on his trial.

classified as one of the promising lions, not promising much in himself, but to his friends. No rational human being would ever suppose Mr. Beales capable of carrying out his benevolent purposes towards mankind in general or the British people in particular. A politician who, like Mr. Beales, promises everything to everybody is not in the way of becoming as distinguished for deeds as words. The amicable role played by this demagogue, has, however, given him an unbounded personal popularity, and he exercises an immense influence. His power is confined to those however, who have no influence, namely: the ignorant classes, whom he easily deludes, and really, therefore, amounts to nothing, at least in so far as the public is concerned. He makes it of some value to himself, for Beales is a selfish lion in the way of securing fees in the petty courts where he practices and expounds what he calls the law, and in obtaining small offices, for which he has a great inclination and of which he has held many, in which he has acquired notoriety—not good fame. Such lions as Mr. Beales, do not present a fair type of the British animal. John Bright, M. P., is of the genuine British genius; it is such as he whose whisper is as loud as a thunder clap and who argue with strong teeth and sharp talons. It is this type which has been chosen as one of the supporters of the Royal arms. As such he is intended to represent the popular opinion of the country, and when he roars and lashes his tail, kings and statesmen know he must not be trifled with. He is, as we have said, not a particularly wise beast. He does not always discriminate rightly between the false and the true. When Sampson was sent of God to be the deliverer of his brethren, a lion came roaring against him at the first setting out. So when, in the present day, a man gets a special mission to deliver mankind from some chain of superstition or ignorance, popular opinion is sure to come roaring against him at first: but, as Sampson rent the lion as if he were a kid, so the power and majesty of truth, in the end, overcomes popular opinion, and effectually stops his roaring. Truth is stronger than a lion, and the triumph of truth is sweeter than honey For as Sampson, on his return, found a honey-comb in the jaws of the lion, so the herald of truth, having overcome the opposition of popular opinion, derives bread from the eater and sweetness from his strength, and the jaws and tongue of the people henceforward flow with honey in his praise.

Nothing is truer than that in the long run truth will overcome error. To time, therefore, may be safely left the solution of those grave problems in government with which Mr. Beales so rashly tampers. We heard with pain the leveling principles of this demagogue, having always believed that the greater the rewards you give to virtue the better men you will get to contend for them.

Mr. Beales has given conclusive evidence of his character, or rather want of character. Having made himself troublesome, if not a dangerous man, in order to quiet him he was appointed to a judgeship in 1870, and ever since has been as silent as the grave. Enjoying the honors and emoluments of the judicial station, this reforming lion no longer roars. Keen as are his optics he no longer sees any defects in the British Constitution ; he only sees a stupid and ignorant people crying out about their wrongs, a people whom he complacently declares have only rights. This is his "official opinion." No longer a reformer, the learned judge rivals the late Earl of Ellenborough in his admiration of English institutions, as at once the pride, the strength and the glory of the Fatherland.

## CHAPTER XXII.

SEVENOAKS — MONTREAL — THE AMHERSTS — KNOLE CASTLE — SHOWMEN — TONBRIDGE WELLS — BATTLE ABBEY — RETURN TO LONDON.

A short trip brought us to the old county town of Sevenoaks, situated in one of the loveliest parts of Kent. Like many English towns, Sevenoaks is remarkable for the clean and tidy air which pervades every part of it. In other respects it is in itself not particularly noteworthy, yet as one of these old places recalling our forefathers it possesses many charms. There are few of us who do not love to linger among the dwelling places of our ancestors, which, although now knowing them no more, appear still to retain a portion of their spirit and exhibit traces of their true and kindly nature. The country surrounding Sevenoaks is unsurpassed for beauty and variety of scenery, and has long been a favorite retreat for city people. During some brief interlude in the monotonous round of their busy lives, it is not only pleasant to steal from the 'mad'ning crowds' ignoble strife' to refresh their minds and bodies by a visit to the country, but the pleasant and holy memories of the good old days, doubtless renovates their jaded spirits.

Some of the finest mansions in England are situated in what may be called the Sevenoaks neighborhood. One of these, which possessed special interest to us, is the old baronial residence of the ancient family of the Amhersts, called "Montreal." A pleasant walk through cornfields, corpses, and shady lanes conducted our pedestrian party to Montreal. It was built by Sir Jeffrey Amherst,* in commemoration of his glorious successes in America, upon the site of an old manor house, originally erected during the Saxon era. When approached, its venerable stone front is seen from amidst a grove of splendid old trees.

The grounds and gardens attached to Montreal are not extensive, but the house is a handsome structure. In the park there is an obelisk to commemorate, as the inscription says "the providential and happy meeting of three brothers, on the 25th of January, 1704, after six years of glorious war, in which the three were successfully engaged." On the other side it runs as follows; "Dedicated to that most noble statesman, during whose administration Cape Breton and Canada were conquered, and from whose influence the British Arms derived a degree of lustre unparalleled in the past ages."

The following record of the victories achieved in the *far West*, is also inscribed upon it :

"Louisburg surrendered, and six French battalions prisoners of war, 26th July, 1758.

Niagara surrendered, 25th July, 1758.

Ticonderago taken possession of 26th July, 1759.

Crown Point taken possession of 4th August, 1759.

Quebec Capitulated 18th September, 1759.

Fort Levi surrendered 25th August, 1760.

Isle au Noix abandoned 28th August, 1760.

Montreal surrendered, and with it all Canada, and ten French battalions layed down their arms, 6th of September, 1760.

St. Johns, Newfoundland, retaken 18th September, 1760."

The most interesting objects, however, in the vicinity of Sevenoaks, are Knole Castle and Park, now the property and residence of Earl Amherst—Lord Delaware. It was originally the property of the Sackvilles, Lords Buckhurst, then of the Earls and Dukes of Dorset and continued in the latter family till 1825, when it was

---

*Jeffrey, Lord Amherst, was born in 1717, entered the army 1731, served under the Duke of Cumberland 1741, Colonel in 1756, Major-General in 1758, served in America against France 1758, Commander-in-Chief in Canada 1758-60, Governor of Virginia 1763 and Governor of Guernsey 1770, Lieut-General 1772, created Lord Amherst of Montreal 1788, died 1797.

inherited by the present, which is a collateral branch of the family of Thomas Sackville, first Earl of Dorset.

The Castle stands in a park of 1,000 acres, dotted over with fine elms and large oaks. Everything about this old domain is so venerable, and at the same time so poetical, that in pacing its grassy glades, one almost expects to encounter the nymphs and satyrs once believed to inhabit its groves. What this splendid park was two centuries ago, it is to day. No modern innovations or improvements have impaired its sylvan beauty and it stands pre eminent amid the romantic nooks of Kent. Occupying an eminence, as its name implies, the building covers 3½ acres of ground, the principal portion of which is of the 15th and 16th centuries, though parts are much older. It is considered by archæologists among the most interesting, as it is certainly one of the most famous of English baronial mansions. Grey, stern and majestic, it is suggestive of those times when might made right, and looks as if any deed of violence might have been committed under the shelter of its stout walls. It was once surrounded by a deep fosse and lofty vellum, but these have long since disappeared, and a well laid out garden occupies their places. The spot which once echoed to the imperious tread of the mailed Baron and his half savage retainers, is now covered with innocent flowers, which send up their offerings of sweet incense. Long occupied by different families as a residence, no part of the buildings, interior or exterior, has been modernized, but are preserved in the quaint old style in which they were originally built. It is remarkable for numerous and extensive subterraneous cavities and vaults, which undermine the gardens and are said to extend in some directions two miles. The furniture with which it was supplied, with the additions of subsequent periods, is also retained. Among this is the Chair of State which was occupied by James I, when on his visit to Knole in 1610.

Passing into the "Stone Court," we enter the "Great Hall" where is preserved the massive oak table at which in accordance with ancient custom, the domestics were wont to dine in the presence of their Lord. The fire place in the Hall is of the requisite capacity for roasting a whole bullock, the hospitable form in which the roast beef of old England was served up on grand occasions by the great Barons. The hall is hung with paintings and old armor, weapons of war and the chase, etc.

From the great hall we were shown successively into the Brown gallery, Lady Betty Germain's rooms, the billiard room, the ball room, the chapel, the cartoon room, the King's bed room, the dining room, &c., in all of which there are many fine paintings, curious pieces of antique furniture, tapestry, and other objects of art.

The ceilings and stair cases are alike painted in fresco, and we are glad to say not by Verrio. The whole atmosphere of the place is impregnated with the odour of a bye gone age, and calls back many charming historical associations of our fatherland.

Among the numerous portraits, many taken from life, we particularly observed a full length portrait of James I, which well expresses in its contracted features, the narrow and pedantic nature of his mind; one of Sir Kenelm Digby, the resolute seeker of the Philosopher's stone; another of Philip II, the haughty and bigoted projector of the Invincible Armada; others of Beaumont, Fletcher, Shakespeare, Goldsmith, Johnson. Waller, Congreve, Cromwell, &c., &c. The portraits are by Gainsborough, Kneller Jansens, Sir Joshua Reynolds, and other native and foreign artists, who vied with each other in the glories of the pencil. In the crimson drawing room is the original of that famous painting of Count Ugolina in the prison at Pisa. The story is too well known to be repeated here, but the stern features of the Count, tortured by the pangs of hunger, recall it to our mind in all its intensity.

The most curious and interesting room of the mansion is that prepared for James I, and which is called the King's bed room.—On the wall in well wrought tapestry is told the story of Nebuchadnezzar. The bed is hung with gold and silver tissues, lined with rose colored satin and is embroidered with threads of the same precious metals. The toilet service, wash-hand stands, tables mirrors, etc. are all of massive silver. Such were the arrangements made by a fawning subject to entertain the King that "thrift might follow fawning." Our visit to Knole recalled Dr. Johnson's remark when visiting Luton Hooe, [to Boswell. "Sir," said Johnson of Lord Bute's home, "this is one of the places I do not regret having come to see. It is a very stately place, indeed; in the house magnificence is not confined to convenience, nor convenience to magnificence. The library is very splendid; the dignity of the room is very great; and the quantity of pictures is beyond expectation, beyond hope."

After spending two days studying the castle and its art treasures, we turned our attention to the park which contains something over a thousand acres and many romantic scenes of hanging woods and green valleys.

One day while wandering amidst these scenes we entered a grassy ravine down which a saucy, gossipping brook babbled and sparkled half in sunlight and half in shade. The voice of the dashing waters deadened all other sounds, and it was not until we had passed out of the park and were almost in the centre of the odd scene we are about to describe, that we were aware of having intruded upon a convocation which was probably intended to be secret. At a point near the opening of the ravine, the brook had expanded into a wide shallow pool, some fifty yards in diameter. The water was surrounded by a tract of waste land covered with moss and shaded by fine oak and beech trees, the survivors of an ancient forest. Their trunks were vast in girth and were covered with mosses and whitening canker stains. These old monarchs of the wood had assumed all the crooked, deformed and fantastic shapes which betoken age and decay. Under their wide spreading branches had encamped a colony of some forty persons, men, women and children. The heavy growth of timber in the Park protected them from view on one side and a range of hills covered with furge separated them from the highway on the other. A number of carts covered with canvass, a load of dirty planks, a couple of rickerty old vans, or rather wooden houses on wheels, furnished with doors, windows and chimnies, a monster puppet show and a couple of Punch and Judy rostrums, had all been pitched down at random upon the ground by their respective owners, the several owners having squatted their families and their properties in the most convenient sites. The succulent grass was being cropped by a cohort of half starved donkeys at the water's edge, and here and there a spavined horse burrowed beneath the moss in search of more savory diet. On top of the pile of plank was a row of small dogs of the poodle breed, with their hinder quarters shorn to the skin. Some had undergone the ceremony of ablution and were shivering with cold, while others, anticipating their turn, shivered from sympathy. Near the wagon an old woman smoking a short pipe, was busy washing in an iron pot the parti colored jackets which formed the dramatic costumes of the shivering canine performers. By her side was a second female plying the needle and thread in behalf of the poodles, in repairing their suits. The rest of the company almost defies description, and presented a spectacle which can scarcely be paralleled in the whole experience of civilization. One and all they had come here to make of it a "washing day," and at this particular crisis were doing business with ludicrous energy and enthusiasm. The pool was the common wash tub in which men and women were standing up to their knees, and rapidly going through those familiar evolutions necessary to the purification of linen. Every possible rag which decency would allow them to dispense with, had been cast off by the entire party, and consigned to the wash; and all were undergoing the cleansing process, some with soap, which seemed to be a scarce article, and others with a soponaceous clay, found in many parts of England and well known to persons who lead a vagabond life. At the point where the pool overflowed and the waters went rippling down the ravine, a number of calico gowns too worn to stand the 'rough handling of the washers, had been pegged fast to the bank, under the water, to derive what benefit they might from a swill. Some vestiges of shirts and spotted neck ties bore them company, and a boy divested of all covering but a shirt, stood knee deep in the water to intercept any that might part from their moorings. The drying was accomplished by women on shore, who spread the articles on the furze bushes or hung them from ropes, running from one van to another.

The most prominent and remarkable of these washers was a tall sallow-faced, intellectual person, with a black beard reaching down to his breast. The spectacle he presented as he soaped and rubbed and smoothed on his long lean arm what seemed to be the remains of a lady's lawn collar, was decidedly grotesque and inharmonious. He pursued his work with a gravity which contrasted strongly with the frivolity of his occupation, but no one seemed conscious that there was anything ridiculous or incongruous in the affair, and without exception pursued their occupation with an order and industry which promised a speedy and satisfactory result.

But this indispensable operation of washing was by no means the only occupation of the hour. At a short distance a fiddler was rehairing his bow from the tail of a spavined horse: the owner of a bass drum was cobbling the leather braces and casting lugubrious glances at a yawning fracture in the tympan. A committee of drivers were holding council over a delapidated vehicle, while axe and saw, hammer and nails were at work on the crazy carts and vans; the peep show completely disembowled, disclosed its mysteries to unheeding eyes, while the owner pottering among the strings and pulleys, sought to repair the dislocated machinery. All the while a hideous booing and braying arose from a distant part of the ground, where a musician was tuning his monster machine, and anything more dismal than the wail of the single notes as they waved and wavered in unison could not be imagined.

Of course we had been too long in England to require any explanation of this singular scene. We saw at once that all these were but the necessary preliminaries to a country fair, which was to come off the next day. They informed us that they came this round regularly twice a year, and never without having a washing day at the brook. They were lodged in the barn (where a hundred were usually furnished with quarters for the night) belonging to the Inn keeper, who charged them nothing for this accommodation provided they paid their score for gin. Unless their wine bill is discharged a portion of their property is detained. Upon the occasion when we saw them, one of their favorite performing poodles was held by the Inn keeper as security for 2s 6d. The showmen said they would redeem him from their first takings at the fair of the next day. After leaving the party we passed the Inn and remained long enough to verify what the showman had said. On approaching the building we heard the plaintive notes of the whining hostage, and on entering the top room found the poor poodle tied up in the bar. The publican said these strolling actors and showmen were not worse as to morals than the run of his customers. That some of the men drank hard, to be sure, but that was the exception and not the rule; that as a class they like nothing better than a hot supper and plentiful supply of edibles, after taking which with a "night cap" of hot gin, they turn into the clean straw of the sheltering barn.

The following day we saw at the fair the entire party we had seen at the pool. They had arrived during the night and selected their ground, arousing the town from sleep by the hammering, lumbering and din of the preparations. The best sites had been monopolized by the first comers who had erected their booths, stages, &c. during the night, thus securing the entire day for business. As the multitudes do not crowd to the fair until evening, there is no particular advantage in this haste. But we will not enter upon the details of the country fair; they are familiar to every one, its fun, its folly and its sin. Among all the curious people attending it none were more curious than our acquaintances of the washing pool. Here was the bold musician who had made the yesterday hideous with his booing and braying machine, which was now all polished and varnished, grinding away at his instrument with a roar that filled the whole ground. Surrounding him was an open-mouthed audience, devouring the inexplicable drama performed by the little wooden figures, which dance, twirl, run and fight together, by the mere turning of the handle, while among the audience the grinder's little daughter, her head covered with a tiara, and her breast covered with a white handkerchief, thrust herself and her tambourine in hopes of pennies. Conspicuous among the performing dogs, all dressed in colors and spangles, moving in a minuet to the music of pipes, and the big drum, with the cobbled tympan, was the captive of yesterday. And there was the sallow-faced, long bearded philosopher, clad in the courtly professional garb of centuries past—a peaked hat upon his head, a waving mantle falling over his limbs and beneath his chin, forming a showy background to his long, black beard, a pointed Vandyke collar, which is recognized at once as the identical gem he was yesterday washing with such deliberate gravity. He was here as Esculapius, and with pill box in hand discoursed "in words of learned length and thundering sound" on the ills that flesh is heir to and the merits of his medicaments, while a boy at his feet makes all sorts of horrible grimaces of countenance, contortions of face in exemplification of the sufferings of those who have not tried the Doctor's remedies. Near is the traveling theatre with its gauzy panorama forty feet long and twenty high, on whose broad platform fools and clowns, and mummers and harlequins and shameless women dance and shout a reel and whirl in one mad rage together, all affording the merest foretaste of the indecency and fooleries within. This is the grandest of the temples of pleasure, and is flanked by the dancing and drinking booths, where drunkenness and wantonness go hand in hand.

These strolling showmen form but a part of that numerous class or varieties of classes who prefer the charms of a wandering life to any other, and who have a rooted antipathy to in-door life and regular occupation. Some of these are known as "tramps," and pass their lives in traversing the Kingdom, professedly in search of employment. They are rarely expert and for the most part loathe the work they seek. The confirmed tramp would upon no account confine himself to one spot, so fixed with him is the habit of vagabondage. To this class belong the itenerant tinkers, the knife grinders, the cane chair plaiters, the umbrella menders, the rat catchers, vermin hunters and the whole tribe of unlicensed hawkers. Some years ago we saw one of these cane chair plaiters industriously plying his occupation in the crowded thoroughfares of Liverpool and months afterwards recognized him in a Sea Side village inn Hants. It is impossible to reduce them into settled habits and indeed no one seems to care to take the trouble, though all are aware that from all their barter Her Majesty's exchequer is none the richer, that they contribute nothing to the support of society. Notwithstanding the strange spectacles witnessed at the fairs, the strangest of all is the people themselves, or as Pope expresses it,

"Let bear or elephant be e'er so white,
The people, sure the people are the sight."

Here we must dismiss the subject. Our plan does not admit of our entering upon the relations which the vagabond tribes bear to and the influence they exercise upon that portion of society with which they are brought in contact. The subject will be better treated by those who give themselves to the consideration and elucidation of social questions.

Proceeding by a route we had previously decided upon, a most circuitous one considering that London was the ultimate object, we arrived the day after leaving Sevenoaks at Battle, having delayed on the way only long enough to take a draught from the celebrated ferruginous spring of Tonbridge wells and to visit Penhurst, commonly called the home of the Sydneys. In the environs of

Tonbridge we visited some curious rocks from 40 to 70 feet high, containing many singular clifts and caverns. One of these which is known as the *Bell Rock*, emits a clear, ringing sound when struck. The lap dog of a lady named Bow, fell through a chasm in this rock during the last century, an event which she caused to be commemorated in the following inscription :

> "This scratch I make that you may know
> On this rock lies ye beauteous Bow;
> Reader, this rock is the Bow's Bell,
> Strik't with thy stick and ring his knell."

Penhurst Park was at the time of the Norman conquest the residence of the Penchester family and so continued for two centuries later. It then passed to the Dukes of Buckingham, subsequently to the Dukes of Northumberland and was finally inherited by that grand old gentleman, the pride of the court of Elizabeth, Sir Philip Sydney.

Great interest attaches to Penhurst as the home of the Sidneys, and especially of the Countess of Pembroke, "the subject of all verse, Sidney's sister." This accomplished woman was born about the middle of the 16th century and was reared with the utmost care, particular attention having been paid to her education. She made remarkable progress in every branch of learning and became the brightest star in the galaxy of brilliant and talented women who ornamented the Court of Elizabeth. At this time one of the most conspicuous men for his rank, religion and learning among Elizabeth's courtiers, was the Earl of Pembroke. A mutual attachment sprung up between them, and in 1576 they were married. Shortly after in conjunction with her brother, Sir Philip Sydney, she composed the *Arcadia*, a work of superior merit, though almost entirely neglected in the present day. Her fame as a poet, however, rests on her version of the Psalms, which were likewise written in conjunction with her distinguished brother. Up to the appearance of her work only two metrical versions of the entire Psalms had been attempted : the first, the well-known translation by Sternhold & Hopkins, and the second by Archbishop Parker. Both were inferior in vigor, dignity and poetic spirit to that by the Sidneys. As a specimen of the excellence of her version we shall here reproduce the opening of that truly magnificent Psalm, the 139th, and her version has never been surpassed :

PSALM CXXXIX—PART I.

O' Lord ! in me there lieth nought,
But to thy search revealed lies :
For when I sit·

Thou markest it,
No less thou notest when I rise ;
Yea, closest closet of my thought
Hath open windows to thine eyes.

Thou walkest with me when I walk,
When to my bed for rest I go,
I find thee there,
And everywhere:
Not youngest thought in me doth grow,
No, not one word I cast to talk,
But yet unuttered thou dost know.

To shun thy notice, leave thine eye,
O whither might I take my way?
To starry sphere?
Thy throne is there.
To dead men's undelightsome stay ?
There is Thy walk, and there to lie
Unknown, in vain I should essay.

O Sun ! whom light nor flight can match.
Suppose thy lightful, flightful wings
Thou lend to me,
And I could flee,
As far as thee the evening brings :
Ev'n led to west he would me catch,
Nor should I lurk with western things.

Do thou thy best, O secret night
In sable veil to cover me;
Thy sable veil
Shall vainly fail :
With day unmask'd my night shall be;
For night is day, and darkness light,
O Father of all lights to Thee.

As a prose writer she was equally elegant in style. The following lines, quoted from her translation of Philip de Mornay's "Discourse of Life and Death" will satisfactorily establish the fact.

"It seems to me strange and a thing much to be marveled, that the labourer to repose himself hasteneth as it were the course of the sun ; that the mariner rows with all his force to obtain the port, and with a joyful cry salutes the descried land ; that the traveller is never quiet nor content till he be at the end of his voyage, and that we, in the meanwhile tied in this world to a perpetual task, tossed with continual tempests, tired with a rough and cumbersome way, cannot yet see the end of our labour but with grief, nor behold our port but with tears, nor approach our home and quiet abode but with horror and trembling. This life is but a Penelope's web, wherein we are always doing and undoing; a sea open to all winds, which sometimes within, sometimes without never ceases to torment us, a weary journey through extreme heats and colds, over high mountains, steep rocks and thievish deserts. And so we term it weaving this web, in rowing at this oar, in passing this miserable way. Yet lo, when death comes to end our work, when she stretcheth out her arms to pull us into the port ; when after so many dangerous passages and loathsome lodgings, she would conduct us to our true home and resting place ; instead of rejoicing at the end of our labour, of taking comfort at the sight of our land, of singing at the approach of our happy mansion, we would (who would believe it?) retake our work in hand, we would again hoist sail to the wind, and willingly undertake our journey anew. No more then remember we our pains ; our shipwrecks and dangers are forgotten ; we fear no more the travails and the thieves. Contrawise, we apprehend death as an extreme pain, we doubt it as a rock, we fly it as a thief. We do as little children, who all the day complain, and when the medicine is brought them, are no longer sick ; as they who all the week long run up and down the streets with pain of the teeth, and seeing the barber coming to pull them out, feel no more pain. We fear more the cure than the disease ; the surgeon than the pain. We have more sense of the medicine's bitterness, soon gone, than of a bitter languishing, long continued ; more feeling of death, the end of our miseries, than the endless misery of our life. We fear that we ought to hope for, and wish for that we ought to fear."

Her profound knowledge of the Hebrew tongue and the classic languages—the models necessary to a perfect knowledge of poetry—made her the admiration of the scholars of the age. Among the truest admirers of her genius and virtues was Spencer, the first poet of the time. To her intellectual gifts she joined rare personal charms, which were celebrated by Ben Johnson. After a life protracted to an advanced age and twenty years of widowhood she died September 25th, 1621, and was buried in Salisbury Cathedral, and though no monument was ever erected to her memory, she has been honored with an epitaph, perhaps better known than any other which has graced the annals of the land, and which cannot fail to perpetuate, in colors durable as the language in which it is written, her beauty, virtue, and mental endowments

> Underneath this sable hearse
> Lies the subject of all verse;
> Sidney's sister, Pembroke's mother.
> Death, ere thou hast kill'd another,
> Fair and learn'd, and good as she,
> Time shall throw a dart at thee.

Let us add a word as to Sir Philip Sidney who was one of England's greatest, noblest men. His father, Sir Henry Sidney, was an Irish gentleman who married a daughter of the Duke of Northumberland, and Philip was born at Penhurst, in 1554. At the age of twenty-five, he became one of the most highly trusted counsellors of Elizabeth, by whom he was sent as Ambassador to the Emperor of Austria.

He proved one of her wisest advisers a few years later when the Duke of Anjou sought her hand in marriage. Though the Queen was 25 years older than the Duke, he visited England to press his suit in person and paid the Queen a secret visit at Greenwich. Though he was not handsome, his manners were pleasing, and he made a decided impression on her heart. The Queen ordered her ministers to fix the terms of the marriage settlement; and a day was appointed for the nuptials. The wisest of her advisers, Sir Philip Sidney, saw the necessity of averting a step which might have been very prejudicial to the interest of England, and had the courage to address a letter to her, in which he dissuaded her from the match with such force of reasoning, that her resolution was shaken. She became irresolute and melancholly as the day of marriage drew near, and is said to have passed several sleepless nights. The advice of Sir Philip prevailed and the Duke of Anjou was dismissed.

In 1585, an English army under the famous Earl of Leicester, was sent to Holland to aid the Prince of Orange. The Earl was a poor general, and did little for the cause, but Sir Philip Sidney so greatly distinguished himself by his courage and conduct, that his reputation rose to the highest pitch throughout Europe. He was invited to accept the Crown of Poland, and would have accepted but for the Queen. On the 17th of October, 1586. he was mortally wounded at the battle of Zutpher. After the battle, while lying mangled with wounds, upon the field, a bottle of water was brought him to relieve his thirst; but observing a soldier near him in a similar condition, he said, "This man's necessity is greater than mine," and resigned the water to the dying man. His body was taken to London and buried in St. Paul's Cathedral.

Besides the beautiful poem of the Arcadia, which places him in a high rank among poets, he wrote a number of smaller pieces, both in prose and verse. By the writers of that age he is described as the most perfect model that could be imagined of a great character. With the wisdom of a statesman, the valor of a soldier and the elegant accomplishments of a gentleman and scholar, he combined high principles of religion, and great purity of life. No person was too low to become an object of his humanity.

Battle is about seven miles from Hastings, and is situated near the spot where William the Conquerer fought his great battle with Harold, on the 4th of October, 1066. Harold was killed by an arrow which passed through the eye into the brain and Norman power was thus founded in England. On the battle field William I, established the Abbey of *St. Martin de bello Loco*, in gratitude for his victory, and as a solemn act for the repose of the souls of those who had fallen. After many ages of splendor the Abbey was despoiled by Henry VIII and much of it was destroyed. A portion of the ruins remain and are open to the inspection of visitors and another part of the Abbey has been restored and is occasionally used by the Duke of Cleveland. Everything connected with this memorable spot is too well known to justify being communicated by us to the reader. Near Battle, we visited Normanhurst —the splendid seat of Thomas Brassey, M. P., who has just been appointed by Mr. Gladstone, first Lord of the Admiralty—and had the pleasure to see his father, Thomas Brassey, Sr., the celebrated Railroad Contractor and millionaire, who founded the family. He was then about 65 years of age and was suffering from the palsy, but was still in the full possession of his mental faculties.

From Battle we proceeded by private conveyance to Hastings, stopping in Warrior Square, and after a few days sight seeing there and at St. Leonard's, returned by Brighton to London. Arriving in the Metropolis about two o'clock and near the tower, and unfatigued by the journey, we determined to avail ourselves of the opportunity to make another visit to this ancient building and have a look at its contents before proceeding to our quarters in Wimpole street. The day was cold and a strong easterly wind searched the very bones of the miserable crowd of sight seers, many of them Americans, whom we found penned in the open air just within the gate. When about 130 persons were gathered together, the gate closed, and while another crowd was allowed to collect outside it, those within were tolled off in batches of thirty and followed a beef-eater, who marched through some portions of the Tower, giving a history of the special features therein, but in such an undertone that few heard a word he said. We were taken through the magnificent collection of Armor and Arms at a pace which forbade the slightest examination of those grand historical relics, telling their wondrous tales of ancient chivalry and bloody battles. There was not a single piece of Armor, but had a volume inscribed upon it, not a lance or sword without a history of its own. In that collection of iron, England's past glories were told over and over again and yet we were compelled to walk past them without a chance of even looking at some articles and with only a cursory glance at others, which left no impression on the mind except of disgust with the authorities. This is what the tourist gets for his trouble in visiting London Tower.

The next morning was Sunday and our amiable and accomplished friend Mrs. Priaulx, who was the follower of the strange man, who has been styled the Plato of Christianity, Swedenborg, not only invited, but insisted upon our taking a seat in her carriage and going to King's Cross to hear a sermon from Dr. Bayley.— Reaching about 10 o'clock the new Jerusalem church, we found it, architecturally, comfortable and commodious. At the East end, beneath the table of mosaic law stands an Altar bearing the sacramental elements, in front of which, to the right and left towers, a brace of imposing pulpits. In looking over the books in Mrs. Priaulx's pew, we found that the new Jerusalem musical arrangements include anthems as well as hymns.* This was an agreeable surprise. As the congregation began to assemble, we discovered that the Swedenborgians are by no means a sombre sect, for the lover and his lass were ubiquitous and there was a pleasing absence of the elongated visage. After awhile the fine toned and well played organ piped up, and then from the vestry emerged two figures—one of them Dr. Bayley—the other an assisting high priest of Emanuel Swedenborg. They wore Geneva gowns of pure white, which exhibited in front a plentitude of waistcoat and watch chain. The two white figures ascended the two lofty pulpits. Now commenced the services, which were conducted with irritating slowness; but in mercy this tardy process is relieved by some capital singing. The professional element, one is glad to think, has received the sanction of Swedenborg and his disciples, and we imagine it forms quite as much an attraction as the two gentlemen in the snowy gowns, or the doctrines of Emanuel himself. Of the service as such little need be said. The ritual bears a strong family resemblance to that of the Morovians. The sermon was dull and the subsequent Eucharist was all the most zealous Protestant could desire. The vagaries and visions of the founder of this phase of religion seemed to be judiciously kept in the background, and there was, indeed, little to offend the susceptibilities of the most rigorously orthodox. One of the pastors invited the working men to a meeting in the week in order that a passage in St. Mathew might be explained by a layman in the light of the prophet Swedenborg, but as no workmen were visible to the naked eye in the church, we were not seriously alarmed for

RAMBLING REMINISCENCES

the spiritual safety of the proletariat. Altogether the service was exceedingly pleasant, especially for those who are fond of good music and some parade. More amused than edified by what we had seen, we returned to Cavendish Square and enjoyed a good dinner and long chit chat with our friends.

The following morning we re-entered upon the prosaic duties of our town life at that period.

## CHAPTER XXIII.

### THE ANGLO-NORMAN ISLE OF GUERNSEY.

England affords so many objects of interest worthy of description that a work of the nature of this might easily be made very voluminous. This we do not desire, nor probably the reader. We shall, therefore, close these reminiscences with a concluding chapter, in order to give some very rambling reminiscences of the Island of Guernsey, where annually, for years, we spent much time.

This pretty little island lies in a favored archipelago in the bay of Lamanche, or the bay of Mount St. Michel, as the English call it, about 85 miles from and S. E. of Weymouth, on the north west coast of France, at the extremity of Cherbourg point. It is a favorite resort of half pay officers and others of limited income, for the necessaries of life are cheap and the luxuries untaxed. It is also much frequented by delicate persons who require a mild winter climate. The gulf stream after leaving America crosses the ocean and expends itself on the shores of Western Europe, to which cause may be attributed the genial climate of the southern counties of England and the Channel Islands. The vast body of tepid water of the gulf stream causes also rapid evaporation and the fogs which hang over this part of the world and which envelope Guernsey with their warm breath, create upon the rocks in the midst of the sea a flora, which the most beautiful islands of the Adriatic and Mediterranean might well envy. The Aloes and the Camelia spring up in the open air and the Passion flower entwines itself around the largest trees.

In London we formed the acquaintance of several Guernseymen and on reaching St. Peter-port were most cordially welcomed, received, indeed, with that warmth and true politeness which come from the heart. By Col. James Priaulx, of Montville, one of Her Majesty's aid-de-camps, we were introduced to the Lieutenant Governor, General C. Rochforth Scott, and Sir Stafford Carey, the Bailiff, or Chief Justice of the Court of Common Pleas. With both we were much pleased, the General uniting to the qualities of the old soldier the accomplishments of the man of letters,* and the Bailiff, who is a graduate of Oxford and former professor of law in the University of London, adding to a profound knowledge of his profession, elegant scholarship and extensive attainments in several branches of learning. Sir Stafford was a tall, strongly built, erect, handsome man of about 65—with dignified, but affable manners and bearing—moreover, a man enjoying that valuable gift, a presence which is said to have carried more men to fortune than intellect. Subsequently a warm friendship grew up between Sir Stafford and the writer, and he takes a sorrowful pleasure in saying of him here, years after his death, that a more noble, honorable, upright man and judge never lived.

Such was the beauty of the island as we looked upon it from the deck of the Weymouth steamer which took us to St. Peterport that we lost no time on our arrival in viewing Castle Cornet, the fort, the docks, the light houses, the columns and statues—all the objects of interest in and about St. Peter Port and then in visiting the bays, inlets and commons, going entirely round the island and through the interior to the Parish churches situated near the centre of each parish, and surrounded by a small cluster of houses, stopping to talk to the peasants, entering their houses and examining their farm buildings, their farms, their stock, etc., and returned to the town so much delighted that we pronounced the island a garden, a veritable earthly paradise, where a few weeks before, the fields had been laden with rich harvests and the orchards covered with fruit.

Let us now plunge, without regard to order, after the advice of Horace, into the midst of what we have to say.

Within a few days after our arrival we dined at Haviland Hall, the Governor's residence, and at Candie, that of Sir Stafford Carey, meeting at both places representatives from the leading

*Gen'l Scott is author of a learned work entitled "Rambles in Egypt and Candia." He was an ensign in the British army in 1812 and present at the battle of New Orleans in 1815.

families of the island. This was during the winter, and the winter is the gay season in Guernsey, and if the entertainments are on a smaller scale than those of London, Paris and New York, they are none the less agreeable.

The resources of the island in the way of society are by no means inconsiderable. The native society is quite large and is reinforced by the Garrison officers and their families, and there are always in the island detachments of Royal Engineers, artillery and infantry. The stranger population, composed of those to whom we have referred, is never less than 3,000, many being English families, who have adopted it as a permanent residence, and there are always many yatchmen and other pleasure seekers who come here at every season, but more particularly in summer. As all are people of leisure, there is no business but pleasure, and Guernsey is a decidedly gay and festive spot, a little, though a very little, Paris. The usual vices and follies of the great world prevail, but probably in a less degree than in larger communities. However this may be, we shall not declaim against them in bitter or indeed, in any terms, as the Guernsey devotees of fashion are no worse, if no better, than others—than modern society in general —against which it is not our purpose to tilt the lance. As to the customs of good society, it is sufficient to say that they are similar to those which prevail in London and New York rather than in Paris, only slightly modified by ancient isl and customs. The people are, in a general way, very much like other people— as fond of dancing as the French, of music as the Italians, and of eating as the English. This brings us to remark that as in England and Guernsey, the dinner is the main institution of society, and as it differs a little in the way it is prepared and served from our American dinner, it will not tire our readers if we say a word about it. In the first place, it may be truly said of them that they are exceedingly good and enjoyable and always select as to company. And the company invited must not arrive too soon or too late, but strictly at the hour invited. They are never crowded, and are spiced with the conversation of educated people—experienced and traveled ladies and gentlemen, and men of talent for talking, if such can be secured, which makes them highly gratifying to the mind and senses. It is customary to dine at five o'clock, but dinner parties rarely occur before half past six and sometimes as late as half past eight o'clock. The place of distinction at the table is the seat at the greatest distance from the door at which the food is brought in, and to the right of the lady of the house. This post is usually assigned to the person of highest rank, or stranger guest, but great eminence in talents sets aside distinctions. These rise superior to rules. All the rest take their places promiscuously, unless, as is often the case, the names of the guests on cards are placed at the seat they are intended to occupy. A servant does the carving for the company. The dinner begins with a light soup; this is followed by fish, potatoes and salad; then follow the *entrees*, then the roast, then the game, then the pastries and puddings, then cheese, and last the fruits and nuts. With the fish, sauterne and sherry are served, then champagne, hock and claret, and the dinner ends with port, claret and sherry, liqueurs and coffee. No healths are drunk by anybody present. Occasionally, however, a foreigner's health is proposed, when he is expected to make a few remarks. After the ices and dessert have gone round, the ladies retire, when everything is removed but the wine and nuts, over which the gentlemen converse until nine or ten o'clock, when the gentlemen join the ladies in the drawing rooms where such guests as have been invited to an "evening" are assembled, and where whist, music and dancing conclude the entertainment. There is a homely old proverb applicable to these Guernsey dinners—"one may go further and fare worse."

Let us indulge in a few more details. To the after dinner receptions, or "evenings," the lady of the house invites the company, and these parties are usually large and the company somewhat promiscuous, often including, if not all, much the greater part of the hostess' acquaintances—consequently like the garrison and other balls, they are crowded and there is no small amount of cramming, squeezing and struggling, especially around the supper table. These suppers are, by the way, always good, consisting of fowls, game, &c., all kinds of made dishes, including one peculiar to the island, and called pickled ormers.* It is a shell fish, something similar to the oyster, only when cooked in Guernsey, by an ancient *chef de cuisine*, much better. Everything is washed down with sherry, claret and champagne. Dancing is always going on somewhere, but little else is visible to the on-looker than a writhing mass of humanity. Even in winter, in this mild climate, the heat on these occasions is oppressive, notwithstanding the pains taken to secure good ventilation, and the rapid passing round of ices. Conspicuous at these balls, are, of course, the subalterns in the army and under graduates fresh from the universities, the latter 'painfully neat,' as Hood says, and known among the Lilies of Guernsey, notwithstanding their irresistible garments, as "featherless bipeds." These gallants, who are always at a premium at dances, now and again feather their nests by marrying the island belles, who are generally heiresses and always pretty.

*The shells of the ormer are converted into work-boxes and pretty toys of one kind or another.

The Guernsey women, we may as well say here, are tall, well proportioned, and of blonde complexion in the high and brunette in the low parishes; their carriage is noble and their tone of voice sweet and tender. Owing to the extreme purity of the atmosphere and their open air exercises, they do not require artificial aid to heighten their beauty, the bloom of the rose and lily vie in their complexions. Their dress is Parisien and, of course, lacks nothing in the way of taste and elegance.

At this point, where we have spoken of the dinner customs and the marrying young man, it may not be out of place to say something in regard to that fashionable event, the marriage breakfast —an event far too rare in the island where there are several thousand more females than males—thousands, indeed, of splendid girls, marriagable, but unmarried. The disproportion is so great that a stranger might well imagine that the men had fallen upon the advice of Mr. Weller to his son Samivel: "I'm a goin' to leave you, Samivel, my boy, and there's no telling ven I shall see you again. Your mother-in-law may have been too much for me, or a thousand things may have happened by the time you next hears any news o' the celebrated Mr. Veller o' the Bell Savage. The family name depends wery much upon you, Samivel, and I hope you'll do wot's right by it. Upon all little pints o' breedin', I know I may trust you as vell as if it was my own self. So I've only this here one little bit of adwice to give you. If ever you gets to up'ards o' fifty, and feels disposed to go a marryin' anybody—no matter who—jist you shut yourself up in your own room, if you've got one, and pison yourself off hand. Hangin's wulgar, so don't you have nothin' to say to that. Pison yourself, Samivel, my boy, pison yourself, and you'll be glad on it arterwards." The real cause of this anomalous state of affairs is simply the fact that most of the Guernsey youths are abroad seeking their fortunes— some in the British army, some tossed about on the seas in men of war, or commercial vessels, some are growing coffee in Ceylon, or wool in Africa or Australia and others are cow boys in Colorado. Wherever there is work to be done or money or glory to be acquired, these Guernsey boys are to the front. Yes these are the causes of the disproportion and not the want of beauty or accomplishments with the ladies.

The customs which prevail in regard to marriage are not very dissimilar to those of the English. People marry after the publication of three banns, and a dispensation of banns is easily obtained by those who do not wish to be thus married, and those who aspire to the habits of good society never do, as the marriage by banns is not considered *comme il faut*. Magnificent breakfasts among the wealthy, and substantial suppers among the peasantry are customary on such occasions, irrespective of expense. These breakfasts are worthy of a slight notice. It is usually arranged on one or more tables, decorated with silver, glass and flowers—the wedding cake is richly ornamented with flowers in sugar and a knot of orange blossoms at the top. At either end of the table are tea and coffee. Generally the viands are cold, consisting of poultry, game, salads, hams, tongues, jellies, cake and indeed sweets of every description, ices, fruits, wines, etc. The wedding cake is cut by the nearest gentleman and handed round. The father—or in case the father be absent, or dead, the nearest friend now proposes the health of the bride and bride-groom. The latter is expected to answer, which we have often heard him do in a most amusing and ridiculous manner, and to propose the bride-grooms-man. The latter returns thanks, and pledges the brides-maids, who answer through the bride-groom. The health of the clergyman, if he is present, is also proposed. The health of our "American cousins," brought us to our legs oftener than we could fitly respond in words that breathe and thoughts that burn to the hospitality of these charming people. A coach and four draws up, after a sufficient time has passed to allow ample justice to be done the breakfast, the company then take leave of the bride in the drawing room, and she is led to the coach as rice and slippers are thrown after the drag, in which she drives off. The rice throwing had its origin in the Kingdom of Macassar, where rice is thrown out of the back windows of the house all day during a wedding. It is supposed that since rice is an emblem of fruitfulness, it is thrown in the hope that it will secure an abundant crop of olive branches

On these occasions presents are given by the bride-groom to the bride and bridesmaids, and by the bridesmaids and friends to the bride. They consist generally of jewelry and are often costly. The servants, too, expect presents and are rarely disappointed, from which it may be rightly inferred that a fashionable wedding in Guernsey is by no means an insignificant affair.

Though from the diminutive character of the island, there are few opportunities of acquiring wealth, there are several families of fortune, not large, but easy and independent, whose money has been made by trade in South America, Spain, Australia, Ceylon and other countries. This is notably the case with the Careys, the Allaires, the MacGregors, the Tuppers and the Dobrees, all of whom have had members distinguished for their intelligence, spirit and enterprise. Having made money by honorable mercantile transactions, they know how to keep it, and they have enjoyed it so long that the taint of trade has gradually disappeared. Their children are brought up to the most exemplary habits of economy and saving.

It is usual to give very young children a few small coins weekly, which they take with regularity on Saturdays and deposit in the savings banks. This is done to teach them habits of accumulation. They are told that the bee gathers honey for the winter, the squirrel nuts against a time of want, and the ant is pointed out as a beautiful example of industrious forethought. They are early impressed with the idea that man forms no exception to the rule, and that in youth he must provide for the necessities of old age. The good results of such teachings are seen in the staid habits and customs of the people, and in their surroundings—in their neat, tidy dwellings, well kept grounds and in their dress and general thrifty appearance. It must not be inferred from this that the virtue of economy is carried to an extreme—far from it. These good people only practice that kind of thrift which leads to thriving. Persons of limited income do not vie with those of larger fortune, nor do they lose caste by it. Often have we been invited to tea by refined and cultivated persons who accompanied their civility with the remark that they were unable to give dinners—hence their invitations to equally agreeable and less expensive entertainments. It gave us genuine pleasure to accept such invitations and we always enjoyed much these quiet reunions. While an enlightened economy prevails with all there is no parsimony or niggardness. No people display a more Christian or charitable spirit in all matters affecting the poor. So large are the voluntary contributions to the poor, especially during the Winter, that little is left to be done by the parochial authorities. And never was a sailor lost at sea, a workman blown to atoms in the quarries, or a family overtaken by any unusual misfortune such as the loss of the head, that a handsome subscription did not follow—often placing the widow and children beyond want. This benevolent spirit, which forms so beautiful a feature in the Guernsey character, is further shown in large contributions in aid of sober, industrious and worthy families who wish to emigrate to America or the British Colonies, and in contributions to alleviate the misfortunes and sufferings of unfortunates in other countries—the victims of fires, earthquakes, floods, disease and pestilence.

The people are physically muscular and active, not so large in person as the English or so small as the French, but a fair mean between the two. In the high parishes the men and women are larger than in the low parishes, which is said to be due to their Breton origin in the vale, and to the deplorable extent to which marrying in-and-in is carried—the rule down there being to marry a cousin if possible. The population of the high parishes claim a Norman origin. In every part of the bailiwick the people are of a vivacious and lively temperament and a stranger walking through the market place, the arcade or high street of an evening, sees gay countenances, hears obstreperous laughing and a universal inclination to jollity, and this among a people far removed from what is styled an ignorant and restless populace.

Regret has been expressed, even by Guernseymen, that the people do not take more pleasure in the manly sports of the English, instead of passing their leisure time at bazaars, or following religious and other processions. The better sort of people among the Islanders are not, it is true, fond of procuring themselves pleasure by means of violent exercise. But it is otherwise with many and especially with the masses, who are fond of cricket, foot ball, tennis, quoits and boating, and these games would be practised more generally, if their occupations admitted of it. Games, of some sort, are common in Summer and every afternoon one or the other of those mentioned is played in Cambridge Park, or some other suitable ground. And it is common for the College, or Garrison Clubs, or the Town clubs, to send challenges to those of Weymouth, Southampton, or Jersey, and invite them to try their skill, contesting for some prize. On such occasions large crowds of people resort to see them play ; and it sometimes happens that gentlemen not members of the clubs, more particularly the collegians and garrison officers, are among the number of the players. The Summer festival of Elizabeth College, or what are styled "the College Sports," occur on a high ground overlooking the sea and are fashionably attended. The young men and boys dressed in light tights, contend in hurdle races, flat races, sack races, hammer throwing, leaping, and in all manner of athletic exercises for prizes, generally awarded by some popular lady.

At the annual races many other sports are common with the peasantry, such as hanging hams, fowls and other eatables at the top of a perfectly smooth pole. The nice things at the top of the pole reward the successful climber. The most vigorous young men make a trial of this fete, but the greater part are unsuccessful—sliding down with great velocity, to the no small merriment of the spectators, men and women. He who is so robust and skillful as to reach the top and throw down the eatables, is the hero of the hour.

When the annual Spring and Autumn races occur, on L'ancresse common in Guernsey or Gorey common in Jersey, these and many other like sports and rustic games prevail. All classes take a deep interest in regattas, and when they occur the islanders turn out *en masse* and many visitors come from the neighboring islands and even from England and France. These are only some of the games and exercises which call forth the powers of the mind as well as those of the body—require strength and dexterity, and the mere mention of these will serve to correct the erroneous impressions on this subject and tend to convey a just idea of the people.

## LITERATURE, ETC.

Guernsey has produced several meritorious poets and there is a brisk vein of poetry running through the population. The most famous poet is Georges Metevier, who made valuable contributions to other departments of literature. He prepared and published some years since a great work with a view to preserving the ancient language of the country, styled "*Dictionnaire Franco-Normand; au Recueil des mots particuliers au Dialecte de Guernsey.*" The book is grand in the design and complete in its execution and reflects infinite honor upon the author and the island. Mr Metevier, who was over 80 years of age when the work was published, had been sixty years employed upon it and had the assistance of Sir Stafford Carey, Sir Edgar MacCulloch, F. B. Tupper, Rev. R. J. Ozanne and Dr. Hoskins. It has added immensely to the stock of knowledge already possessed by the scholars, and teaches the student, by a striking example, of the vast and almost incredible acquisitions the human mind can make, when long and incessantly employed in the pursuit of knowledge.

It is said that the work was undertaken at the suggestion of Lucian Bonaparte, Prince of Canino, who was himself an accomplished philologist, and despite some inaccuracies, is still the best authority on the subject which it treats. Mr. Metevier lived in his books, knew little and cared less about any of the ordinary affairs which exercise the minds of men, and though of the most benevolent and amicable disposition, had little more sympathy with any of the questions of the day than if he had been living in another world. He was the younger brother of Wm. P. Metevier, a Jurat of the Royal Court and one of the most excellent and useful men in the island. This erudite and good man, as also his venerable brother, has descended to the tomb. Hallowed be their memories. Mr. Metevier was a profound etymologist, scholar and poet.*

Several other Guernseymen have succeeded in different departments of learning, notably Ferdinand Brock Tupper, author of the most valuable history extant of the island, who may be described as traveller, archæologist, natural philosopher and historian, combined in one. Frederick Lukis and Dr. MacCulloch, distinguished geologists; Rev J. A. Jeremie, D. D., regius professor of

---

*Mr. Metevier's poetry is smooth and harmonious—much more so in his native French-Normand language than in English—is characterized by fine taste, sound judgment, and lively imagination. It is reason ornamented by imagination and rythm. The reader will find, in appendix A, some lines from his pen, which appeared in the local Guernsey papers shortly after the author's return to America —ED.

Greek at Cambridge; Peter Paul Dobree, hellenist and classical writer; Osmond de B. Priaulx, author of "Questiones Mosaicæ," or the book of Genesis compared with the remains of ancient religion," and other valuable educational works; Dr. Hoskins, author of "Charles II., in the Channel Islands," and other works; Amias C. Andros, author of an interesting work of travels in Spain, etc.; Mrs. Carey Brock, author of several popular religious works.

The island has produced no eminent artist, painter, architect, or sculptor, but there is at present a clever portrait painter, a native of the island,—a Mr. Paul Naftel, winning fame in London. If in these departments they have done little, they have furnished many fine soldiers and sailors to the British army and navy, and the island militia is well drilled and full of martial spirit.

The higher class is known as Sixtys, who have for ages held the first position and enjoyed the best of everything in the island. They are called by the peasantry "the people of the first fashion," and are, in fact, the old manor families. Their society comprises nearly all that is brilliant in art and intellect in the island; all who are distinguished by their wealth, virtues, or knowledge, and has done so from a remote period. Men of fortune are admitted to it because they support the burdens of the state; men of virtue and enlightenment, because they chiefly contribute to its preservation and glory, and men of birth from a presumption that it transmits from father to son more noble sentiments, and a more ardent patriotism than can be found in vulgar minds. Particular regard is therefore paid to the old families, and especially those whose founders have displayed examples of distinguished virtue. Some of the Sixtys trace back their origin more than a thousand years, and are accused of inventing genealogies to establish their pretensions. They enjoy no peculiar privileges or precedency, but their education gives them a claim to the first places and public opinion facilitates their attaining them.

The leading Seigneurs and landed proprietors are the Priaulx's, Seigneurs of Comte, the Andros', Seigneurs of Anneville, the Sausmarez, Seigneurs of Jerbourg, the de Jerseys, proprietors of Oberlands, the Collings', Seigneurs of Serk, the Lefevres, Seigneurs of Blanchmond, the Le Marchants, proprietors of Haye de Puit, and the Mansells, proprietors of the Vaubelets. The present representatives of these families are as different as possible, in all but spirit, from their warlike ancestors, who clad in steel armor and mounted on Percheron chargers often made whole districts tremble. This was their principal employment, during the middle ages, when these Seigneurs exercised a complete mastery over their villeins, making them perform all kinds of menial offices in time of peace and follow their persons in time of war. In those days there were but Sixteen Seigneurs in Guernsey—the rest of the population was in a state of vassalage. As this was the character, position and former state and condition of the Sixtys, it is hardly surprising that they still feel a little pride of position. The Sixtys affect French manners, as well as the French language* and resemble their architypes in affability, easy elegance and alertness. They are not a little proud of their immediate descent from the Norman Conquerers of England and boast, as indeed does the entire population, that they have never been over-run, subjugated or conquered by any race, or nation whatever. Although very exclusive, within recent years many have crept into their social circle, who ought not to be there—these for the most part have been disreputable or what are styled "shady" English.

The second rank is known as Fortys and are said, with what truth we know not, to be descendants of the *fancs tenants* of the middle ages, or those serfs who by superior parts, acquired lands of the Seigneurs exempt from any service, burden, tax or duty to the Lord of the Manor, or lands in which Seignorial rights were, for a valuable consideration, surrendered. The Fortys are sturdy men of affairs, bankers, merchants, manufacturers, care little for learning or the arts, and nothing whatever for the gayeties and frivolities of the fashionable world. They are full of practical ideas, plodding industry and progressive energy. Whatever trade and commerce Guernsey can boast of, is in their hands; if they do not originate they carry out all public improvements, rear blooded stock, apply science to agriculture—they are the men of to-day—the Sixtys of yesterday. The latter will not admit them to social intercourse, however agreeable they may be in manners, in social talents and elevated in character. This is to be regretted since many of the Fortys would be ornaments to the island society. Such men as John D. Utermarch who though descended of humble Dutch origin, and enjoying few advantages of early education, was a man of such perseverance, strength of will and extraordinary audacity that he made the most of every opportunity that came in his way, and rose to a prominent position at the bar, ranking with such eminent jurists as Charles de Jersey and Henry Tupper—the latter the most learned lawyer, comprehensive statesman and unselfish patriot of his day, and Hilary O. Carré and James Gallienne, both of plebian extract, but of such talents and acquirements as to rank with the best advocates of the Royal Court. Ought such men to be neglected and go unhonored in any society? Certainly not, still less for such shams as are every day met, not only in Guernsey, but the world over—men

*A society called the Society de Guernsais has been formed with the special object of preserving the French-Guernsey language.

whom the world calls great and noble, and are only so on the outside, like the giants one sees in the pantomines who are made of paste-board, and have a very ordinary sized man moving about in them.

Mr. Tupper became, in time, one of our warmest friends and we cannot allow the opportunity to pass, when his name is mentioned, without paying a tribute to his memory. He was a man of vigorous intellect, large heart, just and noble sentiments. He was not brought up to enervating luxury. His father was poor—there was more bread than butter in that family, but means were found to enable him, after completing his academic education at Elizabeth College, to enter the celebrated law school at Caen, in Normandy, where he was, in due season, graduated. Returning home, he devoted himself to the law practice and met with large success. Subsequently he was elected to the States and soon became the leader of that body and conspicuous for his liberal and enlightened statesmanship. In private, he was noted for his benevolence and generosity, and in public and private for the warmth of his temper, which occasionally approached to bitterness, in his contests with the narrow party of obstruction, composed of the old school, or men inimical to all change. Sir Stafford Carey, we have said, was a man with a presence. Mr. Tupper was a man with a manner. By manner we mean that invisible quality which insensibly pervades, with the happiest effect, the works of genius, which animates the pencil of the artist, the pen of the poet, and the sentiments of the orator. Such was his manner that he was irresistibly charming. The warmth with which he received his friends, the vivacity with which he spoke, the skill with which he told an anecdote, the charity with which he viewed the short comings of his neighbors, the ardor with which he denounced a wrong, the fidelity with which he adhered to his friends, in good and evil report,in a word his character and his manner drew round him hosts of friends and admirers whom he held by a power no language can express. And yet this irreproachable and magnetic man had ene mies who pursued him with relentless hatred to the grave. Death has placed him beyond their reach. For ourselves, we felt for him the affection of a brother, admired his virtues, his talents, his acquirements, his *soul*—we never met him without a rising sense of pleasure in our breast, feeling a strong desire to be nearer to him. This accomplished man and charming companion, who commenced life poor, and ended it the wealthiest man in the island, died while we were yet in Guernsey; was accorded a public funeral; and we followed his remains to the tomb with profound sorrow.

The peasantry are industrious and thrifty, and make successful farmers, excellent gardeners and fruit growers, skilled mechanics brave soldiers and hardy sailors. Their qualities have been illustrated on many fields, under the lead of such martial spirits and Sarnian heroes as Lord de Saumarez, Major Gen'l Sir Isaac Brock, Captain Charles Andros, R. N., General Sir Gaspard Le Marchant and others.

Whether they be descended from the Seigneurs, or Serfs o the middle ages, we know not, but whatever their origin, they are a staunch. true and steadfast race. Many of them preserve their pedigrees with curious pride, which they would hardly do if sprung from slaves, and have the spirit of a long line of ancestors as honorable as any of the islanders of whatever rank, and they generally begin a history of themselves with a genealogy. A Mr. Guille, a cabinet maker of the Hauteville, gave us on one occasion, when we called to have a chair repaired, an interesting account of the Guilles, and showed his family tree. Mr. Guille knew something of his father, a little of his grandfather, and up to that point his pedigree was history beyond fable and tradition. Yet we went over it with care, though all family history, but our own, is dull reading, and we felt satisfied it was as reliable as a majority of such genealogies, though it made out he was descended from Noah.

Some of the manor houses and country seats are handsome and commodious, and surrounded by park like grounds, ornamented with ancient forest trees and fine shrubberies; they look like English halls. The principal country seats are the Vaubelets, Les Eperons, Oberlands, Haviland Hall, St. Helene, Rosenheim, Vanquiedor, Saumarez, Woodlands, St. George's, Haye de Puits and the Vallon. Like the town houses their interiors are quite artistic. The furniture, much of it old oak, the decorations and all the surroundings are in extremely good taste and are just what one would expect to see in the houses of cultivated people.

This is particularly the case with Rosenheim, the home of Gen. Huysh, a gem in itself, in its furniture, its objects of art, virtu, etc., and in its grounds, conservatories, etc.

The rural population generally reside in substantial stone houses, some of them of great antiquity — one of them in St. Martin's Parish having A. D. 1604, the date of its erection, cut in a round over the front entrance, which has the characteristic Guernsey round-arched stone doorway. These farm houses and cottages while plainly furnished are comfortable and neat, and there is nothing peculiar to them but the round arched stone doorway and the fern bed. This lounge, or bed, is a wooden frame placed always on one side or the other of the principal sitting room or kitchen fire place. It is spread with fern leaves, is called a *lit de fouaille*, and is the resting place of the farmer and his employees when they return of an evening, and of any visitor who may come in. These beds have been used in the island time out of mind, and are connected with all the traditions and habits of the people. The writer has often, when stopping during a pedestrian tour, reposed upon them, finding them soft, elastic, and with an agreeable aromatic or spicy fern odour. The peasants are noted for honesty. Robbery and thieving are scarcely ever known in the country parishes and lost articles, when found, are generally restored. The trades people while fond of getting a good price for their goods and wares, rarely resort to cheatery and we have known them to give extra weight, or an additional quantity of an article, where they considered the customer outwitted in the price. They take pains to explain to strangers the difference in the Guernsey weights and measures from those of France and England and the difference in the value of the foreign and the Island currency, and for the most part they are good humored and obliging.

The fourth rank is composed of the day laborers.

According to ancient custom they were thus ranked, that is to say : 1st, the Seigneurs, or the nobility ; 2d, the Freemen, or franc tenants ; 3d, the Freedmen ; 4th, the Serfs, and as it was the custom, if not the law, that each person should marry in his own rank, their different orders were long preserved uncontaminated. Within the past century there has been a good deal of marrying between the Sixtys and the Fortys, the wealth of the Fortys constituting a very acceptable inducement to the less wealthy of the Sixtys. But the Fortys thus admitted into the higher class feel their dependence and are often humiliated. It is a painful situation to be where they have no authority or influence and it would be wiser probably to marry in their own class.

From what has gone before, the reader will not be surprised to learn that the Sixtys regard trade as derogatory, or *infra dig*, and that no one engaged in it, is admitted to their society, nor are such persons allowed, with their consent, to fill offices of dignity or profit. An election for Judge or Jurat of the Royal Court occurred while we were in the Island. Accepting an invitation to be present, we attended the states of election on the occasion.

Abraham Bishop, a prosperous and wealthy merchant, was nominated for the post. His election was opposed by one of the Sixtys, upon the grounds of Mr. Bishop's connection with trade and his consequent unfitness for the position This ancient policy on part of the old families, has excluded from the States, in times passed and still does so, many men of character and talents for legislative work. And men have been elected merely because they were descendants of the old Seigneurs, who were hopelessly eccentric, or congenitally stupid. The States have not heretofore been noted for the acumen, the efficiency or the learning of its members, though that body has never, at any time, been entirely without men of good parts. To raise the standard of ability in the House by electing the better men of the Fortys was not agreeable to the Sixtys—still less an effort to purge the public councils of all who from great age, incapacity or bad character were unsuited for its duties. While such a policy would have given moral weight and political strength to the States it would have impaired the influence of those who have so long controlled it. And this was something which could not be tolerated. Like Juba, King of Numidia, who had Roman senators in his train, the Sixtys like to have Fortys following at their heels.

The deputy who stood forward to oppose Mr. Bishop's election went on sharply to criticise his presumption in allowing his name to be presented, and this while he admitted Mr. B. to be a man of capacity, of fortune and of deep stake in the community. Though this was not denied, the deputy said Mr. Bishop's business pursuits, his want of social standing, and his lack of special legal training, (something by the way which none of the Jurats had except the Bailiff) altogether disqualified him for the office.

The member who had adventurously nominated Mr. B. feebly essayed to justify his course, as taken in accordance with the liberal tendencies of the age, and in the hope of securing more progressive ideas and efficiency in the States, but his remarks were so badly received that he soon resumed his seat amid the ill suppressed sneers of that haughty aristocracy, which hardly regarded Mr. Bishop as better than a huckster, and, of course, the election went against the Merchant Prince, as Mr. Bishop was sometimes styled.

The ancient Greek gods were jealous of those who tried to vie with them. Apollo slew Marsyas for daring to contend with him on the lyre. Minerva changed Arachne into a spider for boasting superiority to her. The Sovereign of the Gods could not endure the luxury and pride of the earthly despot and it became the business of Nemesis to compass his destruction. She invoked against him Ate or infatuation. Ate darkens his mind and forces him to enter of his own will on the path whose end is destruction. It seems to have been an article of an Athenian creed that there was a sort of wickedness in one free man attempting to rise up to or above the level of his fellow citizens. This was a kind of inverted doctrine of the divine right of kings and traces of this sort of thing may be seen in the history of Guernsey.

The reader must not infer from all this that the Sixtys in the

States are milk sops, far from it. For centuries they looked upon their Jurats as personages of very great dignity. Several of those on the bench in former times were men of ability and learning, some kept up much state in their living, all were of the Seigneur class, and they do not wish the office to decline in dignity by the introduction to it of persons of inferior caste. This it is and nothing more. They consider, in fact, that they owe a duty to society and that it would be a deriliction of duty to vote a Forty, even if the Forty was well qualified and above reproach, into the high office of Jurat. So far from being milk sops, the Guernsey Sixtys as a rule are men of great cleverness, only a little behind the age, or Torys *de fond au comble*; they are men of nicety of principle, a dignified sense of honor, refinement of feeling, in a word of such tastes, sentiments and habits as are engendered and cherished by education, and the pursuit, however desultory, of knowledge, and these qualities impart a kind of serenity and blandness to the whole atmosphere of Sarnian society highly grateful to the cultivated visitor.

### THE SPORTING CLUB.

Some of our most enjoyable days were spent on L'ancresse Common, first as a guest and afterwards as a member of the "Sporting Club." This club is of great antiquity, was no doubt, founded at a time when there was game to be had, which is no longer the case, and when fishing, as an amusement, was more common than now. To-day it is merely a dining club, the members driving to the common and spending the day idly wandering about, looking out upon the ocean, as it rolls on the shore with musical, lapping sound, and inhaling the air, fragrant with the breath of wild flowers. This common, and the cliffs and cotils are famous for the purity of the air, the sweetness of the water which flows from their little springs, the fertile vallies that lie between, and for the plants and herbs which are interspersed with the grass. These are said to give a peculiar flavor and richness to the milk and butter of the cows pasturing on them. Guernsey butter is unquestionably good, but we do not credit this statement any more than the story told of Helicon, whose plants were said to cause the serpents that fed upon them to lose their venom. The Guernsey people believe it all the same.

After the best part of the day is thus spent, the members assemble at the club house at 6 o'clock for dinner, and nowhere are better dinners served than at the Sporting Club. After several hours spent at the table, the Club, with its guests, returns to town by the light of the stars, in omnibusses, reluctant to separate sooner than is absolutely necessary.

The President of the Club, when we first dined with it, was Maj. Genl. Barry, Royal Engineers, a venerable patriarch, who, though past 80, was not infirm, but erect and stately, and full of the peculiar wit and humor of that splendid Irish race from which he was sprung, and of which he was an ornament. At the lower end of the table sat Rear Admiral, Sausmarez Brock, R. N., Vice-President, who was hardly less winsome than the President, and who never failed to entertain us with his experiences afloat and ashore, in India and Africa, but especially in the Crimea, where he was Military Governor of Eupatoria—events to which his memory fondly clung. His anecdotes, equally amusing and instructive, are worthy of a place in the Guernsey library. To the right of the President sat the Lt. Bailiff, the present Sir E. MacCulloch, a tall, thin, refined looking old man, amiable, engaging and entertaining,—mild and circumspect in private and public. To the left of the V. P. sat the late J. Priaulx, the noblest Roman of them all, a man of gentle and polished manners, but who at times of excitement, became somewhat reckless in tone and bearing and oblivious to the conventionalities of society. The generosity of his heart, his inflexible integrity and his noble aspect, gave something of dignity to his language and gestures, however extravagant they might be at times. Opposite Mr. Priaulx sat Col. Durnford, who was regarded as a native born. Sixty, having intermarried with one of the manorial families. He was mild, polite, affable and moderate. He courted the good will of others and imparted to them his own. He was neither wit nor humorist, but in his face, his sentiments and his language, there was something so honest and engaging that one was quickly charmed and attracted. The rest of the members seated themselves promiscuously and were—we take a sad pleasure in preserving their names—:

General Barry, Royal Engineers;
Admiral Brock, Royal Navy;
Sir Edgar MacCulloch, Lt. Bailiff;
Joshua Priaulx, Seigneur of Comte;
Joshua Gosselin, of Springfield;
Julius Carey, Premier Connetable;
Col. Durnford, R. A., of Havalet;
John Le Mottee, Royal Court;
Col. Bell, Q. A. D., of Swiss-ville;
A. D. MacGregor, of Melrose;
P. S. Dobree, of Ronceval;
Le M. Thomas Le Marchant, of Haye de Puits.

Gen. Barry, Admiral Brock, Mr. Priaulx, Col. Durnford and the members generally, had been great travelers and had grown thoroughly liberal and cosmopolitan—were without the limitations and prejudices of nationalities, races and sects. It is the fortune of most men who mingle in the world and attain to. even middle age, to make many friends and lose them in the course of nature. Such has been our fate.

Of the fourteen members above enumerated, eight are in their graves. Their pleasant and familiar faces will be met no more here below, yet the club exists, the music of birds is still heard on the common, the waves murmur ceaselessly on the shore, and the air is still full of the aroma of odoriferous herbs and sweet scented flowers. Man dies, but nature lives, and we recall the sad lament of the poet: "Woe that the linden and the vine should bloom, and a just man be gathered to the tomb." Sausmarez, Brock and his inseperable boon companion, Barry, are gone; Joshua Priaulx and his old crony, Joshua Gosselin, two jovial men who enjoyed life so thoroughly that one could not help wishing they might live forever—their visiting cards are now tombstones. MacGregor and Dobree are gone—but we are getting blue. The dead sleep well. They need neither sympathy nor tears, and as for regrets, they are unavailing. We cannot, as Lamb lamented, "lay our ineffectual fingers on the spokes of the great wheel" and stop where we are. Growing old is a part of the inevitable programme of life. It belongs to the natural process of gradation, by which nature accomplishes all her work, never doing anything abruptly. Men grow and bud and blossom and bear fruit,or live barren like certain trees, and then also like the trees, fade and fall and disappear. We can only accept the situation.

### THE INSTITUTIONS OF THE ISLAND, ETC.

A few words only need be said of the institutions of the island. Guernsey has preserved almost in their original form, her ancient municipal charters and has to day a municipal government precisely what it was in the middle ages, and they enjoy it in security, though it is behind the age. They have preserved their laws, their coinage and their language, though none of them are English. In their Norman language they conduct the pleadings in their courts and the affairs of their States, or local Parliament. Though England garrisons the island for defense, no British soldier dare arrest a Guernseyman, and the Lieutenant Governor himself would long hesitate before he would encroach upon the local police.

These ancient laws and customs of the island are very superannuated in some points and very little in harmony with modern progress. The British Parliament wished, years ago, to introduce many necessary reforms and gradually to substitute for these old Norman laws its own laws and authority, but this the Guernsey people would not hear of. When Parliament sought to obtain its ends by a Royal Commission, the States answers fiercely: "Are you ignorant that you are not our masters? We have never been conquered by, nor submitted to you. Recollect that we are the descendants of the Normans of the Conquest, and that our ancestors imposed their domination over you." Reasons which it is very certain would not hold good before heavy ordinance. The justice of these views was recognized; the island does not appertain to the English government, but belongs to the domain of the Queen, who is its suzerain, and who yet retains the prerogatives of the Norman Kings. Thus the Parliament held in check by these ancient privileges of the crown saw itself powerless, and everything is left to the States. Who are to be most admired in this conflict — the little people who have preserved such a sacred regard for their rights, or the great nation which respects them? Such is nevertheless the cause of the independence of the island. That their liberty has not been sterile is apparant. On every side are seen signs of activity and industry—not only in the smooth and beautiful roads, in the substantial character of their houses, but in the general well-being of the community and at the gigantic granite quays, jetties and docks. In a moral point of view they enjoy religious toleration and a free press. Hence strangers collect in great numbers in all the channel islands, for the condition of all is the same, attracted by the fineness of the climate, the beauty of the scenery and the freedom of the institutions.

Many of the manor houses still standing and occupied, bear the names of the Huguenots, who took refuge here. The Hauteville is the most ancient part of the town, but the Basseville the more populous; it is principally inhabited by merchants and those connected with the trade of the island.

The principal towns are St. Peter-port, with a population of 17,000, and St. Sampson's. Of the latter it is not necessary to say more than that it is the chief port for the export of granite. St. Peter-port is situated on the northern acclivities of the island, nearly opposite and in full view of the islands of Herm, Jeddo and Serk, three miles from the first two and about seven miles from the last. The streets wind up the hills and with the exception of the Avenue St. Julien, are steep and narrow but are well paved, and the houses, which are built of granite, are roomy and substantial. The number of churches is large, but they contain few monuments of note, with the exception of the town church and the Roman Catholic church, in which there are some good pictures and statues.

HAUTEVILLE HOUSE, VICTOR HUGO, PRIVATE THEATRICALS, ETC.

The most famous house in the island is that of the illustrious poet, Victor Hugo, in the Hauteville. On the summit of a cliff, it overlooks the town, the fort and the immense horizon of the sea. The house awakens a lively curiosity in all visitors to the island, and fabulous stories are told in Guernsey of its costly furniture, its massive plate, its gorgeous decorations.

The day after our arrival the poet invited us to breakfast, having been introduced to us by John Talbot, Esq., editor of the Star—an invitation we accepted with much pleasure, and this was the beginning of a lasting friendship between us and his family,* then consisting of Madam Hugo, his sister-in-law, Madam Cheney, and the children of his son, Charles Hugo. This is not the place to give our impressions of Victor Hugo nor his house—we do not wish to recall anything but a little representation which was given in it not long afterwards. A charade was performed upon a subject proposed by Victor Hugo.

In the first scene the shadowy Cymbeline appears enveloped in clouds of tulle-illusion and having at her feet the beautiful Leander, pale as a confirmed poet. Transparent and ideal he pays court to her with rhymes and sighs something after the style of an amorous sonnet of romance.

Leander, immaterial as he appears, is not the less anxious to obtain a nocturnal meeting under the trees and upon the moss. His eloquence is transparent. After some moments of cooing in prose and verse Cymbeline consents, and to the end that her platonic lover may find her without noise, she gives him the key of her chamber, a delicate little key of gold, a real piece of bijou, which one might well believe was made to open the door of the heart of a young girl.

At the moment when Leander disappears the reasonable moral man of the piece enters dressed in blue. He is a fat person and a rich banker. He, like Leander, is enamored with Cymbeline, but he loves as a simple mortal—a staunch man of business. At his sight the shadowy Cymbeline quickly returns to the prose of every day life and descends in smiles from her celestial perch to receive this kind of chrysalis gentleman, at once Marquis and proprietor, who is permitted by her parents to love her when Leander is present, but Cymbeline does not grant him this privilege.

The Marquis explains to her what folly it is to love Leander; how much more advantageous to accept his suit—he will open to her the doors of a luxurious and happy life in his Burgundian Chateau. She shall sleep late, go to bed early as Queen of Yuctot, she shall have four meals a day, and he will attend her with paternal

*Victor Hugo presented the writer, before his departure for America, with his likeness, flatteringly inscribed in his own handwriting. It is preserved at Steephill as a precious souvenir of the immortal poet.

care at them all.  For amusement she shall hunt the wild beast, and enjoy every day young patridges garnished with wild boars' heads. Her Sundays shall be passed at Mass, the grand Mass and at Vespers.  The Marquis ends by laying his heart, his kitchen and his hand at Cymbeline's feet.  The indignant beauty dismisses this prosaic lover, who withdraws defeated, but not discouraged, with a malicious smile in which can be seen the hope of ultimate triumph.

The final soliloquy of Cymbeline :
"This Marquis, fie ! the horrible man ! hast thou ever seen him ? To hear love spoken of by this dolt who always has his spoon at his mouth ! To eat ! who eats to sleep and sleeps to snore.  While Leander, the zephyrs scarcely dare supply him with breath." Suddenly Cymbeline stops stupefied, is a motionless mass, utterly inert.  Some one quickly enters by the window and throws himself at her feet.  It is Leander, his cigar in his mouth, his cravat in disorder, his hair unkempt, drunk as a lord.  The Ex-Endymion throws himself upon Cymbeline, whom he imagines to be the daughter of the porter, a certain Manton, with whose daughter for a long time he has secretly threaded the ways of love.

Stupefied Cymbeline seeks to escape from his arms and make herself known.  Leander holds her by right of conquest and to show that he has come to the promised *rendezvous* draws from his pocket a key which causes Cymbeline to raise a cry of horror. Instead of a key of gold he presents to her a passport, in rusted iron which opens the way to Marton's heart.  It is easy to believe that this ogress key would have eaten up the little key of gold if they had not met in the same pocket.  Happily in the midst of poor Cymbeline's confusion, the Marquis reappears with the key of gold.

The end may be conjectured, the Marquis stupefies Leander by his presence and sobers Cymbeline.  The result of the whole thing is, that Cymbeline and he marry and have many children.

As to the words of the Charade, they were anti-real, improbable and unfindable.  What was this unknown tongue?  No one will ever seek for it.  No one will ever find it.  No one will ever know it.  One laughs at it and that is all.

---

It is usual in the island to provide similar evening amusements for guests and we shall long remember with pleasure the private amateur Theatricals at Candie got up by Sir Stafford and Lady Carey and by Mr. and Mrs. Joshua Priaulx, at the Mount, and the inimitable and side splitting comic songs of Julius Carey and others.

The drama is held in high esteem by the Guernsey people and actors and actresses treated with much civility.  A pretty actress is surrounded by the fops, who do not hesitate to express their admiration for her as a glorious creature. "I say Nash aw—that I am—aw—really not accustomed—to seeing such lovely creatures in the hay market—aw—haw." "You are quite right" responds de Boots, of the Guards, who is leaning against the side of the door. "They are rare, she is--aw a most glorious creature-aw."

There are several halls in Peter-port for the exhibition of plays and a small but comfortable theatre. The exterior is unimposing, but the interior well decorated. During the Winter pantomimes, historical dramas and other plays are performed. The actors and actresses are habited in the costumes of the people at the period when the personages represented were supposed to have lived. While the critics prefer the drama, the people like best comic pieces, in which there is a buffoon, whose grimaces and low jests, like those of buffoons elsewhere, obtain the greatest share of applause. The music which accompanies the acting, or "orchestra," is inferior, unless, as is sometimes the case, the garrison band plays. The island cannot boast of any native dramatists and the plays are generally French, or adaptations from the French, though rarely if ever, from such tragic writers as Corneille or Racine, Crebillon, or Voltaire. Few of these modern adaptations can stand the test of criticism, but are popular with the masses, as they abound in show, noise and nonsense. Though this is so, one must not conclude that the average Guernsey man is miserably ignorant of theatrical matters, that they have banished all sense and propriety from their stage and that they cannot be pleased with anything but farcical buffoonry. At times they have in the island excellent companies and plays acted in the theatre, or in their houses by amateurs, in which there is great purity and force of language, harmony of versification, intricacy of plot, multiplicity of incident, probability of catastrophe, variety of decoration and many other excellencies expected in modern drama. Mr. and Mrs. Wybert Rousby were the lessees of the theatre at the time we are writing about, and the best amateurs were Julius Carey, since Constable, Col. Wm. Bell, Secretary to the Governor, and Charles Carey, son of the Bailiff, whose performances were always rapturously received.

Though the people are French in descent and speak a dialect of the language, their manners and customs are English rather than French. None of the peculiar restraints thrown around the intercourse of young people of opposite sexes in France, exist in Guernsey. On the contrary, their intercourse is without restraint as in England or America and every belle commands as many adorers as she lists, who love her platonically—never disuniting the idea of her beauty from that of her virtue. Love is not considered a mere matter of convenience, or a commerce of libertinism, but as a laudable passion, a powerful mover of the heart, and as a great inducement towards a display of that courage and virtue which characerize heroes.

Depraved men of the style of Hugo's Leander, will not easily be brought to believe that love may be an innocent commerce of gallantry and reciprocal affection, of which no one need be ashamed. Yet in the eyes of these Islanders nothing is more true. The beau makes no concealment of the lady whom he loves and honors. The most modest poet names in his verses the fair one who inspired them; and the chastest lady never blushes to be the object of a guiltless passion, nor scruples to return it publicly. They know how to keep love and vice apart, and though at bottom their passions be still the same with the rest of mankind, yet with them the heart and the senses have different routes and their objects are seldom the same. They know the difference between an ordinary woman and that sublime being, the divine sovereign of their thoughts, an object of the greatest reverence, never to be approached but as an angel clad in human form.

## PUBLIC LECTURES, ETC.

It may be further remarked that learning is not so much cultivated as it might, and under other circumstances probably would be, and when it is, it is not so much for the love of it, as for its use and convenience in common life Yet there are men of learning in the Island, as we have seen, and a well patronized College, which under the late head master, Rev. M. Corfe and his predecessors, acquired much reputation; and a considerable stock of books in the College library and those of the Mechanics Institute and the Guille-Allez collection. Besides this, Osmond de Beauvoir Priaulx, of London, a wealthy and highly cultivated Guernseyman, has presented his large and well selected library to the Island, and at his death it is to be placed in Candie House, which, with its beautiful grounds, was also presented by Mr. Priaulx to the town parish, of which he is a native. This gift adds so largely to the stock of books, in the Island, that students will possess facilities for conducting their investigations, never before enjoyed. Mr. Priaulx's generosity and public spirit are worthy of every praise. In all this man of true nobleness of soul does, he is animated by an ardent desire to promote the public good of Guernsey. The present libraries are largely attended by readers,—so much so, that it entirely refutes the idea sometimes advanced by cockney tourists, that the people are destitute of literary taste.

Among these readers there are some whose lives have been devoted to the acquisition of knowledge, such as Mr. Metevier, and

F. B. Tupper, Osmond Priaulx and Paul Dobree, whose names are not confined to the narrow limits of the Island, but are known to men of science and literature throughout Europe ; men who do honor to their country by their mental acquisitions. A frequent visitor to the libraries and to the fields where the rural population were engaged in cultivating their crops, and to the extensive stone quarries in the vale parish and other spots where work was progressing, we could but admire the quiet demeanor, industry and intelligence of the laborers and were happy to learn that they did not labor in vain. Few working classes in Europe are better off than those of Guernsey ; who have comparatively little to complain of. They are well paid, and are in comfortable circumstances when moderately prudent. Provisions and other necessaries of life are cheap in comparison with the prices in England, and this class deposit out of their modest earnings considerable sums in the savings banks. Much has been done by the more intelligent and progressive portion of the people to amuse and instruct the working classes, and by lectures, penny readings and other pastimes, in which there is a judicious leaven of amusement, to draw them off from restaurants, gin palaces, and other objectionable evening resorts. The plan met with much success, and the rooms where they occurred were crowded week after week. The attractiveness of these reunions was increased by the addition of music and singing. Regarding the movement as wise and well intentioned, it gave us pleasure to encourage them by accepting, from time to time, invitations to preside over them. On one particular occasion, the following is the brief report of what occurred, taken from the "Guernsey Star," (Newspaper).

ST. JOHN'S READINGS.

The first of these interesting and instructive meetings was held yesterday in the St. John's Boy's School, the chair being taken by Col. Peyton, who, on this occasion, spoke in able and eloquent terms of the advantages of education, his whole speech from beginning to end, evincing signs of deep and careful thought, and drawing from the audience continued and hearty applause. His remarks were in substance as follows :

Col. Peyton said that concurring very heartily in the object sought to be secured by the St. John's Society, he had readliy consented to take the chair upon this occasion. No one regretted, however, more than himself that the Committee was under the necessity of extending the invitation to him, as this was due to the fact that his friend, Mr. Blundell, was unable to occupy the chair. He had usually done so the past season, but was prevented now by the melancholy cause of ill health. This amiable and accomplished gentleman had contributed so much, said Col. Peyton, to the success of these *reunions* by his zeal and energy, by the extent and variety of his knowledge and the popular character of his lectures, that his absence this Winter would be seriously felt, not only by the Committee of Management, whose labors he smoothed and lightened, but yet more by the large and appreciative audiences his name and fame always brought together in this Hall. Since, however, we are unfortunately deprived of Mr. Blundell's valuable services, he was glad to supply his place on this occasion, and he trusted it would not be long before we had the pleasure to see him once more in renewed health and strength, occupying his accustomed position on this platform.

Having said this much, Colonel Peyton remarked that he might very well resume his seat, but he would probably be excused, if he availed himself of the opportunity to say a few words in regard to the laudable objects sought to be attained by this and similar societies; namely, the amusement and instruction of the people.

No truth was more fully recognized now-a-days, than that the people must in self defence be educated. It is justly considered necessary to their protection, as well from foes within as without. From the indigenous vandal or gamin, who, according to Lord Macaulay, is growing up under the shadow of our Churches, Universities, Libraries and Museums, as from the foreign invader, who would, on the first appearance of weakness, seek to overrun and desolate the land. In modern times no ignorant and unenlightened people, how numerous and spirited soever, are secure in the presence of a valiant and educated enemy. The history of the recent Franco-German war forcibly illustrated this axiom. The total defeat and overthrow of the French armies, so distinguished in history for their prowess, the breakdown of the government more characterized under the second Empire by an intriguing spirit than a wise diplomacy, and the volatile character of the people, a trait aggravated by their ignorance and superstition, rendered them all but helpless in presence of their educated and enterprising enemy.

A prudent statesmanship deeply impressed with these occurrences, is seeking, for forewarned is forearmed, to provide against the repetition of such disastrous history on British soil— not so much by heavy ordnance, numerous battalions, strong fortresses and iron clads, though these precautions are not neglected, as by popular education.

Colonel Peyton said that he was inculcating no new lessons. Nearly 800 years before Christ, Hosea, one of the minor prophets, declared, "*My people are destroyed for lack of knowledge.*" And it cannot be doubted that the ignorance of the Jewish people betrayed them into many crimes and consequent miseries. And this has been the history of other nations and other and later times, as it is sure to be that of every nation and people who neglect a matter of such gravity. History, like everything human, continued the Colonel, was undergoing a revolution. The idea formerly attached to history was that it was a kind of biography of kings and nobles so written as to inspire a reverence for the Divine and hereditary wisdom. The battles in which these heroes fought were described by particular scenery in which kings had cloven the skulls of their antagonists with the battle axe, or had fought with superhuman pertinacity and success. The world has become tired of such histories, of such fancy pictures. The peoples were forgotten in the accounts of battles which they fought and where they died by thousands. They were not allowed to appear in tournaments, whose silken tents their hands wrought, whose queens of beauty their skill arrayed in brilliant costumes. It was forgotten who built the castle where the petty lord displayed his tyranny, or the vast cathedral towering like a glorious dream from earth to Heaven. How the people progressed from slavery to liberty, how the arts advanced from the rudeness of earlier times had been passed over, totally ignored, though all the spacious, magnificent, the vast and wonderful exhibitions of human enterprise, with which the world is covered, we owe to toil, to the goddess of poverty.

Sir Walter Scott first broke the sleep of history in his novels, and history has assumed a truer and nobler position. It is now written in a different spirit, the people are viewed in a more becoming light and awarded their real position. All the merit is not now given to the warrior and statesman—the artist, the mechanic and the philosopher come in for their share. It is known and acknowledged, at least among Anglo-Saxons the world over, that the source of all political power is the people and the source of all national wealth their industry. Hence their was in America, statues to the tallow chandler's son, Franklin, who in the language of Manilius, as applied by Turgot, "Snatched the lightning from Heaven and the sceptre from tyrants." And in England to Sir Humphrey Davy, the son of a Cornish wood-carver, whose discoveries in chemistry have surrounded his name with extraordinary brilliancy ; and since the Crimean war, monuments to the guardsmen as well as officers. This more just appreciation of the people and what is due to them, is a happy omen of the future. The Omnipitent has taught us the unity of the race, not only by creating us in his own image, but by declaring that he has made of one blood all the nations of the earth. Who then with any broad human sympathy and christianity can look upon the face of a fellow human being, however destitute, degraded and despised, without recognizing in him a brother sprung from the same origin and inheriting the same immortal destiny.

Let us, therefore, unite in our humble way, in the good work of providing a proper moral and intellectual training for the masses. The good and wise of this country and America have long sought to accomplish this mission by scattering abroad the treasures of knowledge by bringing useful information within the reach of all, and thus to exalt, to teach and to bless mankind. One of the most eminent laborers in this field was the late Lord Brougham, who, as principal founder and promoter of the society for the diffusion of useful knowledge, and author of many articles in the Penny Magazine, did yeoman's service in the cause. The chairman regretted that he had not been able to procure in the island a copy of the works of this great scholar, essayist, historian, lawyer, and statesman, else he might have quoted many eloquent passages in support of the general proposition which he had enunciated, namely, that intellectual advancement was the sure forerunner of moral improvement; that we had but to make the people wiser, to refine and make them better.

"We owe it," said Colonel Peyton, "no less to ourselves than to society, that we should shed abroad the light of education. By education he did not mean the simple poring over books, but the whole process by which we draw forth the powers and capacities of the human mind into full and free activity; and it is just in proportion as the inward and originally slumbering powers of the intellect are drawn out, that man rises above the sphere of a mere physical existence and comes to be guided by his reason, his conscience and his feelings.

Such societies as this were laboring successfully in one direction by uniting oral instruction with rational amusement during hours when the most laborious have a little leisure. The long evenings of winter cannot be spent here, where instructive lectures are delivered, well selected extracts from good books—books through which the current of wisdom flows—are read and sweet music is discoursed without a certain cultivation and refinement of both mind and heart following. This is a great result to obtain; there is another. If by the attractive character of these entertainments you keep a single individual from the seductions and charms of the public houses, from the hardening and degrading influences of the gaming table, or if you prevent one from dissipating his time in strenuous idleness, your labors will not have been in vain. All success, then, to your society. (Loud cheers followed this address.)

On another occasion, namely, the 25th of March, 1875, we presided over a meeting of the Workingmen's Association, at their rooms in Pollet street, of which the following is a brief report as it appeared in ths Guernsey Star of the following day :

LECTURE ON ELECTRICITY—WORKING MEN'S ASSOCIATION—
REMARKS BY COLONEL J. L. PEYTON.

A lecture on electricity was delivered last Tuesday evening by Mr. Power at the Temperance Hall Pollet, in connexion with the working Mens' Association. The chair was occupied by Col. Peyton, who expressed his gratification at being able to introduce to the audience, as lecturer, a gentleman of theoretical knowledge and practical experience in everything having reference to the science of electricity, and the useful purposes to which it has been and is likely to be applied—in a word, an electrician *sous tous les rapports*. Many of those present were doubtless acquainted with the history of electricity ; with the fact that it was known to the ancients, though their knowledge was so limited that it served 'no useful purpose, but rather tended to increase the superstition of those primitive times. Thales, of Miletus, knew the effect produced by the friction of amber and other bodies, and the fact is mentioned by Theophrates nearly 315 years before the birth of Christ. Pliny also informs us of the knowledge of animal electricity possessed by the Romans—of its possession not only by the Torpedo, but by other fish, and also by the human body. It is related by writers of old, that certain ancient philosophers, when dressing and undressing, emitted occasionally certain crackling sparks, and of one it is said that his body emitted flames without burning his clothes. To a people prone to place ignorant reliance in omens and prognostics, to believe blindly in supernatural appearances, there was enough in such phenomena to excite their wonder and stimulate their belief in false religions. In the Middle Ages some scanty knowledge of this subtle principle was possessed by the monks, but the world hardly began to emerge from its general ignorance on the subject until the day of Gilbert, who in 1660, by some new discoveries, added much to our stock of knowledge ; and afterwards Boyle, and then Newton, who first constructed an electric machine of glass, extended this knowledge. After Newton, followed Hawshee, Dufay, Leyden, Weston, and others, who still further illustrated the subject by their discoveries ; but it was reserved for the American philosopher, his fellow countryman, Franklin, to raise electricity to the dignity of a science, and to connect it with the thunderbolt, which he not only disarmed of its terrors, but brought down and converted into a useful element. Since then Faraday and others have made many valuable discoveries and now it is recognized as one of the most potent and valuable agencies with which the world is acquainted. We constantly hear of electro-chemistry, electro dynamics, electro-magnetism, electro type, electro plate, electro-telegraphy, &c., words that denote the connection of the sciences and substances with electricity. Of electricity, the Colonel asserted that it might be generally said, that it enters the sick chamber and proves more efficacious than the warm breath of Spring in restoring health to the prostrate frame; raising up from the bed of despair the benumbed and helpless paralytic, and once more nerving him for the contests of the world; that by its aid we write our letters, transmitting them in an instant across the widest seas; by it we will construct the simple instruments of peaceful industry, and forge the thunderbolts of war, blow up the fortresses, sink the fleets and scatter the armies of our enemies. "But," said Colonel Peyton, "I will not pursue this interesting subject further, tempting as it is, but give way to the lecturer, whose particular task it is to-night, and who is far better qualified to do it justice in all its bearings.

"The Chairman sat down amidst loud applause and was followed by the lecturer,"

### PHYSICAL FEATURES, FORMER STATE, ETC.

After having said so much of the manners and customs of the people, it will not be amiss to bestow a few further remarks on the Island they inhabit, its soil, climate, scenery and its former condition, religion, etc.

The Island of Guernsey is about nine miles long and five wide, contains about 15,500 acres, two thirds of which is under cultivation, and a population of 30,000 souls. It is nearly in the shape of a right angle triangle, the highest point being 300 feet above the level of the sea. The Northern parishes, St. Sampson and the vale are low and flat, while the Southern and Eastern, called the high parishes, are elevated and broken, presenting a line of rugged cliffs to the sea. These cliffs begin in St. Peter-port, extend to the sea in St. Martin's, and thence South and South east through the Forest, St. Andrews, St. Peters-in the wood and Torteval. The bays are very beautiful, so much so that it is not unusual to hear gushing maidens style them heavenly. The sea in these bays seems literally to sleep in the arms of the shore. The most romantic and admired are Fermain, Munlin Huet, and Petit Bot bays, all of which are defended by Martello towers. The vallies abound in lovely scenery, and the soil is everywhere singularly fertile. The water lanes are a feature in the scenery. The most beautiful are water lane in St. Martin's and that in the Couture nearer town. The farms are from three to thirty acres in size, the largest farm in the Island, the Vaubelets, having 30 acres, and the fields do not average more than an acre. They are divided by embankments of earth on which furze grows luxuriantly; this furz is used for heating the ovens for baking. There are few gates, but the entrance to a field is guarded by a bar placed across from two stone pillars. The usual crops are hay, turnips, carrots, potatoes, mangolds, wheat, oats, and barley. The ground is plowed by a large trench plow drawn by four or sometimes six horses one after the other, or by oxen—the farmers unite in this work each leading a horse. Nobody, however, well off owns six horses, often not even one. Great attention is paid to their cows, which are, as we have said, larger than in any of the Islands, and are evidently the blending of blood in early days. For many years the races have been kept distinct, and the improvement, in all the Island, is strictly within the lines of pure breeding. They are deep milkers and high colored, the prevailing color being a rich fawn, with much white laid on in large patches. When they dry off they fatten easily and make excellent beef. There is a difference of opinion as to the value of the Guernsey and Jersey cows. It is an open question whether the cows of Jersey or Guernsey are the best. While the Guernsey cattle are the largest of the channel Islands breed, for symmetry, the palm is awarded to those of Jersey. The former do not vary so much in color as the latter, but they are usually red and white. It is the custom to tether cattle when out. The produce of the Jersey and Guernsey cows average the same, for, although the greatest rivalry on this point exists between the farmers of both Islands, on investigation it will be found that the amounts of produce correspond. The fattening of oxen is carried on in both Islands to a certain extent, and it may be computed that one-sixth of the supply of meat is fed on the Island.

The waters surrounding Guernsey abound in fish, of which the most prized are turbot, brill, John Doray, plaice, sole, lobsters, crabs, ormers and shrimps, and two eels—the one small, called the sand eel, the other the conger, weighing often 30 pounds. The peasantry esteem the conger eel highly, and salt it as they do the sand eel for winter use, and as it sells for only one penny a pound it is a boon to them. The cancer crab, sometimes called the Guernsey crab, is one of the most delicate, highly flavored and delicious crustaceous fish ever eaten. It is in great demand in England and France and fetches a high price. As may be readily imagined, the people draw a large part of their support from the sea.

### THE ISLAND ONE HUNDRED YEARS AGO.

It now remains for us to gtve a slight idea of the changes the Island has experienced during the last century. Within this period it has emerged from a very rude and primitive condition.

In 1770 the Governor lived in a mean, comfortless old house—this miserable building is still standing on Tower hill, and is now called the haunted house, and is tenanted by laborers in common with bats and owls ; and the garrison consisted of only four companies of invalids. There were no barracks and many of the soldiers lived in the town and as there were no drills or other military duties to be performed, some of them acted as porters, by way of gaining a few pennies. The Royal Court held its sittings in a store room, and the public records were kept in the cottage of the Greffier, and prisoners were confined in the fort. The meat and vegetable markets were held in the open streets on Saturdays. There was only one teacher in Elizabeth College, and the theatre was a store room in which roving actors performed about once in every four years. The shipping of the Island consisted of one ship, four brigs and a few sloops and cutters. The land transportation was done by oxen and ponies. The shops were small, low and dark, and scantily supplied. There were three or four small breweries and some small factories of rope, tobacco and candles. Barley bread was used six days in the week, wheaten on Sundays, as a treat. There was no printing press, newspaper, or druggist, and not a greenhouse. Little butcher's meat was eaten, the inhabitants living principally on fish, conger eels, and vegetables. There was no post office. The Sixtys then ‘resided in High, Cornet, Smith and Pollet streets—usually dined at one o'clock, tead at four and supped at nine o'clock.

F. B. Tupper's history, from which these particulars are derived, goes on to say, these early hours extended, in some measure, even to company ; and notwithstanding, the inhabitants maintained a constant social intercourse, as the money which is now spent in general entertainments, and in carriage hire, was then devoted to more frequent, genuine, and rational hospitality. It must be added, however, that the convivial meetings of the gentlemen, who had few amusements, or intellectual resources, were often stained by hard drinking, a vice prevalent in Great Britain and Ireland at that time. Unhappily, also, the marriage of near relations was very frequent, although that of first cousins was pronounced unchristian by the Colloquy in 1591, and the ill effects are manifest to this day in many families. The public assemblies were held weekly, in a large room at the bottom of the Pollet ; and the ladies were not the less joyous, or the less lovely, because they walked to parties in hoods and pattens ; indeed, it was not until after the peace of 1815, that hack carriages were introduced.

The language of all classes in their own families was, with few exceptions, either French or Guernsey French, chiefly the latter ; but the upper classes could speak English, as they were generally educated in England, where these Islands were then as little known as the Orkneys are now.

The roads throughout the Island were mere lanes, only wide enough for a cart, but the greater part had a narrow, high footpath, and when two carts met, one had to go into a field, or in a recess called *gensage*, to allow the other to pass; these lanes were, moreover, extremely rough, and often flooded in Winter, and very muddy during the rains of Summer.

In consequence, the inhabitants of the country had so little intercourse with each other, or with the town, that their parishes could be discovered by their different accents. It must be confessed, however, that the lanes formed a most agreeable shady walk for pedestrians in Summer, as the high hedges on either side were planted with trees, and covered with wild primroses, violets and harebells. The gentlemen who cultivated their own small estates, usually dined in the kitchen with their farm servants who sat below the salt, as did the retainers of the lairds in Scotland at that time: One of these gentlemen, of ancient family,—Mr. Chas. Andros, who resided at *Les Piques* in St. Saviour's Parish,—was the Lieut-Bailiff, a man of good property, and highly respected. Carriages were almost useless, as excursions were necessarily made on foot, or on horseback, and the few which existed were either open gigs or close vehicles on two wheels, substantially constructed without springs, the horse in the latter being always led, not driven. It was about this time that Lieut.-Governor Irving introduced the first four-wheel close carriage, with a pair of horses, ever seen in the island.

Thus in 1775, Guernsey was essentially unimproved, badly cultivated, and without easy means of communication, either externally or internally. We have said that parties met at an early hour, and even as late as the year 1796, at a ball and supper given by the gentlemen of the island, at the Assembly rooms in St. Peters port, to Major-General Small and the officers of the garrison, on the 18th day of January, to celebrate the Queen's birth day, "the company," was requested, "to assemble at six o'clock." The late King William IV, while Prince William Henry, visited Guernsey twice, the first time as a midshipman in the Hebe frigate, and the second in command of the Pegassus, of 28 guns. On the latter occasion a ball, apparently without a supper, to prepare which there probably was not time, was given to him by the Guernsey gentlemen, on the 7th of June, 1786, the entire cost for nearly two hundred persons present being only £36.4 5s or 14s. 6d. per head for the 50 gentlemen who subscribed, as we learn by a copy of the account: twenty-five years later, balls and suppers given to the naval and military officers cost about £500, so great was the sad change effected in a few years by a large garrison and squadron, and a greater intercourse with strangers.

In reviewing the state of Guernsey, just 100 years ago, we must not forget that both England and France, the pioneers of European civilization, were then very far behind what they now are in roads, buildings, equipages, literary gratifications, and other comforts and elegancies of life. The steam engine has since given an impetus to every species of improvement, which might otherwise have lain dormant for another century. England was covered with almost Egyptian darkness  The state of the established church and the conduct of most of its bishops and ministers would now be considered lamentable. Highwaymen invested the public roads and education was so little diffused that the lower orders were deplorably ignorant and brutal. All these are notorious facts. One of our informants remembered, when he was at school at Southampton, in 1775, that the stage coaches, of which there were only two, set out thence for London at four o'clock, a. m , and reached their destination at nine o'clock, p. m. Even more than thirty years afterwards, the coaches were thirteen or fourteen hours performing the same distance. Now the journey is performed in less than three hours by rail. The mode of living in Scotland at the same period was very similar and by way of soothing the minds of his Guernsey readers at the truthful picture he drew of them and their antecedents, Mr. Tupper quotes these lines from Chamber's Journal : "The accommodations possessed by families of good figure, in Scotland, were generally limited to three or four rooms, not more than one of which would be unfurnished with a bed. Of the middle ranks, most lived in bed rooms. Arrangements, now deemed indispensable, were unknown " Mr. Tupper, who was a perfectly veracious man, did not intend that the truth should be disguised because it was not palatable to some of his countrymen, and proceeds to say that in 1804, a gentleman of an ancient Guernsey family and a Jurat, sat in his parlor, which had a dirt floor and little furniture. He was, says he, the second richest man in the island, from which it is quite evident that the first in wealth was no Crœsus. The Guersey historian goes on to say that three of his sons became general officers, the fourth a Jurat, the fifth the Dean of Guernsey and the sixth, the Receiver-General, or tax gatherer of the island,while one of the daughters married a distinguished Major-General and was the mother of a baronet. (See Tupper's history of Guernsey, p. 404.)

Mr. Tupper was a pronounced democrat in his political opinions, which he is said to have imbibed during his long residence in North America, and cultivated a certain republican simplicity in his manners and habits. In the above account of the Jurat and his descendants, it crops out, however, unintentionally, that there was nevertheless in Mr. Tupper the usual English latent love of a lord ; since in his opinion the crowning sucess of the floorless tenant's family was his daughter's bearing a son who became a baronet, or a little Baron.

In a historical point it is not necessary to add to what we have said, more than that the Channel Island group of which Guernsey is the most important, with the single exception of Jersey, are the only remains of all the former Norman possessions of England, and these islands have followed the fortunes of England in all changes of religion and government. Their transfer from the Bishop of Coutance to the diocese of Winchester was effected only in A. D. 1500 by a bull of Pope Alexander VI, long after England had ceased to hold any part of Continental France.

Long as the island has been known it can boast of few antiquities. Such as exist are of Druidical and Celtic origin. The ruins of Vale Castle are the most interesting monuments of the more recent past. Mr. Lukis has a private museum containing many archaeological and other curiosities taken from the Cromlechs of the islands—in it there is much unburnt pottery, many stone weapons taken from excavations, where there were found many human bones, etc.

The climate is mild, equable and salubrious—the mean temperature in summer being 59° and of winter 43° Far. or about the climate of Nubia.

Guernsey is fairly well watered with small springs and little rivulets which find their way through the valleys to the sea. The soil is carefully cultivated and is very productive—the yield being increased by the application annually of large quantities of sea weed, or vraic to the ground,the fertilizing properties of which are remarkable. Fruit and vegetables are the principal crops, though some wheat is grown and a considerable part of the land is reserved or pasture, where one sees the Guernsey variety, of what is known in America as the Alderney cow, or more recently the Jersey cow. There is little difference between the cows in any of the Channel islands and in America it is now the rule to class them all as Jerseys. This is our opinion, though some persons will tell you that the Guernsey cows, which are the largest in the Channel Islands, are as different from the Jerseys as is the Ayrshire from the Devon. There is also a fine breed of diminutive horses which originally came from France. They are strong and mettlesome. Though small they are well formed and some of them beautiful—there are no mules, but a few asses and some goats. There is no timber in the island, only a few shade trees in Cambridge Park and round about country houses, and the fuel of the peasants is gorse, that of the wealthy classes coals brought from Newcastle and Wales. The grape only comes to perfection under glass and no wine and little cider is made, though the apple grows well but not in sufficient quantities to be manufactured into cider. The pears are extremely good, especially the Chaumontel, which is peculiar to the Island.

There are no manufactories of iron, cloth, paper, or other articles with the exception of a small factory in the Pollet of candies, jams and sweet meats, and in the country a few mills for grinding corn.

### RELIGION, PAST AND PRESENT, ETC.

The people are pronounced protestants and great respect is paid to religion by all classes. Many of them are enthusiastic christians and illustrate in their lives and conduct, that human societies do not contain the entire man: that there remains in him the noblest part of himself—those lofty faculties by which he soars to God, to a future life, to unknown blisses in an invisible world. These are his religious convictions, that true grandeur of man, the consolation and charm of weakness and misfortune, the inviolable refuge against the tyrannies of this world.

The island is divided into twelve parishes with a Rector for each, several curates for the chapels of ease; a handsome Catholic Church and a number of churches for the various sects who are dissenters, or non-conformists.* The church of the town parish is well worth a visit. It is very old, ornamented with many fine tablets and monuments, and is altogether the finest ecclesiastical building in the Channel Islands. The oldest church building, now in ruins, is the Chapel of St. Apolline.

As far back as 1603-20 there was much dissent in the Channel island group and to counteract it James I appointed a strong churchman, Sir John Peyton, Governor of Jersey. The following is the account of it in Tupper's History of Guernsey, pp. 195-196.

"The circumstances which led to the appointment of Sir John Peyton to the Governorship of Jersey, are not without interest as throwing light upon the religious condition of both Jersey and Guernsey at this period, and may be briefly and not inappropriately referred to at this point. On the accession of James I., the Church in Guernsey and Jersey was in a distracted condition, the principles of Calvin, having to a considerable extent taken root in both Islands. As early as 1555 Calvin had declared, in his epistle to the English Church in Frankfort, that he had observed in the 'public Liturgy many tolerable vanities, the relicts of the

---

*A dissenter is one who differs in opinion and separates from the service of the Church of England. The non-conformist is one who does not differ in opinion on theological points, but refuses to conform to the rites and modes of worship of the established church.

filth of Popery, and there was not in it such piety as was expected.' These views of the eminent reformer and founder of the Calvinistic sect, were adopted by numerous inhabitants of Guernsey and Jersey, particularly among the lower orders. On Sundays there was a slim attendance at the Parish Churches, 'a beggarly account of empty boxes,' in the way of empty pews—and even those who were regularly at divine worship, from motives of worldly policy, lauded the greatness of Calvin's character, while studiously avoiding any open declaration of adherence to the religious creed promulgated by him. All this was extremely distasteful to the orderly and orthordox mind of the new King, for while James had lived among the Scotch Presbyterians, he was not of them. This truth soon became painfully apparent to the Puritans, who had, anterior to the death of Elizabeth, entertained sanguine hopes of aid and comfort from him. These expectations were now dashed, and they had another illustration of the wisdom of the oft quoted biblical aphorism : 'Place not your trust in Princes.' The King evinced a determined purpose to reinstate the bishops in their ancient power and place, and to establish in all the reformed Churches, unity of religion and uniformity of devotion. With this view, when Raleigh was attainted of treason, his Majesty appointed Sir John Peyton, of Doddington, Co. Cambridge, Governor of Jersey, to whom he entrusted the task of bringing back the straying Jerseymen to the fold of the Church of England. King James could scarcely have found one more peculiarly fitted for the responsible duty entrusted to his diplomacy than Sir John Peyton. Sir John had been previously Lieutenant-Governor of the Tower and a member of the Privy Council of Elizabeth. He was conspicuous at once for the dignity of his birth and the vigour of his intellect ; for the extent of his learning and the orthordoxy of his religious opinions, and was, says Le Quesne, 'A man of great spirit and determination.' He was, in the language of an old writer, 'Educated in the politest manner of the age he lived in, by serving in the wars of Flanders under the most able and experienced soldiers and politicians of that time.' Amidst the sunshine of the courts of Elizabeth and James I, and the affluence of a large fortune, his conduct was so regular and temperate, that his life was prolonged to the age of *ninety nine* years in so much health and vigor that he rode on horse back hunting three or four days before his death. Heylin thus relates the downfall of Presbyterianism in Jersey under the administration of Sir John Peyton. The rector of St. John Parish being dead, the Colloquy appointed 'one Brown' (so called by Heylin), to succeed him, and carried their point, although the Governor—who by his patent held the presentation of all the livings in Jersey, deanery excepted—protested against the nomination. Soon afterwards, the Governor, who was well inclined to further the things wished, and Marret, the *procureur du roi*, forwarded several complaints to the Council against the Colloquy, declaring that that body had usurped the patronage of all the benefices in the island, and praying the King to grant them such a form of discipline and church government as would prevent the repetition of similar abuses. These complaints were referred to the two royal cummissioners just named, Gardner and Hussey, when the clergy contended that their right of appointment to the Ministry, and their exercises of ecclesiastical jurisdiction, had been confirmed to them by his Majesty. While the questions at issue were pending, disputes occurred between the clergy and the laity; and the Royal Court annulled the sentences pronounced by the consistory, which was moreover accused of holding secret and treasonable meetings. The parish of St. Peter becoming void, Sir John Peyton presented it in 1613, to a clergyman named Messervey, who had resided at Oxford, and was patronized by the Bishop of that See. The colloquy refused his admission, chiefly on account of his having been ordained by that prelate, as to accept Messervey seemed to them almost an acknowledgment of episcopacy. After considerable trouble growing out of these matters, Jersey was brought under the polity and ritual of the Church of England, and forty years later Guernsey."

At the period of our second visit to the island the very Rev. J. Guille was dean and rector of St. Peter-port. He was a good preacher, pastor and man. The more distinguished of the rectors were Rev. Richard J. Ozanne, a most kind, sympathetic and hospitable man; Rev. C. D. P. Robinson, of St. Martin's, and Rev. J. Geraud, of St. Saviours. These three were very strong men able theologians, eloquent preachers, and men of true piety. The remaining nine Rectors were hardly above mediocrity in talents or acquirements, but like their more distinguished colleagues, were diligent in the performance of their duties, seizing the opportunities which their situation affords to noble minds and pure hearts for the exercise of active virtue. By their pastoral visits to all, especially to the lowly cottagers, they exerted their greatest powers, guiding the mother's hand in rearing her children and teaching them the important lessons of religious education and domestic economy, awakening by kind praise the ambition of the young, and soothing with lenient hand the sorrows of the old. In such occupations they exalt the character of their calling and extend its benefits, shedding upon the poor blessings which mitigate their wants and proverty, teaching them that in religion they can truly find the compensation of all their difficulties and trials,

They thus made themselves fathers of the people, and while employing their benevolence in guiding them in peace through things temporal, with higher christian benevolence guiding them in hope to things eternal. They thus made up for want of brilliant intellectual parts and other deficiencies, and if not all that could be wished, were at least acceptable to their flocks.

The reader will find in appendix C. the names of all Guernseymen who have been prominent in literature and in the public service from 1600 to the present day.

During our repeated visits and long sojourns in Guernsey we made many friends whom we most highly valued and shall ever cherish in affectionate remembrance. Among them was Lady Carey, the amiable and accomplished wife of Sir Stafford Carey, and a relative of the poet and ecclesiastical author, Dr. Jonathan Shipley, bishop of St. Asaph, from 1769 to his death in 1789. Lady Carey had in her possession twenty letters in the hand writing of Dr. Benjamin Franklin, and one from his nephew, Jonathan Williams, which she derived from an aunt to whom they were given at Dr. Shipley's death, and which she placed in our hands to be disposed of as we saw fit. Unwilling to retain the originals we had them carefully copied and now give them, after a quarter of a century, to the American public, who have always manifested an extraordinary interest in everything relating to the wonderful man by whom they were written—a man whose whole conduct and writings, indeed, present the somewhat singular union of great genius united to practical good sense, and of singular worldly shrewdness, with the loftiest integrity of principle. No honors could make him forget or deviate from the principles with which he started life. Remembering his own humble origin and subsequent rise, he rightly considered every man as originally equal as regarded real intrinsic worth, and equally by precept and example contributed more than any one whatever, to breaking down those invidious bars to eminence and success in life, which the conventional habits and artificial feelings of society had heretofore interposed to the elevation of those unblessed by birth and fortune. (For these letters see appendix B.)

To Guernsey, the so called England of the channel Islands, we must now say farewell, and with no small regret. We love her and her people, and love to recall the happy days spent on her shores. No American should fail to visit "sweet little Guernsey." Its climate, its scenery, its history, its inhabitants, its manners and customs, its ancient laws and institutions, its antiquities, its Druidical and Celtic remains, its monuments, its language, its learning and culture, combine to make it for the Western traveler one of the most interesting spots in the old world.

# APPENDICES.

## APPENDIX A.
### TREES.
#### LINES BY GEORGES METEVIER.
Suggested by reading "Over the Alleghanies," &c., by J. L. Peyton.

Look at the sycamores of Blannerhasset,
    At their Titanic trunk, their stretch'd white arms,
As, honour'd friend, John Lewis Peyton, has it,
    A scribe whose ev'ry line displays rare charms!

Still, how forget the tree on whose huge limbs,
    Tost in autumnal gales, unseen, alone,
A boy once caroll'd warm faith's artless hymns,
    Lull'd by the distant wave's incessant moan?

Long ere the houseless myriad, unrepell'd,
    Found here a refuge and o'erflow'd the land,
High and low, rich and poor, had firmly held
    *A people's* old hereditary band.

We know each other, loyal, frank and true,
    Norman, or Angevine, or Aquitanian,
And grey beards laugh at Cockneyland's mad crew,
    The Radical, the Chartist, and the Fenian.

But what am I to them or they to me?
    Nothing; and this is all I wish to say,
He who hews down God's image, our old tree,
    Is God's flint-hearted foe, think what he may.

A name, a legend, record of the past,
    Marks, here and there, some giant undefiled,
But with'ring infidelity's cold blast
    Annihilates the seraph and the child.

The child! Such was Mæonides, who won
    Truth's leafy diadem, though blind and poor,
Such was that meek "Divine," the only one
    Who sits in his Lord's bosom evermore.

And if a truant in our elm's vast womb*
Oft shelter'd innocence, why should he not,
Joyous, near the green threshold of his tomb,
Remember, as he prays, that holy spot ?

Oak, ash, pine, hawthorn, kindly lent a name
To worthy fathers whom the vulgar scorn,
Each homestead's hearth wants its primæval flame ;
Where is eve's glory, hope's fond Angel, morn ?

AOSDANA.

\* "L'Orme du bas du Belle."

Concerning this venerable elm, a volume of delicious reminiscences, even at this very late hour, might be said or sung. Sciolism would, peradventure, laugh at them. Did not, however, one of our early masters, a philosopher and a healer of souls as well as of bodies, warn pretenders who have neither traveled through the world of words nor through the world of facts, that "Nil arrogantius grammatico est,"—"c'est une bete frottee d'esprit."

Let us therefore modestly reproduce the article "BELLE," from a Glossary printed at Jena, six years ago, an elaborate work of which the compiler, still a French scholar, never saw a single proof:—

"Belle, s.m. Cour interieure attenant aux batiments."

"Norm. bel. besle. boil, V. fr. boille, pour cour. jardin."

"L'origine norse de ce terme so demontre par un article des Leges Scaniœ, IV., I."

"Toute la ville se divise en portions egales (partiones) qu'on appele Boel dans la langue maternelle "

"Il y a encore a Vologne une petite place qui se nomme le Bel-Pinaud : la place qui etait au milieu du chateau de Caen etait aussi nommee le Besle." Dumeril. p 39. Voir le reste, p. 59 du Gloss.

## APPENDIX B.

[Dr. Franklin to the Lord Bishop of St. Asaph.]

LONDON, June 24th, 1771.

MY LORD :—I got home in good time and well. But on perusing the letters that were come for me during my absence, and considering the business they require of me, I find it not convenient to return so soon as I had intended. I regret my having been obliged to leave the pleasing society of your L's and family, and that most agreeable retirement good Mrs. Shipley put me so kindly in possession of. I now breath with reluctance the smoke of London, when I think of the sweet air of Twyford: And by the time your races are over, or about the middle of next month (if it should then not be unsuitable to your engagements or other purposes) I promise myself the happiness of spending another week or two where I so pleasantly spent the last.

I have taken the liberty of sending by the Southampton stage, directed to yôur Lordship a parcel containing one of my books for Miss Georgiana, which I hope she will be good enough to accept, as a small mark of my regard for her philosophic genius. And a specimen of the American dry'd apples for Mrs. Shipley, that she may judge whether it will be worth while to try the practice. I should imagine that the sweet Summer apples which cannot otherwise be kept until Winter, are best to be thus preserved. I doubt some dust may have got among these, as I found the cask uncovered ; therefore it will not perhaps be amiss to rinse them a minute or two in warm water, and dry them quick in a napkin.

With the greatest esteem and respect and many thanks for your and Mrs. Shipley's abundant civilities I am, my Lord, Your Lordship's obliged and most obedient humble servant.

B. FRANKLIN.

P. S. The parcel is directed to be left at the Turnpike next beyond Winchester.

---

[Doctor Franklin to Mrs. Shipley, wife of the Bishop of St. Asaph.]

LONDON, Aug. 12, 1771.

DEAR MADAM :—This is just to let you know that we arriv'd safe and well in Marlborough street, about six, where I deliver'd up my charge :—

The above seems too short for a letter; so I will lengthen it by a little account of our journey. The first stage we were rather pensive. I try'd several topics of conversation, but none of them would hold. But after breakfast we began to recover spirits and had a good deal of chat. Will you hear some of it? We talked of her brother and she wished he was married. And don't you wish your sisters were married too? Yes. All but Emily; I would not have her married. Why? Because I can't spare her, I can't part with her. The rest may marry as soon as they please, so they do but get good husbands. We then took upon us to consider for each what sort of husband would be fitted for every one of them. We began with Georgiana.* She thought a coun-

---

*Miss Georgiana Shipley was the eldest daughter of the Bishop of St. Asaph and seems to have been Dr. Franklin's favorite in the family. It was to her that he addressed the following letter on her loss of her American Squirrel, who, escaping from his cage, was killed by a Shepherd dog.

LONDON, Sept. 26, 1772.

DEAR MISS:—I lament with you most sincerely, the unfortunate loss of poor Mungo. Few squirrels were better accomplished; for he had had a good education, had travelled far, and seen much of the world. As he had the honor of being, for his virtues, your favorite, he should not go, like common Skuggs, without an elegy or an epitaph. Let us give him one in the monumental style and measure, which has neither prose nor verse, is perhaps the properest for grief. Since to use common language would look as if we were not affected, and to make rhimes would seem trifling in sorrow.

EPITAPH.

Alas! poor Mungo!<br>
Happy wert thou hadst thou known<br>
Thy own felicity.<br>
Remote from the fierce bal'd eagle,<br>
Tyrant of thy native woods:<br>
Thou hadst naught to fear from his piercing talons,<br>
Nor for the murdering gun<br>
Of the thoughtless sportsman.<br>
Safe in thy wir'd castle,<br>
Grimalkin never could annoy thee.<br>
Daily wert thou fed with the choicest viands,<br>
By the fair hand of an indulgent mistress;<br>
But discontented,<br>
Thou wouldst have more freedom:<br>
Too soon, alas! didst thou obtain it;<br>
And, wandering<br>
Thou art fallen by the fangs of wanton, cruel Ranger!<br>
Learn hence,<br>
Ye who blindly seek more liberty,<br>
Whether subjects, sons, squirrels, or daughters,<br>
That apparant restraint may be real protection;<br>
Yielding peace and plenty<br>
With security.<br>

try gentleman, that lov'd travelling and would take her with him, that lov'd books and would hear her read to him ; I added, that had a good estate and was a member of Parliament and lov'd to see an experiment now and then. This she agreed to ; so we set him down for Georgiana and went on to Betsy. Betsy, says I, seems of a sweet, mild temper, and if we should give her a country Squire, and he should happen to be of a rough, passionate turn, and be angry now and then, it might break her heart! O none of 'em must be so; for then they would not be good husbands. To make sure of this point, however, for Betsy, shall we give her a Bishop? O no that won't do. They all declare against the church, and against the army ; not one of them will marry either a clergyman or an officer ; that they are resolved upon. What can be the reason for that? Why you know, that when a clergyman or an officer dies, the Income goes with 'em ; and then what is there to maintain the family? there's the point. Then suppose we give her a good, honest, sensible city merchant who will love her dearly and is very rich ? I don't know but that may do  We proceeded to Emily, her dear Emily, I was afraid we should hardly find anything good enough for Emily ; but at last, after first settling that, if she did marry, Kitty was to live a good-deal with her ; we agreed that as Emily was very handsome we might expect an Earl for her. So having fix'd her, as I thought, a Countess, we went on to Anna Maria. She, says Kitty, should have a rich man that has a large Family and a great many things to take care of; for she is very good at managing, helps my Mama very much, can look over bills, and order all sorts of family business. Very well, and as there is a grace and dignity in her manner that would become the station, what do you think of giving her a Duke ? O no! I'll have the Duke for Emily. You may give the Earl to Anna Maria if you please : But Emily shall have the Duke. I contested this matter some time ; but at length was forced to give up the point, leave Emily in possession of the Duke, and content myself with the Earl for Anna Maria.

You see, my dear Miss, how much more decent and proper this broken style is, than if we were to say, by way of an epitaph,—

Here Skugg
Lies snug,
As a bug
In a rug, .

And yet, perhaps, there are people in the world of so little feeling as to think this would be a good-enough epitaph for poor Mungo.

If you wish it, I shall procure another to succeed him ; but perhaps you will now choose some other amusement.

Remember me affectionately to all the good family, and believe me ever your affectionate friend, B. FRANKLIN.

And now what shall we do for Kitty? We have forgot her, all this time. Well, and what will you do for her? I suppose that though the rest have resolved against the army, she may not have made so rash a resolution. Yes, but she has: Unless now, an old one, an old general that has done fighting, and is rich, such a one as general Rupare; I like him a good deal; you must know that I like an old man, indeed I do. And some how or other all the old men take to me, all that come to our house like me better than my other sisters: I go to 'em and ask 'em how they do, and they like it mightily; and the maids take notice of it, and say when they see an old man come, there's a friend of yours Miss Kitty. But then as you like an old General, hadn't you better take him while he's a young officer, and let him grow old upon your hands, because then, you'll like him better and better every year as he grows older and older. No, that won't do. He must be an old man of 70 or 80, and take me when I am about 30. And then you know I may be a rich young widow.

We dined at Staines, she was Mrs. Shipley, cut up the chicken pretty handily (with a little direction) and helped me in a very womanly manner. Now, says she. when I commended her, 'my father never likes to see me or Georgiana carve, because we do it, he says, so badly: But how should we learn if we never try? We drank good papa and mama's health, and the healths of the Dutchess, the Countess, the merchant's lady, the country gentleman, and our Welsh Brother. This brought their affairs again under consideration. I doubt, says she, we have not done right for Betsy. I don't think a merchant will do for her. She is much inclined to be a fine gentlewoman; and is indeed already more of the fine gentlewoman, I think, than any of my other sisters; and therefore she shall be a true Countess.

Thus we chatted on and she was very entertaining quite to town.

I have now made my letter as much too long as it was at first too short The Bishop would think it too trifling, therefore don't show it to him. I am afraid too that you will think it so and have a good mind not to send it. Only it tells you Kitty is well at school, and for that I let it go. My love to the whole amiable family, best respects to the Bishop and 1000 thanks for all your kindness, and for the happy days I enjoyed at Twyford.

With the greatest esteem and respect I am Madam, Your most obed't humble servant.

B. FRANKLIN.

(Dr. Franklin to the Bishop of St. Asaph.]

LONDON, Aug. 15th, 1771.

MY DEAR LORD.—Many thanks for your letters to the Primate

and Mr. Jackson, which I shall take care to forward if I shall happen not to have an opportunity of delivering them personally. Your repeated kind invitations are extremely obliging. The enjoyment of your Lordship's conversation, good Mrs. Shipley's kind care of me sick and well, and the ever pleasing countenances of the whole amiable family towards me, make me always very happy when I am with you. But I must not abuse so much goodness, by engrossing it. You have many other friends, and I ought to be contented with my turn.

I own that I do flatter myself that my pamphlet upon colds may be of some use. If I can persuade people not to be afraid of their real friend *fresh air*,* and can put them more upon their guard against those insiduous enemies, *full living* and *indolence*, I imagine they may be somewhat happier and more healthy.

You guessed rightly, but after my fellow traveller had recovered her spirits, we did not want conversation. The story of the Noises at Hinton she did introduce, by intimating that having by accident heard a part, it had been thought proper to tell her the whole. "I do not believe any such thing, not a word of it; and I wonder that so sensible a woman as Mrs. Rickets can be in the least uneasy about it." I had not the smallest suspicion of any plot to draw the story from me; and this declaration, of her not at all believing any such things, was very proper to put me off my guard, and induce me to talk freely on any of the circumstances; so that I might have fallen into the trap, if her *knowing the whole already* had not made me think it useless to mention any of them. I assure you she gave me no kind of trouble on the journey, behaved in the most agreeable, womanly manner all the way, and was very interesting.

I propose to set out on Tuesday next for Ireland. I wish all kinds of happiness to you all, being with the sincerest esteem and veneration for your Lordship, and much *affection* (if that word is

---

*Dr. Franklin wrote as early as 1768 to Monsieur Dubourg on the free use of air, as follows:

"You know the cold bath has long been in vogue here (London) as a tonic; but the shock of the cold water has always appeared to me, generally speaking, as too violent, and I have found it much more agreeable to my constitution to bathe in an another element. I mean cold air. With this view, I rise almost every morning and sit in my chamber without any clothes whatever, half an hour or an hour, owing to the season, either reading or writing. This practice is not in the least painful, but, on the contrary, agreeable: and if I return to bed afterwards, before I dress myself, as sometimes happens, I make a supplement to my night's rest of one or two hours of the most pleasant sleep that can be imagined I find no ill consequences whatever, resulting from it, and that at least it does not injure my health, if it does not in fact, contribute much to its preservation. I shall, therefore, call it for the future, a bracing or tonic bath.

permissible) for Mrs. Shipley, Your most obliged humble servant,
Bishop of St. Asaph.                                  B. FRANKLIN.

[Same to same.]

LONDON, Aug. 19th, 1771.

MY LORD,—By the Southampton coach I have sent your Lordship the Book of State trials, which would have been sent sooner but that I hoped to send the Northumberland book with it. I have searched and enquired among my friends for the book and cannot find it. I suppose I have lent, and do not just recollect to whom.

I dined on Sunday last at Sir John Pringle's with Messrs Banks and Solander, and learned some further particulars. The people of Otahitee (George's Island) are civilized in a great degree, and live under a regular feudal government, a supreme Lord or King, Barons holding districts under him, but with power of making war on each other; Farmholders under the Barons; and an order of working people, servants to the farmholders. They believe in a supreme God and inferior Gods, all spirits, with a celestial government similar to their own. They have some ceremonies of Adoration, but seldom used. They erect temples for their gods; but they are small and stuck up on a pole in the fields, partly to honor the gods and partly for their convenience to lodge in when they happen to come down among men; a little temple being, they say, as commodious for a spirit as a large one. Their morals are very imperfect, as they do not reckon chastity among the virtues, nor theft among the vices. They have honors and distinctions belonging to different ranks but these are paid to a father no longer when he has a son born, they are afterwards paid to the son; and this keeps some from marrying who are unwilling to lose their rank, and occasions others to kill their children that they may resume it. They had no idea of kissing with the lips, it was quite a novelty to them, though they liked it when they were taught it. Their affectionate and respectful salutation is bringing their noses near each other's mouths and snuffing up one another's breath. Their account of the creation is, that the great spirit first begot the waters, then he begot the Earth and threw it, a great mass, it into the waters; then not liking to see it all in one place, and a great part of the waters without any of it, he fastened a strong cord to it and drew it so swiftly through the waters that many of the loose parts broke off from it and remain in the sea, being the islands they are acquainted with. They believe the great mass is still in being somewhere, though they know not where, and they asked our people if they did not come from it. They have a considerable knowledge of the stars, sail by them, and make voyages of three months westward among the islands. Notwithstanding all the advantages our people could show we had from our arts, &c., they were of opinion after much consideration that their condition was preferable to ours.

The inhabitants of New Zealand were found to be a brave and sensible people, and seemed to have a fine country. The inhabitants of New Holland, seemed to our people a stupid race, for they would accept none of our presents. Whatever we gave them they would look at a while, then lay it down and walk away. Finding four children in a hut on one part of the coast, and seeing some people at a distance who were shy and would not be spoken with, we adorned the children with ribbons and beads and left with them a number of little trinkets and some useful things; then retiring to a distance, gave opportunity to the people to fetch away their children, supposing the gifts might conciliate them. But coming afterwards to the hut we found all we had left, the finery we had put upon the children among the rest. We call this stupidity. But if we were disposed to compliment them, we might say, Behold a nation of Philosophers! such as him whom we celebrate for saying as he went through a Fair, *How many things there are in the world that I dont want.*

Please to present my best respects to good Mrs. Shipley. Her kind letter has relieved me from an uneasiness I was under lest by some *sottise* or other in my long hasty scrawl I might have given offense. My love to all the young ladies accompanies the sincere and great esteem and respect with which I am, my Lord, your Lordship's most obedient and most humble servant,

B. FRANKLIN.

Our journey is postponed to Saturday next.

---

[From the same to same.

LONDON, Aug. 21, 1773.

MY DEAR LORD.—Inclosed I send a Boston newspaper in which the sermon is advertised. The speaker of the Assembly of the Massachusetts, in his letter to me says, "The Bishop's sermon is much liked, as it discovers a catholick spirit, and sentiments very favorable with regard to America." Dr. Chauncey an ancient dissenting Minister of Boston writes, "The Bishop of St. Asaph's sermon I got reprinted in 24 hours after it came to hand. 'Tis universally received here with approbation and wonder, and has done much good. It sold amazingly. A second impression was called for in two days."

I daily expect to hear more of it from the other colonies. I hope the good family all continue well and happy.

With sincere esteem and affectionate respect I am ever your Lordship's most obed't humble servant.
Bishop of St, Asaph. B. FRANKLIN.

[Same to same.]

CRAVEN STREET, March 10, 1774.

MY GOOD LORD:—In page 26 and Leg. of the oldest of these pamphlets and page 64 of Leg. of the newest, your Lordship will find the subject of communication with settlements on the Ohio pretty fully handled.

The rarity of goods brought from distant countries makes people willing to give such an additional price for them as more than compensates the charge of carriage. A gentleman assured me that not long since being at a Fair in Transylvania, he saw there a shop full of English Queen's ware, which had been carried up the Rhine and down the Danube. The ware is bulky, of low value proportioned to its bulk and hazardous to carry, and yet the price defrayed the expense and risque.

I send also another pamphlet, at the end of which, page 143, is reprinted a little piece of mine on the differences then arising between the countries.

I apprehend that one view of the intended bill may be the discouraging of emigration. The prospectors may suppose, that if titles to new land cannot be obtained in America, people will not go thither to obtain lands. They will however find themselves mistaken. The natives of America are those who settle new lands, removing from those they have begun to cultivate as fast as they have an opportunity of selling them to new comers, who are not so fit for the woods as themselves. And this will go on for people will confide that Government can never be so unjust, as to turn them off, and indeed it will never be done.

But suppose such an act could be executed, what would be the consequence? The American gentlemen, (not at present in favor here) who are possessors of large tracts of land, fit for settlement, would then have the whole market in their own hands, and their estates would thereby be increased in value beyond imagination. Sir Francis Bernard and his associates (of whom I have the honor to be one) have 120,000 acres in Nova Scotia which we wish to have settled. The settlement on the Ohio is against us, as it draws the people another way. Perhaps he may move the measure for his own sake, and that of his English friends. I ought not to object to it, if I thought only of my own interest; for I have declined my share in the Ohio purchase. But I think people should be left at liberty to go where they can be happiest. I and my son have also some other considerable tracts, so that if such an act should pass, Government will do me more favour than they have done me injury by taking away my place.

With greatest esteem and respect I am, my Lord, your Lordship's most obedient and most humble Servant.

B. FRANKLIN.

[Same to same.]

[This letter is without date, but is supposed to have been written by Dr. Franklin during the autumn of 1774, and before the next letter dated Sep. 28th, 1774. J. L. P.]

EXTRACT FROM KALM'S TRAVELS IN AMERICA.

"It has been found repeatedly that these trees (Peach trees) can "stand the frost much better on hills than in the vallies ; inasmuch "that when those in a valley were killed by the frost, those on a "hill were not hurt at all. It is remarkable that in cold nights, all "the leaves to the height of seven or even of ten feet from the "ground have been killed by the frost, and all the top remained "unhurt. Further, it is observable that the cold nights which hap- "pen in Summer never do any hurt to the high grounds, damag- "ing only the low and moist ones." Vol. 11 page 83.

The above extract shows that the phenomenon mentioned by my dear good friend is not uncommon in North America. I remember to have once travelled through a valley there, on both sides of which the leaves on the trees were killed to a certain height, the line of the blast appearing very even and level as far as the eye could reach, all below the line being blasted, and all above green. I think I have heard it observed here, that frost in a dry night does not hurt so much as when the leaves have been wet. Fogs sometimes lie on low grounds, and one can see over them from the side of a hill. Perhaps a frost with such a fog may affect the trees immersed in it more than those above it. In a hilly country, too, though the vallies are warmest in the day time, while the sun shines, from the many reflections of his rays; yet, as soon as he is set, the contrary takes place ; the cooler air of the hills settles into the vallies, and the warmer air of the vallies ascend to the hills. This I have frequently observed in little excursions from Philadelphia in the Summer season. Riding out in the day I have been sweltered in the vallies, nothwithstanding the thinness of my dress, and refreshed when passing over the hills. Returning in the evening, the same thinness of dress made a sensible of a chilling coolness in the vallies, while the air on the hills was agreeably warm.

Your very kind invitation to Twyford, with the strong impression I have from experience of the happiness I might enjoy there, in a family I so truely love, almost staggers my resolution of visiting America this Summer. But I grow exceedingly home-sick. I long to see my own family once more. I draw towards the conclusion of life and am afraid of being prevented that pleasure. Besides I feel myself become of no consequence here. I find I cannot prevent nor alter measures that I see will be pernicious to us all. But there, where my opinion and advice is a little more regarded, I imagine I may still be of some use, in diminishing or retarding the mischief. It is true, my country pays me well for residing here. But I think a mere labourer, though paid as usual for a day's work, would not be satisfied to turn a grindstone all day, where nothing was to be ground.

Please to present my respectful compliments to good Mrs. Shipley, and all the amiable young ladies, with your valuable son, who, I hear by Mr. and Mrs. Jackson, is at present with you. I had a little of the pleasure of their company before they set out for Spa.

I have not yet heard from America how the sermon was received there. But expect it will have several editions in different places and be greatly applauded, as indeed it is here among all the friends of Liberty and the common rights of mankind. I think even the New Englanders will for once have a good opinion of a Bishop.

With the sincerest esteem and most affectionate respect, I am, my Lord, your much obliged and most obedient servant,

B. FRANKLIN.

---

[Same to same.]

LONDON, Sept. 28, 1774.

I received my dear friend's letter of the 8th post and should have written sooner but that I have been in continual expectation of being able to visit you. A succession of thwarting businesses has prevented my giving myself that pleasure hitherto. And writing by post is now attended with such inconvenience, that I am apt to postpone it.

I am glad the conduct of my countrymen meets your approbation, who are so good a judge of what is right and prudent. I think I can answer for them that whatever is agreed on at the Congress will be executed with universal resolution, firmness and perseverance. There may be a few personal exceptions, but of little moment. Your information is true that great orders for goods have been sent over by some in expectation that a *new importation* agreement would probably take place; but the managers there apprehending that the merchants were not all to be relied on, have set on foot a *new consumption* assessment, among the country people, which since Gage's absurd proclamation against it has made great progress; and this has occasioned already several counter orders, as the importation can answer no end if the people will not buy. I suppose you must have heard that some steps are taken to form a coalition if possible among those of our great folks who agree in disapproving the present measures, though they have not had a good understanding on other accounts. If they can unite, they will have greater weight in endeavouring to unhorse the present wild riders, and thereby prevent the ruin that seems to threaten our great political building by their mad management.

I had the great pleasure of hearing in all companies the speech extolled as a master piece of eloquence and wisdom. Great numbers of them have been printed and dispersed over the nation: And I think one may see already its beginning effect. The abuse of America in the papers is of late much diminished, and new advocates for her are arising daily. I send you inclosed one of the smaller edition. The publishers who have put their names to it, have as yet only delivered quantities to the subscribers, (who distribute them gratis) being afraid of offending Cadell if they should advertise it and sell it at the price mentioned; though they think they could sell great numbers if they had the author's leave.

I had the honor of a long conversation lately with Lord Chatham, whose sentiments upon American affairs, I found such as I could wish. I hear the same of Lord Camden's. And I know the same of so many others, that I think if the proposals of the Congress should appear tolerably reasonable, a strong push may be made the ensuing session for the repeal of all the mischievous acts that have of late almost dissolved our union. I hope nothing will prevent your being present. It was said the Parliament would meet in November. But I hear now that January is intended.

Please to present my best respects to all the good family with whom I long to be. I am a letter in debt to Georgiana; which I will pen when I can. With the sincerest esteem and respect I am ever, my dear Lord, your obliged and affectionate humble servant,

B. FRANKLIN.

[Same to same.]

LONDON, Jan. 7th, 1775.

I find it impossible to visit my dear friends at Twyford as I promised myself, my time is so fully occupied by business.

The petition from the Congress has been presented to the King by Lord Dartmouth to whom we delivered it for that purpose. The answer we received was, that his Majesty had been pleased to receive it very graciously, and had commanded him to tell us, "It contained matters of such importance that he should as soon as they met lay it before his two Houses of Parliament." We have been advised not to let it be printed till it has been communicated to Parliament as an immediate publication might be deemed disrespectful to the King. But I inclose a copy for your perusal. It will fall short of what you wish in the manner, not equalling the admirable remonstrances of the French Parliaments or the *Cour des Aides*; but having made some allowances for unpolished America, you will not, I hope, think it much amiss. When I consider that Congress, as consisting of men, the free, unbiased, unsolicited choice of the freeholders of a great country, selected from no other motive, than the general opinion of the wisdom and integrity, to transact affairs of the greatest importance to their constituents, and indeed of as great consequence as any that have come under consideration in any great council for ages past ; and that they have gone through them with so much coolness, though under great provocations to resentment ; so much firmness under cause to apprehend danger, and so much unanimity under every endeavour to divide and sow dissentions among them ; I cannot but look upon them with great veneration. And I question whether I should be so proud of any honor, any King could confer upon me, as I am of that I received by only having my health drank by that Assembly. By the way I am well informed they drank the Bishop of St. Asaph in three successive bumpers ; but it was not so mentioned in the papers, lest some other friends might be displeased. I have cut out of a Boston paper and inclose an advertisement of the speech* by which may be seen something of the esteem in which it is held there. My best wishes attend the whole good family. Miss Georgiana will be so good as to excuse my not writing to her at present.

With sincerest respect and affection, I am ever your Lordship's most obedient and most humble servant, B. FRANKLIN.

[Same to same.]

PHILADELPHIA, May 15th, 1775.

MY DEAR LORD.—I arrived here well the 5th, after a pleasant

*The following is the advertisement cut from the Boston paper and enclosed to the Bishop by Dr. Franklin :
"The Bishop of St. Asaph's excellent SPEECH intended to have been spoken on the Bill for altering the Constitution of this Government, will be published tomorrow in a Pamphlet, and to be sold by the Printers. It was fold in England for One Shilling, but the price here is no more than Six Coppers. We set it at this low price in order that it may be immediately purchased and read. It is (at the particular desire of many gentlemen,) printed in a Pamphlet, rather than News-Papers, that the contents of so truly valuable a performance, may be more effectually preserved for the perusal of future generations.

passage of six weeks. I met with a most cordial reception, I should say from all parties, but that all parties are now extinguished here. Britain has found means to unite us. I had not been here a day before I was unanimously elected by our Assembly a delegate to the Congress, which met the 10th, and is now sitting. All the governors have been instructed by the Ministry to call their Assemblies and propose to them Lord North's pacific plan. Gen. Gage called his; but before they could meet, drew the sword; and a war is commenced, which the youngest of us may not see the end of. My endeavours will be if possible to quench it, as I know yours will be; but the satisfaction of endeavouring to do good, is perhaps all we can obtain or effect. Being much hurried I can only add my best wishes of happiness to you and all the dear family, with thanks for your many kindnesses. I am ever, with the highest esteem and respect my Lord, your Lp's most obliged and obed't humble servant, B. FRANKLIN.
Lord Bp St. Asaph.

[Same to same.]

PHILAD'A, July 7th, 1775.

I received with great pleasure my dear friend's very kind letter of April 19, as it informed me of his welfare and that of the amiable family in Jermyn Street. I am much obliged by the information of what passed in Parliament after my departure; in return I will endeavor to give you a short sketch of the state of affairs here.

I found at my arrival all America from one end of the 12 united Provences, to the other, busily employed in learning the use of arms. The attack upon the country people near Boston by the army had roused everybody and exasperated the whole Continent. The tradesmen of this city were in the field twice a day, at 5 in the morning and six in the afternoon, disciplining with the utmost diligence, all being volunteers. We have now three Battalions, a troop of Light Horse and a company of Artillery, who have made surprising progress. The same spirit appears every where, and the unanimity is amazing.

The day after my arrival, I was unanimously chosen by our Assembly, then sitting, an additional delegate to the Congress, which met the next week. The numerous visits of old friends and the public business have since devoured all my time; for we meet at nine in the morning and often sit till four. I am also upon a Committee of Safety appointed by the Assembly, which meets at six, and sits till near nine. The members attend closely without being bribed to it, by either salary, place or pension, or the hopes of any; which I mention for your reflection on the difference, between a new, virtuous people, who have publick spirit, and an old corrupt one, who have not so much as an idea that such a thing exists in nature. There has not been a dissenting voice among us in any Resolution for defence, and our army, which is already formed, will soon consist of above 20,000 men.

You will have heard before this reaches you of the defeat of the Ministerial troops in their first *sortie*; the several small advantages we have since had of them, and the more considerable affair of the 17th, when after two severe repulses, they carry'd the unfinished trenches of the post we had just taken on a hill near Charlestown. They suffered greatly, however, and I believe are convinced by this time, that they have men to deal with, tho' unexperienced, and not yet well arm'd. In their way to this action, without the least necessity, they barbarously plundered and burnt a fine, undefended town, opposite to Boston, called Charlestown, consisting of about 400 houses, many of them elegantly built; some sick, aged, and decrepit, poor persons, who could not be carried off in time, perished in the flames. In all our wars, from our first settlement in America, to the present time, we never received so much damage from the Indian *Savages*, as in this one day there. Perhaps Ministers may think this a means of disposing us to reconciliation. I feel and see every where the reverse. Most of the little property I have, consists of houses in the sea -port towns, which I suppose may all soon be destroyed in the same way, and yet I think I am not half so reconcileable now as I was a month ago.

The Congress will send one more petition to the King, which I suppose will be treated as the former was, and therefore will be the last; for tho' this may afford Britain one chance more of recovering our affections and retaining the connection, I think she has neither temper nor wisdom enough to seize the golden opportunity. When I look forward to the consequences, I see an end to all commerce between us; on our sea coasts she may hold some fortified places as the Spaniards do on the coast of Africa, but can penetrate as little into the country; a very numerous fleet, extending 1500 miles at an immense expense may prevent other nations trading with us; but as we have or may have within ourselves everything necessary to the comfort of life, and generally import only luxuries and superfluities, her preventing our doing that, will in some respects contribute to our prosperity. By the present stoppage of our trade, we save between four and five millions per annum, which will do something towards the expense of the war. What *she* will get by it, I must leave to be computed by her own political arithmeticians. These are some of my present ideas which I throw out to you in the freedom of friendship. Perhaps I am too sanguine in my opinion of our abilities for the defence of our country after we shall have given up our sea ports to destruction, but a little time will show.

General Gage, we understand entered into a treaty with the inhabitants of Boston, whom he had confined by his works, in which treaty it was agreed that if they delivered ther arms to the select men, their own magistrates, they were to be permitted to go out with their *effects*.

As soon as they had delivered their arms, he seized them and cavil'd about the meaning of the word *effects*, which he said was only wearing apparel and household furniture, and not merchandize or shop goods, which he therefore detains: And the continual injuries and insults they met with from the soldiery, made them glad to get out by relinquishing all that kind of property. How much those people have suffered, and are now suffering rather than submit to what they think unconstitutional acts of Parliament, is really amazing. Two or three letters I send you inclosed, may give you some, tho' a faint idea of it. Gage's perfidy has now made him universally detested. When I consider that all this mischief is done my country, by Englishmen and Protestant Christians, of a nation among whom I have so many personal friends, I am ashamed to feel any consolation in a prospect of revenge; I chuse to draw it rather from a confidence that we shall sooner or later obtain reparation; I have proposed therefore to our people, that they keep just accounts, and never resume the commerce or the union, 'till satisfaction is made. If it is refused for 20 years, I think we shall be able to take it with interest.

Your excellent advice was, that if we are to have a war, let it be carried on as between nations who had once been friends, and wish to be so again. In this ministerial war against us, all Europe is conjur'd not to sell us arms or amunition, that we may be found defenceless, and more easily murdered. The humane Sir W. Draper, who had been hospitably entertained in every one of our Colonies, proposes in his papers called the Traveller, to excite the domestic slaves, you have sold us, to cut their master's throats. Dr. Johnson, a Court Pensioner, in his *Taxation no Tyranny*, adopts and recommends that measure, together with another of hireing the Indian Savages to assassinate our Planters in the Back Settlements. They are the poorest and most innocent of all people; and the Indian manner is to murder and scalp men, women and children. This book I heard applauded by Lord Sandwich, in Parliament, and all the ministerial people recommended it. Lord Dunmore and Governor Martin, have already, we are told, taken some steps towards carrying one part of the project into execution, by inciting an insurrection among the Blacks. And Governor Carleton, we have certain accounts, has been very industrious in engaging the Indians to begin their horrid work. This is making war like nations who never had been friends and never wish to be such while the world stands. You see I am warm; and if a temper naturally cool and phlegmatic can, in old age, which often cools the warmest, be thus heated, you will judge by that of the general temper here, which is now little short of madness. We have however, as yet asked no foreign power to assist us, nor made any offer of our commerce to other nations for their friendship. What another year's persecution may drive us to, is yet uncertain. I drop this disagreeable subject; and will take up one that I know must afford you and the good family, as my friends, some pleasure. It is the state of my own family, which I found in good health; my children affectionately dutiful and attentive to everything that can be agreeable to me; with three very promising grandsons, in whom I take great delight. So if it were not for our public troubles and the being absent from so many that I love in England, my present felicity would be as perfect, as in this world one could well expect it. I enjoy, however, what there is of it, while it lasts, mindfull at the same time that its continuance is like other earthly goods, uncertain. Adieu my dear friends, and believe me ever, with sincere and great esteem, yours most affectionately, B. FRANKLIN.

My respectful compliments to Mrs. Shipley.

Your health on this side of the water is everywhere drank by the name of THE Bishop.

I send for your amusement a parcel of our newspapers. When you have perused them please to give them to Mr. Hartley, of Golden Square.

---

[NOTE.—In reference to the conduct of General Gage and Dr. Johnson, Dr. Franklin remarks in his Papers entitled "The retort courteous," vol. 11, page 485 of his Posthumous Works:

"General Gage being with his army, (before the declaration of open war) in peaceable possession of Boston, shut its gates, and placed guards all around to prevent its communication with the country. The inhabitants were on the point of starving. The General, though they were evidently at his mercy, fearing that while they had any arms in their hands, frantic desperation might possibly do him some mischief, proposed to them to capitulate, in which he stipulated, that if they would deliver up their arms, they might leave the town with their family and *goods*. In faith of this agreement, they delivered their arms. But when they began to pack up for their departure, they were informed, that by the word *goods*, the General understood only household goods, that is, their beds, chairs, and tables, not *merchant goods*; those he was informed they were indebted for to the merchants of England, and he must secure them for the creditors. They were accordingly all seized, to an immense value, *what had been paid for not, excepted.* It is to be supposed, though we never heard of it, that this very honorable General, when he returned home, made a just distribution of those goods, or their value, among the said creditors. But the cry nevertheless continued, *These Boston people do not pay their debts!*

The army having thus ruined Boston, proceeded to different parts of the Continent. They got possession of all the capital trading towns. The troops gorged themselves with plunder. They stopped all the trade of Philadelphia for near a year, of Rhode Island longer, of New York near eight years, of Charleston in South Carolina, and Savannah in Georgia, I forget how long. This continued interruption of their commerce, ruined many merchants. The army also burnt to the ground the fine towns of Falmouth and Charlestown near Boston, New London, Fairfield, Norwalk, Esopus, Norfolk, the chief trading town in Virginia, besides innumerable tenements and private farm houses. This wanton destruction of property operated doubly to the disabling of our merchants, who were importers from Britain, in making their payments, by the immoderate loss they sustained themselves, and also the loss suffered by their country debtors, who had bought of them the British goods, and who were now rendered unable to pay. The debts to Britain of course remained undischarged, and the clamor continued, *These knavish Americans will not pay us!*

Many of the British debts, particularly in Virginia and the Carolinas, arose from the sales made of negroes in those provinces by the British Guinea Merchants. These, with all before in the country, were employed when the war came on, in raising tobacco and rice for remittance in payment of British debts. An order arrives from England, advised by one of their most celebrated moralists, Dr. Johnson, in his Taxation no Tyranny, to excite these slaves to rise, cut the throats of their purchasers, and resort to the British army, where they should be rewarded with freedom. This was done, and the planters were thus deprived of near 30,000 of these working people. Yet the demand for those sold and unpaid still exists; and the cry continues against the Virginians and Carolinians, *they do not pay their debts!*"]

PHILAD'L, Sep. 13, 1775.

MY DEAR FRIEND:—I write but seldom to you, because at this time the most innocent correspondence with me may be suspected, and attended with inconvenience to yourself. Our united wishes for a reconciliation of the two countries, are not I fear soon to be accomplished; for I hear your ministry are determined to persevere in their mad measures, and here I find the firmest determination to resist at all hazards. The event may be doubtful, but it is clear to me that if the contest is only to be ended by our submission, it will not be a short one. We have given up our commerce; our best ships, 34 sail left this port on the 9th instant. And in our minds we give up the sea coast, tho' part may be a little disputed, to the barberous ravages of your ships of war ; but the internal country we shall defend. It is a good one and fruitful. It is, with our liberties, worth defending, and it will itself, by its fertility enable us to defend it. Agriculture is the great source of wealth and plenty. By cutting off our trade you have thrown us *to the Earth*, whence like *Antæus* we shall rise yearly with fresh strength and vigor.

This will be delivered to you by Mr. Jonathan Williams, a nephew of mine, whom I left in my lodgings. Anything you see fit to send me, may be safely trusted to his care and direction. He is a valuable young man, having, with great industry and excellent talents for business, a very honest and good heart. If he should stay in London, I beg leave to recommend him to a little of your notice.

I am here immersed in so much business that I have scarce time to eat or sleep. The Winter, I promise myself, will bring with it some relaxation. This bustle is unsuitable to age. How happy I was in the sweet retirement of Twyford, where my only business was a little scribling in the Garden Study, and my pleasure, your conversation, with that of your family!

With sincere and great esteem and respect, I am ever, my dear friend, your affectionate and most obed't and hum'le Servant,

B. FRANKLIN.

Upon the third page of this letter is the following memoranda in Dr. Franklin's hand writing:

The perfidy of General Gage in breaking his capitulation with Boston and detaining their effects ;

The firing of Broadsides from men of war in defenceless towns and villages filled with women and children ;

The burning of Charleston, wantonly, without the least reason or provocation ;

The encouraging our Blacks to rise and murder their masters;

But above all, the exciting of the Savages to fall upon our innoxious outsettlers, farmers (who have no concern in, and from their situation can scarce have any knowledge of this dispute) especially when it is considered that the Indian manner of making war, is by surprising families in the night and killing all, without distinctions of age or sex! What would be thought of it, if the Congress should hire an Italian Bravo to break into the house of one of your

ministers and murder him in his bed ?  All his friends would open
in full cry against us as *assassins, murderers* and *villians*, and the
walls of our Parliament House would resound with their *execra-
tions !*  Of these two damnable crimes, which is the greatest?

These proceedings of officers of the Crown, who it is presumed,
either act by *Instruction*, or know they shall *please* by such conduct,
give people here a horrid idea of the *spirit* of your Government.

Passy near Paris, Feb. 9th, 1778.

My very dear Lord :—I flatter myself that notwithstanding distance, absence, and the interruption of friendly correspondence
which the circumstances of the times occasion, you may still be
pleased to hear (what I wish to hear of you and your truly amiable
family) that health continues, and as much happiness as public
calamities will permit to sensible minds.  We both of us have the
satisfaction of having join'd in endeavours to prevent these calamities ; and I know you join with me in the sincerest wishes of seeing an end to them.  But the time is not yet come.

The bearer of this line is Mr. Alexander, son of an intimate and
dear friend of mine.  He is ambitious of the honor of being known
to so good a man as the Bishop of St. Asaph.  He is a young
gentleman of very promising parts, and bears an excellent character.  I beg leave to recommend him to your Lordship's notice.
I am sure he will endeavor to merit it.  With the greatest esteem
and respect I am ever most affectionately your Lordship's obedient
humble servant, .                                                            B. F.

[Same to same.]

Passy, June 10th, 1782.

I received and read the letter from my dear and much respected
friend with infinite pleasure.  After so long a silence, and the long
continuance of its unfortunate causes, a line from you was a prog-
nostic of happier times approaching, when we might converse and
communicate without danger from the malevolence of men en-
raged by the ill success of their destracted projects.

I long with you for the return of peace, on the general principles of humanity.  The hope of being able to pass a few more of
my last days happily in the sweet conversations of company I
once enjoyed at Twyford, is a particular motive that adds strength
to the general wish, and quickens my industry to procure that
best of blessings.  After much occasion to consider the folly and
mischiefs of a state of warfare and the little or no advantage obtained even by those nations who have conducted it with the most
success, I have been apt to think that there has never been or ever
will be any such thing as a good war, or a bad peace.

You ask if I still relish my old studies? I relish them but I cannot pursue them. My time is engross'd, unhappily, with other concerns. I requested of the Congress last year my discharge from this public station, that I might enjoy a little leisure in the evening of a long life of business; but it was refused me; and I have been obliged to drudge on a little longer.

You are happy as your years come on in having that dear and most amiable family about you. Four daughters—how rich! I have but one, and she necessarily detained from me at 1,000 leagues distance. I feel the want of that tender care of me which might be expected from a daughter and would give the world for one. Your shades are all placed in a row over my fire place, so that I not only have you always in my mind, but constantly before my eyes.

The cause of liberty and America has been greatly obliged to you. I hope you will live long to see that country flourish under its new constitution, which I am sure will give you great pleasure. Will you permit me to express another hope, that now your friends are in power, they will take the first opportunity of showing the sense they ought to have of your virtues and your merit.

Please to make my best respects acceptable to Mrs. Shipley, and embrace for me tenderly all our dear children. With the utmost esteem, respect and veneration, I am ever my dear friend yours most affectionately,

B. FRANKLIN.

[Same to same.]

PASSY, March 17th. 1783.

I received with great pleasure my dear and respected friend's letter of the 5th inst., as it informed me of the welfare of a family I so much esteem and love.

The clamor against the peace in your parliament would alarm me for its duration, if I were not of opinion with you, that the attack is rather against the minister. I am confident none of the opposition would have made a better peace for England 'if they had been in his place; at least I am sure that Lord Stormont, who seems loudest in railing at it, is not the man that could have mended it. The reasons I will give you when I shall have, what I hope to have, the great happiness of seeing you once more, and conversing with you. They talk much of there being no reciprocity in our treaty. They think nothing then of our passing over in silence the atrocities committed by their troops, and demanding no satisfaction for their wanton burnings and devastations of our fair towns and countries. They have heretofore confest the war to be unjust, and nothing is plainer in reasoning than that the mischiefs done in an unjust war should be repaired. Can Englishmen be so partial to themselves, as to imagine they have a right to plunder and destroy as much as they please, and then without satisfying for the injuries they have done, to have peace on equal terms? We were favorable and did not demand what justice entitled us to. We shall probably be blamed for it by our constituents. And I still think it would be the interest of England voluntarily to offer reparation of those injuries, and effect it as much as may be in her power. But this is an interest she will never see.

Let us now forgive and forget. Let each country seek its advancement in its own internal advantages of arts and agriculture, not in retarding or preventing the prosperty of the other. America will, with God's blessing, become a great and happy country; and England, if she has at length gained wisdom, will have gained something more valuable and more essential to her prosperity, than all she has lost; and will still be a great and respectable nation. Her great disease at present, is the number and enormous salaries and emoluments of office. Avarice and ambition are strong passions, and separately act with great tone, on the human mind; but when both are united and may be gratified in the same object, their violence is almost irresistible, and they hurry men headlong into factions and contentions destructive of all good government. As long, therefore, as these great emoluments subsist, your Parliament will be a stormy sea and your public Counsels confounded by private interests. But it requires much public spirit and virtue to abolish them; more, perhaps, than can now be found in a nation so long corrupted.

Please to present my affectionate respects to Mrs. Shipley, and all my young friends, whom I long to see once more before I die. I hope soon to congratulate you on the marriages that I hear are in contemplation. Everything interests me that regards the happiness of your family; being ever, with the sincerest esteem and affection, my dear Sir, your most obedient and most humble servant, B. FRANKLIN.

[Same to same.]

PASSY, Aug. 22nd, 1784.

DEAR FRIEND.—When I am long without hearing from you, I please myself with re-perusing some of your former letters. In your last of April 24th, '83, you mention the departure of Anna Maria with her husband for Bengal.* I hope you have since heard often of their welfare there. When you next favor me with

*Note. Anna Maria married Mr. Jones, afterwards Sir William Jones, a learned Indian Judge and celebrated linguist and Oriental scholar,

a line, please to be particular in letting me know how they do. My grandson, a good young man, (who as a son makes up to me my loss by the estrangement of his father,) will have the honor of delivering you this line, and will bring me, I trust, good accounts of your health, and that of the rest of your family. I beg leave to recommend him to your civilities and counsels. As to myself, I am at present well and hearty, the stone excepted, which, however, gives me but little pain and not often, its chief inconvenience being that it prevents my using a carriage on the pavement; but I can take some exercise in walking, am cheerful and enjoy my friends as usual. God be thanked!

Your kind invitation to spend some time at Twyford with the family I love, affects me sensibly. Nothing would make me happier. I have solicited the Congress to discharge me, but they have sent me another Commission, that will employ me another year at least; and it seems my fate, constantly to wish for repose, and never to obtain it.

With the greatest and most sincere esteem and respect, I am ever, my dear friend, yours most affectionately,   B FRANKLIN

[Same to same.]
STAR INN, Southampton, Aug. 1785.

DEAR FRIEND, I am just arrived here from Havre de Grace, not at all fatigued by my journey thither, being favored with one of the King's letters carried by large mules who walk very easy. But I cannot bear a wheel carriage or I would do myself the great pleasure of going to see you and the family I love at Twyford. I hear that my cousin William, who is coming from London to join us, proposed to stay a day or two on a visit to you. I write the inclosed note to hasten his coming hither, as we want his assistance in our preparations, and shall probably sail sooner than he expects. My respects and best wishes attend you and yours. Adieu my very dear, dear friend, and believe me ever your's most affectionately   B. FRANKLIN.

My Grand-son desires to be respectfully remembered.

[Jonathan Williams* to the Bishop of St. Asaph.]
PHILADELPHIA, Sep. 19th, 1785.

MY LORD:—I have already given your Lordship an account of our agreeable passage and safe arrival; least that letter should fail, I shall repeat the substance of it.

Our venerable friend, the Doctor, was, I think, better at sea, than he had been ashore; there was but one day, in which he suffered any pain and that was not severe. There never was on the

---
*Nephew of Dr. Franklin.

ocean, a better ship, better provided, nor better commanded. We were six weeks at sea and then landed on the wharf amid the acclamations of thousands of grateful people, who rejoiced to see their benefactor return to spend the remainder of his life among them; every public mark of respect was immediately shown him, and in spight of his desire of retirement, the people insist unanimously on being governed by him.

Your Lordship will see by the public prints what are the general sentiments, and you will see nothing exaggerated.

When I hear of another opportunity I will write a third letter; for Miss Shipley's last command made so strong an impression on my mind, that my conscience would not be at rest, if I did not take at least three chances of conveying to her so agreeable news, as that of the welfare and happiness of her lover.

With my most respectful compliments to your Lady and daughter, I have the honor to be, with the greatest respect, my Lord, your Lordship's most obedient and most humble servant,

JON. WILLIAMS.

[Dr. Franklin to the Lord Bishop of St. Asaph.]

PHILADELPHIA, Feb. 24, 1786.

DEAR FRIEND:—I received lately your kind letter of Nov. 27th. My reception here, was, as you have heard, very honourable indeed: but I was betray'd by it, and some remains of ambition, from which I had imagined myself free, to accept the Chair of Government for the State of Pennsylvania, when the proper thing for me was repose and a private life. I hope, however, to be able to bear the fatigue for one year, and then to retire.

I have much regretted our having so little opportunity for conversation when we last met. You could have given me information and counsels that I wanted, but we were scarce a minute together without being broke in upon. I am to thank you, however, for the pleasure I had after our parting, in reading the new book you gave me, which I think generally well written, and likely to do good. Tho' the reading time of most people is of late so taken up with newspapers and little periodical pamphlets, that few now-adays venture to attempt reading a Quarto Volume. I have admired to see that in the last century, a Folio, *Burton on Melancholly*, went thro' six editions in about twenty years. We have I believe more readers now, but not of such large books.

You seem desirous of knowing what progress we make here in improving our Governments. We are, I think, in the right road of improvement, for we are making experiments. I do not oppose all that seems wrong, for the multitude are more effectually set right by experience, than kept from going wrong by reasoning with them. And I think we are daily more and more enlightened: So that I have no doubt of our obtaining in a few years as much public felicity as good government is capable of affording. Your newspapers are filled with fictitious accounts of anarchy and confusion, distresses and miseries we are supposed to be involved in, as consequences of the revolution; and the few remaining friends of the old Government among us, take pains to magnify every little inconvenience a change in the course of commerce may have occasioned. To obviate the complaints they endeavour to excite, was written the enclosed little piece, from which you may form a truer idea of our situation than your own public prints would give you. And I can assure you that the great body of our nation, find themselves happy in the change, and have not the smallest inclination to return to the Domination of Britain. There could not be a stronger proof of the general approbation of the measures that promoted the change itself, than has been given by the assembly and council of the State, in the nearly unanimous choice for their Governor of one who had been so much concerned in those measures; the assembly being themselves the unbribed choice of the people, and therefore may be truly supposed, of the same sentiments. I say nearly unanimous, because of between 70 and 80 votes, there were only my own and one other in the negative.

As to my domestic circumstances, of which you kindly desire to hear something, they are at present as happy as I could wish them. I am surrounded by my offspring, a dutiful, affectionate daughter in my house, with six grand children, the eldest of which you have seen, who is now at College in the next street, finishing the learned part of his education; the others promising, both for parts and good dispositions. What their conduct may be when they grow up and enter the important scenes of life, I shall not live to *see* and I cannot *foresee*. I therefore enjoy among them the present hour, and leave the future to Providence. He that raises a large family, does indeed, while he lives to observe them, *stand*, as Watts says, *a broader mark for sorrow;* but then he stands a broader mark for pleasure too. When we launch our little Fleet of barques into the ocean, bound to different ports, we hope for each a prosperous voyage; but contrary winds, hidden shoals, storms and enemies, come in for a share in the disposition of events; and though these occasion a mixture of disappointment, yet considering the risque when we can make no insurance, we should think ourselves happy if some return with success. My son's son, whom you have also seen, having had a fine farm of 600 acres conveyed to him by his father when he was at Southampton, has dropt for the present his views of acting in the political line, and applies himself ardently to the study and practice of agriculture. This is much more agreeable to me, who esteem it the most useful, the most independent, and therefore the noblest of employments. His lands are on navigable waters, communicating with the Delaware, and but about sixteen miles from this city. He has associated to himself a very skilful English farmer, lately arrived here, who is to instruct him in the business, and partake, for a term, of the profits; so that there is a great apparent probability of their success.

You will kindly expect a word or two concerning myself. My health and spirits continue, thanks to God, as when you saw me. The only complaint I then had, does not grow worse, and is tolerable. I still have enjoyment in the company of my friends; and being easy in my circumstances, have many reasons to like living. But the course of nature must soon put a period to my present mode of existence. This I shall submit to with less regret, as, having seen during a long life, a good deal of *this* world, I feel a growing curiosity to be acquainted with *some other*, and can cheerfully with filial confidence resign my spirit to the conduct of that great and good Parent of mankind, who created it, and who has so graciously protected and prospered me from my birth to the present hour. Wherever I am, I hope always to retain the pleasing remembrance of your friendship, being with sincere and great esteem, my dear friend, yours most affectionately, B. FRANKLIN.

We all join in respects to Madame Shipley and best wishes for the whole amiable family.

---

[Dr. Franklin to Miss Catherine Louisa Shipley.]

PHILAD'A. May 2nd, 1786.

MY DEAR YOUNG FRIEND.—I received both your kind letters, that of Aug. 2nd, and that of Sep. 30th, together with the charming purse of 13 stripes and stars, which you have so obligingly made for me and sent me. In return I have knit for you and send enclosed, the art of procuring pleasant dreams, the little piece you demanded of me. Accept it with my thanks both for the purse and our dear Georgiana's pleasing verses. I write to her by this opportunity, and to my inestimable friend your father. Will you be good enough to excuse, therefore, the shortness of this to you. My time is so cut to pieces with everybody's business, that I can neither do or say all I would. My love to all, and believe me ever, my dear friend, your most affectionately. B. FRANKLIN.

---

[Dr Franklin to Miss C. L. Shipley.]

PHILAD'A. April 27th, 1789.

It is only a few days since the kind letter of my dear young friend, dated Dec. 24th, came to my hand. I had before in the public papers met with the affecting news that letter contained. That excellent man has then left us! His departure is a loss, not to his family and friends only, but to his nation and to the world, For he was intent on doing good, had wisdom to devise the means, and talents to promote them. His sermon before the Society for propagating the Gospel, and his speech intended to be spoken, are proofs of his ability, as well as his humanity. Had his counsels in those pieces been attended to by the Ministers, how much bloodshed might have been prevented, and how much expense and disgrace to the nation avoided!

Your reflections on the constant calmness and composure attending his death, are very sensible. Such instances seem to show, that the good sometimes enjoy in dying a foretaste of the happy state they are about to enter.

According to course of years, I should have quitted this world before him. I shall, however, not be long in following. I am now in my 84th year, and the last year has considerably enfeebled me, so that I hardly expect to remain another. You will then, my dear friend, consider this probably the last line to be received from me, and as a taking leave, present my best and most sincere respects to your good mother, and love to the rest of the family, to whom I wish all happiness; and believe me to be while I do live,* your most affectionately, B. FRANKLIN.

REMARKS ON CHAPTER XI OF THE CONSIDERATION ON POLICY, TRADE, &C., BY DR. FRANKLIN.

Suppose husbandry well understood and thoroughly practiced in a country, and all the lands fully cultivated.

Those employed in the cultivation, will then raise more corn and other provisions, than they can consume.

But they will want manufactures.

Suppose each family may make all that is necessary for itself.

Then the surplus corn must be sold and exported.

Farms near the sea or navigable rivers may do this easily, But those distant will find it difficult. From some the expense of carriage will exceed the value of the commodity. Therefore, if some other means of making an advantage of it are not discovered, the cultivatior will abate of his labors and raise no more than he can consume in his family.

But tho' his corn may not bear the expense of carriege to market, nor his flax, nor his wool, yet possibly linnen and woolen cloth may bear it.

*Dr. Franklin died April 17th, 1790.

Therefore, if he can draw around him working people who have no lands on which to subsist, and who will for the corn and other subsistence he can furnish them with, work up his flax and wool into cloth, then is his corn, also, turned into cloth, and with his flax and wool rendered profitable, so that it may easily be carried to market, and the value brought home in money. This seems the chief advantage in manufactures. For those working people seldom receive more than a bare subsistence for their labour ; and the very reason why six penny worth of flax is worth perhaps twenty shillings after they have wrought it into cloth, is, that they have during the operation consumed nineteen shillings and six pence worth of provisions.

So that the value of manufactures arises out of the earth, and is not the creation of labour as commonly supposed.

When a grain of corn is put into the ground it may produce ten grains. After defraying the expense, here is a real increase of wealth. Above we see that manufactures make no addition to it, they only change its form. So trade or the exchange of manufactures, makes no increase of wealth among mankind in general ; no more than the game of commerce at cards makes any increase of money among the company, tho' particular persons may be gainers while others are losers. But the clear produce of agriculture is clear additional wealth.

## APPENDIX C.

The following are the names of the more prominent Guernseymen since 1650:

Sir Edmund Andros, Colonial Governor of New York and Virginia, etc.
Maj.-Gen. Sir Isaac Brock.
Daniel de Lisle Brock, Bailiff.
Col. Saumarez Brock, Knight of Hanover.
Mrs. Carey Brock, Author.
Sir Octavius Carey.
Sir Stafford Carey, Jurist.
Rev. Peter Paul Dobree, Scholar.
Dr. Hoskins, Author.
Sir Jno. Jeremie, Governor of Sierra Leone.
Dr. John MacCulloch, Author.
Sir Edgar MacCulloch, Bailiff.
Georges Metevier, Author.
Osmond de B. Priaulx, Author.
Maj-Gen. Le Marchant.
Col. H. Le Mesurier.
Admiral Lord Saumerez.
Gen. Sir Thomas de Sausmarez,
Gen. Sir George Smith.
Charles de Jersey, Jurist, and Procureur du Roi.
Henry Tupper, Jurist and Liberal Statesmen.

FINIS.

# WORKS BY THE SAME AUTHOR.

"THE AMERICAN CRISIS,
OR PAGES FROM THE NOTE BOOK OF A (FOREIGN) STATE AGENT DURING THE CIVIL WAR."
BY
JOHN LEWIS PEYTON,
Bachelor of Law, University of Virginia, Corresponding member of the Virginia and Wisconsin Historical Societies, Fellow of the Royal Geographical Society, London, etc., etc., in two vols. 8 vo., London, 1866, Saunders, Otley & Co., Brooke St. West.

NOTICES OF THE PRESS.

"Here we pause reluctantly; the extreme interest we take in the political portion of Col. Peyton's most valuable and instructive work, has induced us to discuss somewhat at large what we may venture to entitle 'Sentiments proper to the present Crisis,' and that with reference as well to England as to America. It is not, however, to the statesman or historian alone that these volumes will be interesting. Their author has mingled largely in the best society on either side of the Atlantic; public and private life in both hemispheres, with their leading warriors, orators, statesmen, artists and men of letters, have come as a matter of course under his notice, and are sketched ably by his graphic pen;—he is in turn a Hogarth and a Watteau, as eccentricities and absurdities, graces and amenities are to be delineated. Nor is graver information wanting; his work is replete with historical anecdotes, valuable statistics and sound and apposite reflections upon subjects of contemporary or social interest."—*British Press.*

"We have seen no work upon the American Civil War, more entertaining and thoroughly readable than that by Colonel Peyton, the style of which is terse and vigorous."—*London Cosmopolitan.*

"Some of the most interesting portions of these charming volumes contain a summary of Col. Peyton's experiences, as well in the political, as in the literary worlds. His sketches are graphic, and beyond all controversy, life-like. We commend these volumes cordially and conscientiously to perusal, and we err if their circulation be not extensive. Their author was, we believe, some two or three years ago, resident for a little while amongst us, and has since been for a longer season domesticated in Jersey. It is not improbable that he may, ere long, once more be a visitor to the Channel Islands, and in that case we are sure that we may promise him for ourselves, and equally confident that we may prognosticate for him from our neighbors, a very hearty welcome. What Sidney Smith called 'stress of politics,' has driven many an honored exile for freedom or for conscience sake, upon our shores, but surely none more worthy of our esteem than this intelligent and gallant gentleman of whom—his enemies themselves being judges—the very worst that can be said must be 'Victrix causa Dies placuit, victa Peytoni."—*Guernsey Star.*

Colonel Peyton's book is a half narrative of his reminiscences of the Great Civil War, or rather of his personal intercourse with the chief actors, both military and political, and half a description of his experiences in England and his impressions of English society. He exhibits considerable skill in blending his adverse feeling towards Jefferson Davis (whom he regards as a commonplace politician and not a genius at all) with the necessary amount of attachment for the Confederate cause. Some of the chapters which he devotes to his personal observations while in this country, will be read with interest, and portions of them with amusement. Of course he does not like Mr. Cobden or Mr. Bright. Of Lord Russell's appearance and manner he speaks with contempt which is not wholly unmerited, but ill-becomes a panegyrist of Mr. Alexander Stephens, of whose outer man, he has given the most unflattering of descriptions. But he is at all events impartial in his satirical judgments. When he presents what is on the whole a very uncomplimentary portrait of Mr. Roebuck, he is perhaps more true to life, but he makes a poor return for much zealous service."
—*London Daily Star*.

"This subject is unrivalled in importance to Americans, and a very arduous one with which to deal; the interests involved are so manifold, and the questions connected with it are so complicated that it requires a master mind to do them justice. Col. Peyton has taken very elevated views of all these great questions. We have rarely met with a writer who combines so much impressive earnestness with so much sound sense and masculine depth of thought."
—*London Gazette.*

"The American Crisis is a work of great interest, written in a most spirited and masterly style."—*Thanet Advertiser.* (England.)

"The American Crisis is a highly entertaining work, and one in which the reader's interest will seldom or ever flag. Many of the sketches are hit off with much skill and effect."—*Herald.*

"The earlier portions of Colonel Peyton's work draws a lively picture of the feelings which prevailed in the South, and especially in Virginia, during the first month of the war. The sanguine advocates of Secession were full of hope and animation, predicting a speedy triumph for their cause, which should force Massachusetts itself to return all fugitive slaves, and place the prosperity of New England at the mercy of the Southern Confederacy.

Colonel Peyton's second volume is devoted, for the most part, to life in England. He gives us particulars about Hotels and Lodging-houses, describes our railway management and railway carriages ; sketches some of our great men ; tells us about our dinners, our evening parties, our country houses, and our manner of living in them ; in point of fact, is communicative to Englishmen; and the other, on England, for the use of Americans. But we can imagine many reasons which may have made it more convenient to treat together the two countries which have been connected by his own experience. He is not at all a fatiguing writer to follow ; we may read with tolerable care what he has to tell us about America, and may then proceed with undiminished energy to glance at his remarks on a subject which, after all, has an interest for most of us—ourselves."—*The Guardian.*

"Full of spirited sketches and interesting descriptions."—*The Month.* English Magazine of the Catholics.

"The work contains some admirable sketches of distinguished Southern leaders, among them, President Davis, Secretary of State, Hunter ; Sec'ys of Navy and War, Mallory and Benjamin ; Gen's Lee, Johnston, Presston, and others, and of such Federalists as President Lincoln, V. P. Johnson, Gen. B. F. Butler, Parson Brownlow, etc. They are original and striking in style, showing very great discrimination and acuteness."—*The Standard.*

"It is curious to see with what contempt this gentleman of high birth and solid position, looks down on the mushroom leaders of Secession. Most of these men are sketched by Colonel Peyton in sharp and biting acid."—Hepworth Dixon, in the London *Athenæum.*

"These volumes are compiled from notes of the author, who was an agent in Europe from one of the late Confederate States. The incidents commence from the outbreak of the war and there are numerous authentic facts and data given, which will throw light upon many circumstances connected with the long struggle between the Northern and Southern States. The description of scenes visited, the reflections on social subjects and the statements connected with the secret history of the war, acquired by the author in his official capacity, are of the highest interest and importance."—*The London Sunday Observer.*

"The American Crisis rises to the rank of a voluminous State paper. Colonel Peyton's work is destined, we believe, to be the text book for posterity, as far as regards the political questions opened up by this Civil war, the most gigantic conflict the world has ever witnessed. The author gives very spirited sketches of the preparations for the fight, and the interest taken in them by the veterans of the South. Throughout he proves his sound common sense and perfect mastery over the difficult science of political economy. Colonel Peyton has told the history of the American Civil war, its commencement, progress, and ultimate close, with precision, and with considerable historic care. He has woven with the main thread of his story, too, so many strands of minor interest, so many sketches, and so many glances at English and American domestic and country life, that each succeeding year cannot fail to add to its value as a photograph of its own times."--*Jersey Express.*

"The book impresses us like the animated conversation of an intelligent and philosophic traveler, a man of cosmopolitan tastes and catholic views, not writing so much as talking of that he has observed and very entertainingly and instructively."— *The Monthly Journal.*

"This sprightly, chatty, interesting volume, from the facile pen of Colonel Peyton, shows how an exiled Virginian is spending his time abroad in contributing to a better knowledge of our people and country among the English, while he furnishes delightful reading to countrymen at home. The free, easy, off-hand style of the volume, cannot fail to entice the reader to the end of the work, while it gives him glimpses "behind the scenes," which will often amuse, sometimes startle, and occasionally provoke him."— *The Richmond (Va.) Whig.*

"In these two handsome volumes the author presents a candid, interesting, and valuable series of sketches of men, events, etc., at the commencement of the war of 1861. He enters, in the first chapter of his work, at considerable length into the question, not so much of the right of secession as of its feasibility and desirability at that time. Upon these points there will always exist many modifications of opinion even in the South, and it is only necessary to say here that, accepting a mission from North Carolina as State agent in the interest of the Confederacy, the author proceeded through the blockade of Charleston, S. C., in the C. S., man of war, Nashville, to England, stopping on his way at the Bermudas, and in London found himself thrown in familiar contact with other Southern Commissioners, and English sympathizers of rank and influence. The reader will find the work very entertaining. The views and comments of Col. Peyton are those of a liberal minded traveler, cosmopolitan in taste, with a quick eye for the characteristic, the humorous, and the picturesque. We repeat what we said in the beginning of this paper, that Col. Peyton's style is direct, lucid, unassuming, and at all times full of simplicity and ease. He observes keenly and narrates incidents and adventures as he describes character, with the art of the *raconteur* and succeeds in rivetting the attention."—Jno. Esten Cook in *The Southern Review*, Baltimore.

# THE ADVENTURES OF MY GRANDFATHER,

BY JOHN LEWIS PEYTON, L. B., F. B. G. S., &c.,

Author of "The American Crisis;" A Historical and Statistical View of the State of Illinois, etc., etc. In One Volume, demi. 8vo. Price, 16s.

NOTICES OF THE PRESS.

"A very interesting and remarkable work."—*Sir Bernard Burke.*

"We have rarely risen from the perusal of any work with greater satisfaction. It is an interesting and elegantly written volume."—*Weymouth Paper.*

"Le livre est 'ecrit de main de maitre. La biographic et les laisons qui tiennent les lettres, sont d'un style parfait, et, èn somne, le livre est des plus interessant."—*Gazette de Guernsey.*

"The adventures are in themselves as fully fraught with interest as those of Robinson Crusoe, or the pioneers who first penetrated into the far West, and had to combat with the terrors of the Rocky mountains, or the hostilities of the red Indians. His agreeable volume will give him an additional claim to the esteem which has been already, and so deservedly, accorded to his character and talents by all classes of our society."—*Guernsey Star.*

"We again heartily commend this volume to the attention of the reading public who will, we are sure, heartily join us in thanking its enlightened and accomplished author for the literary treat which he has afforded them."—*British Press.*

"He has produced a very able and graphic biography. It possesses all the qualities necessary to become popular, and there is nothing to hinder the work from having an extensive run."—*Mail and Telegraph.*

JOHN WILSON, Publisher, 93 Great Russet Street, London, W. C., England.

By the same author.
## OVER THE ALLEGHANIES AND ACROSS THE PRAIRIES.
PERSONAL RECOLLECTIONS OF THE FAR WEST, ONE AND TWENTY YEARS AGO.
Simpkin Marshall & Co., Stationers Hall Court, London, England, 1870, I. Vol. 8vo.

NOTICES OF THE PRESS.

"Colonel Peyton, who is favorably known to the British public by his previous works, is an intelligent and observant traveler, who tells well what he has seen, so that his narrative makes a volume of very pleasant reading."—*Notes and Queries*, London.

"The production of a scholar and a gentleman. We can but recommend our readers to possess themselves of it, assured that they will find that they have secured a fund of pleasant reading."—London *United Service Magazine.*.

"The reminiscences are very interesting and give an excellent and truthful idea of the North American Indians, their mode of life and warfare."—*The Athenœum*, London.

"Colonel Peyton's work is of historic value, and we heartily commend it to all."—*The London Review.*

"Full of personal reminiscences of an interesting character. Some of the episodes are full of the romance of real life. He shows himself to have been a keen observer."—*Public Opinion*, London.

—"Colonel Peyton's work is agreeably written."—*The Guardian*, London.

"His chapters are fraught with a fresher interest than we get in these days of railway and fast traveling."—*Low's Publishers Circular*, London.

"This volume written in a very lively and entertaining style has more claims upon readers' attention, than a glance at the title might lead one to suppose."—*Illustrated London News.*

"As a useful and reliable companion, few can compare in interest with Colonel Peyton, whose agreeable volume we have read with much pleasure."—*The Weekly Times*, London.

"We commend this volume of stirring stories to the lovers of adventure."—*Lloyd's Weekly*, London.

"An exceedingly interesting volume, abounding in pleasant reminiscences, by the well known Colonel Peyton, son of Senator John Howe Peyton of Virginia. Colonel Peyton is author of two other very clever works well known in England, "*The American Crisis*," "*The Adventures of My Grand-Father.*" To Englishmen the work will prove more interesting than fiction, and Americans will find it a living history of their own day and generation." *The Cosmopolitan*, London.

"A pleasant, amusing, and charming volume."—*Norwood News*, London.

"A sprightly, chatty, interesting volume."—*Richmond (Va.) Whig*.

"An interesting contribution to the history of the recent past in the rapidly developing regions of the West and North West." —*The Courier*, (Georgetown, District of Columbia.)

"Books that illustrate the rapid growth of the great empire of the United States are always interesting, and that is done by both of the volumes before us (Colonel Peyton's) and Parker Gilmore's "A hunters adventures in the great West." Mr. Gilmore's work, however, is far less valuable than Colonel Peyton's. His book is amusing as well as instructive, &c."—*The Examiner*, London.

"Many pages might be called illustrative of Col. Peyton's genial, descriptive style and great native abilities."—*Guernsey Cornet.*

"Col. Peyton is a most desirable traveling companion, he is genial and good natured, and sees the bright side of everything, as well as the dark, and thinks it best to make the most of the former. * * The book is exceedingly entertaining, and the easy, friendly style in which it is written, will engage the attention from the first page to the last."—*The News of the World*, London.

"In description, whether of scenery or incidents, Col. Peyton's pen is graphic and his narrative is characterized by an easy, natural flowing style, combined with elegance of diction,"—*The Telegraph*, London.

"Indeed the book whether taken up for mere amusement or studied for solid instruction, is one that must commend itself to all classes of readers."—*The Guernsey Star.*

"We are very much pleased to observe that the author, if not a Catholic, is at all events above the narrow minded prejudices of most Protestant writers."—*The Month*, of London.

"His book abounds in lively sketches of the rough, manly temper of the western Americans, different alike from the unhealthy activity of the Northerners, and the comparative indolence of the

Southerners. He is not tender with their weaknesses—weaknesses which, in a paragraph of his preface, he shows to be really elements of strength. 'The wonderful growth of the United States in their western territories,' etc., The book is of historic value.— *The Review*, London.

"To Americans, this book is of great historical value for its reminiscences of celebrated men and newly born cities, while the general reader will find in its pages much new information. We have no doubt that an American edition would be received with great favor."— *Canadian News*.

HAUTEVILLE HOUSE, Guernsey, 2d Jan. 1870.

Mon Cher Colonel :—J'ai lu avec le plus vif interet votre excellent ouvrage. Vous m'exprimez, sur le primierie page, des sentiments qui me tonchent vivement. Je suis votre concitoyen en liberte et en humanite.

L'abolition de l'esclavage a rendu l'Amerique a elle-meme; d'esormais il n'y a plus ni nord, ni sud ; il y-a la Grande Republique. J'en suis comme vous.

Recevez, Colonel, mon cordial shake (of the) hand.

To Colonel John Lewis Peyton.   VICTOR HUGO.

"That these works possess unusual merits, we feel safe in asserting. One merit—it is not in our eyes a slight one—is that Col. Peyton everywhere writes like a gentleman. The age we live in has carried its 'fast' and 'slap dash' propensities into literature. Repose, simplicity, and that charming *unreserve* which characterizes the well-bred author, as it characterizes the well-bred gentleman writing for persons of culture and intelligence is his. His descriptions and comments possess great directness and picturesqueness, mingled with a natural and agreeable humor; and render his volumes extremely agreeable reading. * * The works would prove highly successful, we think, if republished in America."   JOHN ESTEN COOKE,
(In the Southern Review.)

# HISTORY OF AUGUSTA COUNTY, VIRGINIA,

BY J. LEWIS PEYTON,

Author of "The American Crisis," "Over the Alleghanies," "A Statistical View of the State of Illinois," etc., etc.

---

Extracts from some of the NOTICES OF THE PRESS, etc.:

From the Lynchburg (Va.) Daily News.

"It is a work of immense labor and research and embodies many facts and documents of great value to the future historian of Virginia. Written in an easy, flowing, scholarly style, it every where indicates the high cultivation of its distinguished author. He may well be proud of his work, and trust it to carry his name and fame down to a remote posterity."

From the Norfolk Virginian.

"This is an able record of the great county which once embraced the States of Ohio, Indiana and Illinois. It is characterized by the most careful and intelligent research, and possesses great literary and historical value. Colonel Peyton has done himself much honor, and his State much service in the production of this valuable work."

From the Richmond (Va.) State.

"This is an invaluable addition to Virginia historical literature. The field was fruitful, and the distinguished author has made exceptionally good use of it. The work bears evidence of indefatigable research, but the tedium of a purely historical narrative is relieved by the introduction of a great deal of folk-lore, which is presented in a very entertaining style. We trust this work is an earnest of farther historical investigation on the part of Colonel Peyton."

From the Virginian.

"The laborious research which has been bestowed upon it, the lucid and graphic style of the composition, the tragic events detailed of border warfare, and the vast fund of historical information it contains, will command for the book a warm reception from the public."

From the Saturday Review, London, England,

"It is an able and elaborate work. It is, of course, in great part a history of Virginia, especially in her earlier position as a British

Colony ; but contains, also, many geographical. historical and biographical details of purely local interest. That part of the narrative which relates to the civil war deserves a special word of commendation, as illustrating forcibly both the thorough loyalty to the Confederacy of the men who protested most earnestly against secession and the cruelties perpetrated by Sheridan and the other federal commanders. Northern sympathizers would do well to study at least one such work as Colonel Peyton's before they again refer to the treatment of the southern rebels as an example of democratic lenity."

From the Atlantic Monthly, Boston, Mass.

"The History of Augusta County, Va., by Col. J. Lewis Peyton, is a substantial county history, in which is gathered much local material. Many curious details are preserved in it, and the work will take its place as one of the storehouses for the future historian."

From the Staunton Vindicator.

"It is one of the most popular as it is one of the most readable works of the day."

From the Rockbridge Enterprise.

"Colonel Peyton's previous works had well prepared him for this one—works which have given him an English as well as an American reputation. In point of polish and elegance of style, of fullness and minuteness of detail, and in glowing interest, it ranks with the best books of this country. It is a sound, instructive history, with the charm of one of the Indian romances of Fenimore Cooper. Every public and private library in the State should have a copy."

From the Augusta Democrat.

"While the author modestly calls it a history of the county, it has no small claims to be called a 'History of the State,' so carefully has he traced all the great events of the early and later days of the Republic with which Augusta had any connection,"

From the Farmville (Va.) Journal.

"Colonel Peyton, the author, is the son of the Hon. John Howe Peyton, one of Virginia's most eminent lawyers, and is a man of fine literary taste and extensive scholarly attainments, a practised, forcible and elegant writer. These qualifications embodied with an ardent affection for his native county and a laudable feeling of ancestral pride, being a descendant of the Lewis family so greatly distinguished in the early history of Virginia, make him eminently fitted for the task he has undertaken and so admirably accomplished."

From the Alleghany (Pa.)Tribune.

"From Colonel Peyton's acknowledged ability and learning the book must prove a valuable edition to the history of Virginia."

From the Lynchburg Virginian.

"Colonel J. L. Peyton's History of Augusta is a work of great interest and value, especially to the people of Virginia. It contains the history of Augusta from its first settlement by Europeans, down to the present time—a county once extending from the Blue Ridge to the Mississippi. It deals with the Indian tribes, their habits and customs, and contains sketches of Augusta's most distinguished sons."

From the Philadelphia Press.

"It is a valuable history of Augusta county, but there is much in it to interest and instruct the general reader."

From the Richmond Dispatch.

"This is an interesting book, and gives not only a history of the formation of Augusta county, but all sorts of valuable information concerning it. It is an essential contribution to Virginia's history and is characterized by careful research and fullness of detail.

From the New York Publishers' Weekly.

"The work will be found full of interest and valuable information."

From the Highland Recorder.

"This is a complete history of the great county of Augusta, and abounds in valuable information not to be found in any other work. Colonel Peyton's style is incisive, clear and vigorous, and the work written with great minuteness of detail."

From the Los Angelos Herald.

"The glowing narrative will deeply interest the general reader and will be fascinating in the extreme to every Virginian. Their blood has flowed in the veins of many Californians, among them the silver-tongued orator, Balie Peyton, and the eminent lawyers, Baldwin, Marshall and Weller."

From the Greenbrier Independent

"The 'History of Augusta County' is deeply interesting, and ought to have a wide circulation."

From the Virginias.

"Colonel Peyton combines the qualifications of the laborious student and the finished scholar. A native of the county, a descendant of the heroic founder, Col. John Lewis, an ardent student and lover of local annals, experienced as an author and trained by extensive travels to observe men and manners, Colonel Peyton is peculiarly fitted for the task of writing the history of this grand county."

From the Staunton Spectator.

"In point of historic information, conveyed in clear, graceful and classic language, it is one of the most valuable and readable works of the times. The distinguished author has been imbued with the laudable and noble purpose of embodying in recorded form the historical and legendary learning he has amassed. The work will captivate old and young. It should be a text book in the schools and colleges of the State."

From the Valley Virginian.

"It abounds in glowing descriptions of nature, profound thoughts and lofty sentiments, the style everywhere being characterized by warmth and animation. This excellent work, with Col. Peyton's previous contributions to our literature, justly entitle him to take rank with the great Virginians who have conferred honor on their native land by their splendid and commanding talents."

From the Watchman, Richmond.

"It is a book of rare interest from the distinguished Virginian, Colonel J. Lewis Peyton, and contains a fund of historical, geographical and biographical information."

From the Richmond Whig.

The book displays great ability, laborious research and is written in a vigorous and elegant style."

From the Industrial South, Richmond.

"It is a work of wide spread interest and permanent historic value."

From the Christian Observer, [Louisville.]

"The work is of special interest, and is a valuable addition to the history of Virginia."

JUDGE R. W. HUGHES, United States District Judge, says: "I have read your history of Augusta with deep interest. It contains a great deal not elsewhere to be found, and you have entitled yourself to the public gratitude by rescuing from oblivion and embodying in enduring form historical treasures which ought not to have been left to perish."

HON. ROBERT W. WITHERS, late United States Senator, says: "I have read your able and elaborate work with deep interest. It will take its place among the standard histories of the country."

PROF. GEORGE F. HOLMES, of the University of Virginia, says: "It is an able and exhaustive record of the history of the county."

PROF. J. B. MINOR, of the University of Virginia, says: "It is a most able and interesting work upon your county—a county famous for the important part it took in the early history of the State, for its superior population and in the past hundred years for its great and virtuous lawyers. The work displays great industry and acuteness."

PROF. SCHELE DE VERE, University of Virginia, says: "I have delayed acknowledging the receipt of your 'History of Augusta County,' that I might read it before doing so. Its perusal has afforded me much pleasure and instruction. The interest of the narrative is absorbing. I congratulate you on your success. It is a model work of its kind."

REV. MONCURE D. CONWAY, of London, England, says: "It is written with great care and is a most interesting and valuable work."

HON. ROBERT C. WINTHROP, of Boston, Mass., says: "I thank you warmly for the opportunity you have given me of reading your really valuable history of Augusta county."

JOHN ESTEN COOKE, says: "You have written what seems to me not only a most interesting, but also a most valuable book I have recently been re-reading your excellent 'American Crisis,' and think it your most attractive work. You should employ your leisure, I think, in adding to these life-like sketches, which I think you have the art to make more interesting than any other author of the time."

DR. FRANCIS GALTON, L. L. D., of London, England, author of *Hereditary Genius*, says: "There seems much in the book of interest. You say, p. 307, in respect to the Preston family, "that it is not improbable there are hundreds of grand and great grand children who will sustain the character of this great American family for brains, bravery and beauty.' Why not work out the family to show first, 2nd and 3rd ?" &c., &c.

"Had I possessed the volume in time, I would have used parts of its investigations in my vol. I. of American Literature. The town meeting, the starting point of civilization, was a good but not perfect thing; and so, it seems to me, the manor house you so eloquently describe, was a good but not a perfect thing. Northerners cannot comprehend the strength and the meaning of Virginia's noble history until they study the causes of the development of her families."—*Prof. Chas. F. Richardson*, writing to the author.

"Such county histories are of very high value now, and in the future will be well nigh priceless, * * to all who love their country. Virginia is the nurse of heroes."—*Theodore W. Dwight*, Pres't. of Columbia College Law School, N. Y.

"I assure you that I have read your history of Augusta Co. Va., with much pleasure and profit. I have always had a fondness for local history of that sort, for in them we get a fineness of detail, and a local coloring that are lost in more pretentious books."—*H. W. Grady*, Editor of Atlanta Constitution.

"It is a most interesting and admirably executed work, and apart from its historical worth, can hardly fail to have a considerable influence on both sides of the Atlantic in the chain which binds together the branches of the English-speaking race."—*Lloyd Sanders*, of London, English author.

"You have laid the county of Augusta, and the entire State under great obligations, and fixed your name upon the annals of history. I congratulate you upon your success, and hope it may stimulate to further exertions in the same line."—*Col. Thos. L. Preston*, of Charlottesville.

The distinguished author has received similar complimentary letters from scores of statesmen, literary men, etc., in this country and Europe,among whom may be mentioned President Cleveland, Hon. T. F. Bayard, Hon. Geo. Bancroft, late Minister to Prussia, Edgar Fawcett, novelist, &c., Prof. T. A. Lounsbury, of Yale, Prof. Young, of Princeton, Prof. Swift, of Rochester, N. Y., Prof. Gilman, of John Hopkins University, Prof. Chas. Manly, of Furman's University, S. C., The Head Master of Victoria College, Jersey, Sir Edgar MacCulloch, Bailiff of Guernsey, Eugene Defosse, Paris, Sig Nicolini, Pisa,Italy,and others too numerous to mention. —[SAM'L. M. YOST & SON, Publishers, Staunton, Va.]

www.ingramcontent.com/pod-product-compliance
Lightning Source LLC
Chambersburg PA
CBHW030748230426
43667CB00007B/887